A Shooting People book
Get your documentary
funded and distributed

Published by Shooting People Ltd.
Shooting People
8 Hoxton Street
London
N1 6NG

© 2005 Shooting People

ISBN 0 9544874 1
Printed May 2005

Design by Pixeco, www.pixeco.com

Cover photography by Jet, info@jetshot.com

Note
This is the first edition and there will be some errors and oversights. If you'd like to point out
any inaccuracies or items we've missed, or if you have any comments, please contact us via
docsbook@shootingpeople.org

Copies of this book are available via www.shootingpeople.org/docsbook

Preface

Who is this book for, what's its purpose, and what's in it?

This book is written for independent documentary filmmakers, directors and producers, but if you aren't one of those or a member of my immediate family, I hope you enjoy it anyway.

Though it's primarily for British filmmakers, I hope the book will also prove useful to our friends overseas, either because they want to find out more about how things work over here or because the book does pull together useful information about Europe and North America (although filtered for what is most relevant to a British filmmaker).

One half of this book is very practical information about funding sources and distribution avenues. The book has the names, deadlines, URLs and phone numbers you need. You will find the details of the UK TV broadcasters here. But this book is also designed for people who have already been rejected by commissioners and, still determined to make the film, are wondering how the hell to do so outside of British broadcasting.

The other half of the book is precision interviews and success stories intended to inspire and encourage or at very least cheer you up – after all, you are a documentarian, so you need it. We have interviewed the new star filmmakers like Morgan Spurlock, the festival directors such as John Cooper who programmes Sundance, the directors of the Amsterdam and Hot Docs pitching Forums, and the distributors who select the docs that make it to the cinema. We have covered some big, breakthrough films like 'Super Size Me' and 'One Day in September', but also smaller films, shorts such as 'Paperboys' or niche features like 'Trembling Before G-d', chosen because they demonstrate something particularly interesting. We've gone directly to the people who are at the heart of making new opportunities for doc filmmakers. So in Chapter 3, John Smithson describes in person how the new UK Film Council's Documentary Development Slate funding will work; in Chapter 9 Claire Aguilar of ITVS, the leading funder of US public TV, announces a new production fund open to non-US filmmakers; and in Chapter 3 there is the first description of the new British Documentary Foundation. Throughout the book you'll see how the interviewees explain things in their own words, rather than just reading what the press releases have to say.

You will notice some emphasis on American films and box office dollars. This is intentional; the US still dominates the international film industry, Sundance is still regarded as the best opener for a documentary and many US documentaries provide the best case studies for new and innovative ways to do things.

So far so good.

I would also like this book to be a manifesto for the future of the documentary in Britain. Times are changing and we need to react if we want to preserve and grow our lucky documentary tradition in this country. It's important to retain a sense of the glorious tradition that exists in documentary filmmaking. And that brings us to the glasses on our front cover. They used to belong to legendary American documentary maker Albert Maysles, who made my day when he gave them to me. I found that a lot of people wanted to see the world through Albert's eyes and there's a website we created with all of their portraits on it: www. albertmayslesglasses.com. If you go to the same documentary festival as me – I'll take your picture in them too.

But back to the future. We need to be brutally realistic about what television can do for documentaries these days. We need to remember that documentary filmmaking existed before television came along and we should wonder why we decided that this was the only place to make and show documentaries. We need to reposition the British documentary in our cultural life and rediscover its range and power. We need to raise our heads and start scanning the horizon for new opportunities, and we need to think laterally to invent whole new models of funding and distribution.

Many familiar doors have shut but exciting new ones can be opened and with a few sticks of dynamite I'm told you can put doors where there never were doors before.

Jess Search

Authors:

Melissa McCarthy is a writer. She is editor of the Shooting People documentary network and has curated film festivals, screenings and seasons, and compered Q&As with directors, throughout London and elsewhere. Her work apart from documentary involves writing fiction, talking about art and culture, and running art projects in all media.

Jess Search is a co-founder of Shooting People. She is the executive producer of Sundance feature documentary 'Unknown White Male' (www.unknownwhitemale.com), an ex-commissioning editor for documentary at Channel 4 and now leads the Channel 4 British Documentary Film Foundation (www.britdoc.org).

Contributors:

A graduate of The Richard Ivey School of Business, **Shamir Allibhai** worked for the BBC until September 2003, when he joined Linx Productions, as an Associate Producer working on documentary and new media projects in the Middle East, East Africa and India. Shamir works with Shooting People and The British Documentary Film Foundation and is active in the community and with alumni organizations.

Vibeke Bryld is a filmmaker who works in London and Denmark.

Ava Fedorov studied filmmaking at Bard College, in upstate New York. After spending several years traveling and teaching in Mexico, she settled in New York, where she became involved in several documentary projects, including the 'Soy Andina' production with director/producer Mitch Teplitsky.

Before joining the Channel 4 Documentary Film Foundation, a new company dedicated to aiding new and established filmmakers, **Maxyne Franklin** worked at Channel 4 as editor for the new talent initiative the '3 Minute Wonder' and co-curator of the late night innovation zone 'Outside'.

Kathy Leichter is a producer/director, fundraising and outreach consultant and the co-founder of Mint Leaf Productions, a film and television company based in New York City and Martha's Vineyard. Her most recent film, 'A Day's Work, a Day's Pay', received funding from ITVS and was the recipient of the Harry Chapin Media Award for excellence in films addressing issues of poverty and hunger. She is the mother of two children.

Julie Moggan is a recent graduate from the National Film & Television School. Her graduation film 'Waiting for a Lift' has been screened at a number of festivals and broadcast on BBC Four. Julie is currently working as a researcher for Nick Broomfield and preparing to direct her first feature-length documentary in June 2005.

Mitch Teplitsky is a producer and marketing/fundraising consultant based in New York and Lima, Peru. He was the long-time marketing director for the Film Society of Lincoln Center prior to making the forthcoming documentary 'Soy Andina' (www.soyandina.com).

Kathy and Mitch would like to extend special thanks to **Gail Silva**, President of the Film Arts Foundation in San Francisco, CA.

Simon Tzu is a filmmaker and former editor-in-chief of Shooting People. To find out more about his work visit www.simontzu.org

Shooting People

Shooting People is the UK's leading filmmakers networking organisation which continues from strength to strength in the UK and New York. See www.shootingpeople.org for more information and to become a member.

Throughout the book the symbol ⭐ shows where members of Shooting People can receive a discount on goods and services. These offers are correct at the time of going to press but may change at any time.

Interviews

By Maxyn Franklin:
Arthur Bradford; Michael Thornton; David Koh; Josh Braun; Cactus 3

By Julie Moggan:
Carol Morley and Cairo Cannon; Arthur Howes; Kersti Uibo; Lucy Walker; Stefan Nadelman; Franny Armstrong; Marc Isaacs; Sophie Fiennes; Mike Mills; Nikki Parrott; Cosima Spender; John Battsek; Sasha Snow; Alex Cooke; Jason Massot; Kerri Davenport-Burton

By Melissa McCarthy:
Xiaolu Guo; Sirkka Mueller; Fleur Knopperts; Jan Rofekamp; Jo Lapping; Agnieszka Moody; Andre Singer; John Smithson; Jonathan Goodman Levitt; Stuart Bamforth; Nick Higgins; Daniela Zanzotto; John Edginton; Fabien Riggall; Elizabeth Wood; Amy Hardie; Emily Renshaw Smith; Edward Fletcher; Himesh Kar; Alex Stolz

By Jess Search:
John Cooper; Diane Weyermann; Sandi Dubowski; Morgan Spurlock; Robert Greenwald; Peter Broderick; Michaelle McLean

Thanks to:

All of our interviewees;

The contributors, for their hard work;

Nadja Jones, Nick Atkinson and the many others in film and television roles who have been very generous with their time and information;

Stuart Tilly, George Graham, Brendan Eagar

Contents

Chapter One
Introduction: the time of the documentary

Part One: Funding

Chapter Two
You, television and production companies

Chapter Three
Nationwide public funding

Chapter Four
Public funding, Scotland

Chapter Five
Public funding, Wales and Northern Ireland

Chapter Six
Public funding, England

Chapter Seven
Private funding in the UK

Chapter Eight
European funding, television & events

Chapter Nine
North America

Part Two: Distribution

Chapter Ten
Introduction to distribution

Chapter Eleven
Short documentaries

Chapter Twelve
Festivals and markets

Chapter Thirteen

Competitions and awards

Chapter Fourteen
High end distribution

Chapter Fifteen
DIY distribution

Appendix

Chapter One
Introduction: the time
of the documentary

By Jess Search

Jess Search is a co-founder of Shooting People - the UK's leading filmmakers networking organisation which continues from strength to strength in the UK and New York (www.shootingpeople.org). She is the executive producer of Sundance feature documentary 'Unknown White Male' (www.unknownwhitemale.com), an ex-commissioning editor for documentary at Channel 4, and is now leading the Channel 4 British Documentary Film Foundation (www.britdoc.org).

Wow, what a year 2004 turned out to be. It was the year that saw Michael Moore take the Palm D'Or and break the $100 million mark in the US with 'Fahrenheit 9/11' whilst a British feature by the Oscar-winning Kevin Macdonald, 'Touching the Void', topped the UK box office setting a new record at £2.3 million. There was also 'Super Size Me' which came from nowhere (and Spurlock's credit cards) to take $11 million in the US, 'Metallica: Some Kind of Monster', 'The Corporation', 'Control Room', 'Outfoxed', 'Riding Giants' and 'The Story of the Weeping Camel'.

2003 had already been a breakthrough year for documentaries. 'Winged Migration', a wildlife film that wasn't a big story in the UK, took almost $12 million in the US and is still number thre in their all-time documentary chart (just beneath the two Moore films). There was also 'Spellbound', 'Etre et Avoir' (released in the US as 'To be and To Have'), 'Fog of War' and the Sundance winner 'Capturing the Friedmans' ($3 million). But 2004 was to go even bigger and has cemented the confidence of distributors and film companies that this is a trend here to stay.

Of course documentaries have been in the cinema as long as there has been cinema and there were breakthrough hits in the last century too. 'Hoop Dreams', which followed the aspirations of African American basketball hopefuls was released in 1994 and took a very impressive $7.8 million. Remember also 'Paris is Burning' (1991)? Muhammad Ali epic 'When We Were Kings' (1996)? 'Buena Vista Social Club' (1999)? But the last four years alone have given us 25 out of the top 50 US theatrical documentaries since 1982.

Errol Morris' 'The Thin Blue Line' is arguably the seed of the whole trend. Back in 1988 it grossed $1.2 million, setting a new record (it is now at number 39) after the adventurous new distributor Miramax surprised everyone by taking on a documentary and paying a huge advance for it of $400,000. Boss Harvey Weinstein told his team that it was on no account to be described as a 'documentary' because that was such a dirty word and box-office death. It was released as a 'non-fiction feature' and, as Peter Biskind amusingly records in 'Down and Dirty Pictures',

"Harvey caught Errol being interviewed on national public radio and hated him. He sent the director a 'Dear Errol' letter dated August 13, 1988 in which he wrote, 'You were being boring,' and led him through a Socratic dialogue that went in part: 'Let's rehearse:

Q: What is this movie about?

A: It's a mystery that traces an injustice. It's scarier than 'Nightmare on Elm Street'. It's a trip to the Twilight Zone.' Harvey continued in this vein, furnishing Morris with his lines. he concluded with, 'If you continue to be boring. I will hire an actor in New York to pretend that he's Errol Morris.'" *

'The Thin Blue Line' grossed $1.2 million so Miramax had been right about something. But 15 years later after Errol won the Oscar for Fog of War, it went into 261 screens across the US as THE Oscar documentary and grossed over $4 million.

So things have changed, but why? The Sundance Film Festival has long placed documentaries on a nearly equal footing with fiction films (the festival showcases equal numbers of American premier docs and fiction films). Director of Programming John Cooper has seen both documentaries themselves and press and

*'Down and Dirty Pictures: Miramax, Sundance, and the Rise of Independent Film', Simon & Schuster, 2005

audience perception of them change enormously over the last fifteen years. He told me, "In the early years you couldn't talk people into going to the documentaries. They thought it was academic, they thought it was like church, they thought it was good for them."

Audiences used to see documentaries as a very different proposition to a fiction film. Self-improving but less entertaining, often very niche in their subject, serious and perhaps even pious, 'you should watch this' rather than 'you want to watch this'. Two things have happened. Firstly, documentaries have had a bit of a shower and a shave: they are often made with more humour, and even though they have often remained resolutely political they are more aware of the need to engage and entertain an audience. Secondly, fiction has started to wear documentary's clothes, appropriating its camera techniques (following rather than anticipating action) and moving actors to a 'verité' style of speaking and moving (not blocking action). Documentary directors who once found it a struggle to 'move over' to drama have been headhunted. The result is that documentary no longer smells like fiction's librarian cousin; instead, fiction's search for realism has honoured documentary's perceived closeness to 'real life', flattering by emulation.

Tom Grievson of the British distributors Metrodome names the 1998 'Buena Vista Social Club' as the documentary at the beginning of the new trend on the grounds that "It was a feel good documentary. You watched it and you came out and you were really happy from seeing it, and that promoted a lot of word of mouth on it. Instead of it being a documentary that went into the cinema and grossed £100k or something like that, it went on to make a million."

What is certain is that documentaries are now seen as films not as documentaries by the market place. In the UK distributors such as Optimum, Metrodome and Tartan Films have moved to capitalised on documentary's new success but on a panel at the 2004 Resfest in London, representatives of all three companies confirmed that documentaries are no longer regarded, bought, sold or marketed by distributors any differently from their other films.

What role has television played in the emergence of documentary at the cinema? In Britain, as multi-channel choice has grown, so terrestrial television's range of documentaries has narrowed. I do believe that audiences are becoming more ready to pay money in the cinema for documentaries which would once have felt less special, less distinct from films which could regularly be seen for free on TV. But 'Super Size Me' director Morgan Spurlock told us in an interview in Sheffield in 2004, "People love to disagree with me but I really am a firm believer that reality television has helped documentaries, especially in America. It's made people in middle America suddenly go, 'Wow, watching shows about regular people is interesting. In fact, they're just as interesting as watching a big Hollywood blockbuster, they're just as dramatic, they're just as engaging, as entertaining.'"

All the Americans I spoke to including Spurlock also underlined a growing sense in the US that truths about this world are less likely to be delivered from the corporately controlled media and that independent filmmakers have something more personal and direct to offer. Indeed, no US broadcasters have rushed to acquire 'Super Size Me', perhaps because of the impact on their advertising revenues of a McDonalds boycott. Orlando Bagwell is a media programme officer at the Ford Foundation and he has a background in documentary production. He told me that he thought the shocking events of 9/11 had created an environment in which documentary could thrive because Americans realised they needed to understand the world outside their televisions. And in fact two of 2004's most interesting documentaries take the control of the media as their subject: 'Control Room' (about al-Jazeera, the Arab news station branded terrorist by Rumsfeld) and 'Outfoxed' (about the Murdoch empire). Battle for versions of the truth is also the inspiration behind Moore's emotive polemic 'Fahrenheit 9/11', of course.

So perhaps television's role, at least in America, has been to familiarise the audience with watching reality whilst frustrating them that the reality they were watching was too limited and controlled.

Returning to Moore's phenomenal success, it is worth remembering that whilst 'Fahrenheit 9/11' did break the $100 million mark, the next most successful doc is a) also one of Michael Moore's and b) only took one fifth of that amount. Number three took one tenth. The documentary spoils have not been divided equally and the circumstances which led to Moore's success on 'Fahrenheit 9/11' were rather special, including a brilliant manipulation of the Disney censorship story on the eve of the Cannes film festival. The results enabled this documentary to be opened as if it was a traditional major studio fiction film across over two thousand screens, with a huge marketing spend.

What will prove more significant to us mere mortals is likely to be the changes in distribution that are opening up, in particular DVD sales and internet marketing. Peter Broderick, who was president of Next Wave films and is now having adventures in documentary distribution, urges filmmakers to keep and exploit the right to sell their films on-line because a documentary with an in-built niche audience can do very well in this environment. 'Trembling Before G-d' and 'Outfoxed' are two recent films profiled in this book which demonstrate another way of building an audience for films with clever use of targeted screenings and press, word of mouth campaigns, and internet marketing over a more prolonged period.

2005 has started extremely well for British documentaries with not one but two British feature docs being accepted to Sundance's World Documentary Competition section (for which only twelve films are selected). One was 'Unknown White Male' (directed by Rupert Murray, produced by Beadie Finzi and executive produced by me), which was picked up for a US theatrical distribution deal at the festival and which I am happy to say Shooting People will be distributing in the UK. The other film was Sean McAllister's 'The Liberace of Baghdad' which scooped a Special Jury mention.

It's an exciting time to be making documentaries.

Part One: Funding

Chapter Two
You, television and production companies

Funding your documentary

How much money do you need? You could go guerilla and do it all yourself: hire a camera from an arts community centre (found through the recommendation of your regional screen agency or local council arts liaison officer); use the visual editing software that comes bundled into most computers; burn a DVD at a high street copyshop or camera shop, and show it to anyone who'll watch. That's your first doc out of the way.

From that point, the price tends to escalate, but the fact remains that with the ever-decreasing costs of equipment, it becomes constantly easier to get your hands on the equipment for filming, editing and outputting your film. This book isn't a how-to guide to filmmaking, though – there are many books and courses on the market covering those topics. What we're offering here is the nitty-gritty of the bits that, in an ideal world, would come on either side of filming: raising funds before you film, and getting it seen and perhaps sold once you've finished. We look at the second part of this later on in, in Part Two: Distribution.

Like everything else in documentary filmmaking, arranging your funding calls for patience, preparation and some good luck. It pays to think laterally about funding sources (is there a way you could tweak your film to be eligible for something else?); to be aware of how the land lies for the people from whom you're requesting funding (whether it's the Film Council, your mum, or an arts charity, have you investigated what they want to get out of funding, not just what you want?); and to read the instructions and make sure you're eligible.

Cairo Cannon, producer, with Carol Morley: *"You need to be a little creative and think outside the box and not just go to Independent Film and Video, who are absolutely groaning with applications. Look for ways, even in the television system, for things to get made."*

Jason Massot made 'Seafarers' in 2003.

"I did take the idea to commissioning editors before I went off to make it, but very half-heartedly. The production company I was working out of decided that they were going to try pitching it at the BBC, but I never really wanted to do that. I let them just for the hell of it and of course the BBC were profoundly uninterested in it, because it's not a narrative as far as television understands it and it's not a film that tells you something. One of the reasons there are so few documentaries that I really admire is because documentaries are constantly trying to tell me stuff and I'd rather read an article in a newspaper to be told something.

The BBC rejected it I imagine because a) there wasn't a coherent story and b) they thought it's not a sexy subject, its just about a bunch of men and worst of all they are not even exciting men, just normal guys doing a pretty thankless job. In a way I was very pleased they turned it down because it wouldn't have been the film that it now is if there'd been any television involvement in it.

I wanted to make this film in a very contemplative, meditative way. I wanted to give a much more total portrait of the people by resisting the temptation of tidying them up, either in terms of the sync they were saying or in terms of giving a precise explanation as to why they are as they are. For example, there's a two and a half minute take of one of the guys going round the engine room doing his checks. I could have quite easily just had him say, "I spend hours doing these engine checks and it's really dreadful," but I thought it's more fun to show it and to also feel the weight of time; you have to be with them experiencing it. I knew there was no way that TV would allow that kind of thing to get through, but for better or worse, whatever people think of it, that was the kind of film I wanted to make.

The problems is, I've made fourteen programmes for television and if one actually felt that one could make the films that you want to make within that forum then of course you wouldn't bother spending all your own money. It's not television's fault because television has a very clear mandate to reach out to as many people as possible and that's fine and I'm not knocking that. But certainly with the kinds of films that I want to make British television just wouldn't buy them."

So, assuming that you're technically competent (but, we've listed UK training organisations in the appendix, in case you want to improve your basic skills), you've got a cracking idea for the film you really want to make and you can get access to the subject matter and to as much of a filmmaking team as you need... What are the options open to you, and how do you decide which ones to take?

This book is aimed at considering a broader picture than just UK television, but we start there because a great many filmmakers will want to try for TV, and then, if, like most of us, you're not successful, to consider other options. British documentary television has a world-wide reputation for quality, and we continue to have a strong tradition of training top-class filmmakers, both through film education and at work. But increasingly TV isn't the right outlet, because of the subject matter or style of your film.

Sometimes there are very practical obstructions to having your film made with, or shown on, television. It can be as simple as length – Jonathan Goodman Levitt couldn't get his film acquisitioned because *"I was sending them 89 minute cuts but they all wanted 60'* – or for legal reasons. Franny Armstrong couldn't sell 'McLibel' when it was first completed: *"Alan Hayling at Channel Four wanted to buy it, but that was a much more clear-cut legal problem. He wanted to buy it and the lawyers said no, end of story."* If you are heading for TV, make it easy for yourself by following the rules as far as you can.

British broadcasters are becoming more insistent that all commissioning is carried out through recognised production companies; as an individual filmmaker the opportunities to approach a commissioning editor and persuade them to fund your film are extremely limited, going down to zero if you have no track record (the situation is slightly different when it comes to acquisitions – offering a completed work for sale, as opposed to asking for investment in order to make a film). Commissioning editors all say that a breath-takingly original idea from an unknown could blow them away, but still, if you can't demonstrate any successful filmmaking, even at a smaller and non-professional level in the past, they won't give you the responsibility. The involvement of a production company should give peace of mind to both the commissioner and the filmmaker; someone is on board who knows how to co-ordinate the matter of your film reaching the screen, so the broadcaster is dealing with someone they trust, and the filmmaker has some support and access to the filmmaking infrastructure.

How do you find a production company?

Independent production companies started to emerge when Channel 4, the first UK broadcaster that didn't make any of its own programming but purchased it entirely from outside producers, was established in 1982. During the following ten years, the BBC and the ITV companies began to commission more and more from the independent sector as well as having their own staff working in-house. Once the newer digital broadcasters such as Sky, Discovery and MTV Europe entered the picture also commissioning original programming, there was really quite a lot of work to be shared by the independent sector. PACT (the organisation which represents these independent companies) was founded in 1991 and has over 1000 members, ranging from the small (one or two permanent staff), to the extremely large or super-indie (employing hundreds of people across production, distribution, format sales, talent management, etc). A lot has been written about the transformation of this sector from the mid-90s to the present. It is the current wisdom that more and more of the work being given out by the broadcasters will go to fewer and fewer of the larger companies and there have been a lot of mergers and acquisitions as smaller companies are amalgamated to make larger, smarter, more business-orientated entities. In the documentary pool, it is probably the middle-sized outfits with overheads to cover that will find the next few years hardest, whilst the tiny companies centered around one or two creatives will happily swim along, oblivious to the sharks.

You can start your own company, but without any past productions to your name, this won't cut much ice with a broadcaster, even if it is a useful business structure. Otherwise you'll need to track down a suitable existing production company.

To do this:

• watch films on television or at the cinema and make a note of production companies that make work you're interested in. The Radio Times lists production companies of programmes. Read trade magazines, eg. 'Broadcast', to keep an eye on what production companies are up to and who's working in a field you're interested in. Shooting People has arranged a partnership deal with 'Broadcast': full members can get 50 issues for £21.25 quarterly by Direct Debit (that works out at £85/year, saving £55 on the standard subscription); part members can get 50 issues for £23.75 (£95/year, saving £45). See www.shootingpeople.org/offers/broadcast.php for details.

• look in the PACT Directory or The UK Directory of Independent Producers 2005, as it is formally known. 'Founded in 1991, Pact is the UK trade association that represents and promotes the commercial interests of independent feature film, television, animation and interactive media companies' – www.pact.co.uk. The directory lists most of the main TV production companies but not all. Not everyone is a member of PACT, especially smaller companies, as it is expensive, and not every member chooses to be included in the book, but it is still the best single place to see as many companies as possible. Each entry includes contact and key personnel details and lists the recent productions a company has made so you can see who it was that made the documentaries you loved, and who made the ones you hated before you get in touch. The only problem is that the book is expensive - £50 to non-members of PACT. Luckily, Shooting People has a partnership deal with PACT to offer the books to our full members at a whopping 50% discount.
See www.shootingpeople.org/offers/pact.php

• 'Filmbang' is another listing, specifically for Scotland, available online at www.filmbang.com, with the first hard copy version appearing at the end of 2005.

Almost every production company is looking for good ideas to take on and as long as they are within their genre area, they don't mind if they come from outside the company, so in theory you can approach anyone you like with a suitable idea. In practice, though, you may have to be quite persistent to get through, as every company is besieged by people looking for work and people sending in tapes of their work hoping to impress. The rules are the same rules as for approaching a commissioning editor: email the right person with a very succinct explanation of what the idea is and who you are. If you send a letter and a tape it might take weeks for them to get around to you.

Once you are in the door having a meeting about your idea, the golden rule is CLARITY: be extremely clear about what you want and don't want, and try to draw them out into being as clear as you. These relationships between companies and outsiders usually breakdown over miscommunications and then one or both parties can feel jerked around. Exactly how much potential do they think the idea has? What needs to happen now? Who will do the work? What are the deadlines? Who is the idea to be sent to? When?

There are three more complex issues that often cause trouble because they are not clearly discussed:

1. What role will you have on your idea if it gets commissioned?
Is it realistic that you direct it? Are you prepared to assistant produce for the experience if the only way it can get commissioned is with a more experienced director? Will you get the right to help choose this director? Talk about it up front!

2. What financial benefit will you get if it is commissioned?
Are you expecting a percentage of the production fee, assuming the project does not overspend? What is reasonable on this project? Depending on the circumstances, your percentage could be anything from 10% up to 50%. Talk about it up front.

3. If the idea is not commissioned, when and how will ownership of the idea revert to the original proposer?
This is particularly complex. By the time your idea is rejected it has probably evolved with the help and input of the production company, but if they can't get it commissioned or have lost interest and impetus, then how can you take it back and take it elsewhere with no bad feeling? Discuss up front how many months you will give it with them, and when you will judge that the relationship is over. Ask them to agree

up front that you will be able to take the idea as it has evolved away with you. If they are very unwilling, maybe you want to accept some payment from them so that you are paid to develop it with them but it's agreed that it will be their idea and not yours at the end. There are many ways to structure these things, which is why you must establish at the get-go how things will be.

And get everything in writing – an email trail is fine, a letter of intent is also very good. There is no need to get lawyers to do contracts, but people in TV have very faulty memories (too many cathode rays!), so it is helpful to be able to remind them what they agreed many months before.

TV opportunities for you and your production company

Research by Julie Moggan

Collaborating with your prodco, here are the television opportunites that you could access.

Marc Isaacs is director of 'Lift' and 'Calais':
"Spending a few days at film festivals with people from different parts of Europe, or all over the world, and talking about films, I began to realise how privileged we are in England in terms of the money that is available. People would always ask me, 'What, do you make films for a living?' and I'd turn round and say yes and they were amazed, really impressed and kind of jealous. Because people were with films that they'd been struggling for years to make or that had just been a one-off project and they'd have a day job. You start to get a slightly different perception of your own position. It was really interesting to learn we are in a privileged position, because we always moan about the state of television and I'm as guilty as anybody else of doing that, but at the same time it's much easier to make films here than anywhere else, probably."

Commissioning editors in the main broadcasters' documentary departments don't stay in place forever, and both the slots available to them and the type of film they are looking change all the time. Check the websites for the most up-to-date information, but in this section is an overview of the position as at May 2005.

If you're thinking of pitching, do your background research: look on the channel's website for information for producers; attend events such as conferences held by 'Broadcast' magazine, the Discovery Campus Masterschool, and channel open days, to hear what commissioners have to say about what they're looking for. Watch TV.

Although they say that there is discussion among colleagues, and that a good idea can be passed on to another part of the organisation, commissioners want to know that you've gone to the trouble of thinking about why their slot is the best place for your film. If there's drawback to the fine documentary resurgence that we seem to be enjoying, it's that there are many more documentaries being made, without much more time in the schedules for them.

In this chapter we also list each channel's attitude towards acquisitions – the buying of a completed film. Having your film acquired is not something you can bank on. If you first submitted it for commission and were rejected, it's unlikely that without any input from the commissioner, you'll have ended up making just the film they eventually want. The licence fee from selling a completed doc is generally not high, and of course it only goes to recovering money that you have already spent. The good points of acquisition are that any income from selling your film is rarely unwelcome; you might decide in favour of a sale, in the trade-off between small income and the benefit of the exposure of your film being bought and broadcast; and on a non-financial plane, you'll have had more freedom to make the film as you wanted (depending on where the rest of the finance came from).

Some news programmes have room for investigations of under ten minutes or so, going into a story for a deeper view, particularly if you have a short film based on good primary research. Alfred de Montesquiou explains, *"My partner and I made 'Dancing on the Rubble', a self-funded hour-long film on the contrast between Beirut's political tensions and its place as a party capital. When the former Lebanese Prime Minister Rafic Hariri was assassinated, we cut down the film to a eight-minute news piece. We signed with the distributor Journeyman. They sold it to the main Danish TV station DR, and to APTN, the broadcast service of the Associated Press, bringing in a welcome £2,000, which I'm using to return to Beirut to work on a 26-minute film about the youth and the democracy movement, 'Tents in Beirut'. I think the broadcasters were keen to get their hands on an item that gave a bit of background to the breaking news that was then developing in Lebanon."*

Carol Morley and Cairo Cannon's methods won't work for everyone, but the producer-director team has had good TV exposure for 'The Alcohol Years' and 'Everyday Something'.

Carol: *"I think everyone should pitch to TV. It's very difficult to get a commission but I don't think you should turn that option down. One really good bit of advice is that when you approach someone in TV or wherever they be, approach them in a way that they've got options other than to just say no. So you approach them maybe for advice, or maybe you go and meet them before you put an application in; you try to get to know people first. That's one of the most important things, because actually sometimes when you put an application together you can do it in a way that's inappropriate for the funding body that you're approaching.*

Cairo: *"It's good to know who they are, what are they really interested in, what's their job title, spell their name right, give them a little bit of respect. You don't want to be taking something that's impossible to someone who's thinking, 'Why are you here?' They've got so little time and you're not going to help yourself. It doesn't take that long to do a bit of research to find out a little bit more. You can even call up because you'll get somebody's secretary. You just ask them. Just do a little bit of research to show respect."*

Carol: *"The other thing is to get really good publicity materials together. I think documentary gets neglected, but you've got to have your stills, you've got to have your blurb right. And even before that you have to write good treatments that are exciting, that are page turners, that make people want to know more. I don't know how commissioning editors feel about it, but my treatment for 'The Alcohol Years' was just insane, it wasn't a proper treatment. I wrote a story about my life, really, and I had a top page and then four pages and I remember meeting some guy at the BBC and he said, 'When I got this I thought, 'What the fuck is this?'' But I got so gripped that I couldn't stop reading it, it was like a story from Granta.' I think you get told to do two pages to do this and that, but it can become very boring for people to read. So I'd just be careful of reproducing the formula, like those courses that they're running. I think it's worth thinking about that - how best to present your idea."*

The BBC

 BBC Television Centre
London
W12 7RJ

0208 743 8000

 www.bbc.co.uk

The BBC both makes programmes in-house, and commissions from outside production companies. It is proposing a move towards a system whereby 50% of programming would be made within the BBC, 25% by independent production companies, and the remaining 25% (a 'window of creative competition') would be open to proposals from any filmmaker, whether inside or outside.

There are different ways to get proposals to BBC commissioners: you can pitch to whoever is in charge of the specific strand you think your film is suited to; to the documentaries commissioning editor; to a genre commissioner; or, if you're in the nations and regions, to a local commissioner who oversees your genre. www.bbc.co.uk/commissioning has up-to-date information.

Acquisitions

BBC FOUR's Storyville shows a combination of co-productions and acquisitions and so is the place to which most people send their completed documentaries. It is an international strand, open to subjects and filmmakers outside the UK. They do get overwhelmed with submissions, and watching tapes takes time. Try to meet one of the team at a festival or documentary event and prime them, or go through someone who knows them who can recommend your film to Jo Lapping or Nick Fraser.

Central commissioning

The Documentaries and Contemporary Factual department of the BBC covers a broad range of commissioning, from documentary singles and strands to factual and leisure entertainment. The department commissions across all four channels: BBC ONE, BBC TWO, BBC THREE and BBC FOUR. Contemporary documentaries can cover any subject and can be commissioned as singles or series. Singles can also be commissioned via contemporary factual strands.

Each channel has a different identity and commissioning requirements. Examples of programmes from each channel include:

ONE 'Victoria Wood's Big Fat Documentary', 'Twins: The Identity Test', 'Rail Cops', 'Nap Attack'

TWO 'The Hunt for Britain's Paedophiles', 'My Family and Autism', 'When Michael Portillo Became a Single Mum', 'Notorious', 'Crackhouse'

THREE 'Dead Man Walking', 'The Nine Lives of Alice Martineau'

FOUR 'North Korea: a State of Mind', 'Baader Meinhof: in Love with Terror', 'Care House'

Submissions process

In spring 2005 there was a rearrangement within the BBC's documentary department and in the procedures for commissioning from independent producers. Instead of needing approval from both the channel controller and the genre controller or commissioning editor, producers submit their proposal just to the relevant commissioner at any time. There will be acknowledgement within two weeks, a decision to reject outright or to progress the proposal by six weeks after submission, and a final decision within twenty weeks of submission. Most decisions will be made in commissioning meetings once every four months, where commissioning editors and the channel controllers can compare ideas. After each meeting, the commissioners will report back to producers at 'pitchback sessions', where they'll also give preliminary briefings on priorities for the next round. In line with these open channels of communication, the commissioners will also make visits to nations and regions to brief independent producers.

People

Richard Klein, based in Bristol as part of the BBC's flight out of London, is Commissioning Editor, Documentaries, working with independent production companies. Proposals for documentaries outside of the strand described below should go to Richard, and he has eight slots a year for single docs on BBC TWO. Send proposals by email to docs.proposals@bbc.co.uk

Alan Hayling is Head of Documentaries at the BBC, overseeing its inhouse documentary producers. He comments, *"The current changes at the BBC mean that there will be significantly more work commissioned from independent producers; there's a real shift towards external production. We're also seeing, throughout the industry, a move towards a greater emphasis on authorship in documentary making. This is a welcome development because for the past few years the rise of formats and docu-soaps has required directors who could guarantee repeatability rather than originality. In other words what broadcasters and Executive Producers of these kinds of programmes wanted was a director who could reproduce an existing show to a high standard; someone with strong craft skills but not necessarily strong innovative skills or imagination. At the BBC I'm trying to encourage a move away from that, to the idea that personal vision and authorship are what's needed to create powerful and memorable documentary."*

For the two main docs strands, the editors are:

ONE life

✉ Todd Austin, Commissioning Editor, Documentaries
Room 5503
BBC White City
201 Wood Lane
London
W12 7TS

☎ 020 8752 6608

 onelife.documentaries@bbc.co.uk

ONE life airs on BBC ONE at 10:35pm. It's a strand for high impact 40-minute films which reflect life in contemporary Britain, with strong, developing narratives which concentrate on a few central characters. They must have instant audience appeal and find accessible and innovative ways through potentially bleak subjects. They must be moving, thought provoking, revelatory and ambitious. 'Lager, Mum and Me' was a ONE life which went on to win the BAFTA Flaherty award for best doc. Send single page proposals only, including details of any producer/director you have in mind for the film.

Storyville

 Nick Fraser, Commissioning Editor
Jo Lapping, Strand Executive
Room 201
1 Mortimer Street
London
W1T 3JA

 020 7765 5211

storyville@bbc.co.uk

Storyville is the BBC strand for single, international documentary films. Transmitting weekly on BBC
FOUR and also delivering an increasing number of titles a year to BBC TWO, the strand looks for
ambitious contemporary films from all over the world, as co-productions, pre-buys or acquisitions.
Storyville films can be extremely varied in terms of style, attitude and subject matter. The only requirement
is that they should be strongly narrative. The commissioning editor of the strand, Nick Fraser, prefers to
receive a taster tape with a proposal. Past Storyvilles include: Rodrigo Vazquez's 'Condor: Axis of Evil',
Marc Singer's 'Dark Days', Ben Hopkins' 'Footprints', and Sophie Fiennes' 'Hoover Street Revival'.

Fresh

Fresh is a scheme for new British directors on BBC THREE, giving a budget of up to £50,000 for a first-
time, half-hour film. Announced in 2004, the six films selected for the slot are being shown around spring
2005, although the promotion for these individual films, which include Lawrence Barraclough's 'My Penis
and I', (co-directed with Sam Grace) has gone rather quiet about their connection with the scheme. Check
the BBC commissioning site to see whether the scheme is repeated.

Other opportunities for docs

For specialist factual programming, the commissioning editors are:
Adam Kemp,   Commissioning Editor, Arts, Performance & Religion
Emma Swain,   Commissioning Editor, Specialist Factual
       (which includes History, Natural History, Science and Business)
Peter Horrocks,   Commissioning Editor, Current Affairs and Investigations
Glenwyn Benson   Controller, Factual Commissioning
There is an unfilled post of Commissioning Editor, Factual Features

Strand editors are:
Matthew Barrett,   Editor, Horizon
Clive Edwards,   Executive Producer, The Money Programme
Fiona Pitcher,   Executive Editor, Wild
John Farren,   Editor, Timewatch
Tim Martin,   series editor, Natural World
Janet Lee,   Series Producer, Imagine (Single arts documentaries for BBC ONE's flagship strand)
Anthony Wall,   Series Editor, Arena
Karen O'Connor,   Editor, This World

Hugh Faupel in Manchester is Executive Producer, BBC Religion & Ethics

BBC commissioning in the nations

The BBC transmits some dedicated programming for different areas of Britain. As well as going direct to the relevant commissioner with a documentary proposal, filmmakers in the nations can also submit proposals for network programming via their national section. The national channels also create and commission programming for broadcast on national, as opposed to network, TV.

BBC Scotland

 BBC Scotland
Broadcasting House
Glasgow
G12 8DG

✆ 0870 010 0222

 www.bbc.co.uk/scotland/aboutus/commissioning

BBC Scotland has slots for opt-out programming (ie. commissioned or produced locally, rather than through network BBC) on the channels BBC One Scotland and BBC Two Scotland. This cross-genre programming must have a particularly Scottish focus, 'embracing the experience of life in Scotland, both contemporary and historical, and reflecting the distinctive social, cultural and political activities of the nation.' Proposals should indicate how the programme would help achieve BBC Scotland's ends of reflecting the diverse nature of modern Scotland. Andrea Miller is Head of Factual Programmes, Scotland. BBC Scotland programmes popular and specialist factual programming, including longer-term landmark factual series, human interest series, religion series and sustained narrative series such as 'Adoption Scotland'. For general submissions, commissioned on a rolling basis, send a brief initial proposal to ascertain the level of interest. Include any reasons why the film is timely, such as significant new developments in the field, anniversaries, new exhibitions or performances in the pipeline etc; and state any relevant expertise on the filmmaker's part. Initial proposals will be responded to within a month, after which a full proposal might be requested. Send proposals to:

Ewan Angus
Commissioning Editor, Television,
BBC Scotland
Room 113, Broadcasting House
Queen Margaret Drive
Glasgow, G12 8DG

There are two factual strands that include one-off docs that are of particular interest to independent documentary filmmakers:

EX:S

This is BBC Scotland's popular single subject documentary strand, returning January 2006. From July 2005, BBC Scotland will be looking for four 30-minute programmes for this strand. The remit is 'real stories about real lives and Scottish culture in its broadest sense.' Previous programmes have covered stories ranging from a psychic barber to the Ibrox disaster. The brief is for strong characters, compelling narratives, fascination of viewers. EX:S is primarily concerned with real lives today but will also consider stories about recent historical events and well-known cultural figures if there is a strong narrative and contemporary relevance. Send an outline of proposal to: Pauline Law, Series Producer, EX:S, Room 3166, BBC Scotland, or e-mail to pauline.law@bbc.co.uk.

ArtWorks Scotland

This is a series of half-hour documentaries about the arts in Scotland. The intention is to commission four programmes from the independent sector, for transmission around August 2005. The series is varied in terms of subject matter and geographical location but is rooted in contemporary arts practice in Scotland, including not only the traditional arts such as theatre, music and visual arts, but also broader cultural areas such as design, architecture and popular culture. Historical or nostalgic stories are generally not accepted unless they have a strong contemporary aspect. Profiles of influential cultural figures, process pieces following work being made and topical, opinionated pieces are all welcome. The brief is for strong stories, good characters, and a good sense of how these stories will be told rather than just suggestions of interesting subject areas. Ideas should be sent as outline proposals in the first instance to Nicola White, Series Producer, ArtWorks Scotland, Room 3191, BBC Scotland, or e-mail to nicola.white@bbc.co.uk.

BBC Craoladh nan Gaidheal

The Gaelic-language section of BBC Scotland (BBC Alba is the Gaelic name for BBC Scotland) offers services on television, radio and online. The aim is to support a diversity of output, and to expanding the existing audience while targeting the 25-40 age group and learners of Gaelic.

Proposals are invited for stand-alone documentary programmes, particularly ideas which reflect 'the life of Gaels as it is lived today.' Following the template available via the BBC Scotland website, short outlines of proposals should be sent to:

Ishbel MacLennan
BBC Craoladh nan Gaidheal
Rosebank
Church Street
Stornoway
Isle of Lewis

Tel: 01851 880 727
email : ishbel.maclennan@bbc.co.uk

BBC Wales

 Broadcasting House
BBC Wales
Llandaff
Cardiff
CF5 2YQ

02920 32 2000

www.bbc.co.uk/wales/info/commissioning

BBC Wales opts out of network broadcasting for slots on its channels BBC ONE Wales, BBC TWO Wales, and the new digital channel 2W, which broadcasts on weekdays between 8:30 and 10pm, sometimes previewing programming that then migrates to the main Welsh channels. BBC Wales is keen to work with independent production companies on factual programming both for Wales and network BBC programming. Its programming seeks to reflect the multicultural aspects of Wales, both in subject matter and in the production process. Recent independent productions for BBC Wales include 'Hearts of Steel', a documentary on steel workers from Ebbw Vale, and 'The Story of Welsh', a landmark series on the Welsh language from the 11th century onwards. BBC Wales' Network Factual programming is split into two areas, General Factual and Specialist Factual. BBC Wales plays into both genres but has been particularly designated as an area for the development of history programming, with programmes such as 'The Iron Duke', on Wellington. There is Welsh-language programming on BBC Cymru, the Welsh name for the channel. Adrian Davies is Head of the Factual Department; Martyn Ingram is BBC Wales Commissioning Editor, Independents and 2W.

Commissioning rounds take place throughout the year, initiated by a commissioning brief which gives details of strands, desired programmes, target budgets and timescales. Most independent commissions for factual programmes are decided at specific commissioning rounds, which are advertised on the BBC Wales site (you can subscribe to a mailing list which keeps you informed of new rounds) and through PACT and TAC (Teledwyr Annibynol Cymru, the Welsh association for independent producers; see www.teledwyr. com).

In addition, BBC Wales is happy to look at a brief outline at any time, with an eye to finding 'the next big idea'. For proposals that aren't taken forward, BBC Wales offers feedback and, conscientiously, guarantees to respond to all queries. Regular open meetings are scheduled for independents, with the aim of developing 'reciprocal programme-producing partnerships'. The website offers a guide on how to lay out proposals. Email ideas in the first instance to commissioningwales@bbc.co.uk, phone 029 20323128 or write to:

Martyn Ingram
Room 3021
Broadcasting House
BBC Wales
Llandaff
Cardiff
CF5 2YQ

Capture Wales

www.bbc.co.uk/wales/capturewales

Capture Wales is a digital storytelling scheme. Workshops are run all over Wales at which members of the public are guided through using video technology, their imaginations, photo albums, anything, to create short film pieces of around three minutes. It's a modern form of digital, documentary, oral history. Participants get copies of their work, which is also uploaded to the website, and some are screened on 2W. To apply to take part, see the website. The scheme has also expanded to Humber and Lancashire. Vimal Madhavan took part in a Capture Wales workshop to make his film about his life as a journalist exiled from Fiji, 'Mangoes in a Cold Climate', which was then entered into the Commonwealth Film Festival, Manchester, in 2005.

BBC Northern Ireland

BBC Northern Ireland
Broadcasting House
Ormeau Avenue
Belfast BT2 8HQ

02890 33 8000

 www.bbc.co.uk/northernireland

BBC Northern Ireland commissions from an in-house production base in Belfast and from the independent sector. Commissioning rounds for factual programming take place twice a year, in spring and autumn, for developing and shortlisting proposals. Guidelines are provided outlining slots available, the kind of programmes desired, prices and timings. See the website for commissioning windows. Peter Johnston is Head of Broadcasting. Fergus Keeling, Commissioning Editor Broadcasting, is the television commissioner for Independent producers.

BBC regional commissioning

There are twelve regions of BBC programming, each of which locally produces material for opt-out programming on regional news shows. The emphasis is therefore on politics, local news and current affairs, particularly through the Inside Out strand. Independents are also sometimes commissioned to produce programming with a regional or local emphasis that can tie in with major network output, such as the six-part BBC ONE series 'A Picture of Britain' in summer 2005, which will be complemented by local programming. See via www.bbc.co.uk/commissioning/contacts for regional contact details.

ITV

✉ ITV Network Centre
200 Gray's Inn Road
London
WC1X 8HF

✆ 0207 843 8000

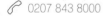 www.itv.com

ITV is made up of a network of regional licensees which broadcast to 15 separate regions. They also compete with independent producers for commissions from the ITV Network Centre to produce documentaries for the network, which broadcasts over all regions except for during opt-out periods of regional scheduling. At least 25% of ITV's output comes from independent producers. Independent producers can choose whether to sell their programme via an ITV regional company or straight to ITV Network.

Acquisitions

It is very rare for ITV to make acquisitions of documentaries.

ITV network commissioning

Bridget Boseley is Controller of Factual.

Daniela Neumann is Controller of Commissioned Programmes ITV2 and Editor, Factual, ITV1 She is responsible for commissioning and overseeing all programming for ITV2.

Dominic Crossley-Holland is Controller of news, current affairs, arts and religion.

ITV seeks to commission original documentaries with broad, populist appeal, including three or four-part series of one-hour docs and some seven or eigh-part series of 30 minutes. New filmmakers should approach ITV via an ITV company or via an independent production company, preferably one with an existing relationship with the channel. At the least, a new director would need to come with an expereinced exec producer with strong links with the channel. See www.itv.com/producers.

Real Life

This is ITV's flagship documentary strand, for 'stories of people living extraordinary and challenging lives.' The tone of the strand is emotive but uplifing, often with stories about an individual or family and with a British slant, eg. 'A Mother's Journey', about a Scottish woman travelling to the middle east, where her son was killed in a bombing attack. There are usually six Real Lifes made a year, with the 2005 strand filled. Proposals for 2006 should be made preferably prior to the September offer round (commissioning rounds are help each year in March and September), firstly by a phone call to the factual department, who can advise on the next stage for proposals.

ITV regional commissioning

Of the 15 regional ITV companies, some transmit only a small amount of their own programming each week, none of which is independently-produced documentary. Some of the larger companies, however, work closely with independent producers in their regions for programming for regional transmission. But these companies can also themselves function as independent production companies who pitch to the broadcasters for network transmission, so in this case they have no need to work with external production companies. But to complicate the picture still further, some of these production companies welcome approaches from independent filmmakers, with ideas that the regional production companies could take to the networks for commissioning. Go via www.itvregions.com for links to each of the regions, and to see up-to-date information on programming.

Documentaries at the regional level are often commissioned within a broader factual features department, and sometimes within the news and current affairs department. Regional non-news programming is undergoing a shake-up. In Spring 2005 Ofcom (the regulatory body overseeing telecommunications) carried out consultation and a review into the role of the ITV regional companies, looking at questions of fairness and competition between the difference components of the ITV network. The expectation is that regional broadcasters will be obliged to commission more work from independent production companies, with a view first to externalising regional documentary production and then abolishing it altogether. See www. ofcom.org.uk for updates on this.

The regional broadcasters are:

ANGLIA TELEVISION

 Anglia House
Norwich
NR1 3JG

✆ 01603 615151

🖰 www.angliatv.com

Neil Thompson is Head of Programming. Anglia is good for doc schemes with new directors; keep an eye on the website.

BORDER TELEVISION

 The Television Centre
Carlisle
CA1 3NT

01228 525 101

 www.border-tv.com

For regionally-relevant docs, send proposals to Jane Bolesworth, Head of Features, at above address.

ITV CENTRAL

ITV Central does no work with independent doc production companies

CHANNEL TV

 Television Centre
La Pouquelaye
St Helier
Jersey
JE1 3ZD

01534 816816

 www.channeltv.co.uk

Karen Rankine is Director of Programmes, responsible for local production; queries to broadcast@channeltv.co.uk

GRAMPIAN

Television Centre
Craigshaw Business Park
West Tullos, Aberdeen
AB12 3QH

01224 848848

www.grampiantv.co.uk

Grampian is strong on docs and works with Scottish Screen on the This Scotland funding strand for new filmmakers, for which see Chapter 4, Public Funding, Scotland.

GRANADA

 ITV1 Granada
Quay Street
Manchester
M60 9EA

📞 0161 832 7211

🖱 www.granadatv.com

ITV LONDON

✉ London Television Centre
Upper Ground
London
SE1 9LT

ITV London was created by a merger of Carlton and LWT, who before 2004 were responsible for London's weekday and weekend programming, respectively.

MERIDIAN

Meridian does no work with independent doc production companies

SCOTTISH TV

✉ 200 Renfield Street
Glasgow G2 3PR

📞 0141 300 3000

🖱 www.scottishtv.co.uk

Agnes Wilkie and Bobby Hain are commissioners.

TYNE TEES TV

✉ City Road
Newcastle Upon Tyne
NE1 2AL

📞 0191 261 0181

🖱 www.tynetees.tv

An increasing number of docs are made by independents. Send proposals to Jane Bolesworth at this address.

ULSTER TV

 Havelock House
Belfast
BT7 1EB

 02890 328122

 www.u.tv

Alan Bremner is Director of Television. He says, *"UTV commissions about 40 hours of regional programmes from independents, both North and South. These programmes cover almost all our programme genres and independents should feel free to make proposals for any type of programmes. The independent programmes, like in-house programmes, are scheduled at 7.30pm on Tuesdays and Thursdays (against BBC's 'Eastenders'), at 11pm on Thursday nights and at Sunday teatime. We create programme proposals for the ITV network and for other channels: almost 90% of these proposals come from partnerships between UTV and independents.*

Filmmakers should feel free to send us, in the first instance, a very short outline proposal and they should expect a reply within two weeks of our receiving the programme outline. They should bear in mind that we want programmes which have a strong sense of place and which will attract a good audience. All proposals should be sent to myself or, if they are Current Affairs or news features, they should go directly to Rob Morrison, our Head of News, Current Affairs and Sport."

ITV WALES

ITV Wales produces only a small amount of programming.

ITV WEST

 Television Centre
Bath Road
Bristol BS4 3HG

 0117 972 2722

 go via www.itvregions.com

Strong on docs. Proposals and outlines should be sent to the Head of Features and Current Affairs, currently James Garrett (James.Garrett@itv.com), who explains, *"The slot - and the likely audience for it - dictates what we commission; documentaries appeal to the Eastenders avoider who's our likeliest viewer at 7:30pm. I'm happy to commission programming from indies within the region, including new firms; in the latter case I'd want to check out their track records, see some past shows, etc. They should bear in mind that, with pressure on slots now so tight, they'll likely be waiting some time to make a series for us unless it's exactly what we're looking for at a particular moment. Indies from outside the region will now only get to make programmes for us if a) it's a co-production with the ITV region in which they're based (a maximum of up to eight hours per year) or b) it's such a must have that I'd be mad to turn it down. I'm happy to receive proposals by post or, more usefully, by email. Due to programme budgets being squeezed I'm increasingly influenced by the question 'Who else might be interested in this programme/ series?' in deciding whether or not to commission. Faced with two proposals from different companies, one of which would attract co-production money from elsewhere and another which didn't, chances are I'd go for the former. It allows me to make the programme budget go further, enhance the quality of the programme and either get or maintain*

a toehold on another channel, to the obvious benefit of both ITV and the indie producer.

We were very happy with 'Wacky Racers', commissioned from an indie that was then called SN Productions and is now 123 Media, set up by producer / director Stuart Napier. The film won prizes both at the RTS regional awards and at the Houston Independent Film and Video Festival."

ITV WESTCOUNTRY

 Langage Science Park
Western Wood Way
Plymouth

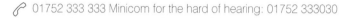 01752 333 333 Minicom for the hard of hearing: 01752 333030

 go via www.itvregions.com

Both the features and current affairs departments work with independent producers. Send one A4 page with a synopsis to Jane Blanchard, Head of Features.

YORKSHIRE TV

 The Television Centre
Kirkstall Road
Leeds
West Yorkshire
LS3 1JS

 0113 243 82 83

 www.yorkshiretv.com

Sally Cieslik is Production Manager, Regional programming.

Channel 4

✉ 124 Horseferry Road
London
SW1P 2TX

☎ 0207 396 4444

🖱 www.channel4.co.uk

Channel 4 makes no programmes in-house.

Acquisitions

With 95% of documentaries commissioned by Channel 4 there are very few acquisition slots available and those that there are tend to be for feature length cinematic releases such as Super Size Me and Spellbound. There is some potential for acquisitions at More4 but again this is limited and a synopsis should be submitted before sending other materials.

Commissioning

People

Channel 4's documentary department consists of:

Danny Cohen,	Head of Documentaries
Kate Vogel,	Editorial Administrator and Editor for 3 Minute Wonder
Meredith Chambers,	Commissioning Editor, Documentaries

Simon Dickson,	Commissioning Editor, Documentaries
Candice Gumble,	Assistant
Hilary Bell,	Commissioning Editor, Documentaries (currently on leave)
Dominique Walker,	Commissioning Editor, Documentaries

the role of a deputy commissioning editor are unfilled, as at May 2005

Peter Dale,	Head of More4 and Documentary Events
Katie Speight,	Editor, More4

Emily Renshaw Smith, producer at FourDocs, for which see Chapter 15, DIY distribution

For detailed information on the specific output and requirements of each commissioner check out www.4producers.co.uk.

Beyond the documentary department

Outside the documentary department, other parts of the channel also accept docs on some subjects.
Ralph Lee, Commissioning Editor, History
Editorial Assistant, Caron Copek
Louisa Bolch, Editor, Science
Editorial Assistant, Caron Copek
Aaqil Ahmed, Commissioning Editor, Religion
Jan Younghusband, Commissioning Editor, Arts & Performance
Edwina Waddy, Assistant Editor, Arts
Mark Rubens, Commissioning Editor, News and Current Affairs

Channel 4's Nations and Regions department exists to oversee the successful growth of regional production. It has two main requirements, to 'reflect the diversity of life across the UK' and to commission 30% of originated programmes from producers outside London, ie with a business base outside the M25, and with 70% of the qualifying production budget and at least 50% of the key production staff spent regionally. (see www.ofcom.org.uk). Development money is specially ring-fenced for regional producers. They must have an idea that Channel 4 wishes to pursue, then funds are then allocated by the Nations and Regions commissioning team.

Producers with ideas in the area of contemporary factual programmes should approach the department's editor Andrew MacKenzie. He represents Nations and Regions on Channel 4's contemporary factual group and will assess the viability of ideas. There is an R&D task team to support independent producers in the Nations and Regions, and the department hosts an EU-funded Research Centre, to deliver business development programmes and support company growth.

Channel 4 Nations & Regions
4th Floor
227 West George Street
Glasgow
G2 2ND
Phone: 0141 568 7100

Director of Nations and Regions Stuart Cosgrove
Office Manager: Debbie Walker, dwalker@channel4.co.uk

Output

Channel 4 commissions various formats and series, looking for films with authorship, narrative and popularity. Cutting Edge is the main documentary strand of ten films a year, a mixture of observational and past-tense stories, including personal, domestic stories, and more journalistic works. Recent programmes include: 'Snatched' and 'Bad Behaviour'. Other recent programming includes one-off singles such as 'Alex Best: My Life with George' and 'The Great Reality TV Swindle' and limited-run documentary series (of two to four parts). Simon Dickson commissions the BodyShock strand, about 'the intersection of extraordinary people with extraordinary science.'

The documentaries department has a number of new talent initiatives for emerging directors and producers. These used to be run by Independent Film and Video, which has been subsumed into the main documentary department.

3 Minute Wonder

Assistant Editor: Kate Vogel
This is the documentary shorts strand after the Channel 4 News at 7.55pm. Its aim is to encourage new talent and take risks at the heart of the primetime schedule. It is an opportunity for directors who have not worked for Channel 4, those who to wish to cross genres and first time directors/APs.

3 Minute Wonder shows a different series each week and is usually made up of four programmes (three during cricket season). The budget is a fixed price £4,000 per episode in 2005. Proposals should have a sense of purpose and a strong narrative, and be clever and intriguing stories that have a surprising way of reflecting who we are today. They can be about any subject, but must be suitable for pre-watershed transmission. New styles of filmmaking are encouraged; the films should be engaging and inventive in form. Send proposals to Kate Vogel.

The Other Side

IWC (previously the production company Ideal World) run this Channel 4 scheme to produce one-hour documentaries from first-time directors. Eight films are commissioned each year, on budgets ranging from £50,000 to £70,000. They are all made at IWC so only directors, not other production companies, can apply. The finished films are screened in a slot between 9pm and midnight, depending on the film. Experience in documentary is preferred, but ideas are welcome from people new to the field who think they could handle the demands of a one-hour film made to a tight schedule with a relatively low budget.

They call for 'original ideas with a clear narrative and popular appeal. The most successful directors have found remarkable characters that an audience can engage with. Their films also have a strong sense of authorship, unique access and the ability to confront contemporary issues in a fresh and intelligent way.' Recent Other Sides include 'Siamese Survivors', dir. Simon Gilchrist, 2003, and 'Studs of Suburbia', dir. Vicky Crawley, 2004, while subjects have ranged from films about American anti-war protestors in Gaza to teenage dwarves on dates. Many directors have done well from the scheme, using it as a chance to prove their ability to find popular stories, cast them well and tell a story over the course of an hour, thereby enabling them to move on to bigger Channel 4 jobs.

To apply: check via www.iwcmedia.co.uk/theotherside/ to see whether the submissions window is open; send in a maximum of one side of A4 with a CV of relevant experience, no tapes. They say, 'Don't worry if your idea isn't fully formed or worked up. It's still worth sending it in, even if you only have a paragraph or two.'

Submissions

Channel 4 only accepts programme proposals that come to them via an independent production company, with the exception of the the 3 Minute Wonders strand. A paragraph outlining your idea and approach is enough in the first instance, no tapes. Ideas should be submitted to specific commissioning editors via the channel's online proposal system which can be accessed through the producer's website (www.4producers. co.uk). You will also need to include additional information on the programme length, budget and the time in the schedule you see it best working at. The channel tries to respond to proposals within two weeks. If they are interested in your idea they will either ask you for more information or invite you to come in for a meeting. The commissioner's assistants, who are also listed on the producer's website, should be your first point of contact with regard to any queries you may have.

Channel 4 Sheffield Pitch

The Channel 4 Sheffield Pitch has been running since 2002. New directors are invited to compete to win a commission to make an hour-long documentary on a budget of £30,000. Applicants need to submit an idea for a one-hour documentary (on no more than one to two pages) and a copy of their CV to Channel 4. Twelve applicants are then invited to the Sheffield International Documentary Festival (held annually in November) to pitch their ideas on stage to a panel of Channel 4 commissioning editors. From this initial pitching round, four applicants are selected to go through to the finals. It is nerve wracking for the directors and extremely instructive for the audience, who not only get to hear the Channel commissioners talking about they like and don't like about each idea, but also get to think about what makes a good pitch and what under-sells an idea. Even if you don't apply, it's worth attending.

In 2003 the commissioners chose two winners. Lee Kern's idea (and brilliantly provocative pitch) about challenging the BNP to a football match against a team of players of mixed races proved impossible to pull off. But Lee went on to make a set of short films for The Slot (which is now the 3 Minute Wonder strand) and another film, 'The Edgeware Walker'. Joshua Whitehead got to make his idea about Britain's best scrabble players. 'Lost for Words' premiered at the Sheffield International Documentary festival in 2004 and was broadcast on Channel 4. The 2004 winner was Dominic Waugh with an idea called 'Good Vibrations', about a deaf club organiser called Troi who wants to win the UK air guitar championships. It was a great pitch: confident, well timed, witty and based around an inventive use of prompt cards.

The competition is open to anyone who hasn't already made a one-hour documentary for network primetime TV. Individual applicants do not need to be attached to an independent production company in order to compete. The commissioners are looking for strong one-off ideas with the potential to get noticed. In 2005 the festival is running in October so the deadline is likely to be early September; see www.sidf.co.uk for details.

More4

Headed by Peter Dale and Katie Speight, More4 is a digital channel launching in October 2005. It will run from 4pm to midnight every night, then repeat until 6am, and while it's billed as 'the home of documentaries, films, drama, news and current affairs', there's a welcome documentary slant. The aim is to work towards one big programming event each month, to screen on 9pm on a weekday night, then repeated through the month. These might be authored, new documentaries, or acquisitions of big foreign docs, or good things from the Channel 4 archives, perhaps revisited by the filmmaker. About 30% of the output will be original commissioning, with roughly £20 million to spend on original programming. Budgets will range from £250,000 - £1million for the big pieces, depending on the genre and ambition, to around £50k-£100k for one-hour midweek docs. Submissions to the channel should go through the normal Channel 4 commissioning routes, specifying that it's a propsal with More4 in mind, then ideas will be passed up to More4. See details via www.4producers.co.uk

Peter Dale described his ambitions:

"We want the channel to be mainstream, original and intelligent: not as rarefied as BBC4, but smarter than the Chubby Chasers programming on ITV2. The plan is to combat the blandness that I feel permeates some television; be prepared to be argumentative; and to be responsive to the world around us. I want viewers to feel that there are thinking people running this channel, who care about what's on it, and aren't just putting in some tapes to run for the night and then going home. I'm not sure there'd be a slot at the level of Alt-TV, but we certainly want to make room to give promising filmmakers a break. There's interesting filmmaking going on regardless of television, and we have to get back into that and support it.

More4 is a step towards preparing for analogue switch-off. Digital television doesn't have to be the poor relation of analogue TV; we want to be in the thick of it, offering it in an interesting and grown-up way."

The Channel 4 British Documentary Film Foundation

This is a new initiative set up by Jess Search, who used to run Channel 4's new talent and innovation department Independent Film and Video. The Foundation's funding comes from Kevin Lygo, the director of programmes at Channel 4, but it is an independent, non-profit organisation with separate offices from the Channel and so is listed in the 'Trusts and charities' section of Chapter 7, Private funding.

FIVE

✉ 22 Long Acre
London
WC2E 9LY

 www.five.tv

Acquisitions

Five acquires 100 to 150 factual documentaries a year in the genres of science and technology; wildlife; history and adventure. Independent directors/producers with a film they are looking to sell should send Bethan Corney (Factual Acquisitions Executive) a one paragraph synopsis. If the synopsis appeals to Bethan she will request a screening of the work. If she acquires the film for Five it may, if necessary, be put it through a re-versioning process with an independent production company.

People

Relevant commissioning editors as at May 2005 are:

Jeff Ford,	Managing Editor & Director of Acquisitions
Chris Shaw,	Senior Programme Controller (News, Current Affairs and Docs)
Ian Russell,	Deputy Controller, News, Current Affairs and Documentaries
Sham Sandhu,	Controller of Special Events and Pop Features
Kim Peat,	Controller of Daytime, Arts and Religion
Peter Grimsdale,	Controller of Science
Alex Sutherland,	Controller of History
Bethan Corney,	Factual Acquisitions Executive

Output

News, Current Affairs and Docs
Chris Shaw looks for prime time documentaries covering topical subjects. The department specialises in crime, royalty and popular contemporary topics, with the majority having a strong tabloid sensibility. It also does a small number of observational hours and series. The bulk of the output has to be suitable for transmission at 8 or 9pm. The department also commissions late-night documentaries with a sexual or crime theme, and low cost celebrity documentaries. With proposals, first contact Emma Rowlands, Assistant, on 020 7421 7123, or emma.rowlands@five.tv .

Special Events and Popular Features
Sham Sandhu is interested in commissioning high-profile, celebrity-led documentaries and reality series that will appeal to a twenty to thirty-something audience. Ideas can be pitched at various peak time slots, both pre and post-watershed. Sham also commissions late-night entertaining and fun 'adult' singles and series. With proposals, first contact Sam Heaver, Assistant, on 020 7421 7197, or sam.heaver@five.tv

Daytime, Arts and Religion
Kim Peat looks for arts series of 30-minute programmes and one-off documentaries marking events or anniversaries. Arts programmes need to have an accessible approach and appeal to the loyal arts audience and the interested viewer. Kim is also interested in religious programmes that reflect multi-faith Britain. Budgets are £35,000 per half hour for arts, £10 – 20,000 per half hour for religion. With proposals, first contact Rachel Wilkinson, Assistant, on 020 7421 7113, or rachel.wilkinson@five.tv .

Science
The main opportunity here is for hour-long, peak-time documentaries for the Extraordinary People strand, consisting of character-led narratives about individuals with an extraordinary power, ability or medical condition. The Stranger Than Fiction strand is for 'real stories or events that appear at first sight to sound counter-intuitive but have a rational explanation.' These two strands could attract a budget of up to £180,000. There are some 10pm slots for popular programming, and room for limited series on extreme medicine, surgery or psychology, or human interest.

History
Alex Sutherland is looking for historical documentaries that have an appealing new proposition, or that take a fresh look at British history, or focus on an event with a live element to it. She is also keen to find new ways of doing biographies, finding landmark series with big ideas at their core and finding more ways of telling contemporary or social history with a popular appeal. With proposals for science and history, first contact Cherri Dunlop, Assistant, on 020 7550 5653, or cherri.dunlop@five.tv .

Submissions
New directors should come via an established independent production company. Submit a brief synopsis in writing to the relevant controller's assistant. Five aims to respond within four weeks.

Other broadcasters

Artsworld

✉ 80 Silverthorne Road
London
SW8 3XA

✆ 0207 819 1160

 www.artsworld.com

Artsworld is an independent digital TV channel dedicated to the arts. From 2pm to midnight every day it broadcasts features, performance, documentaries and shorts on all aspects of the arts including opera, dance, classical music, blues, jazz, architecture, photography, visual arts, design arts, literature, drama, paintings and antiques. Artsworld does not commission programmes but acquire most of their programming from the international TV markets MIP-TV and MIPCOM. Programmes can be of any length and can be series or individual programmes. Artsworld seek exclusive cable and satellite rights in the UK and Eire usually for a period of two to three years. Independent directors/producers with a finished arts-related film should send a VHS and a covering note to James Wills, Head of Acquisitions.

Discovery Network Europe

✉ Discovery House
Chiswick Park Building 2
566 Chiswick High Road
London W4 5YB

☎ 020 8811 3000

🖱 www.discoveryeurope.com

Discovery UK's core genres are history – particularly contemporary, military, and biography – and science, especially 'entertaining, passion-driven programmes that explain the world around us.' 30 and 60 minutes programmes are preferred. Discovery UK only considers proposals pitched to them via independent production companies, accredited scientists and scientific organisations. Around 30% of Discovery's output is acquired programming. Submissions can be made by post to the Commissioning Editor at the address above, or go via http://producers.discovery.com/ , an online submissions process for all parts of the international Discovery Network.

The History Channel / The Biography Channel UK

✉ Grant Way
Isleworth
Middlesex
TW7 5QD

☎ 0207 941 5185

🖱 www.thehistorychannel.co.uk
www.thebiographychannel.co.uk

The History Channel and the Biography Channel are joint ventures between A&E Television networks and BSkyB. The History Channel's output ranges from classical historical documentary to reality history programmes and movies. The Biography Channel concentrates on profiles of famous names from politics, history, Hollywood, music, the arts and sport. The Channel is always interested in A-list celebrities and gossip, and runs true life stories including crime.

The Channels acquires around 50% of its programming from A&E (their US parent company), 30% from other sources, and about 20% is co-produced and commissioned. The History Channel/Biography Channel UK is primarily interested in British subjects and does not often fully commission. It can, however, serve as a good source of co-production top-up funding.

The History and the Biography Channels run a rolling commissioning process. Proposals from anywhere are considered and individual filmmakers do not have to approach via an independent production company. The Channels make a practice of introducing new programme makers to established independents. Proposals should be emailed to Richard Melman, Channel Director. Proposals should feature an excellent story, idea or concept and also show how the director intends to make the film. They are helped by access to unique resources, whether people, archives or places. If a director's work is unknown to the Channels, a pilot tape is a useful introduction. The Channels attend major markets and liaise with distributors worldwide to make acquisitions. Individual directors/producers with a programme to sell should contact Louise Dillon, Acquisitions Manager, with a synopsis.

Teachers' TV

 16-18 Berners Street
London
W1T 3LN

 www.teachers.tv

Teachers' TV is a digital and cable channel funded by the DFES and run by Education Digital, an independent consortium composed of Brook Lapping Productions, ITV and the Institute of Education, which provides programming, including plenty of factual and docs, for those working in education. Launched in February 2005, Teachers' TV informs independent producers that it will not consider proposals until later in 2005; check the website for details. A VHS of a completed programme for acquisition can be sent to the Acquisitions Team at the above address.

Chapter Three
Nationwide public funding

Introduction

You're an independent filmmaker. You might well be a UK taxpayer. You wonder whether any of your taxes ever come back to you in the form of public subsidy for your filmmaking endeavours. The answer is yes, by very round-about routes. Money from general taxation filters through the system and comes to filmmakers, with the other major source being money from the National Lottery. In this section you'll find an overview of public funding: how it's split up, sums and figures, who's eligible, and where to look for it.

In addition to hard funding – money that you're given – public policy has an effect on your film finances in terms of soft money, or what you don't have to pay; see Chapter 7 on funding, financing and tax breaks for more on this. And public policy affects filmmakers in many, stranger ways: do you ever feel that we're swamped in American imports and there's no room for your film? Government policy abolishing the Eady Levy had a hand in that. The decisions Channel 4 takes on showing cutting edge, alternative docs, or churning out the profitable ones? Policy choices to keep the channel publicly owned or to consider letting it go private have an effect on what's commissioned. Accounting rules for freelance workers? The list goes on. And for a lucky handful each year, public subsidy supports their studies on the documentary direction MA course at the NFTS.

The Department for Culture, Media and Sport

✉ 2-4 Cockspur Street
London
SW1Y 5DH

✆ 020 7211 6200

🖥 www.culture.gov.uk

The DCMS is the government department that has film within its remit. It gives grant-in-aid (money from central government) to the UK Film Council, and sets its tasks. It develops legislation that affects national policy towards film. In the context of funding films, the other government bodies that can have an impact are the Treasury, which decides tax policy (again, see Chapter 7), and The Department for International Development (DFID), which also supports filmmakers (see below).

The DCMS oversees the National Lottery and sets guidelines for its distribution. Established in 1994, the Lottery has awarded over £1.4 billion through its 15 distributing bodies, to support good causes in arts, heritage, health, education, environment, community and charity sectors. Most Lottery money for filmmakers is channelled through the Film Council, its regional screen agencies or RSA, the Arts Councils, and NESTA, described below, but certain film and video projects may also be eligible for funding directly through Lottery schemes. Bear in mind that this funding will not be given just 'to make my film', however much you feel that you and your doc are worthy recipients. The funding is awarded to pursue charitable aims, so only a small proportion of documentaries, for which either the subject or the means of production have a wider aim, will be eligible. But if you do fall into the right category, or if you can tailor your film in such a way, then no funding is to be sniffed at.

The main thing to remember with Lottery funding (and this is a phrase that keeps cropping up in this book) is to do your preparation. Lottery cash is there and a large infrastructure has been established just to give it away, so make use of it: speak to your regional office, find out exactly how your project can match what's available, and use their support systems to give your application the best chance.

Lottery funding

Awards for All

'Awards for All' is a Lottery grants scheme aimed at local communities. It funds projects that enable people to take part in art, sport, heritage and community activities. The aims are to:

• Extend access and participation by encouraging more people to become actively involved in local groups and projects, and by supporting activities that aim to be open and accessible to everyone who wishes to take part

• Increase skill and creativity by supporting activities which help to develop people and organisations, encourage talent and raise standards

• Improve quality of life by supporting local projects that improve people's opportunities, welfare, environment or local facilities, for example through voluntary action, self-help projects, local projects or events.

Not-for-profit organisations can apply for grants between £500 and £5,000 to fund a specific project or activity that meets at least one of the above aims. Examples of film projects that have received funding include: Workhouse Films, a community-based arts organisation, which was given an award of £3,600 to run a short film project with 16-25 year-olds in disadvantaged areas of Sheffield; the Northampton Bangladeshi Association, which received an award of £4,700 to produce a video with 13-19 year-old Bangladeshi women about the issues facing young women in everyday life. The final product was made available to local schools and community groups for educational purposes; and the North Wing Project: Care for the Elderly, which used an award of £3,200 to make a film about the problem of bogus callers for the elderly.

It is a rolling awards scheme and grants must be used within one year. Companies which aim to distribute a profit and individuals may not apply. 'Awards for All' is a national programme operating through nine regional offices in England. Each region has areas of special emphasis on which it wishes to focus and it is advisable to contact your local awards office to establish their particular priorities before submitting an application. Details can be found on the website of each regional distributor:

AWARDS FOR ALL ENGLAND PROGRAMME OFFICE

✉ Ground Floor
St Nicholas Court
25-27 Castle Gate
Nottingham, NG1 7AR

✆ 0115 934 9350

 julia.palmer@awardsforall.org.uk
www.awardsforall.org.uk

NORTH WEST

✉ Ground Floor
Dallam Court
Dallam Lane
Warrington, WA2 7LU

✆ 01925 626845
Textphone: 01925 231241

🖱 north.west@awardsforall.org.uk

WEST MIDLANDS

✉ 8th Floor
Edmund House
12-22 Newhall Street
Birmingham, B3 3NL

✆ 0121 200 3511
Textphone: 0121 212 3523

🖱 west.midlands@awardsforall.org.uk

SOUTH WEST

✉ Beaufort House
51 New North Road
Exeter, EX4 4EQ

✆ 01392 849705
Textphone: 01392 490633

🖱 south.west@awardsforall.org.uk

NORTH EAST

✉ 6th Floor
Baron House
4 Neville Street
Newcastle upon Tyne, NE1 5NL

✆ 0191 255 1111
Textphone: 0191 233 2099

🖱 north.east@awardsforall.org.uk

EAST MIDLANDS

✉ Ground Floor
St Nicholas Court
25 - 27 Castle Gate
Nottingham, NG1 7AR

✆ 0115 934 9304
Textphone: 0115 934 9360

🖱 east.midlands@awardsforall.org.uk

YORKSHIRE AND THE HUMBER

✉ 3rd Floor
Carlton Tower
34 St Pauls Street
Leeds, LS1 2AT

✆ 0113 224 5345
Textphone: 0113 245 4104

🖱 yorkshire.humber@awardsforall.org.uk

EASTERN

✉ 2nd Floor
Elizabeth House
1 High Street
Chesterton
Cambridge, CB4 1YW

✆ 01223 449009
Textphone: 01223 352041

🖱 eastern@awardsforall.org.uk

LONDON

✉ 9th Floor
Camelford House
89 Albert
Embankment
London SE1 7UF

✆ 020 7587 6659
Textphone: 020 7587 6620

🖱 london@awardsforall.org.uk

SOUTH EAST

✉ 3rd Floor
Dominion House
Woodbridge Road
Guildford
Surrey, GU1 4BN

✆ Tel: 01483 462943
Textphone: 01483 568764

🖱 south.east@awardsforall.org.uk

WALES

✆ Tel: 01686 611740

🖱 Email:enquiries.wales@biglotteryfund.org.uk

SCOTLAND

✉ Highlander House
58 Waterloo St
Glasgow, G2 7DB

✆ 0141 242 1200

🖱 Scotland@awardsforall.org.uk

NORTHERN IRELAND

✉ 1 Cromac Quay
Cromac Wood
Ormeau Road
Belfast, BT7 2JD

✆ 028 9055 9090

🖱 enquiries.ni@awardsforall.org

Heritage Lottery Fund

🖱 www.hlf.org.uk
enquire@hlf.org.uk

The Heritage Lottery Fund gives grants to support a wide range of projects involving the local, regional and national heritage of the UK. The fund was set up in 1993 by the National Heritage Memorial Fund, which was established in 1980 to protect the nation's heritage and award grants in memory of people who have lost their lives for the United Kingdom. The Heritage Lottery Fund can only fund projects that take place in the UK and can provide both capital grants (for buildings and equipment) and time-limited activity grants. It offers grants through the 'Awards for All' programme, and as separate funding streams. The fund aims to support work designed to care for heritage and to help people experience it. It also supports activities that will increase people's understanding and enjoyment of their heritage.

For the period 2002 – 2007, the fund has four specific agendas; to encourage more people to be involved and make decisions about their heritage; to conserve and enhance the UK's diverse heritage; to ensure that everyone can learn about, have access to and enjoy their heritage; and to achieve a more equitable distribution of grants across the UK, by making more grants available to those parts of the UK and those communities which have received little funding from the fund to date.

Film and video projects will be supported as long as they record and increase public understanding and involvement in Britain's heritage, and form part of a wider heritage project. The fund does not support filmmaking for its own sake.

For further information on the range of grants available go to www.hlf.org.uk or contact your local Heritage Lottery Fund team:

HEAD OFFICE & LONDON OFFICE & SOUTH EAST OFFICE

✉ 7 Holbein Place,
London, SW1W 8NR

☎ 020 7591 6000
Textphone: 020 7591 6255

EAST OF ENGLAND OFFICE

✉ Kett House
Station Road
Cambridge, CB1 2JT

☎ 01223 224870

EAST MIDLANDS OFFICE

✉ Chiltern House
St Nicholas Court
25-27 Castle Gate
Nottingham, NG1 7AR

NORTH EAST OFFICE

✉ St Nicholas Building
St Nicholas Street
Newcastle upon Tyne, NE1 1RF

☎ 0191 255 7570

NORTH WEST OFFICE

✉ 9th Floor
82 King Street
Manchester, M2 4WQ

☎ 0161 831 0850

NORTHERN IRELAND OFFICE

✉ 51-53 Adelaide Street
Belfast, BT2 8FE

☎ 028 9031 0120

SCOTLAND OFFICE

✉ 28 Thistle Street
Edinburgh, EH2 1EN

☎ 0131 225 9450

SOUTH WEST OFFICE

✉ Trinity Court
Southernhay East
Exeter, EX1 1PG

☎ 01392 223950

WALES OFFICE

✉ Suite 5A
Hodge House
Guildhall Place
St Mary's Street
Cardiff, CF10 1DY

☎ 029 2034 3413

WEST MIDLANDS OFFICE

✉ Bank House
8 Cherry Street
Birmingham, B2 5AL

☎ 0121 616 6870

YORKSHIRE AND HUMBER OFFICE

✉ Carlton Tower
34 St Paul's Street
Leeds, LS1 2QB

☎ 0113 388 8030

Millennium Awards

 The Millennium Commission
Portland House
Stag Place
London, SW1E 5EZ

Tel: 020 7880 2001

info@millenium.gov.uk
www.millennium.gov.uk

The Millennium Commission was created in 1993, with the aim of funding projects to celebrate the new millennium. Its Millennium Awards Scheme distributed awards of around £2,000 to 32,000 individual people for projects which benefited themselves and their community. The scheme is now closed, but the Commission left a £100 million endowment, the Millennium Awards Trust, that is administered by the charity UnLtd.

The Millennium Awards provide practical and financial support to social entrepreneurs: individuals who have the ideas and commitment to develop projects which will benefit their community. UnLtd currently offers two levels of award. Level 1 awards are between £500 and £5,000 (with an average award size of £2,000), and cover project start-up costs: materials, equipment, renting rooms, meetings and so on. Level 2 awards, between £5,000 and £15,000, are for powerful, original ideas that are sustainable after the award has finished and have the potential to operate on a wider scale or be replicated in other parts of the UK. Funding at this level covers living costs as well as project development.

UnLtd can fund an average of 1,000 awards per year, for applicants over the age of 16, living in the UK and applying as an individual or informal group. Previous award winners can reapply but priority will be given to people who are developing projects for the first time, and where there is a clear learning opportunity for that individual. Projects must: benefit the public or a community in the UK; be in need of an UnLtd Millennium Award to ensure their success; offer a learning opportunity for the applicant; be either a new initiative or a clear expansion of an existing project.

Film and video projects have been funded where they clearly match the aims of the fund in bringing together a group or community for a project. For example, in 2004, Carlisle Antonio received a Millennium Award to make 'Colouring the Media'. This documentary film about the role of people of colour in the media begins with the premise that Native Americans were the first people to be documented photographically, with the camera used as a propaganda tool to depict them as less than human. See via the Britfilms catalogue (www.britfilms.com) for more information, or contact Carlisle on american.indian@blueyonder.co.uk.

Carlisle had been working in the media for over twelve years as an actor, director and producer when he went to a careers fair in Bristol and learnt about a strand of Millunnium funding, in conjunction with the BBC and Skillset, the UK national training body overseeing the audiovisual industries. This particular strand of funding is no longer available.

"Having looked at the Skillset criteria I decided to put a proposal together. It actually took me half an hour to format it and put it together. This wasn't an idea that was in my mind at the time, I was trying to produce bigger projects for various independent productions. There were I believe two thousand applications, out of which forty were selected for the award. There were only twelve others in the film category; the rest did other things such as radio and print journalism. The package that we'd gained access to consisted of BBC training and production, as well as full media support from Skillset and other media organisations such as ITV, Granada, etc. To win an award, you had to meet strict criteria, in front of a Skillset panel consisting of BBC and other media professionals. There was also a producer who worked closely with projects. The money was

distributed in quite a complicated process really.

Screening of the film has gone well. It was screened at BAFTA and the RSA and a host of media pros attended. I'm not sure where I'd liked to see it placed. I have had enquiries about it since completion, from Sundance, which in the end it didn't make, and Genoa, where it will be showing. I have been lazy with the film and not done much about it."

Rebecca Johnson is a filmmaker who lives in Brixton, London. She applied to UnLtd in 2004 for funding to make a documentary about Top Cats, a local youth organisation and basketball club for underprivileged children. Her award covers the costs of film and camera equipment. Sean Atkinson applied for a Millennium Award to fund an international video exchange project. He produced a video about 24 hours on the Meridian line for two children from Cleethorpes, then took the video to show children in a school in Ghana. He then made an equivalent film about two children in Ghana and brought it back to show children in the UK. He says, *"Fantastic...I hope this scheme continues for many other people to benefit from. I feel so lucky to be able to realise some of my ideas!"*

UnLtd has six offices throughout the UK and a head office in London:

HEAD OFFICE/LONDON OFFICE:

📧 123 Whitecross Street
Islington, London, EC1Y 8JJ

☎ 0207 566 1100

🖱 info@unltd.org.uk

BRADFORD OFFICE

📧 Second Floor, Highpoint Building
Westgate, Bradford, BD1 2TT

☎ 01274 750 630

🖱 zulfiqarahmed@unltd.org.uk

NORTHERN IRELAND OFFICE

📧 Room 70/71, Scottish Mutual Building
16 Donegal Square South
Belfast, BT1 5JG

☎ 028 9024 4007

🖱 stephaniereid@unltd.org.uk

BIRMINGHAM OFFICE

📧 Unit G2, The Ground Floor
The Arch, 48-52 Floodgate Street
Birmingham, B5 5SL

☎ 0121 766 4570

🖱 dawndcaccia@unltd.org.uk

SCOTLAND UNLTD OFFICE

📧 54 Manor Place
Edinburgh, EH3 7EH

☎ 0131 226 7333

🖱 jimbennett@unltd.org.uk

WALES OFFICE

📧 Fourth Floor, Baltic House
Mount Stuart Square
Cardiff, CF10 5FH

☎ 02920 484811

🖱 garethbickerton@unltd.org.uk

NESTA

 Fishmongers' Chambers
110 Upper Thames Street
London, EC4R 3TW

✆ 020 7645 9500

✍ nesta@nesta.org.uk
www.nesta.org.uk

The National Endowment for Science, Technology and the Arts, established in 1998, aims to give individuals the time, space and money to challenge conventional thinking, develop fresh approaches and come up with new ideas across all disciplines. NESTA uses interest on a National Lottery endowment to invest in a diverse range of people, including scientists, inventors, engineers, medical practitioners, educators, artists, writers, filmmakers and musicians. The aim of NESTA is to support creative individuals and new ideas, particularly those that cross normal categories of art, science and technology. Its broader aim is 'to improve the climate for creativity in the UK'; to this end it runs a number of award programmes.

The Invention and Innovation Programme invests in cutting-edge ideas that have the potential to break new ground in their field, supporting them with professional support and early-stage financial investment of between £5,000 and £150,000. Arts-based applicants are required to supply evidence to support the innovation and creativity of their project.

Dream Time Fellowships are for exceptional achievers with at least ten years' experience in their field who wish to take structured time away from their work. The awards are for a maximum value of £40,000, lasting up to a year.

The Creative Pioneer funding initiative encourages recent graduates from the design and moving image world to develop their business skills, while the Crucible project is a year-long set of seminar weekends for science and engineering researchers who want to broaden their engagement with other fields. One of these researchers is Barry Gibb, of the Wolfson Institute for Biomedical Research, who is studying how brain cells communicate. He is also a digital filmmaker and is interested in finding new approaches to science communication. Currently he is developing a project to try and create 'a new visual language for science'.

On the Pocket Shorts scheme (www.pocketshorts.com), filmmakers can apply for up to £2,000 funding to create innovative short films that are viewable on mobile phones and distributed via Bluetooth, WAP and Multimedia Messages (MMS). Pocket Shorts is an extension of NESTA's Creative Pioneer Programme, in conjunction with Yorkshire-based media body Short Circuits, and is aimed at filmmakers who have graduated in the last five years and now live in Yorkshire and Humberside, the North West and North East. The scheme offers up to eight individuals financial support, training sessions in filmmaking and technology, and an industry-professional mentor. At the end of each project, awardees will have produced a 1 minute-long film (downloadable from a WAP site) or four 15 second-long films (which can be sent from phones as well as downloaded) and will have their films showcased at UK film festivals. In 2004 there was an October application deadline for the scheme. Before applying, interested filmmakers can find out more at workshops held in each of the three regions.

NESTA Fellowships

NESTA support also comes in the form of the Fellowship programme, which gives exceptional individuals the time, space, resources and support to develop their ideas, pursue their goals, experiment and push the boundaries of knowledge and practice. Awardees come from all branches of the sciences, arts and technology and receive up to £75,000 to develop their work over a period of up to five years. The award can help with research, education, training, travel, access to facilities, securing intellectual property and displaying work. Each awardee is assigned a NESTA programme manager and a mentor. Awardees must have a record of achievement at a high level in their field, but may not have had the opportunity of the means to develop their talent to the full.

Individuals must be nominated for the award. NESTA's UK-wide network of nominators is made up of experts in their field and is continually refreshed. The fund seeks to make a range of awards spread across disciplines and communities. In certain geographical areas NESTA have appointed talent scouts to draw attention to outstanding individuals and offered certain organizations serving 'niche' communities the chance to make one nomination. All applications go through a rigorous assessment process, including independent, external assessment and consideration by the Fellowship Committee which is made up of both trustees and independent experts.

credit: Gisela Getty

Sophie Fiennes held a NESTA fellowship while making her documentary 'Hoover Street Revival'.

"It's a great organisation - it's specifically encouraging things that are not conforming to the basic frameworks of commissioning and commerce and I was nominated by someone who I had worked for. Having that kind of frame around my work was a real encouragement in a very un-English way, to say, ok, so this is a fund for people who don't quite fit in. NESTA was about creative development for me, and my fellowship covers a certain experimentation and development of my work rather than of a particular project. But I felt that in order to make the transition from small video to big cinema I needed to force the relationship between how people would perceive that, so I argued with NESTA that this particular project was part of my creative development. I wanted to have the money to make a transfer of my film to 35mm print, because if I could get the money to make the transition to a cinema screen then that was about traversing the boundary between TV and cinema. They said, 'If we look at your project further down the line and we think it's going to work like that then we will give you £25,000 to pay towards the transfer.' So that covered the transfer from video to film that would come later on."

CBA – DFID Broadcast Media Scheme

✉ Commonwealth Broadcasting Association
17 Fleet Street
London
EC4Y 1AA

📞 01508 538941 or 020 7583 5550

✉ sally-ann@cba.org.uk dfidfund@cba.org.uk
www.cba.org.uk

The Commonwealth Broadcasting Association (CBA) was founded in 1945 to promote quality broadcasting throughout the Commonwealth. The CBA administers the CBA-DFID Broadcast Media Scheme which is funded by the Department for International Development (DFID). The scheme aims to raise development awareness in the UK via mainstream media and it consists of two funds.

The DFID Programme Development Fund

The fund provides grants to help UK television producers research and develop factual programmes about developing countries. Up to £8,000 is available per project, as 80% of a programme development budget. Funding is available for up to 20 projects per year. Its objectives are:

• To support established television documentary makers wishing to produce programmes, for UK mainstream transmission, that promote understanding of the developing world.

• To fund development work on factual television programmes made in and about developing countries. Grants are intended to cover the costs of research, development, pilot filming and the procurement of filming rights and access.

• To improve the quality and quantity of viable programme proposals in this area of output, likely to interest commissioning editors.

Eligibility: The fund is open to established UK television production companies. Individual producers are not excluded from applying, but are encouraged to approach DFID via an established production company. Grants are for use on projects to be made in developing countries or for programmes that focus on development issues.

Selection Criteria

• Suitability of subject matter in expanding understanding of developing countries (as demonstrated by the treatment)

• Broadcast potential (as demonstrated by a letter of interest from a mainstream broadcaster)

• Originality of approach to subject matter

• Track record of the applicant, company/producer

• Production company is eligible only if has produced a project for UK broadcast within a period of 18 months (as demonstrated by detailed programme history)

• Track record of producer/director (as demonstrated by a CV)

There are three deadlines for the submission of proposals each year. The 2004 deadlines were 14 April, 28 July and 20 October. A previous recipient of funding was the production company True Vision, which was awarded development funding for their proposal 'Dying for Drugs' soon after the scheme was launched. The programme was an exposé of the international drugs industry requiring a great deal of patient investigation and overseas shooting. 'Dying for Drugs' was shown on Channel 4 in 2003. The Scotsman newspaper wrote of the programme, "The pharmaceutical industry is such a money-spinner that only the naive among us still believe that its actions are pure of heart. This documentary still threatens to open eyes and make jaws drop to the floor, though, as it exposes the lengths to which drugs companies will go in search of a profit, whether it's experimenting on unsuspecting children or exploiting the developing world. You'll never look at a painkiller the same way again."

DFID Travel Bursary Fund

Objectives:

• To enable UK television producers and television journalists to extend their knowledge of the developing world by working for up to three months in a Commonwealth developing country or countries.

• To create opportunities for UK television producers to expand their range and contacts and to work on programme ideas in Commonwealth country.

• To encourage UK television producers and television journalists to contribute to improving the quality and quantity of output about the developing world on UK TV.

Applying: The bursary is open to any experienced UK television producer or television journalist working for established broadcasters or production companies, wishing to work on programmes/stories in a Commonwealth developing country for transmission on UKTV. Applicants should be staff of, or on contract to, a UK television organisation or independent production company. Established freelancers are also encouraged to apply if they can indicate support from an organisation or commissioning editor for whom they work.

Successful applicants will spend up to three months in a Commonwealth developing country of their choice. They will use this time either to work for a local broadcasting organisation or television company, while developing programme ideas for use back in the UK, or to research a specific programme idea intended for transmission in the UK.

The scheme operates as a rolling programme. Before completing an application form, potential applicants should contact Sally-Ann Wilson (the CBA DFID Fund Executive) to discuss their interest by emailing sally-ann@cba.org.uk. The bursary is of variable value, depending on the destination and duration of stay, but is offered up to the value of £10,000.

BBC Producer David Olusago took up a DFID Travel Bursary to travel to Namibia and follow up leads on a story that had intrigued him for some while. He shot sequences and returned to the UK where the BBC eventually commissioned his film 'Genocide and the Second Reich'. David's film, shown on BBC Four in December 2004, is a powerful and disturbing film that uncovers a brutal and obscure chapter in the history of imperialism in Africa - the genocide of 85,000 Herero people by the German army in Namibia in 1904. The programme offers an original historical insight while providing a disturbing contemporary resonance.

Applicants will be asked to outline their proposed destination and workplace, the purpose of their work, how they plan to carry it out and the benefits to their own organisation. They will also need to submit a budget and references from their Head of Department or equivalent. Where appropriate, an endorsement by a commissioning editor should be provided, indicating a positive interest in transmitting material generated by the project.

The British Council

 Film and Literature Department
The British Council
10 Spring Gardens
London SW1A 2BN

✆ 020 7389 3051

✉ filmandliterature@britishcouncil.org
www.britishcouncil.org

The British Council is a non-departmental public body funded largely by the Foreign and Commonwealth Office and by the sale of services such as language teaching. Its remit is 'to build mutually beneficial relationships between people in the UK and other countries and to increase appreciation of the UK's creative ideas and achievements.' To this end, it funds various trips abroad by artists, and the promotion of British work including film. It does not fund film production, but is very useful as an information resource, via its sites www.britfilms.org, and www.creativexport.com. The British Council offers some support for distribution and promotion of British films abroad; see Chapter 12, Festivals and markets.

It may be seventy years old but is by no means stuffy: fashion design, pop bands and digital content get as much of a look-in as more established art forms, perhaps more, as the target audience abroad is young people, on the grounds that they will be more receptive to exposure to British culture than are oldies.

The British Council's film advisory committee consists of:

Chairman: Duncan Kenworthy, Producer; Chairman, DNA Films

Members: Michelle Kass, Agent - Michelle Kass Associates
Cameron McCracken, Deputy Managing Director, Pathe UK
Susan Richards, Director, European Humanities Network
Nicole Mackey, Head of International Sales, Capitol Films
Asif Kapadia, Director
Paul Webster, Independent producer
Jill Tandy, Producer, Qwerty Films
Charlotte Macleod, Director, The Script Factory

The UK Film Council

 The UK FILM COUNCIL
10 Little Portland Street
London W1W 7JG

 020 7861 7861
Fax: 020 7861 7862

 General enquiries info@ukfilmcouncil.org.uk
Press enquiries press@ukfilmcouncil.org.uk
Premiere Fund premiere@ukfilmcouncil.org.uk
New Cinema Fund newcinemafund@ukfilmcouncil.org.uk
Development Fund development@ukfilmcouncil.org.uk
Shorts shorts@ukfilmcouncil.org.uk
Distribution and Exhibition Fund def.administrator@ukfilmcouncil.org.uk

The Film Council came into existence in 2000, with the name changing to UK Film Council in 2003. Its role is to be 'the Government's strategic agency for film in the UK. Its aim is to stimulate a competitive, successful and vibrant British film industry and culture, and to promote the widest possible enjoyment and understanding of cinema throughout the nations and regions of the UK.'

In the year ending 2004, the UKFC received £30 million from the Lottery and £24 million from grant-in-aid. It gave out £20 million as grant-in-aid (that is, to organisations, including £14 million to the BFI); £21 million to single film projects or film slates; £0.8 million on training; £1 million on assisting with specialised print and advertising; £0.3 millon on cinema equipment schemes; £0.1 million on publication awards; £12 million to franchise projects; and £4 million to RSAs, Skillset (training to improve the industry's skills base) and First Light (filmmaking with young people).

(Annual Reports and Financial Statements, the Statistical Yearbook and the Annual Review are available from www.ukfilmcouncil.org.uk/filmindustry/annrprtsaccts/ or by contacting the press office. The financial statements list all the recipients of Film Council funding, and lets you know senior staff earnings.)

A setback for documentary filmmakers is the fact that the Film Council was not set up with any particular responsibility for, or interest in, documentary film, but many of its schemes are open to docs.

At a management level, there are two board members, Gurinder Chadha and Parvinder Vir, whose biographies specifically include documentary, although both have moved on to fiction features.

Chairman:	Stewart Till, Chairman and Chief Executive Officer of UIP.
CEO:	John Woodward, former Director of the British Film Institute.
Board:	
Colin Brown,	Chairman of Cinesite Worldwide (Kodak subsidiaries) – a vendor of film effects, from practical through to computer-based visual effects, to the international film industry.
Andrew Eaton,	company director of Revolution Films, which has produced films including 'Bright Young Things' and 'Wonderland'.
Gurinder Chadha,	director, 'Bend it Like Beckham', began her career as a BBC news reporter. She went on to direct award-winning documentaries for the British Film Institute, BBC and Channel 4.
Mark Devereux	is a solicitor, specialising in media, and is the Senior Partner of the law firm Olswang. He has worked in the film industry for 24 years.
Nigel Green,	joint Managing Director of UK distribution company Entertainment Film Distributors: 'Lord of the Rings', 'Gosford Park' and 'Traffic'.
Stephen Knibbs,	Chief Operating Officer at Vue Entertainment, which bought the former Warner Village UK cinema circuit in 2003.
Anthony Minghella,	chair of the BFI, director, 'The English Patient', 'Truly Madly Deeply'. Since 2000 has been joint owner of Mirage Enterprises, which has supported a number of distinctive filmmakers and their projects including Tom Tykwer's 'Heaven' and Richard Eyre's 'Iris'.
Alison Owen,	co-director of Ruby Films, producer of 'Sylvia', 'Proof', 'Elizabeth'.
Marc Samuelson,	producer and exec producer, 'Wilde', 'Arlington Road' and 'The Libertine'.
Heather Rabbatts,	Managing Director of Channel 4's education arm, 4Learning.
Iain Smith,	producer, 'Seven Years in Tibet', 'The Fifth Element' and 'Entrapment'.
David Sproxton,	co-founder and Director of animation studio Aardman Animations.
Parminder Vir,	independent producer. A background in TV documentary: 'Single Voices', 'Algeria: Women at War', 'The Sex Warriors and the Samurai', two series of Developing Stories. Now developing a range of fiction feature films.

The establishment of the Film Council meant that some public funding became differently distributed, and some schemes were phased out or adjusted:

The British Film Institute (BFI) is now funded through the Film Council, although it functions as an independent body delivering cultural and educational objectives as set by the Film Council. The BFI's production department was assimilated into the production funding of the Film Council. British Screen Finance, and the British Screen European Co-Production Fund went the same way. The British Film Commission is now the International Department of the UK Film Council, with a role of encouraging inward investment to the UK from international production companies.

UK Film Council development and funding schemes

The UKFC is both a strategic body, trying to develop and enact a plan for the film sector, and a funding body. Apart from shorts funding, dealt with below, it has three UK-wide development and production funds:

The Premier Fund is headed by Sally Caplan, who has £8 million a year to invest in major feature films that are expected to do well internationally and provide a good return on the investment.

The annual £4 million Development Fund, headed by Jenny Borgars, aims to broaden the quality, range and ambition of British film projects and talent being developed, particularly the screenplays. Over time, the fund aims to build creatively focused relationships, with a breadth of talent, from 'first timers' to experienced practitioners. The fund also seeks to help British film companies to grow sustainable businesses. There is funding for single projects at the stages of seed funding, partnered development, and pre-pre-production.

Although it has no specific remit to do so, the New Cinema Fund, below, deals most often with documentary.

An exception to this is the Development Fund's support for:

The Documentary Development Slate

In December 2004, the UK Film Council announced the successful applicants to its three-year development slates scheme. Seven partnerships share £7.5 million over three years in a scheme aimed at creating stronger links between British producers, international sales companies and distributors. The successful proposal from Darlow Smithson is the only one that aims exclusively at documentary production.

John Smithson is Executive Chair and Creative Director of Darlow Smithson Productions, a London-based production company (co-founded by John in 1989) which has a track record of docu-dramas and factual series for international broadcast. Smithson's first foray into feature filmmaking was the 2003 'Touching the Void', directed by Oscar-winner (and Shooting People Documentary Network patron) Kevin Macdonald, for which Smithson corralled support and funding from PBS, Channel 4 (then FilmFour), the Film Council, and distributors Pathé. The film was a remarkable critical and commercial success, becoming the highest-grossing documentary in UK box office history and screening in more than twenty-eight countries. It also helped push open the door for documentaries in the cinema.

In December 2004 the UK Film Council announced that Darlow Smithson was one of the seven successful applicants to the new Development Slate Fund. This three-year fund offers £250,000 of Lottery money yearly to a group led by Darlow Smithson and including Pathé Pictures, FilmFour and Channel 4 as primary partners, and IFC Entertainment and the Tricycle Theatre. This annual investment from the Film Council is matched by investment from the partners. On top of this core investment, funding for each project is then sought from within and beyond the partnership, and could range from £500,000 to £10 million.

John Smithson explains:

"We're a successful factual television company used to making docs for UK TV, and increasingly, doing complicated co-production for the international market. We'd never really considered theatrical documentary until 'Touching the Void'; there hadn't been a critically and commercially succesful documentary and I didn't have a high opinion of that market. But that film gave us the opportunity to move from TV to theatrical, and its success opened my eyes to the potential. It made me wonder, given the talent in the UK and the documentaries that do manage to get made for TV, even without a strong theatrical outlet, how come there weren't more successful documentaries of this type. I wondered why we shouldn't try to develop a centre of

excellence, using our experience to get more projects going and to make them work.

So when the Film Council announced the Development Slate funding, we thought of making an application based on theatrical films of true stories: hybrid and regular docs, and straight docudrama. We got our old partners back on board and made the pitch, and the project has just started as of April 2005, with Elinor Day as Head. There will probably be about four people running it, when it's up and going. I think the Film Council were happy with our proposal because we made a focussed bid and, with the track record of 'Touching the Void' that we'd already all been involved in, we were an attractive partnership.

So what we have in place are the production company, the broadcaster, the distributor, the sales agent, international links: it's a great opportunity. How it works is that Darlow Smithson are the initial filter. People will come to us, or we'll initiate some projects, and if there's an idea we like and want to develop, we then need to get the approval of all the backers, that is, the other partners in our partnership. The beauty of it is that if the backers don't like an idea and don't think it has the creative and commercial potential, we won't waste more time on it. But if they do like it, we know that there's interest in place, and there's the structure of all our partners in place, which puts the project on a good footing already.

We're obliged to invest at least 30% of the funding in other organisations, so some of the projects will originate with us, but some will start with and be made by others, and in that case they'll still be under the umbrella of the partnership. We want to be a talent magnet, so that the best ideas, the best directors, come through us and work with us. Already we've had some good proposals that would work on TV, but they haven't had the X-factor that would really make them work theatrically. It's hard enough to get single docs to work well on TV, and the problem's amplified when it comes to theatrical release.

But it's very early days and we aren't prescribing what sort of films they'll be or who could come up with them. It could be that we'll also play a matchmaking role, putting directors who we know are good onto projects that came from elsewhere. We have an open view as to who will come to the Fund. We don't want to close any doors, but we must be picky about who we select, who we put forward to our partners. The chances are that the financiers will expect any filmmakers to have a track record, but the story is the vital thing. That's our challenge: to find and develop the great story and craft it into a film that audiences want to spend their money on seeing. That's what we managed to do with 'Touching the Void'; we knew it could go beyond TV and that it had our vital components: great story idea, financial potential, talent round the film, access.

As to distribution, we're not looking to change the whole structure of cinema-going in the UK. The film has to do the work of pulling the audience in. We have Pathé in our partnership, and that's part of what our role is, to make films that distributors will want to show. Perhaps our films won't be exclusively mainstream; we might not get into every multiplex, but we would seek wide distribution. 'Touching the Void', for example, was in fifty screens. And films chosen for the Fund also have to be able to work beyond the UK.

So we're after high-quality, criticallly acclaimed, commercially successful films, based on great stories, that can benefit from the cross-fertilisation and the snowballing effect that comes from us working with these partners in place. There can't be hundreds; we're working now, just as the funding actually starts, to get the first shortlist of ten ideas in place. And it's exciting, a fantastic opportunity."

The New Cinema Fund

Of most relevance to doc filmmakers, however, is the New Cinema Fund of £5 million, headed by Paul Trijbits (until September 2006), which encourages unique ideas, innovative approaches and new voices. The fund intends to finance films with passion and verve that connect with a broad range of audiences. The normal investment is between 15 – 50% of the feature film's production budget, as equity investment.

Himesh Kar is Senior Executive of the New Cinema Fund at the UK Film Council.

"When we first began supporting documentary it was below the wire; there was no provision or mention of it in the original Film Council set up. The first two films we supported were 'Hoover Street Revival' and 'Live Forever'. We worked with Nick Fraser (from Storyville) on these, and like all our feature films (and docs) they had a UK theatrical distributor and a theatrical sales agent.

The next stage was setting up the World Documentary Fund, working, again, with Nick Fraser, and with the National Film Board of Canada. We were looking for like-minded partners to work with, and the Canadians were willing and able to move things along. The point of the WDF was to be a one-stop shop for feature documentaries of the highest calibre, and it was a useful exercise; we got to see how docs are approached by other countries and other big organisations. So that resulted in 'Game Over: Kasparov and the Machine', and we're just in post-production for 'Diameter of the Bomb'. However, our rationale for feature docs has evolved over this period of time and whilst we are happy to work with both the BBC and NFB on a case by case basis, we are no longer running docs through this initiative

Around this time we also supported 'Touching the Void', and this really raised our game for feature documentaries. The rationale we have now is to approach feature documentaries as feature films, just as we do for the fiction films that are submitted to the New Cinema Fund. We support approximately 8 films a year, and if all the best proposals were docs then we'd be quite happy taking them; there is no cap on the number of feature docs we could do. Any film, and that includes the docs, that we support needs to come to us with the film components set up in the first instance: there needs to be a UK distributor and theatrical sales agent attached. For feature docs we would like to see the same ambition and scale that would make it work in cinema as we would demand from a fiction film; there needs to be a real sense that this is a film that will get the audience away from their televisions and paying a tenner to see it in a cinema. Ideally it should also be attractive to a broadcaster and we hope for them. to put in a larger license fee than the regular TV doc fee.

As well as funding the production of these NCF films, we also at our discretion fund some pilots. The pilot is not an assesment, it is a practical way of unlocking process from the treatment. For fiction, what we'd do is work with the director on a couple of scenes from the script, seeing at that close level how they would make decisions about genre, style, use of technology and so on. It is used in a slightly altered way with docs. What happens is that we get the proposal, and on assessment of this and other material (including the director's previous work) if we feel it has the potential to work as a feature film we will bring in the creative team for a meeting So we ask them, 'How will this work in the cinema?' and we ask how we can help them achieve the realisation of this. We're helping them turn the idea into a structure that works. So the process might involve, for a couple of scenes or elements of the film, hiring a script editor to work with the director on the treatment then selecting archive material and treating it as script, writing out exactly what happens, and then cutting these scenes with a film editor. On a recent pilot project we engaged the production team with Empire design, having them work together to create a trailer for the film they wished to make and thus providing them with a further tool to initiate talks with UK distributors and sales agents and start thinking in depth about the production path they would need to follow to reach that end goal The pilot is not a development or conceptual tool; it's meant to be a practical tool, clarifying the structure, the aim, the thought processes behind the film over a couple of months, helping the filmmaker to engage with the end user, even at this early stage.

It's early days for the pilot scheme in terms of feature docs, but I think we've arrived at a good point, we're more confident in what our rationale is. An important element for us is that we're part of a collaborative process. We don't just want to get the film funded, we want to engage with those who can get the film out to the public. So we're finding ways of bringing the sales agents and distributors into the process earlier on, rather than waiting until the film's finished, and then asking them if they want it. Because if by that point, they say, 'We'll think about it,' I take that as a no; we need to be working on the basis that everyone wants to be in on it now, at the start.

Markets are becoming saturated with docs, and like much of the film industry it's the survival of the fittest. If there are only two or three cinema docs a year, but they're successful ones, then this helps to keep the market buoyant for everyone else. It's better for us to support a filmmaker on a project with the potential to reach a wider cinema audience, than for us to support a doc whose honest place is on TV, that, however good it is, gets audiences of only a couple of hundred in the cinema. There's little benefit to the filmmaker for that; their films would be better off on TV where they would be seen by more people, so it's just no use for us funding at that level (we cannot fund TV programmes anyway!). And for the filmmakers we support, we want them to go on to successful careers, we want our backing to help them make a swifter transition to feature films, drama, whatever their next step is.

We support docs just as we do our feature films and provide the same resources to help them get into production. I do have sympathy with the view that docs are in some ways different and have specific requirements, but with limited resources and our rules for funding, this is the route that enables us to fund docs. Our role remains upbeat and we continue in the belief that feature docs can attract a cinema audience. Otherwise you end up supporting films but no audience goes, so no distributors want to pick up that or subsequent films... It's a balance between commercial and cultural demands.

What I've noticed about submissions is that the numbers went up massively after 'Touching the Void'. Before then, we'd get a doc submitted to the NCF for production funding every two or three months, but now it's not uncommon to have three applications in a week. As for the content of the proposals, 90% would be better for TV. They're the sort of film that, yes, you could watch and enjoy for 60 minutes, but for 90 minutes, in a cinema? It's important to think about where your film is best placed. Another common thing is that we get ideas that we feel we've seen before. Everyone says their idea is new and original, but you sometimes think, 'Well, I read about that in a magazine recently, or I saw it on Channel 4.' I'm not being glib to say that there are no truly original ideas; it's your take on it that matters. So we could see an idea that isn't wholly unique, but the proposal can elevate it into something special that we'd want to support. We look at the whole proposal: the director, the team behind them, etc.

We're not the Development Fund; we're specifically production, and we work separately from the new documentary Development Slate that John Smithson is in charge of. But it's great having them beside us, because it puts us all within a better structure for film."

Production

The New Cinema Fund has supported these feature documentaries:

'Touching the Void', 2003, producer: John Smithson, director: Kevin Macdonald, co-financed by FilmFour, Channel 4 and PBS. 'Touching the Void' screened at Telluride, Toronto, Dinard and London 2003 before being released by Pathé in the UK in December 2003. IFC released 'Touching the Void' in the US, where it recorded the highest per screen average in the week of the 25th January, 2004, and accumulated a box office of over $3.8 million. Short-listed for the 2005 Academy Award for Best Documentary Feature.

'Game Over: Kasparov and the Machine', 2003, producer: Hal Vogel, director: Vikram Jayanti. Vikram Jayanti is the award-winning documentary producer of 'When We Were Kings'. 'Game Over' follows Gary Kasparov as he guides us into the world of professional chess players, and investigates his allegation that IBM cheated during the infamous Man vs. Machine tournament in 1997. The first feature documentary to be co-financed by the National Film Board of Canada and the BBC through the World Documentary Fund, it premiered at Toronto 2003. 'Game Over' received its UK premiere at the Sheffield Documentary Festival 2003, screened at London 2003 and was released in the UK by Momentum.

'Diameter of the Bomb', 2003, producers: Georgina Townley & Paul Goldin, director: Stephen Silver. The second feature documentary to be jointly funded by the NCF, BBC Storyville and National Film Board of Canada through the World Documentary Fund. The story of a suicide bombing of a bus in Israel in June 2002, and ten ordinary people whose lives were irreparably changed. To be distributed in the UK by Redbus.

'Hoover Street Revival', 2001, executive producer: Kees Kasander, producer/director: Sophie Fiennes. The first feature documentary from the New Cinema Fund in partnership with BBC Storyville. This compelling film moves like a kaleidoscope through life in South Central Los Angeles, focusing on the Greater Bethany Community Church where preacher Bishop Noel Jones is setting the minds of his congregation on fire. Premiering at Locarno, it went on to screen at Edinburgh and London 2002. Released in the UK by Metro Tartan.

'Live Forever', 2002, producer: John Battsek, director: John Dower
The New Cinema Fund's second feature documentary co-financed with BBC Storyville, 'Live Forever' charts the highs and lows of British rock 'n' roll in the 1990s, and the cultural explosion of 'Cool Britannia'. It premiered at London 2002 and was released by Helkon Redbus in the UK in 2003.

Other NCF funding

At its own discretion and instigation, the NCF can offer to pay for the production costs, excluding above the line costs, of up to £10,000 for a pilot film. Pilot film funding will usually take the form of equity investment repayable to the UK Film Council upon commencement of principal photography of a feature film based upon, or connected to, the pilot film.

Post-production/completion funding: The New Cinema Fund will accept applications for feature film projects which have begun the production process but which require completion through post production funding. Producers can apply at any stage of the production or post-production process, but print and advertising costs are not eligible. To apply: return the regular NCF application form accompanied by a VHS or DVD of a rough-cut/assembly of the film, a budget for completion, details of how the project has been funded to date, and letter(s) of interest from UK distributors. If the film is still being shot, the New Cinema Fund's assessment process will be aided by a selection of footage and the shooting script, if available. The New Cinema Fund may: make an offer of funding for completion of the film, turn the project down, or, at its discretion, make an interim award of funding to examine the viability of the film and then use the results of that interim award to determine whether to proceed with any further award.

In 2003 and 2004, the NCF contracted the company MayaVision to run a separate Short Film Completion Fund. This was a £50,000 fund to support the completion of films under ten minutes long, which in 2003 was awarded to ten films. At printing in May 2005, the Film Council was unable to give details of whether or not this would run again. Again, at May 2005, the Low Budget Feature Project was still only in the process of inviting tenders to run the scheme, so it won't be open to filmmakers for a while yet.

Cinema Extreme

Matthieu de Braconier
The Bureau
PO Box No 5366
London W1A 2WW

www.thebureau.co.uk

The Film Council has commissioned production company The Bureau to run its funding and development scheme Cinema Extreme, which is to help filmmakers with a track record make the next step towards feature directing, by financing development and production of an innovative short film (ten to thirty minutes long) for the cinema. This is the funding scheme that perhaps has most ambitious aims, asking potential applicants to consider 'What kind of stories do you want to tell? What kinds of stories are missing from British cinema? What kind of voice and vision do you want to have as a filmmaker now and in the future?'

Through the 2005 scheme, there will be two sets of workshops for up to 80 applicants, the first in July 2005, and the second in November. Before, during and after the workshops there will be further development of the individual projects, which may involve working with script editors and mentors. As the development programme progresses, four teams will be commissioned by the UK Film Council and FilmFour to produce up to four short films, for delivery within six months and screening at the Edinburgh, Brief Encounters or London Film Festivals in 2006.

Submissions: Cinema Extreme is a director-led scheme, so applications must come from an individual or team with a director in it, although the scheme can pair up individuals with production companies if necessary. Each director can submit up to three ideas for a short film "that explores new storytelling methods and pushes the boundaries of contemporary cinema", and can be realised on a £50,000 budget. A film must be predominantly in English and have substantially British main elements (e.g. producer, writer, director, location, story). It is not an entry level or beginners' scheme; you need a demonstrable track record in filmmaking, such as having directed a film that's been shown at significant international festivals, or directing single drama or documentaries for a network broadcaster. The aim is to provide filmmakers with a level of experience and expertise so that the next step in their careers will be the making of their first feature film. Crossing over from other disciplines and genres is encouraged. None of the Cinema Extreme films of the past couple of years (the scheme has been running since 2002) were docs, but, as the FAQs describe, "If you are a documentary filmmaker who wants to make feature-length documentaries that will play in the cinema and can demonstrate that this film is a stepping stone for you into features, then you can apply with a documentary proposal; if you are a documentary filmmaker who wants to cross over into fiction or use a combination of media and styles then you can apply."

There will be two calls for applications during the year. The first call is 11th April to 6th May; the second is 8th August to 9th September. Applications must include director's showreel and CV, an outline of the idea, notes on how to develop it, and director's statement of intent; see the website for further details. Within eight weeks of the closing date you'll be notified if you've been short-listed for the development process, then within two days of interview if you've been selected. If you're selected, you must agree to commit to the whole development process: attending the workshops and providing FilmFour and UK Film Council with a first option to finance your developed project, if it's one of the final four. During the development process, projects will join and leave the scheme, following quarterly assessments on the progress of each project.

Digital Shorts

Digital Shorts is a nationwide scheme that ran its first bout from 2001 to 2005, encouraging creativity, new talent and cutting-edge filmmaking by funding the production of short films from new filmmakers. New and emerging filmmakers from diverse backgrounds used digital technology to make innovative short and develop their skills and talent. There were no restrictions in terms of genre or theme, but the scheme was intended to focus on narrative fiction, documentary and animation filmmaking rather than artists' film and video. Films had to be for theatrical distribution not TV. The budget for each film was up to £10,000.

The Digital Shorts scheme is a really good opportunity for newer filmmakers, or people wanting to move genre or go down a new route in their filmmaking career. The funding is useful, and the support from the organising body can be extremely helpful in getting the filmmaker into the loop of understanding how public funding and distribution work. Digital Shorts made during the first bout are sometimes toured by the partnering body, depending on their level of enthusiasm or activity; it can be quite hard to find out about the films after the event. Also confusing is the fact that the various schemes can have different names; the London scheme, for example, was called 'Pulse', but was still that region's Digital Shorts.

The Film Council has allocated £700,000 each year to continue the Digital Shorts scheme for a further three years from 2005. This will support the production of approximately 120 low-budget shorts a year, and will encourage new talent across the UK. The Film Council does not run the scheme, but selects participating partners to co-fund and run the schemes in each area. The partners for a further three years are to be announced in June 2005, but it's probable that as in the last round, each RSA (or an RSA in partnership with a local organisation) would win the tender for running the scheme in that region. There are nine regional schemes, plus one each in Northern Ireland, Wales, and Scotland. New to the 2005 – 2007 round is the addition of one scheme that will support eight filmmakers with disabilities, and, as in the previous round, one scheme is specifically for filmmakers from Black and Ethnic Minority backgrounds.

See the Film Council's website for news of the announcement of the partners, then you'll need to check the guidelines and restrictions for the scheme or schemes relevant to you, as each partner can impose different rules. In the previous round, for example, one or two schemes did not accept documentary submissions, but on the whole they were keen to support ideas for docs aimed at theatrical exhibition.

There is also Digital Shorts Plus, as a progression route for directors who have previously made a Digital Short and demonstrated particular directorial merit. Each organising body for Digital Shorts will be able to propose one filmmaker from their scheme to make a further short film at a maximum budget of £20,000. All films produced during the first year must be delivered by 31st March 2006. The UK Film Council is determined that successful films should reach as wide an audience as possible through cinema screenings, festival screenings, TV screenings, internet distribution and all other distribution methods. Digital Shorts actively explores new ideas and possibilities for distribution and the UK Film Council intends to coordinate a single exhibition strategy to ensure that the films and associated talent are promoted as widely as possible.

Chapter Four
Public funding, Scotland

Research by Julie Moggan

Scottish Screen

✉ Second Floor
249 West George Street1
Glasgow, G2 4QE

☎ 0141 302 1700

✆ info@scottishscreen.com
www.scottishscreen.com

The UK Film Council delegates money to Scottish Screen, for which funding of almost £3 million a year also comes through the Scottish Executive. The interim chief executive is Alyson Hagan, the Head of Operations is Alan Knowles, and Emma Valentine is coordinator of the Scottish MEDIA Antenna (see Chapter 8, European Funding, for more on this).

Scottish Screen develops and promotes film, television and new media in Scotland. Its aims are:

• To develop world class production business in Scotland.
• To attract major productions to Scotland.
• To champion a culture of investment in screen industries.
• To nurture and develop talent and audiences.
• To preserve and present Scottish screen production.
• To encourage and support international outlook.
• To drive screen policy from school to statute.

Scottish Screen allocates National Lottery funds to the development and production of feature films (both fiction and documentary) that are intended for theatrical release. It runs a number of short film production schemes in partnership with other screen organisations, several of which are open to documentary projects. Other support for doc filmmakers could come through support of distribution and exhibition, including a presence at major festivals, through promotion of archive resources, or through script feedback.

Scottish Screen put up one third of the budget for 'Rivers and Tides' (2001) - a feature documentary about Scottish sculptor Andy Goldsworthy, directed by Thomas Riedelsheimers. Partner funders included WDR/Arte, YLE (the Finnish national broadcasting company) and Filmboard Berlin-Brandenburg. 'Rivers and Tides' has won a host of awards on the international film festival circuit. It was distributed in a number of countries and did particularly well at the box office in America and Germany.

'Orwell - Against the Tide' (2003) is a feature documentary about George Orwell's life and his love/hate relationship with Scotland, directed by Mark Littlewood. Scottish Screen put up 39% of the budget and the financial picture was completed by a total of 14 different European cultural and broadcasting organisations. The film was selected by the Observer/Guardian to open their two-month-long tribute to George Orwell and it has been nominated for BAFTA and Prix Italia awards.

Director (and Shooting People patron) Kevin Macdonald, working with 4 Way Pictures, received Lottery funding in 2004 to make 'The Lost City of Bam', a documentary about the destruction of the city, told through the eyes of people who know it.

Scottish Screen funding strands

Feature film production funding

Funding is available for up to £500,000 per project for feature films (including feature-length documentaries) aimed at theatrical distribution. Scottish Screen will fund up to 25% of a production's cost. There are five application deadlines a year.

Short film production funding

This fund supports the production of short films, documentaries and animation intended for theatrical release. The films must have core Scottish elements. Applications for awards under £25,000 are accepted on a continuous basis. Applications for awards over £25,000 have four deadlines a year. Scottish Screen will generally not fund more than 50% of the total budget. If some of the partnership funding is 'in kind', applicants must find at least the same amount in cash.

In 2004, producer Jason Hall working with Edinburgh Mediabase was awarded £14,000 for 'Paris - EC100', a short doc celebrating the centenary of the entente cordiale.

Project development funding

Funding of up to £75,000 is available for second-stage development of Scottish feature films, documentaries and animation projects intended for theatrical release. The fund is aimed at projects already at a relatively advanced stage. It will support elements such as schedule preparation and budget, packaging for financiers etc. Applications for under £25,000 are accepted on a continuous basis. Applications for awards over £25,000 have four deadlines a year. Scottish Screen will normally contribute between 10% and 50% of the total development costs. The full amount of any development award will be repayable to Scottish Screen, plus a 50% premium.

Producer Noe Mendelle and director Kalunga Lima, working with the Scottish Documentary Institute, were awarded £5,000 towards 'My Country's Photo Album: A Journey Through Angola', a photographic journey to the filmmaker's ancestral homeland.

Script development funding

Funding between £5000 and £25,000 is available to projects which would benefit from further development of the script prior to packaging and financing. The fund is open to fiction, documentary and animation projects intended for theatrical release. Applications are accepted on a continuous basis, and Scottish Screen can fund up to 90% of the total costs. The full amount of any Script Development award will be repayable to Scottish Screen, plus a 50% premium.

Submissions

Applying: Only commercial companies or organisations, with substantial Scottish core elements and with a formal constitution, are eligible to apply. Applications from companies not normally based in Scotland must demonstrate material benefit to the broader Scottish industry. International co-productions with a strong Scottish element are also eligible. Application forms should be accompanied by additional information including storyboard, research papers, character descriptions, project history, production schedule, budget, financing plan, CVs and details of rights.

Each application will be assessed in relation to the benefit of the project to the Scottish general public; the benefit to the Scottish film industry; the development stage of the project; the creative and commercial quality; the potential to reach audiences in Scotland and beyond; the added improvements lottery funding will bring to the project; applicant's ability to manage the project affectively; a realistic budget and schedule; the level of partnership funding in place.

Conditions: Scottish Screen aims to invest in films in which it has a good chance of recouping its investment. They will recoup from film revenues according to established industry practice. Their share will be in proportion to their level of investment. With each of the production funds (except the short film award), a contribution to the Skills Investment Fund of 0.5% of the production budget up to a maximum contribution of £39,400 is mandatory. Scottish Screen will also expect the production budget to contain provision for any appropriate trade association fees.

Archive Live

This was a scheme run in 2004, with the aim of promoting awareness of the wealth of material (over 3,000 hours of film) held in the Scottish Screen Archive, by encouraging its creative use. Archive Live was designed to encourage experimentation and interactive creativity, using Archive materials and new digital technologies. In November 2004, two projects were selected to publicly present their projects which made use of the Archive. One of these was The Tomorrows Project, created by leading web artists Dan Norton and Gair Dunlop, which was also recently nominated for a BAFTA Scotland Award. Their live internet demonstration, with live music, involved the projection of words, moving images and sounds from the Archive onto a cinema screen, to show visions of Scotland's future which were created in the past. www.tompro.co.uk

Archive Live was a pilot; check via the http://data.scottishscreen.com for 2005 information.

Scottish Screen and external partners

This Scotland

This Scotland is a digital documentary production scheme run by Scottish Screen and the two ITV regional broadcasters Scottish TV and Grampian TV, to commission six single, 30-minute television documentaries from new and existing talent. For the 2005 scheme, the closing date for applications was December 2004, and the six successful programmes, broadcast in 2005 include: Katrina McPherson's 'Catching the Tide', and 'Gold Fever', a musical doc about gold panning, directed by Ruth Barrie and produced by Alice Stilgoe.

To be kept informed of subsequent rounds, email thisscotland@scottishscreen.com or telephone 0141 302 1742

Alt-W

Alt-W
23 Springfield
Dundee, DD1 4JE

01382 348631

info@alt-w.com
www.alt-w.com

This scheme supports Scottish-based creative entrepreneurial talent to produce innovative digital productions, particularly experimental and interactive, that can be delivered via the web. Production grants of up to £2,500 are awarded. Alt-W partner organisations may provide equipment resources for successful applicants. Training and mentoring support is also offered. Alt-W's partner organisations include Scottish Screen, Dundee City Council, Scottish Enterprise Tayside, Dundee College, University of Abertay and the University of Dundee.

Applying: Applicants must live in Scotland. Individuals, students, artists' groups and teams of professionals are eligible to apply. Applicants can come from varying backgrounds, including visual artists, designers, film and video makers, audio artists, musicians, and games and programme developers. Applicants should submit an application form along with a CV and website address relating to their practice. Short-listed candidates are invited to attend an interview which usually takes place within four weeks of the advertised deadline. In 2005 there was a January deadline for applications.

Applicants are assessed on the quality and originality of their proposal, evidence of their ability and commitment to successfully manage and deliver the project, and the degree to which their project takes into consideration both the limitations and advantages of using the web as a tool for interactivity and delivery.

Previous recipients of funding from the 2004 scheme include: 'Reproduced', dir. Sam Hill, a series of interactive guides to sex education for different age groups including young children, teenagers and adults; and 'Anticipation', dir. Holger Mohaupt, a web-based, non-linear documentary revealing the cultural backgrounds of individuals engaging in scientific research into Myotonic Dystrophy across the world. A Research And Development award went to 'Bodies of Water', dir. Maud Sulter, which explores the legacy of the Atlantic slave trade.

Bridging the Gap

 Scottish Documentary Institute
eca, 74 Lauriston Place
Edinburgh
EH3 9DF
Scotland, UK

 0131 221 6125

 www.scottishdocinstitute.com

Bridging the Gap aims to nurture filmmaking talent in Scotland by supporting the production of creative documentaries that push the boundaries between fiction and non-fiction. Ten short-listed projects were selected for a development period of six weeks and then pitched to a panel of experts who selected the five filmmakers to take their project to completion. Those filmmakers work with the support of individual mentors, but free from the restrictions of a TV strand. The scheme commissions five 10 minute digital documentaries, each year with a budget of £16,000 (half in cash and half in production support). In 2004, the films were commissioned on the theme of silence. The five commissioned filmmakers also receive training and mentoring over a 6 month period. The final films are intended for distribution in cinemas and festivals. The scheme is run by the Scottish Documentary Institute (www.scottishdocinstitute.com) at the Edinburgh College of Art and the Angus Digital Media Centre.

Applying: The scheme is open to all filmmakers based in Scotland, and particularly aims to bridge the gap between training/graduation and a first broadcast. Along with the application form, applicants must submit a treatment and a VHS of their latest relevant work. In 2004 there was an October deadline for the scheme. Bridging the Gap is looking for strong visual ideas from filmmakers who are keen to explore cinematic documentary storytelling. Ten ideas will be short-listed on the basis of the treatment and supporting materials. They will be taken into a six week development period and then pitched to a panel of experts who will commission the final five projects.

Cineworks

 Cineworks
Glasgow Media Access Centre
3rd Floor
34 Albion Street
GLASGOW
G11 1LH

☏ 0141 553 2620

✉ info@cineworks.co.uk

Cineworks is an initiative run by Glasgow Media Access Centre and Mediabase, Edinburgh, and funded by Scottish Screen, the UK Film Council's New Cinema Fund and BBC Scotland. It funds five short documentaries a year, with the 2006 scheme announced in the summer of 2005. For 2005, the deadline was November 2004.

Assessments will be based on the following:

• Quality of script/idea to be realised in 10 minutes or less
• Suitability of the project for an international festival audience
• The achievability of the project on a budget of between £10,000 - £15,000
• Eligibility of the applicant
• The impact on the applicant's career in the film and television industry. Because of the sizeable investment, Cineworks looks closely at the applicant's potential.

 Under the Cineworks scheme 2003 Scottish director Stephen Bennett made 'Pig Story' – a quirky ten-minute documentary about his efforts to find a cure for his nine-year insomnia problem. 'Pig Story' was broadcast on BBC1 Scotland and screened at the Edinburgh Film Festival and the Sheffield International Documentary Festival.

"The Cineworks scheme is great – there's not a lot of money granted, but it does force a person to think hard before shooting. Development help is on hand and producers are sent on a number of amazing courses. I went on a two-day documentary storytelling course which was invaluable and I still use the structure system I was taught to this day. Additionally they put you in touch with key people to help give advice – I even met Sirkka Moeller who is the programmer of the Sheffield Documentary Festival. To hear what a programmer thinks firsthand is really useful – it reminds me of the wake up call I once had as I watched an executive producer watch showreels on fast forward.

Amazingly, I had full editorial control. The executive producers for Cineworks and the UK Film Council suggested changes both before shooting and mid-way though the editing – no less than I expected. However, at no point was I forced into something which I did not whole-heartedly agree on.

Unlike drama, where shorts are often a calling card for the directors, I don't think this is the case in documentary – or at least in the TV documentary world. Really, I don't think many people give a damn about this sort of thing, or even understand why someone would do this. I had taken the idea to Channel 4 and suchlike but to no avail, so it became a Cineworks, which in the end I think was the best place for it since I could concentrate on making it the way I wanted. Once finished, I also sent it out to many companies but again not much resulted.

All that said, one executive producer, Chris Kelly at Lion TV, did see it and was hugely supportive. So much so, I have worked with him ever since making the film. He executive produced a 30 minute observational documentary which I produced/ directed about a village under siege from boy racers, then gave me a huge break by executive producing my first one hour international drama documentary for BBC, BBC worldwide and the History Channel about Cold War spies. So, life is good, and Cineworks was a personal success."

Other Scottish funding

Glasgow Film Office

 City Chambers
Glasgow
Lanarkshire
Scotland
G2 1DU

0141 287 0424

film.office@drs.glasgow.gov.uk
www.glasgowfilm.org.uk

GFO is supported by Glasgow City Council, Scottish Enterprise Glasgow (the largest Local Enterprise Company within the Scottish Enterprise Network, the National body promoting economic development), Strathclyde European Partnership (the grouping of public sector bodies who access monies from the European Structural Funds to carry out economic regeneration projects in the west of Scotland).

Since 1997, GFO has supported in excess of 40 high-value productions which have spent over £36 million in Glasgow. Its current aim is to offer grants that expand the city's production capacity by supporting production by both local companies and mobile high-value producers. High-impact film productions, including docs, are those with a budget in excess of £200,000, or which directly contribute more than £100,000 to the local economy. High value TV has a commissioned value of at least £50,000. Grants from GFO need the beneficiaries to raise at least 50% of the cost from their own resources or by introducing private sector funds. Contact by phone or email to discuss funding.

Funding for production companies is available through:

The Product Commercialisation scheme, which offers advice, guidance and some funding, to assist companies with identification of buyers and commissioners to develop, exploit and complete projects; and

The New Writer Integration scheme, in which GFO offers grants of £5,000, £3,000 and £1,000 towards the development costs of projects that go for innovation and aim to develop fresh ideas.

For other media professionals, there is also funding for facilities and service companies, freelance personnel, technical skills development and infrastructure support for high-budget productions considering locating in Glasgow.

Triptych

Triptych
Top floor
15 N Claremont Street
Glasgow G3 7NR

www.triptych05.com

Triptych is an annual arts and music festival held in Edinburgh, Aberdeen and Glasgow. Supported by G-Mac, Edinburgh Mediabase and Peacock Visual Arts, it runs a documentary competition, with the winners receiving professional assistance, access to equipment, and screenings in cinemas.

Scottish Arts Council

📧 Scottish Arts Council
12 Manor Place
Edinburgh, EH3 7DD

📞 0845 603 6000

🖱 help.desk@scottisharts.org.uk
www.scottisharts.org.uk

The Scottish Arts Council is the main distributor of public funding for the arts in Scotland. It distributes National Lottery funding to arts projects that make a difference to the quality of life of people in Scotland and also provides information and advice. Funding is divided into different streams covering Crafts, Dance, Drama, Literature, Music, Visual Arts and Capital Funds. Under the Visual Arts scheme, film and video artists are eligible to apply for Professional Development, Creative Development, the Artist Film and Video Fund and residencies in Amsterdam and New York. Projects must be intended for gallery exhibition and not commercial distribution.

Funding

Artist Film and Video

A fund run by the Scottish Arts Council and Scottish Screen to support visual artists working in film and video to develop new, innovative and experimental work. A total of £50,000 is available; awards of up to £15,000 can be applied for. Successful applicants also receive guidance on promoting their work to international and UK festivals, as well as sourcing exhibition opportunities, such as in galleries and cinemas. This fund is exclusively for visual artists, not for filmmakers making films about artists or the visual arts. Application deadlines are in April and October.

Creative and professional development

Awards of £1,000 to £5,000 are available to assist individual artists with the immediate costs involved in producing and presenting work, with deadlines in April, October and January. Bursaries of up to £15,000 are available to enable the exploration of new ideas and the realisation of significant projects, with an October deadline.

Residencies

One artist is funded with a £16,000 bursary and accommodation to spend a year in Amsterdam; one to live and work in New York for nine months, with accommodation and a £12,000 bursary. The New Media Residency supports an artist to work at the University of Abertay, Dundee, for nine months, with a bursary of £10,000. All these have July deadlines.

Submissions

Visual artists are eligible, including film and video artists at any stage of development in their work, with a body of work outside formal education and who are based in Scotland. Film and video artists applying for funding must provide a VHS copy of previous work and describe how work in film progresses their artistic practice. Applicants will be assessed against the following core criteria: the Scottish Arts Council's funding priorities, artistic quality, public benefit/demand, the financial and operational viability of the project, and the potential impact the award will have on the applicant and their work.

Chapter Five
Public funding, Wales
and Northern Ireland

Research by Julie Moggan

Sgrîn Cymru Wales

✉ The Bank
10 Mount Stuart Square
Cardiff Bay
Cardiff, CF10 5EE

✆ sgrin@sgrin.co.uk
www.sgrin.co.uk

Established in 1997, Sgrîn is the national body responsible for the development of the economic and cultural aspects of film, television and new media in Wales. It undertakes activity in five key areas: New Talent, Content Development, Access and Education, Marketing and Information and Business Support. Sgrîn's objective is 'to develop entrepreneurship and skills within the media industries to ensure that Welsh practitioners are able to confidently compete in European and international markets. It also aims to develop audiences and skilled personnel through its cultural and educational programmes'. Sgrîn runs a number of short film schemes in partnership with other organisations. The chair of Sgrîn is Elis Owen, Director of Programmes for ITV Wales. Sgrîn aims to encourage the indigenous film industry and to increase 'the quality, number and range of films made with significant Welsh elements', which include writers, directors, producers, heads of departments and talent.

Sgrîn places emphasis on the provision of advice and guidance for filmmakers, in the areas of script and project development, production finance, and all creative and financial aspects of production. It can assist producers who have secured Lottery or other funding in making approaches to potential investors, including other public sector funders, and it can advise on Lottery funding applications; filmmakers thinking of going for funding are invited to contact Sgrîn for advice first. The main opportunity to find out about funding developments is the annual Focus On event, held in November as part of the Cardiff Screen Festival (www.cardiffscreenfestival.co.uk).

Lottery funding

Sgrîn oversees the assigning of Lottery funding for film on behalf of and in conjunction with the Arts Council of Wales. Sgrîn's Production Department and the Arts Council of Wales Capital Unit are responsible for this. The Production Department details are as for Sgrîn, above, while the Capital Unit is:

Arts Council of Wales Capital Unit
Museum Place
Cardiff CF10 3NX
Tel: 029 20 376500
Minicom: 029 20 390027
information@ccc-acw.org.uk

Script development

Funding is available for the development of features (including fiction, documentary and animation) intended for theatrical release and/or screenings in other public places, such as film festivals. Short films are generally not eligible, but exceptions may be made for animated short films. A Development Executive will be allotted to successful applicants to act as a script editor, provide advice and to report back to Sgrîn.

Applicants who contribute all necessary partnership funding through their own company funds may request development loans of up to £7,000, or 75% of eligible costs (whichever is lower). Applicants who have attracted third party partnership finance may request development loans of up to £20,000, or 75% of eligible costs (whichever is lower). Partnership funding in kind must be no more than 12.5% of the overall budget. Partnership funding must be in place when the application is made.

Feature film production

Production funding is available for fully developed features (including fiction, documentary and animation) intended for theatrical release and/or screenings in other public places, such as festivals.

Projects intended exclusively for broadcast on television or video release will not be accepted. Applicants for production awards may apply for conditional offers of funding before sources of partnership finance are in place, as long as they submit a viable finance plan and provide evidence of interest from proposed financiers. Applicants may normally request a maximum award of £250,000, or 50% of eligible costs (whichever is lower) towards the production of a feature length film.

Sgrîn has so far put money into just one documentary feature – 'Beautiful Mistake' directed by Marc Evans. The film aimed to celebrate the existence of several world class music acts working in Wales at that time and shows John Cale, collaborating in his native Cardiff with bands such as Catatonia and The Super Furry Animals. Sgrîn awarded £100,000 towards the production of 'Beautiful Mistake' and it premiered at the Cardiff International Film Festival in 2000.

Short film production

This fund supports the production of short films (including fiction, documentary, animation or experimental) of no more than 10 minutes, intended for theatrical release and/or screening in other public places. Projects intended exclusively for broadcast on television or video release will not be accepted.

Applicants may request production funding of between 50% and 90% of the total production costs, up to a limit of £36,000, whichever is lower. Production companies can submit two applications to the fund, but only one award will be made per company. There is an annual deadline in April. Along with the application form, applicants may submit additional supporting documentation if they wish.

General guidelines

Eligibility: Applicants must be part of a limited company. New companies must provide evidence of the steps they have taken towards incorporating the company. Eligible projects must include significant Welsh elements, in most cases, with both the company and the filmmakers based in Wales. Other applicants must demonstrate material benefit to the broader Welsh industry.

Partnership Funding: Sgrîn cannot fully fund projects. There must be an element of non-Lottery partnership funding, although more than one Lottery body may contribute funds to any given project. Lottery contributions cannot amount to more than half of a film's production finance. Broadcaster finance is permitted as partnership funding, although supported projects must be clearly intended for theatrical release. Other sources of partnership funding may include, for example: equity investment, distribution advances, gap finance (generally via a bank), tax-based financing, subsidies (perhaps by way of an official co-production relationship, or regional spend). For short films and development, an element of 'in kind' contribution is acceptable, but deferrals are not. Finance must be in place by the first day of principal photography; before then, the filmmaker should be able to demonstrate both a viable plan for attaining full funding, and interest from potential partners.

Applications: Applicants should first contact Sgrîn to discuss their project and complete an Advance Notification Form, providing brief details of the project, partners, production company and key personnel. This form will be submitted to the production advisory group members who will then indicate their interest in the project, proceeding to full application stage. Unless otherwise stated, applications can be submitted at any time. Sgrîn aim to reach a decision within three months for applications under £50,000, and within four months for applicants requesting larger sums.

Assessment: Applications will be assessed according to the following criteria: public benefit, the artistic quality of the project, the need for lottery funding, financial viability, partnership funding, the likelihood of gaining distribution and the applicant's ability to effectively manage the project. These criteria are particularly important:

• The extent to which key Welsh personnel are involved;
• The contribution the project makes to the development of an indigenous Welsh film industry;
• The relevance to Wales in cultural and aesthetic terms; and
• The percentage spent within Wales during pre-production, production and post-production.

Conditions: Sgrîn expects to recoup its investment in the form of a profit share in the film's revenues, in proportion to its investment. Funds will only be recouped for the development awards if the project proceeds into production. Sgrîn will require screen and publicity credit and regular cost and production reports during production. Wherever possible, each production should employ an appropriate number of trainees (preferably from Wales).

Non-Lottery production schemes

The following short film production schemes are open to documentary makers:

Welsh Micros

Welsh Micros is a new initiative launched jointly by Sgrîn, the Arts Council of Wales, S4C and FilmFour. Using lottery funds, the scheme aims to support the production of micro-budget feature films in Wales. In 2004, two features with budgets of no more than £400,000 were commissioned. The scheme looks to fund feature ideas that are contemporary and distinctive and which are likely to succeed in the marketplace. Sgrîn will prioritise projects where there is substantial Welsh involvement. In 2004 there was a July deadline and there is a strong likelihood the scheme will be repeated again in 2005. Check the Sgrîn website for updated information.

Mini Masterpieces

(also applicable in EM Media, South West Screen, and North West Vision regional screen agencies).

In conjunction with the Bristol Brief Encounters Short Film Festival, Sgrîn offers a trip to Bristol, professional filmmaking support, and broadcast on BBC3 for the winning project from Wales. The competition aims to put into production the best proposal for a film of under three minutes, shot in three days, following dogme-style rules.

This is a competition with various knockout stages. In 2004 the train of events was:

Sept 2004: Deadline for application with a one-page treatment, a lead filmmaker biog, and a clip of your shortest film or extract.
Oct 2004: Ten filmmakers from each region attend a Pitch Day in Bristol. Two finalists survive this to have their script developed by BBC Fiction Lab.
Nov 2004: One film crew from each screen agency comes to Bristol to make a film in three days during Brief Encounters 2004. They get: travel, accommodation and food; a day of specialist advice from an industry pro; tech and production support and use of a DVCam kit; edit facilities, editor, professional audio; ten VHSs of finished film; a festival pass.

The winning film is shown on BBC3 and at the festival.

And the Bristol Dogme rules are this:

· The film will be shot on DVCam tape
· The film should be completed in no more than ten shots
· No props or sets (unless you find them on location)
· Music is not allowed unless it occurs on location (you must clear copyright yourself)
· Only minimal lighting will be available
· The camera should be hand held
· No genre movies
· No 'superficial action' (murders, weapons etc)
· The film must take place in the here and now
· The film must be filmed within a mile of the Watershed in Bristol

Other Welsh funds

Arts Council of Wales

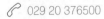 Central & South Wales Office
9 Museum Place
Cardiff, CF10 3NX

☎ 029 20 376500

🖱 south@artswales.org.uk
www.artswales.org.uk

MID & WEST WALES OFFICE

 6 Gardd Llydaw
Jackson Lane
Carmarthen, SA31 1QD

☎ 01267 234248

🖱 midandwest@artswales.org.uk
www.artswales.org.uk

NORTH WALES OFFICE

 36 Prince's Drive
Colwyn Bay, LL29 8LA

☎ 01492 533440

 north@artswales.org.uk
www.artswales.org.uk

The Arts Council of Wales is the national development and funding body for the arts in Wales. It distributes lottery funding and its four key objectives are to develop and improve knowledge, understanding and practice of the arts; increase the accessibility of the arts to the public; advise and co-operate with other public bodies; and work through the medium of Welsh and English.

The Arts Council of Wales does not fund film production intended for theatrical distribution, but film and video artists making work intended for gallery installation are eligible to apply for funding towards development, production, exhibition and skills development and training.

The Creative Wales Awards

The aim of this award is to support individual artists creating new, experimental and innovative work. The awards enable practicing artists working in any creative discipline, or across disciplines, to refresh their skills and creativity and/or make new creative partnerships and take time away from their usual commitments in order to concentrate on developing their work. Individuals can apply for costs directly related to the development of their practice such as time out salary, travel, research and development, the acquisition of new skills, networking, materials and space in which to work. It is also possible to apply for costs related to showing their work and capital equipment costs.

Sean O'Reilly is a visual artist whose work has been exhibited nationally and internationally. He received a Creative Wales Award of £9,000 for his project – 'Shorelines' – in which he proposes alternative ways of viewing the landscape through the creation of a number of landscape prints and video pieces.

Applicants may apply for between £5,000 and £20,000 and must secure partnership funding for at least 10% of the total costs. Applicants must be professional artists whose works shows originality and excellence and who have been in practice for at least two years. Individuals must be living in Wales and planning to spend the majority of their time in Wales whilst undertaking the project. Along with the application form, applicants need to submit a CV, references and recent work. In 2004 there was an October deadline for applications.

Katja Stiller is a video development worker who facilitates work with individuals to create their own representations using video. She received £9,000 from the Arts Council of Wales for her video project 'Person-Centred Community Arts' – a research project into the development of a new person-centred approach to community arts practice.

Each application is assessed against the following criteria: the creative ambition and quality of the project idea; the calibre of artists involved; the value of the project for audiences or participants; the degree to which the project compliments ACW's priorities and regional plans; the need for funding; the applicant's track record, capability, and experience; evidence of how the project will contribute to the long-term development of the individual or organisation; the marketing plan; evidence of strong partnership involvement; and demand from the project's beneficiaries.

Professional development: training

This award supports individuals and organisations wishing to undertake or purchase training in the arts within Wales, the UK, or abroad. The scheme can cover costs such as training fees, conference fees, travel and accommodation. The scheme will not support applications to attend full-time courses in higher or further education.

Individuals undertaking training can apply for between £250 and £2,000. Organisations can apply for between £250 and £5,000. Individuals over the age of 16 who are living in Wales and who are not in full-time education are eligible to apply for the award. Organisations must be based in Wales and must be legally constituted, or at least have a written statement of their aims, objectives and the way they operate. Along with the application form, individuals will need to provide full details of the training course or professional development programme. Organisations will also need to submit a training strategy identifying why the training is required. Applications can be submitted at any time for this fund and there are ten decision points a year.

Applications will be assessed according to the following criteria: the degree to which the training fits with ACW strategic priorities and regional plans; the reasons why this particular training course has been chosen; how the training will benefit the individual or the organisation and the Welsh public in the longer term; the quality or potential of the applicant's recent involvement; the need to ensure a broad spread of awards across art forms.

Capacity building & development

This scheme aims to help artists and arts organisations in Wales to develop their economic potential and build sustainability in the arts. The range of support offered within this scheme includes start-up and development grants for individual artists; research development and initialisation grants; community development; organisational development; business planning; marketing initiatives; and artistic management reviews.

Individuals can apply for grants of between £250 and £5,000. Organisations can apply for between £250 and £50,000. Individuals and organisations must be based in Wales to be eligible for this award. Along with an application form, organisations must submit evidence to support their proposed development such as business plans, marketing plans, fund-raising strategies or research briefs to undertake such work. Individuals must include a career development plan or business plan along with their application form. Applications for grants of less than £5,000 can be made at any time and will be assessed at one of ten decision points over the year. There are four application deadlines a year for grants over £5,000 in January, April, July and October.

Each application is assessed against the following criteria: the creative ambition and quality of the project; the calibre of artists involved; the value of the project for audiences or participants; the degree to which the project compliments ACW's priorities and regional plans; the need for funding; the applicant's track record, capability and experience; evidence of how the project will contribute to the long-term development of the individual or organisation; the marketing plan; evidence of strong partnership involvement; and demand from the project's beneficiaries.

D.M. Davies Award

✉ Cardiff Screen Festival
10 Mount Stuart Square
Cardiff, CF10 5EE

☎ 02920 333324

 sarah@sgrin.co.uk
www.iffw.co.uk

This award, held by the Cardiff Screen Festival, supports up-and-coming Welsh filmmakers by awarding to the best short film in competition a comprehensive package of funding, facilities and assistance, to enable the production of a new ten-minute film which must be made in Wales. The competition is open to documentary films; work should be no longer than 25 minutes and completed within two years preceding the competition. It must not have been screened publicly before (except at another festival) and should not have been previously submitted to the festival.

The director of the film must be either born in Wales, a full-time resident in Wales for two consecutive years or more, or a graduate of a Welsh College or University. All films entered into the competition will be screened at the Cardiff Film Festival. In 2004 there was a September deadline for submissions.

Northern Ireland

Northern Ireland Film and Television Commission

✉ Alfred House
21 Alfred Street
Belfast, BT2 8ED

☎ 028 9023 2444

✉ info@niftc.co.uk
www.niftc.co.uk

The NIFTC was established in 1997 to accelerate the development of a dynamic and sustainable film and television industry in Northern Ireland. It is primarily funded by the Department of Culture, Arts and Leisure and Invest Northern Ireland, the UK Film Council; it is designated by the Arts Council of NI to administer Lottery Funding for film in Northern Ireland. Its work is divided into the following key areas: film development and production funding; promoting Northern Ireland as a base for production; company development support for local production companies; training; providing information services; developing education policy; improving access to audiovisual heritage; and specialist film exhibition development.

Lottery funding

The following Lottery funding schemes are open to documentary filmmakers:

Script development

The NIFTC funds up to £20,000 or 50% of the total development costs of the following kinds of projects: feature films and television films, short narrative films, short experimental films, culturally relevant documentaries, animation, digital media projects with a high proportion of moving image content. Applications for this award can be made at any time of the year.

MINI – Made in Northern Ireland

The NIFTC funds the production of single documentary films or documentary series of cultural relevance to NI, which cannot be 100% funded by a broadcaster. The funding is offered on four levels:

Individuals (up to £2,500)
In this category, the NIFTC offers support to individuals who are new to filmmaking to produce ultra-low-budget short experimental films (up to 5 mins) and single documentaries (no longer than 30 mins). For productions that have a total budget of less than £2,500, a contribution of up to 90% of the budget may be awarded. The NIFTC does not have a recoupment policy on projects awarded funding in this ultra-low-budget category. Applications for this fund can be made at any time.

Small Awards (£2,501 - £5,000)
In this category, the NIFTC accepts applications from small, formally structured groups, as well as constituted companies, for support for new filmmakers to produce low budget experimental films (up to 5 mins) and single documentaries (up to 30 mins). For productions with a total budget of less than £5,000, a contribution of up to 90% of the budget may be awarded. The NIFTC does not have a recoupment policy on

projects awarded in this low-budget category. Applications for this fund can be made at any time.

Low Budget Awards (£5,001 - £30,000)
In this category, funding is available for single documentaries or series which cannot be 100% funded by a broadcaster. For productions that have a total budget of less than £30,000, a contribution of up to 75% of the budget may be awarded. Applications for this award can be made at any time.

High Budget Awards (£30,000+)
In this category, funding is available for single documentaries or series which cannot be 100% funded by a broadcaster. For productions with a total budget of more than £30,001, the NIFTC will not usually contribute more than 50% of the budget, to a maximum of £50,000. There are four application deadlines for this award in February, May, August and December.

Distribution and promotion support

Funding towards distribution and promotion costs is available for single short films and packages of short films made in Northern Ireland since 1994. The kinds of costs that can be covered include negative cutting, tape-to-film transfers, 35mm prints, telecine transfers, tape masters, copies, festival costs and promotional materials. The maximum support available is 10% of the actual production costs, up to a maximum of £5,000 for a single film. Applications for this funding can be made at any time.

Product Development Fund

The NIFTC provides recoupable loans of between £10,000 and £20,000 to support a production company's slate of projects intended for network and international audiences. The NIFTC defines a slate of projects as meaning five or more. Only Northern Ireland-based independent production companies are eligible for financial assistance towards the development costs of programme proposals. There are three application deadlines for this funding in February, August, and November.

The NIFTC put money into Vinny Cunningham's 'Battle of the Bogside' – a documentary that looks behind the barricades at the riots that took place in the Bogside district of Derry, Northern Ireland, in 1969. The NIFTC co-produced the film with the Irish Film Board in association with Northland Broadcast and Raw Nerve Productions and stumped up £50,000 of the total £140,000 budget. The film was broadcast on BBC Four and BBC Two in 2004 and was screened at a number of festivals, winning 'Best Documentary' at the IFTA Awards in Dublin.

General guidelines

Eligibility: Individuals living in Northern Ireland are eligible to apply for awards of £2,500 or under. Companies based in Northern Ireland are eligible to apply for all funds. Companies from elsewhere are also eligible to apply, but at least 50% of the film must be shot in Northern Ireland and at least 40% of the total budget must be spent in Northern Ireland. Lottery funding for film is not intended for productions which would normally be fully commissioned by a broadcaster.

Applications: Applicants are advised to apply early. In addition to the application form, applicants must submit various items depending on the fund for which they are applying; see the NIFTC website for specific requirements. Normally a decision will be taken within two months of receipt of the application (up to £25,000) or within three months (over £25,000).

Assessment: All applications will be assessed according to the following criteria: the benefit to the general public in Northern Ireland; the cultural relevance to Northern Ireland; regional, national and international significance; and the percentage of the budget to be spent in Northern Ireland. Applications for production funding will also be assessed according to the following criteria: distribution and broadcast potential; percentage of pre-production, production and post-production to take place in Northern Ireland with Northern Irish cast and crew; artistic quality; project management and financial viability; partnership funding; and the need for lottery money.

Conditions: Unless otherwise stated, applicants must demonstrate an element of partnership funding. Funding from broadcasters, trusts or public sector agencies is eligible as partnership funding. Contributions in kind (non-cash elements) may be acceptable as partnership funding if the applicant can prove the equivalent cash value of such contributions. With the exception of the Script Development Award and projects with a budget of less than £5,000, NIFTC will fund projects in the form of an investment, with their agreed recoupment based on the NIFTC's contribution in relation to other investors. Producers will also be expected to pay 0.5% of the budget with a ceiling of £39,500 to the Skills Investment Fund. The films must be intended for distribution and broadcast in Northern Ireland.

Funding is also available from NIFTC for financial support to attend markets and festivals; for bursaries to attend training and development courses, for 75% of total costs up to a maximum of £15,000; for company development, in conjunction with Invest Northern Ireland. This fund is designed to assist independent production companies' strategies for growth. Up to £3,000, or 50% of costs, is available for the development of a business plan. Up to £80,000, or 40% of the total budget is available to support a business strategy.

Arts Council of Northern Ireland

 MacNeice House
77 Malone Road
Belfast, BT9 6AQ

 028 90 385200

publicaffairs@artscouncil-ni.org
www.artscouncil-ni.org

The Arts Council of Northern Ireland supports the development of film and video artists making work intended for gallery installation. Production companies and individual filmmakers making films for broadcast and theatrical distribution are not eligible to apply for funding.

General Art Awards Scheme

This scheme supports artists of all disciplines, with awards of up to £5,000 for specific projects, specialised research, personal artistic development and materials/equipment. The Arts Council is particularly keen to support work that is challenging and innovative, especially in areas of new technology. Collaborative applications from individual artists working together in cross-discipline projects/activities are encouraged.

Artists must have been living in Northern Ireland for the twelve months preceding the submission of their application, and must have made a previous contribution to artistic activities in Northern Ireland. Established artists from Northern Ireland currently living elsewhere will be considered only in exceptional circumstances. Along with the application form, applicants should submit a CV and a single example of their previous work. Applicants will be notified of Council decisions within two months. There is an annual deadline for the scheme in September.

Applications are assessed according to the following criteria: previous artistic achievement; viability of proposal; relevance of proposal to advancement of skills, expertise and career; evidence of involvement in specific events/courses; the quality and ambition of the proposal.

Major Individual Awards Scheme

The Arts Council offers three major awards of £15,000 each, to enable established artists to develop and attempt extended or ambitious work. The awards are open to established artists of all disciplines, but each year one of the awards will be discipline-specific. In 2004/05 the discipline was architecture.

Established artists must have been living in Northern Ireland for twelve months prior to the submission of their application, and have made a contribution to artistic activities in Northern Ireland. Established artists from Northern Ireland currently living elsewhere may be considered only in exceptional circumstances. Along with the application form, applicants will need to submit a CV and an example of recent work. Applicants will be notified of Council decisions within three months. There is an annual deadline in June.

Applicants will have to demonstrate evidence of continuing professional practice, evidence of national/ international recognition in the arts, viability of proposal, relevance of proposal to the creation of extended or ambitious work, potential of the award to develop the individual artist.

Seamus Harahan is an artist and filmmaker living in Belfast. He received funding from the Arts Council of Northern Ireland to make 'Holylands' – a film shot through the artist's window over a period of a year and a half about the goings-on in a student area of Belfast. The film depicts the people of the neighbourhood, showing fragments of their passage through this territory. These images are spliced together with a soundtrack that includes hip-hop, traditional Irish and classical music. 'Holylands' has been exhibited in a number of European galleries.

Arts and Artists Abroad

The Arts Council offers awards to help support individual artists and arts organisations/groups of all disciplines to present their work abroad. The artist's work must have a proven potential for exhibition or other artistic presentation in the international arena. New work from Northern Ireland is prioritised. Applications from individual artists and arts organisations/groups wishing to present their work in other regions of the UK will also be considered. The total annual budget available through this scheme is £100,000. The Arts Council normally funds up to 50% (for organisations) or 75% (for individuals) of travel, accommodation, visas, subsistence, carriage, insurance and approved exhibition/performance costs.

Arts organisations/groups must be based in Northern Ireland and have a proven track record of contributing to artistic activities in Northern Ireland and a commitment to continue to do so. Applications from arts organisations/groups with experience of international work will be prioritised. Individual applicants must have been living in Northern Ireland for the twelve months prior to the submission of their application and must have made a contribution to artistic activities in Northern Ireland. Along with the application form, applications must include a CV, or for organisations/groups a summary of previous exhibitions relevant to the proposal, examples of recent work, evidence of invitation from the venues and venue information. Applicants will be notified of Council decisions within two months. There are four deadlines for the scheme each year in March, June, October and December.

Applicants must demonstrate evidence of artistic achievement, experience of and/or proven potential for international work, quality, ambition and viability of the proposal, relevance of proposal to the advancement of international or UK-wide awareness of artistic production in Northern Ireland, evidence of invitation from appropriate venues. Partnership funding is required. The proportion of partnership funding considered appropriate will be determined by the Arts Council on a case by case basis, but must be at least 50% (for organisations/groups) or 25% (for individuals). Partnership funding need not be confirmed at the time of application.

Travel Awards Scheme

The Arts Council offers travel awards to artists of all disciplines working in Northern Ireland to travel outside Northern Ireland in order to advance their skills, expertise and career. The awards cover travel costs and associated costs and vary depending upon the country of destination.

Artists must be living in Northern Ireland and have made a contribution to artistic activities in Northern Ireland for a minimum period of one year. Priority is given to practising individual artists. Applicants must submit a CV along with their application form. The Travel Awards scheme is administered on a rolling basis. Applications must be received no later than four weeks in advance of intended travel. Applicants have to demonstrate evidence of artistic achievement, relevance of travel to advancement of skills, expertise and career, evidence of invitation/offer of acceptance for specific events/courses, evidence of venue/contact reputation (where applicable).

International Artists' Profile Scheme

The Arts Council offers assistance with profiling and marketing material for individual artists who have experience in or proven potential for exhibition, or other artistic presentation in the international arena. The scheme offers the services of a specialist PR/Marketing consultancy in order to compile and collate relevant material for publicity and profile. There will be up to four 'in kind' awards made each year.

Individual artists of all disciplines who have been living in Northern Ireland for the twelve months preceding submission of the application and have made a contribution to artistic activities in Northern Ireland are eligible to apply. Established artists from Northern Ireland currently living elsewhere may be considered only in exceptional circumstances. Along with the application form, applicants need to include a CV and examples of recent work. Applicants will be notified of Council decisions within two months. There is an annual deadline for applications in September.

Applicants have to demonstrate evidence of artistic achievement, experience of and/or proven potential for international work, quality, innovation and ambition and the use they intend to make of the profile material. Artists also have to demonstrate that they have a sufficient body of work which can form the basis of producing international profile material.

Chapter Six
Public funding, England

Research by Julie Moggan

Regional Screen Agencies

The UK Film Council invests £7.5 million a year in regional film activities through the Regional Investment Fund for England (RIFE). The fund is administered by nine appointed regional film agencies across the UK. RIFE emerged from an intensive review of film infrastructure and activity across England, undertaken by the UK Film Council in 2000. It brought together a number of existing regional film bodies, commissions and media development agencies. The objectives for RIFE are based on the UK Film Council's overall aims. They are:

• To contribute towards the development of a sustainable UK film industry by: developing a pool of creative skills and talent; developing entrepreneurial acumen and business clusters; and developing an industrial infrastructure.

• To contribute towards the development of film culture in the UK by improving access to, and education about, film and the moving image by ensuring that the public has access to: a broader range of British and world cinema; opportunities for learning about film; access to the UK's film heritage; and opportunities to participate in film production.

• To promote cultural and ethnic diversity in film industry and culture.

• To maximise inclusion for all disadvantaged groups in film and the moving image.

• Each agency is self-governing, distributing funding in the key areas of production, exhibition, distribution, education, archive, training, development and audience development. Their remits extend across film, broadcast and interactive media. Individual agencies determine their own set of priorities in relation to the specific needs of the region and structure their Lottery funding programme accordingly. The priorities of individual screening agencies, and therefore the funding opportunities they provide, vary widely from region to region. Where you live, or choose to live, could make a considerable difference to the kind of funding opportunities that are open to you.

These aims give the RSAs a wide remit, and correspondingly they offer a broad and varied range of support and services to filmmakers, ranging from funding programmes, through business and skills support, to Screen West Midlands' fine 2003 conference 'Documentary is Dead, Long Live Documentary'.

Each regional screen agency offers a specific range of funding provisions for documentary filmmaking. In light of the recent success of documentaries at the box office, most of the screen agencies seem to be increasingly open to co-financing theatrical documentaries for cinematic distribution. A couple of the agencies are also willing to offer support to documentaries intended for broadcast, whilst Film London administers a scheme that is specifically intended for artists working in film and video. Three of the agencies run documentary schemes for new talent, whilst others open up their digital shorts schemes to documentary shorts. In addition to these production and development opportunities, documentary filmmakers are also eligible to apply for funding towards training courses in many regions. Various kinds of support are also often available to small documentary production companies.

In the case of all of the regional screen agencies, there seem to be no hard and fast rules governing the various streams of funding they offer, particularly in relation to documentary projects. Nearly all the agencies recommend that individuals/companies seeking funding should contact their regional screen agency to discuss their project on a case by case basis, to find out how their project might compliment the specific priorities of the region and thereby qualify for RIFE funding.

RSAs are also well-placed to advise on exhibition and distribution. With the advent of the UK Film Council's Digital Screen Network and its central funding for exhibition, there is a sense of excitement within some RSAs that a stronger infrastructure is coming into place. The RSAs have the local knowledge and the contact with filmmakers to be able to capitalise on these developments and really get new film out into every nook of film-viewing Britain.

RSAs are there to support filmmakers who reside or work in that area. If you don't live and work in a place, you can borrow an address, but the point of the RSA is to stimulate film in that region, so if you can't explain during the application process that their funding you will help film in the area, you weaken your case. If you're an individual working with a production company based in an area, that's okay.

Our message is that you should investigate and contact your RSA – they are there to help.

Regional Screen Agency areas

Screen East	East of England (Bedfordshire, Cambridgeshire, Essex, Hertfordshire, Norfolk and Suffolk)
EM Media	East Midlands (Derbyshire, Leicestershire, Lincolnshire, Northamptonshire and Rutland)
Northern Film & Media	North (Tyne & Wear, Northumberland, Durham, Tees Valley)
North West Vision	North West (Cheshire, Cumbria, Greater Manchester, Lancashire, Merseyside)
Screen South	South of England (Kent, Buckinghamshire, Oxfordshire, Hampshire, Surrey, Berkshire, East and West Sussex, and the Isle of Wight)
South West Screen	South West (Gloucestershire, Wiltshire, Bristol, Somerset, Dorset, Devon and Cornwall)
Screen West Midlands	West Midlands (Herefordshire, Staffordshire, Shropshire, Birmingham, Coventry, Walsall, Wolverhampton, Warwickshire, Worcestershire, Telford and The Wrekin)
Screen Yorkshire	Yorkshire & Humberside (North Yorkshire, South Yorkshire, West Yorkshire and Humberside)

Screen East

✉ 2 Millennium Plain
Norwich
Norfolk, NR1 3RR

✆ 01603 776 920

✆ info@screeneast.co.uk
www.screeneast.co.uk

Covering: Bedfordshire, Cambridgeshire, Essex, Hertfordshire, Norfolk and Suffolk and the unitary areas of Luton, Peterborough, Southend-on-Sea and Thurrock.

Screen East is dedicated to developing, supporting and promoting the film and media industries in the East of England, through the activities of its four departments: Locations, Production, Enterprise and Skills, and Audiences and Education. Funding is targeted at three priority areas: enterprise and skills, audience development, and talent and content development, which includes production funding.

Guidelines

Production funding is available for individuals and companies based in the region. Regionally-based companies and writer/producer teams are a support priority, but applicants seeking cross-regional, international co-production or broadcaster partnerships can apply with a project demonstrating a strong East of England element. Film projects must be intended primarily for cinema audiences. Applications can be for fiction, documentary, digital media or animation projects. Projects must display creative vision, a strategic plan for realisation, and market and audience awareness. Full project funding is not provided; other funding is necessary from other sources. Not eligible for funding are: projects that have already started; undergraduate students; projects made exclusively for TV broadcast or video and DVD release.

Individuals can receive between £1,000 and £5,000; companies a maximum of £20,000. There is no completion funding for short films, which are unlikely to be funded outside the official schemes. Screen East encourages applications for feature length docs with international cinematic potential. These do not have to be about or filmed in the East of England; they must have large-scale appeal and an international dimension.

marketing@screeneast.co.uk can offer advice on getting shorts screened.

Funding

Production investment for two or three low-budget films (£50,000 to £3 million), up to £75,000, is available.

Funding of £1,000 to £2,000 is available for project and script development. Rolling deadlines are set for applications, with the funding committee meeting every six weeks. For further information on Screen East funding, contact Annabel Grundy (Funding and Performance Officer) on 01603 776923, funding@screeneast.co.uk

Business Development Funding of up to £20,000 is available, as is Careers and Skills advice; see the website for further details. There is also a Small Awards Fund of twenty bursaries of £500, across the three priority areas.

Screen East aim to invest in projects that are likely to return their investment. The full amount of any development award will be repayable to Screen East, plus a 50% premium on the first day of principal photography.

New Voices

New Voices is a production and training scheme for new talent in the East of England, commissioned by Screen East and broadcast on Anglia Television. Each year, six half-hour documentaries are commissioned for the scheme. Working with an experienced production team, filmmakers research, develop and film their documentaries. The scheme looks for fresh, challenging stories that the filmmakers passionately feel they want to tell and that can capture a television audience's imagination. Stories must be based in the East of England and preference will be given to directors living in the region. Applicants may have broadcast credits in other areas of film, but must be looking to attain their first documentary directing credit. See the website for details of future rounds.

EM Media

⊠ 35—37 St Mary's Gate
   Nottingham, NG1 1PU

✆ 0115 934 9090

✉ info@em-media.org.uk
   www.em-media.org.uk

Covering: Derbyshire, Leicestershire, Lincolnshire, Northamptonshire, Nottinghamshire and Rutland.

EM Media invests in four broad areas of projects and activities in the East Midlands region: Audience and Market Development, Business Development, Product Development, and Production and Skills Development. Its priorities are to develop viable film and media businesses, promote regional talent and improve opportunities for audiences. EM Media would not normally invest more than £20,000 in any given project or activity, up to a maximum of 75% of total project cost.

EM Media support projects that:
• Develop audiences for film and media product, particularly for specialised film.
• Develop knowledge and understanding of film and media product.
• Assist in getting film and media product to market.

EM Media supports business development for media companies within its ambit, and can award up to £1,000 for individual skills development. Within development and production, there is support for product development which includes script development, slate development, individual production awards and production co-finance. Investment levels vary according to the type of project. Individual production awards for short films range from £500 to £5,000 and are unlikely to exceed more than £10,000. Investment in the development of larger scale projects such as feature films (including documentaries) and projects for television is likely to range from very small initial investment up to a maximum of £95,000 for the development of slates. Production co-finance for features and large scale projects will be up to a maximum of £250,000.

Guidelines

Applicants must either be a resident or have a trading address in the East Midlands region. Individuals applying must be over 18 and must have been demonstrably working in the media industry for at least six months. Projects, ideas or the applicant's business must be focused on or within the region's media industry.

Applications may be made at any time. In addition to the application form, additional material will be required, dependent on the type of investment being applied for. EM Media assesses all applications against the following conditions and criteria: how the project contributes to EM Media's objectives; the short and long term impacts of the project; the risks associated with the project; and the application's financial viability. EM Media seeks to recoup investment in line with, and appropriate to, the scale and nature of each particular project. For example, a definite financial return is sought on large-scale commercial investments, but a smaller project might require only a time commitment from recipients. Repayment can be a combination of the following: financial returns; equity investment; loan repaid with a premium of up to 5% APR (variable) for all or part of the investment; time commitment; goodwill; commitment to attend EM Media events and/or submit a project case study; jobs created/secured; increase in audience numbers; additional investment secured.

EM Media will not invest in the following: projects that have no strategy for reaching an audience; projects in which EM Media's finance becomes pure subsidy and will neither be recouped nor generate future economic benefit for the region; projects where finance is replacing or topping up commercial money with no additional benefit to the region; capital projects and individuals or organisations that have already received over 100,000 euros worth of public sector support in the past three years.

First Cut

First Cut is a broadcast initiative for first-time directors based in the East Midlands to make films of 5-10 minutes focused on regional stories. The films are commissioned by EM Media and ITV Central, and receive a maximum budget of £10,000 per project. The scheme is open to anyone living in the region with no previous broadcast credit as a director, and projects must aim to use local crew and resources.

Each year, 30 minutes of programming (three or four films) are commissioned through this scheme and broadcast on ITV Central. Successful applicants are provided with an induction workshop on the technical, legal and marketing aspects of producing. In 2004 there was a January deadline for the scheme.

Film London

 20 Euston Centre
Regents Place
London, NW1 3JH

☎ 020 7387 8787

✉ info@filmlondon.org.uk
www.filmlondon.org.uk

Film London supports film and media production, exhibition, education, and economic development across the capital. It aims to enhance London's status as a world-class film location, and to create opportunities for people from all communities to engage with moving image technologies. Film London's activities incorporate the distribution of Lottery money through the RIFE and other funding programmes. It has assumed the responsibilities of the LFVDA (London Film and Video Development Agency) and the London Film Commission. Film London does not invest in film production outside its designated funding schemes.

Film London intends to set up a new production fund for low budget feature films but this is still in the pipeline.

The London Production Fund was a popular scheme supported by Carlton TV that ran between 1993 and 2002, funding features, 30-minute TV projects, documentaries and short films. It is under review and will not be running in 2005.

Film London EAST is a project aiming to develop film and media businesses in East London and create a sustainable sector in this region. It supersedes the East London Moving Image Initiative (ELMII). Film London EAST is part-funded by the European Regional Development Fund, and is formed as a partnership with 13 organisations in the area. It will provide business development support; short film production; information, networking and contacts; and advice. The scheme covers the boroughs of Greenwich, Hackney, Tower Hamlets, Havering, Newham, Barking and Dagenham and Bexley. To be able to participate in any of the schemes you must be a resident of one of these London boroughs.

The Film London website also holds information on filming within the city, and it has information on the film liaison people for each borough.

London Artists Film & Video Award (LAFVA)

This scheme, open to established and emergent artists resident in London, is focussed on artists who engage with contemporary moving image practice. Awards from £2,000 to £20,000 are available to artists who are engaged with contemporary moving image practice and producing work that is intended for exhibition in galleries, cinemas or specific sites. The scheme is funded by Arts Council England and, in 2004, awards were given to 14 projects for production and completion. Recipients included Kutlug Ataman with his project 'Küba', for which the artist immersed himself in the culture of a Turkish ghetto for two years to create forty individual DVD portraits. Awards are for individuals (or artists working in collaboration), but the fund welcomes proposals with a producer, production company or commissioning organisation attached as a partner. In 2004 there was a December deadline for proposals. Film London intends for the scheme to run again in late 2005.

Borough production schemes

Film London supports and works closely with eight local London borough production funds.

Greenwich Film Fund

Greenwich Film Fund is co-ordinated by Greenwich Films and is normally open for applications in October with a deadline in December. For information contact Liza Brown at Greenwich Films on 020 8694 2211 or email fund@greenwichfilms.demon.co.uk

London Borough of Enfield Film Fund

The LB Enfield Film Fund is normally open for applications in March with a deadline in April. This year the fund made one award of £1,000 for 16-24 year-olds with little or no experience and two awards of £2,000 for film or video makers aged over 18 with previous filmmaking experience. Contact Enfield Arts Unit on 020 8379 1466 or email julia.harriman@enfield.gov.uk.

London Borough of Newham Film Fund

LB Newham Film Fund is normally open from February with a deadline in April. This year the fund provided up to £5,000 for the production of a 10-minute film, animation or 25-minute documentary. Contact Carole Thomas at Newham Regeneration on 020 8430 2793 or email Carole.Thomas@newham.gov.uk

Tower Hamlets and Hackney Film Fund

The Tower Hamlets and Hackney Film Fund supports a new generation of filmmakers with awards of up to £4,000 to make short dramas, animations or documentaries. Filmmakers must live, work or study in Tower Hamlets or Hackney. For an application form and guidelines contact the Tower Hamlets Films Office direct on 020 7364 7920 or email filmsoffice@towerhamlets.gov.uk

Wandsworth Film Awards

Wandsworth Arts Office, the Wandsworth Film Office and Film London run an annual film awards scheme, open to film makers who live, work or study full-time in the Borough of Wandsworth. Awards of up to £5,000 are offered. For more information about the next scheme, contact the arts office on 020 8871 8711 or visit www.wandsworth.gov.uk/Home/LeisureandTourism/Arts/artsgrants.htm

City of Westminster Arts Council (CWAC) Film and Photography Bursary

Applicants must work, live or study in Westminster. Awards of up to £1,000 are available. In 2005 the deadline was the end of May. For further information contact Paula Price-Davies on 020 7641 1017 or by email paula@cwac.org.uk or visit www.cwac.org.uk.

Other London borough film funds

The following Film Funds are also available. They are not supported by Film London, but the Film London website is the best place to find out about these and all available London funds.

Waltham Forest Arts Council Alfred Hitchcock Memorial Awards

For information on the LB Waltham Forest's annual film fund contact Martin O'Connor, Waltham Forest Arts Council on 020 8527 8750 or email cllrm.oconnor@lbwf.gov.uk

West London Film Fund Awards (Focus West)

A scheme to support media businesses in the London Boroughs of Hammersmith and Fulham, Brent and Ealing, Focus West is funded by the London Development Agency (LDA). For more information register at: www.focuswest.co.uk. Awards of up to £3,000 are available.

Northern Film & Media

 Central Square
Newcastle Upon Tyne, NE1 3PJ

0191 269 9200

info@northernmedia.org
www.northernmedia.org

Covering: Tyne and Wear, Northumberland, County Durham, Tees Valley

Northern Film & Media aims to promote and build a sustainable moving image industry in the North East; to promote an accessible screen culture; maximise opportunities for the development of regional talent and celebrate the region's cultural identity; to encourage the sector's growing importance to the regional economy; and promote world-class creativity within it. Since Northern Film & Media began in 2002, it has funded more than 550 projects, ranging from community cinema to major feature films.

Northern Film & Media operates five different funding schemes.
Development of People is for professional development that can make a significant contribution to an individual's career and can help stimulate a skilled and professional media workforce in the North East. The fund supports both those wishing to deliver these schemes and those wishing to participate in them. Individuals can claim a maximum of £5,000 while organisations can claim a maximum of £10,000. Development of Companies supports regional companies and organisations involved in production, facilities and exhibition. Audience development is for festivals, access, education and archive, with the aim of increasing and educating audiences. By grants to companies, Development of Networks helps further the creation of regional networks, international partnerships, attendance at events, regional conferences, trade visits, and screenings to showcase regional talent.

Development of Content
This scheme tries to develop strong projects with a significant chance of being produced and finding a market.

It covers:
Development – Treatments, scripts and feature development packages
Production – Across a range of genres
Completion – for post-production, effects or format conversions

Up to £10,000 is available for individuals and £40,000 for organisations. Feature documentaries intended for theatrical distribution would be eligible to receive funding from this scheme. Northern Film and Media would also consider funding the early development of documentary ideas for television. For further information contact Helen Stearman: Helen@northernmedia.org or 0191 269 9216

Guidelines

Prospective applicants must discuss their proposal with NF&M before submitting an official application. Organisations and Individuals must live or work in the North East region to be eligible for funding. Applicants may apply for more than one fund and are expected to find at least 25% of their total budget from a source other than Northern Film & Media. Applications can be made at any time of the year and are assessed according to:
• Quality of proposed project
• Contribution to Northern Film & Media's strategic objectives

- Ability to fulfill the planned proposal
- Financial viability
- Value for money

Applications over £1,500 are considered by a funding panel and decisions can take up to 10 weeks.

North West Vision

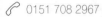 233, The Tea Factory
82 Wood Street
Liverpool
L1 4DQ

0151 708 2967

General email: jacquir@northwestvision.co.uk
Production & Funding: tomg@northwestvision.co.uk
www.northwestvision.co.uk

Covering: Cheshire, Cumbria, Greater Manchester, Lancashire and Merseyside.

North West Vision is the regional screen agency for the North West of England, set up to champion the region's film and TV industry, celebrate the region's talent and diversity, and build on the region's production success. North West Vision distributes Lottery money on behalf of the UK Film Council and is committed to assisting filmmakers, cultural/arts organisations and training providers with funding, advice and support. The funding is split into three stands and has, so far, mainly supported narrative drama projects. However, documentary filmmakers are also eligible to apply for all the three areas of funding, and North West Vision would be particularly interested in funding theatrical documentary projects.

North West Vision can also support training, sector-specific support for companies and organisations, professional development, and audience development.

Guidelines

Applications are eligible from legally constituted organisations, and in some cases individuals, living or operating in the North West region of England. Freelance individuals residing in the North West region can make applications for specific strands. Awards to individuals are limited to a maximum of £5,000.

North West Vision welcome applications from film and moving image media organisations and from organisations whose normal activity may not be film and moving image media related, but whose specific proposal deals with this area. These can include private companies, voluntary organisations, community groups, local authorities and other public organisations and registered charities. Organisations must have a written constitution or set of rules that shows how their activities and finances are managed. National organisations can apply for Lottery funding if the beneficiaries are resident in the North West region and North West Vision welcomes applications from national organisations running pan-regional schemes that benefit the North West's film and moving image industry.

North West Vision cannot fund projects retrospectively or projects that have started before the decision has been made. Applications can only be accepted for projects which take place in the current funding year. North West Vision is unable to support projects spanning more than one year. If a project spans two financial years, this must be discussed with the Lottery Department prior to submission. All applicants must contact the North West Vision's Lottery Department to discuss project proposals prior to submitting an application. Applications can be made at any time for funding under the Organisational & Individual Development and Production & Development strands.

When assessing proposals, North West Vision considers:
• The quality of the proposed activity (projects must be of the highest standard)
• Public benefit (projects must benefit the region, the industry and the public, and must contribute to social inclusion, cultural diversity and access to film and moving image activity)
• Ability and commitment (applicants must provide evidence of ability and demonstrate commitment to the regional film industry)
• The financial viability of the proposal (projects must be financially viable, represent value for money and lever a suitable level of partnership funding)

North West Vision encourages projects which demonstrate a good level and range of partnership commitment. Projects with a budget of up to £2,000 require minimum partnership funding of 25%, of which half must be cash from external sources; budgets over this call for 30% partnership funding, at least two thirds in cash. Awards for script development and individual training bursaries may not require partnership funding. North West Vision Schemes that are funded through the Lottery but advertised separately (such as funding for short films), will have their own partnership/match funding requirements that will be published alongside the schemes guidelines.

Funding

Production & Development
North West Vision intends to invest in creative people and products that are diverse, distinctive and dynamic; that originate from a broad range of cultures, backgrounds and experiences; and that contribute to the economic, social and cultural prosperity in the North West. They will support:

Development
Feature Film Script development (applications up to £5,000 - advertised quarterly)

Development of feature film projects. This can include feature film seed funding to secure further finance (up to £5,000; applications can be made at anytime).

Film Production
Completion awards for short films (up to £5,000; applications can be made at any time)

Innovative feature film production projects which exploit the unique properties of new media technologies (up to £20,000; applications can be made at any time).

Virgin Shorts

Approximately 12 first-time filmmakers will be offered £1,000 to make short narrative films of any genre. Several documentaries have been made through this scheme.

Screen South

 Folkestone Enterprise Centre
Shearway Road
Folkestone, CT19 4RH

✆ 01303 298 222

 info@ screensouth.co.uk
www.screensouth.co.uk

Covering: Kent, Buckinghamshire, Oxfordshire, Hampshire, Surrey, Berkshire, East and West Sussex and the Isle of Wight

Screen South aims to promote talent, support the studios, locations and regional facilities and find ways of presenting exciting film to new audiences. The areas of activity that Screen South covers are archive, exhibition, education, production and development, vocational training, film commission and inward investment. Filmmakers can apply for funding through one of its production or training schemes or through the RIFE open funds, where projects should fit with the agency's priorities.

Guidelines

Individuals and organisations based or working in the region are eligible to apply. Organisations must be registered as limited companies, charities, consortia, schools, societies, colleges, libraries, universities or sole traders.

Screen South encourages people in the region who are thinking of applying for funding to attend one of their regular funding information days. In addition to the application form, individuals must submit CVs for all personnel involved. Organisations must submit CVs, a set of the most recent accounts and the constitution or rules of the organisation. Feature film applicants should also include a full script/treatment and a cash flow projection. Festival applications should include a detailed cash flow projection, a detailed budget, a programming schedule and a full festival description. Applications to the RIFE Open Fund may be made at any time. Screen South's contributions are made in the form of an investment, which will be recouped from income generated by the project.

Funding

Through the RIFE Open Fund, Screen South supports funding applications from the community and a range of media industry sectors. Applications will be assessed in terms of how they fulfill at least one of the following regional priorities:

• To support a sustainable, professional film community and infrastructure
• To support the development of companies and individual talent within the region
• To act as an advocate and leader for the film and television industry
• To find creative ways of developing opportunities for audiences of film and the moving image
• To raise the standard of community filmmaking and help bring the professionals to the community
• To encourage access to our visual heritage

Screen South's criteria for assessing documentary applications, as with most other applications for the RIFE fund, is strongly based on the market and audience potential of the project. Screen South would generally expect to see interest from other partners before considering funding a documentary. The kind of documentary-related projects that have so far received support from the RIFE fund include:

• Development finance for feature documentaries
• Assistance with packaging and trailers
• Short schemes with broadcasters
• Support for documentary festivals
• Support to access European Commissioners
• Support for theatrical distribution.

Organisations can apply for a maximum £10,000. Individuals can apply for a maximum of £5,000. Partnership funding is required.

Good Foundations Creative Team Scheme

An intensive and practical foundation course designed to equip producers with the skills and knowledge to survive the world of film production from development through financing to exploitation. Participants will have at least one feature film project (documentary or drama) in development. They will have either produced one or more short films or gained experience in another sector of film production. Writers or writer/directors may also apply, as long as they are acting as producers in their current stage of development. Successful applicants will be invited to take part in a six-month programme of development, marketing and financing workshops where they will work towards attending one or more film markets. The scheme is intended to be a reality check and awareness programme for media professionals in the Screen South region who are looking to get their first feature film off the ground.

South West Screen

 St Bartholomews Court
Lewins Mead
Bristol, BS1 5BT

 0117 952 9977

✆ info@swscreen.co.uk
www.swscreen.co.uk

Covering: Gloucestershire, Wiltshire, Bristol, Somerset, Dorset, Devon, Cornwall, unitary authorities of Bath, Bournemouth, Plymouth, Poole, Swindon and Torbay

South West Screen is the film, television and digital media agency for the South West of England. It is committed to developing a vibrant, dynamic and constantly evolving screen culture throughout the region. South West Screen organises its funding schemes into three priority areas:

Strand 1 is the development of the film, television and digital content sector, including trade missions, staff development, training, marketing, etc.

Stand 2 is the development of talent and innovation. South West Screen looks to support:

• The development of feature film projects – through both script development and project development awards. Cinematic documentaries intended for theatrical release would be considered for this funding.
• The professional development of individuals based in the region
• Innovative projects which develop the regional sector's resources. For example, Screen East might be able to offer a contribution to project development costs, funding to cover training costs of an individual working in the production sector, or support for a new approach to skills and training provisions.

Strand 3 is the development of film and moving image culture, and increasing access, including support for film festivals, audience development, archive and preservation, and exhibition.

Guidelines

South West Screen strongly recommends that applicants discuss their proposals with their screen development and Lottery Manager before requesting an application form. All applicants need to secure match funding from other sources. Funds are offered in a two-stage process.

Screen Shift

South West Screen and Kuumba (an arts and community organisation in Bristol) have teamed up to offer a scheme for African and Caribbean artists working in the South West, to develop short moving image proposals which contain a significant cross-artform element, for example: dance and film; sound and film; poetry and film; visual sculpture and film. This scheme is funded by Arts Council England and ten artists will each be given an award of up to £500 for proposal development. From these, six artists will be selected for an award of £2,000 for production and a materials budget of up to £5,000. In 2004 the scheme had an October deadline. For further information contact Lmcleod@Kuumba.org.uk or sarah-jane@swscreen.co.uk

Screen West Midlands

 31/41 Bromley Street
Birmingham, B9 4AN

 0121 766 1470

 info@screenwm.co.uk
www.screenwm.co.uk

Covering: Birmingham and The Black Country, Herefordshire, Shropshire, Staffordshire, Warwickshire and Worcestershire.

Screen West Midlands supports, promotes and develops the screen media industry in the West Midlands through six operational areas: production, education, exhibition, training, archive and locations. Screen West Midlands receives Lottery money through the Film Council, which it channels into funding strands that offer individuals and companies the chance to apply for production and sector development.

To support freelance development, Screen West Midlands offers three training schemes that are part-funded by the European Union through the European Social Fund. Moving Up is a 14-week personal development programme aimed at new entrants into the screen media industry. Screen Plan & Select is for professional freelancers and those on contracts of under nine months; it helps to identify and achieve career goals. Enhance & Advance is a scheme for companies wanting to evaluate and increase the skills of their workforce for better productivity.

Guidelines

Individuals can apply for Lottery Script Grants, but only companies can apply for Development Loans and Production Investments, as long as they're based in and operating from the West Midlands region. The funds are also open to companies located outside of the region if their project can contribute to building a sustainable screen media economy in the West Midlands region. All of the funding strands have set deadlines; check the website for further information. Applicants should first register an expression of interest with Screen West Midlands using the appropriate downloadable form. Screen West Midlands will then make contact to discuss the project. Online, there are detailed lists of submission requirements for each part of the fund. Screen West Midlands aims to complete all decision making within 10 weeks of the application deadline. For Development Loans and Production Investments, short-listed applicants will be invited to an interview with a panel containing the CEO, a board member and industry experts, to pitch their project and discuss it in more detail. Applications will be assessed against: public benefit; the ability of the applicant to deliver the project; the extent to which the project fits with the priorities of Screen West Midlands; financial viability. Loans made by the fund are not speculative; projects will need to demonstrate that they have sound market potential, are appropriate to their proposed budget and are likely to recoup all development and production costs. Screen West Midlands expects partnership funding for each investment.

Funding

Through its Screen Fund, Screen West Midlands funds all kinds of projects including fiction/documentary feature films, TV films, TV series or dramas, and digital media projects and animation. Projects must have good market potential and a strong idea about their target audience. Applicants need to know what kind of investors, development executives and distributors they're planning to sell their project to. This Screen Fund is composed of three distinct areas of funding:

Lottery Script Grants

For the development of scripts to a first or second draft, and open to individual scriptwriters and those working as part of a production team. Applicants can apply for up to £5,000 as a one-off grant to cover their writer costs and up to £2,000 on top for an industry script editor if their project needs one.

Development Loans

To enable medium- to large-scale screen media projects to become 'market ready' up to pre-production. The fund is for low-budget (£1.5 million to £4 million) feature film development or similar medium-scale screen media projects. Screen West Midlands is looking for a package with a producer attached and significant partnership support. Investment is between £15,000 and £50,000 for any one project.

Production Investment

For productions that can contribute to building a sustainable screen media economy in the West Midlands region of England. Projects should clearly demonstrate that Screen West Midlands will be able to make a return on the loan. Projects should be almost ready to go and Screen West Midlands can invest up to 25% of the overall project budget, up to a maximum of £250,000.

First Cut

First Cut is a broadcast initiative for first-time directors based in the West Midlands to make films of 5-10 minutes, focused on regional stories. The films are commissioned by Screen West Midlands and ITV Central, and will receive a maximum budget of £8,500 per project. The scheme is open to anyone living in the region with no previous broadcast credit as a director, and projects must aim to use local crew and resources.

Each year, 40 minutes of programming (four or five films) are commissioned through this scheme and broadcast on ITV Central. Successful applicants will be provided with an induction workshop on the technical, legal and marketing aspects of producing. Screen West Midlands also provides training opportunities and Production Executive support.

For further information on the scheme contact production@screenwm.co.uk or desna.atkinson@itv.com

Screen Yorkshire

✉ Studio 22
  46 The Calls
  Leeds, LS2 7EY

✆ 0113 294 4410

 info@screenyorkshire.co.uk
  www.screenyorkshire.co.uk

Covering: Humberside, North Yorkshire, South Yorkshire and West Yorkshire

Screen Yorkshire is the regional agency for film, broadcast and interactive media for Yorkshire and Humber. It aims to develop talent in the region, attract people and productions to the area and encourage technical and creative innovation. Its Lottery programme is organised into four priority streams:

Priority 1: Production and development of Projects
Awards in this category range between £500 and £20,000.

Element 1: Development finance for feature films scripts, documentaries, digital media and animation. Screen Yorkshire supports script development, screenwriting talent and innovation in content for the screen industries. With feature film projects, individuals should be able to demonstrate the potential of their project to reach a significant audience. As part of the award, Screen Yorkshire appoints a script editor and provides training where necessary. Film projects must be primarily intended for cinema audiences; projects made exclusively for broadcast on television or release on video/DVD are not normally accepted. A development award will only be repayable to Screen Yorkshire in the event that the project goes into production. The full amount of the award plus a 50% premium will be repayable on the first day of principal photography. Screen Yorkshire also expects to receive 2.5% of the producer's net profits.

Element 2: Production, completion and distribution of short films, digital media and animation under 30 minutes' duration.
Screen Yorkshire aims to support the career development of new directors and producers through short film production, supporting up to 12 short films (maximum five minutes) per year, as part of a scheme that also offers mentoring and assistance with equipment and post-production facilities. First time and second time filmmakers participate in a series of workshops and are encouraged to form writer/director/producer relationships as early as possible.

Applications can be for fiction, documentary, digital media or animation projects, including partnership with broadcasters. Coherent plans for distribution must be included in the application. All industry production formats are eligible, providing the project is capable of resulting in a 35mm print. Projects must be primarily intended for theatrical distribution and exhibition. Projects made primarily for broadcast on television or for video release are not eligible.

Priority 2: Development of skills and people

Element 1: Developing individual professional skills, with funding of up to £2,000.

Element 2: Short films script development for new and emerging writers
These awards are made through a series of courses.

Emerging writers: a 10-week programme with up to five tutorial sessions, leading to a three to five minute short film script.

New Writers: for writers with at least one completed script. A ten-week programme with up to five tutorial sessions, leading to a ten minute short film script.

Screen Yorkshire welcomes applications from writers with a passion for film regardless of background or experience.

Priority 3: Audiences, Programming & Education

Priority 4: Community and Youth projects

This priority supports projects involving young people and/or under-represented or excluded sectors of the community for filmmaking, documentaries, digital media and animation projects. Projects should offer access to learning opportunities and skills development, and raise the aspirations and creativity of participants. Awards made under Priority 4 range from £500 to £20,000.

Guidelines

Individuals can apply for awards under Priorities 1 and 2. Organisations can apply for all awards if they are registered as limited companies, charities, consortia or public bodies. Normally, awards are only available to organisations and individuals based in or working in the Yorkshire and Humber region, but Screen Yorkshire will consider applications from outside the region if the project will be carried out in the region, using local talent and resources. Applications can be made at any time of the year and applicants are advised to discuss their project with Screen Yorkshire before submitting an application. Screen Yorkshire meets to assess applications in May, August, November and February and aims to process each proposal within six weeks. Applications are assessed according to the following criteria: benefit of the project to the general public in the Yorkshire and Humber region; creative and commercial quality; financial viability; and applicant's ability to manage the project effectively. Under all priorities, a minimum of 30% of the total production costs must come from funding sources other than Lottery awards. In kind contributions can make up 10% or more of your total budget, provided that applicants have raised 20% of cash match funding (this does not need to be in place at the time of application). Examples of in kind contributions might include using a venue free of charge, someone giving time to the project without being paid, reasonable costing for the use of equipment or reasonable costing for applicant's own time on the project.

Screen Yorkshire Production Fund

Screen Yorkshire's Production Fund is a separate funding initiative to the Lottery funding scheme. It is supported by the regional development agency Yorkshire Forward and run in partnership with other public and private sector financiers. It is an investment fund and Screen Yorkshire looks for returns on investments, which might include benefits to the sector and recoupable money. This fund supports any genre (including documentary) in the following categories:

Features: high-concept, low-budget feature filmmaking, especially from production companies based in the region. Applications with a distributor and/or sales agent attached are more likely to be successful.

Television: normally proposals are only accepted from regionally based companies, for programmes that have sales potential in more than one market and that demonstrate the value to the company of retaining ancillary rights.

Short films: occasional one-off shorts, if they make an exceptional case for current or future economic impact.

Funding

Development: For individual projects, Screen Yorkshire can offer up to 50% of the total development budget. Applications with match funding from a third party of at least 30% are more likely to win support. Individual projects normally receive up to £20,000 but in exceptional circumstances this can be increased to £40,000. For multiple projects, Screen Yorkshire can offer up to a maximum of £100,000 for high growth, high risk companies, across a number of projects, and up to 50% of a total development budget. Development finance is only repayable, with a premium, if a project goes into production.

Production: Screen Yorkshire can offer up to £250,000 and up to 25% of the total production budget, or 50% in the case of low budget features created in the region. This is normally in the form of an equity investment in the project, which is recoupable and will give Screen Yorkshire a share in profits on a pro rata basis with other finance partners. Screen Yorkshire aims to support production companies based in the region by reinvesting part of their share of profits in the development and production of subsequent projects.

There are no set funding deadlines for the Production Fund and applications will be considered on a rolling basis. For further information on Screen Yorkshire's funding schemes contact Louise Donoghue on 0113 2944410 or at louise@screenyorkshire.co.uk

Arts Council England

 14 Great Peter Street
London, SW1P 3NQ

✆ 0845 300 6200
Textphone: 020 7973 6564

✉ enquiries@artscouncil.org.uk
www.artscouncil.org.uk

Arts Council England is the national development agency for the arts in England, distributing public money from the Government and the National Lottery. Arts Council England aims to promote the arts at the heart of national life and to enable people throughout England to experience arts activities of the highest quality.

Grants for the Arts are England-wide grants for individuals, arts organisations, national touring and other people who use arts in their work. They are divided into grants for individuals, organisations and national touring; for stabilisation and recovery; and for capital. Though the awards are England-wide, applicants must apply through their regional Arts Council office.

Arts Council England does not fund production companies or film/video work intended for cinema exhibition, but an individual film and video artist with a project intended for gallery installation would be eligible for an individual award under the Individuals, Organisations and National Touring funding scheme.

Grants for the Arts – Individuals, Organisations and National Touring

Individuals can apply for grants for arts-related activities, which might include projects and events, commissions and productions, research and development, capital items, professional development, training and travel grants, bursaries, fellowships, residencies and touring.

Artists, performers, writers, promoters, presenters, curators, producers and other individuals working in the arts and living in England are eligible to apply. The activity must take place mainly in England (with the exception of professional development applications) and be arts-related. Film-based projects must be intended for gallery installation, not commercial distribution.

Grants normally range from £200 to a maximum of £30,000, and can cover activities lasting up to three years. Larger grants can be awarded for major projects and residencies. Partnership funding of at least 10% is required, this can include earned income from your activity, funding from public organisations such as local authorities, grants from trust and foundations and a contribution from you or your organisation.

Applicants must submit an application form and a project proposal, including information about themselves and their work, how they will carry out the activity, financial details, the benefits, how the project fulfills the Arts Council's aims, and how they will evaluate the project. Applications will be assessed for the artistic quality, project management, financial feasibility, public benefit and the contribution of the activity towards meeting the Arts Council's aims. Various deadlines arise throughout the year. Decisions can take up to six working weeks for applications under £5,000 and 12 working weeks for applications over £5,000.

Other funding

The Arts Council has other funding schemes in operation, some of which support the creative industries. Film qualifies as a creative industry, so production companies can qualify for these schemes, provided they are based in the relevant region. These initiatives are listed here.

Advantage Creative Fund

 PO Box 6613
Kings Bromley
Burton on Trent, DE13 7ZD

✆ 0121 643 4733

✉ interest@acfwm.co.uk
www.acfwm.co.uk

Covering: Herefordshire, Shropshire, Staffordshire, Warwickshire, West Midlands Metropolitan Area, Worcestershire

The Advantage Creative Fund invests in creative industries companies located in the West Midlands Region, or those that are prepared to move there. The fund looks to invest in start-up enterprises or established companies capable of sustainability in profitability and robust to economic downturn. It invests in commercially viable businesses with a view to making a profit to be fed back into the fund, and is supported by Advantage West Midlands, European Regional Development Fund and Arts Council England.

The Fund plans to make between 50 and 60 investments by 2008. ACF is open to investment proposals from all kinds of creative businesses with the potential to grow rapidly. Investments fall into three categories: investments of less than £50,000; those between £50,000-£100,000; and those over £100,000. Match funding from other sources will normally be expected. Commercially exploitable projects are the focus of the scheme.

Guidelines

Creative businesses based in the West Midlands with a range of activities or a slate of films in development. Individual projects will not be seen as viable investments. Applicants must first complete and submit a statement of interest online, which includes a basic proposal outline. If the fund is interested in this initial outline, applicants will then be requested to submit a comprehensive business proposal. The fund is a virtual company and therefore requires business plans to be electronically submitted. Applications will be assessed on the quality of the business plan and the potential of the proposal to be a commercial success. The business plan should contain the following details to be considered: summary/introduction, key facts, key individuals, business description, products and services, competitors, market research, prices, production and facilities, suppliers, risks, SWOT Analysis, organisation, past accounts, projections, sensitivity analysis, and finance required. This is a rolling programme and applications may be made at any time.

Chapter Seven
Private funding in the UK

Introduction

One doesn't need to look to the state for funding. There are various other bodies which provide support for filmmaking endeavours and come from a charitable or non-profit standpoint. Additionally, as outlined in the third section of this chapter, there are investors who provide finance to filmmaking because they consider it a vehicle for getting returns on investments. Clearly, these two routes to funding differ in terms of the sums of money involved as well as in the level of direct philanthropy. Feature film funding is for expensive films, but we include it here because we're seeing a growth in the attitude that documentaries can be large, profitable, theatrical-release films, just like fiction films. All the professional advice suggests that the proper market for docs is set to grow and grow, so we explain this model, with tips from the inside.

This chapter concentrates on the UK and on elements of private funding that apply across the board; see Chapter 9, North America, for information on specifically American options.

Trusts and charities

Trusts and charities section by Julie Moggan

The UK trusts and charities listed in this chapter are open to offering film-related funding. Each fund has specific agendas and criteria for eligibility, and none of them are solely devoted to supporting film-related projects. However, if your project strikes a chord with the agendas and interests of a specific organisation, they may well consider funding your film, even if they have never funded a film before. This route may not offer the same prestige as making a film for television, but it has its own advantages – funded by a trust, you will invariably be offered a great deal more creative freedom and control than is usual.

There are no hard and fast rules about how to get funding from organisations. Get to know the charity and NGO network related to the subject matter of your film, for example, if your film is about disability, do your research on charities working in this area and attempt to make direct contact with them. If any of these organisations are open to the idea, then present them with a proposal and a show reel of previous work to give them some idea of your capabilities and approach. Remember to tailor your proposal more specifically to a charity/NGO perspective, as opposed to a television commissioner's perspective. If possible, try to shoot a taster tape (no more than 10 minutes) to give them a sense of your ability and vision for the film and its relevance to their cause.

Charities/NGOs and human rights organisations also increasingly look for filmmakers to shoot promotional videos for them. Though this route may not enable you to make 'your own' film, it can be a rewarding and interesting way of building up your filmmaking experience, coming across new film ideas and earning some money.

Some useful resources:

'Asking Properly: The Art of Creative Fundraising' – George Smith. Ideas and suggestions to help revolutionise your fundraising (White Lion Press)

'Fundraising from America: The Complete Guide for Charitable Organisations outside the USA' – guide to funding given to organisations outside the US by American funders: individuals, companies and foundations (Chapel & York)

'Fundraising from Europe' – Christopher Carnie. Guide to fundraising from individuals and thousands of companies, trusts and foundations in Europe (Chapel & York)

'The International Development Directory' – Sarah Harland & Dave Griffiths. Information on 250 voluntary organisations involved in campaigning and development in the developing world and details of funding sources for such work.

www.sponsorship.co.uk – a search for 'arts sponsorship' will provide the names of companies that sponsor the arts.

The Directory of Social Change provides information and support for non-profit and voluntary organisations. It produces several guides that might be useful for pointing funding-seeking filmmakers in the right direction:

'The Directory of Grant-Making Trusts' 2003/04

'The Guide to UK Company Giving' 2004/05 – John Smyth

www.trustfunding.org.uk – access to this database of over 4,000 trusts is by CD-ROM or password-protected website, costing £120 for voluntary organisations, £170 for for-profit organisations.

www.grantsforindividuals.org.uk offers access to information on over 2,600 grant-making trusts that provide funding for individuals in need, and for educational purposes. Again, has option to search on specific criteria relevant to users and allows them to save searches, save specific trust details, and receive automated updates on new or updated trusts.

These can be consulted for free at the reference library of the DSC; for CD-ROMs an appointment is needed:

The Directory of Social Change
24 Stephenson Way
London NW1 2DP
tel. 08459 777 707
9am - 5pm Mondays to Fridays, except public holidays.
library@dsc.org.uk

The Jerwood Charity

 22 Fitzroy Square
London, W1T 6EN

 020 7388 6287

 info@jerwood.org
www.jerwood.org

The Jerwood Charity, formerly the Jerwood Charitable Foundation, was set up by the Jerwood Foundation in 1998 to administer a range of grants and activities. The majority of its work is in the arts, with small grants to international projects in Nepal. In 2004, the Jerwood Charity launched the Jerwood First Cuts Documentary Award at the Sheffield International Documentary Festival (see Chapter 13, Competitions and Awards, for details).

The charity aims to support outstanding national institutions and provide seed funding to smaller projects at the early stages of an initiative when other grant-making bodies might not be able or willing to act. In particular, it seeks to develop support and rewards for young people who have demonstrated achievement and excellence, and who will benefit from a final lift to launch their careers. The Jerwood Charity has certain primary fields of interest which are constantly being reviewed and developed. The charity is a major sponsor of all areas of the performing and visual arts. Film is not a priority in the funding budget, but film-related projects that aim to reward excellence or encourage young people's achievement will be considered. The Jerwood Charity is also interested in projects which enable an organisation to become viable and self financing. The Jerwood Charity will not consider applications on behalf of: individuals; single performances or arts events (such as festivals); building or capital costs (including purchase of equipment); projects in

Arthur Howes says, "'Nuba Conversations' was NGO funded. I really struggled, but I got some support from Comic Relief. Comic Relief could not fund me directly so they had to fund me though Christian Aid. There was a lot of work involved in getting that funding and I've got whole boxes full of letters and paperwork to prove it - it was a real hustle, a very hard process. You have to really tailor these letters to an NGO perspective as opposed to a filmic perspective. There were budgets galore, so many different budgets, then then got changed depending various factors.

'Benjamin and his Brother' was a much cheaper film, even though there was a lot of travelling. 'Benjamin' became cheaper because more editing was done in my home on my computer in a non-linear way and I had more control.

'Benjamin' was supported through getting a research fellowship in Edinburgh and then teaching at the London Institute so that supported a certain salary over a period of time. Then I got money from Oxfam to pay for the first journey to Africa and later money from another aid NGO to pay for the trip to America. So in the end the film was supported through bits and pieces like that.

At the moment NGOs seem to be making lots of films. Now the difference is that I'm making the films I chose to make that happen to fit into an NGO criteria. The way it usually tends to work is the that filmmakers are commissioned by the NGO to make exactly the film that the NGO want.

I managed to secure NGO funding to make the film I wanted to make – 'Benjamin' - because I'd been invited to Nairobi by a Swiss NGO called Ecotera to do a screening at the UN of 'Nuba Conversations' and 'Kafi's Story'. They invited all the key players in the Sudan conflict, so the screening was really dynamic and powerful because you had all these key players and all the church groups. At the end of the screening I mentioned that I was about to make a new film and that I would need some support, so that's how I made some more contacts and got some further funding at that moment.

I almost feel more comfortable making films with minimal budgets and having to struggle. For example in Sudan I would have found it really obscene if I was on a huge salary and documenting poverty and wars. I don't think I could have coped if I was on a huge budget, slumming it in a refugee camp for half an hour and then going back to the Hilton. We used to travel by lorries, wrap the camera in a towel and jump on top of a lorry or walk places. That way I feel I'm part of it."

Kersti Uibo got funding for 'Narrow is the Gate', a film on life in the Balkans, from a reconciliation fund of the Catholic Church of Germany.

"There are lots of different funding organisations, it depends on your theme. I had a lot to do with reconciliation networks, NGOs and people I met there. You don't get necessarily get money from NGOs but they might give you contacts. It is very much dependent on your subject matter. If you go to the Middle East, for instance, there would be funding organisations that are supporting that area, if it is homeless people in Britain then you try to start meeting people who are in that network. You have to be very flexible, you need to do a lot of research on the internet or at libraries and you ask around. Somehow by reading a lot, by meeting people you will start finding your way.

Foundations that normally wouldn't fund a film can make exceptions. For instance, the foundation I received money from had never funded a documentary before and they probably never will again, but as a one-off they decided to do it. Because they somehow see that you have the conviction and then they think, 'Ok then, let's do it, let's try it.' I had complete freedom, absolutely no conditions and they also gave me the money for a print. In the end they have found it a controversial film - they didn't expect a film like that. I've been letting them know that the film has been winning prizes and they thank me for that but they haven't used it in anyway at all. But that's their problem not mine, I can only keep them informed. It's a complicated route to take but somehow you will find these people who will let you make your film, but it took me two years to find these people."

the fields of religion, sport, animal rights or welfare; appeals for matching funding for National Lottery applications; projects which are mainly of local appeal; and retrospective awards.

The charity makes revenue donations on a one-off basis and there is a strong element of match funding. The charity rarely commits to funding over a fixed number of years, but in many cases maintains support if consistency will secure better results, and if the partnership is producing good results. Applications are made and assessed throughout the year and decisions can normally be expected within six weeks. Grants vary between the lower range of up to £10,000 (often plus or minus £5,000), and more substantial grants in excess of £10,000 and up to £50,000.

Applicants should first email a paragraph to the Jerwood Charity outlining the aims and objectives of their organisation, and the proposed project. If the charity is interested in the project, a written application is required, including: a budget, details of match funding, details of management and staffing structure, the annual report, and audited and current accounts of the organisation.

One World Broadcasting Trust

 3-7 Euston Centre
Regents Place
London, NW1 3JG

✆ 020 7874 7609

 oneworld@owbt.org
www.owbt.org

The One World Broadcasting Trust was established in 1987 by broadcasters from ITV and the BBC. Through broadcast it aims to increase knowledge about the developing world and promote balanced awareness of human rights and global development issues. For its annual awards see Chapter 13.

One World Film Bursaries

Each year the trust offers grants of up to £1,000 to student filmmakers wishing to make films about or in the developing world. These grants are available to film/video students and postgraduates studying in the UK with documentary-making experience. Overseas students based in the UK are also eligible to apply. In addition, the trust offers editorial assistance and holds a screening of completed films in London. In 2004, the trust awarded grants to eight student filmmakers. Applicants should submit a proposal (no more than two pages) and budget, along with the application form. Ideally film proposals should be 'story-led', with a strong emphasis on local voices. Films are expected to be around 20 minutes. In 2005 there was an April deadline for the scheme.

NFTS student Caroline Deeds was awarded a One World Film Bursary to make 'Walking Backwards' – a film about her homeland Ghana and the meaning of independence. The film has been screened at a number of international film festivals and was short-listed for the Jerwood First Cuts Award.

The Prince's Trust

✉ Head Office, 18 Park Square East
London, NW1 4LH

☏ 0800 842 842

🖳 www.princes-trust.co.uk

The Prince's Trust is a UK charity that helps young people overcome barriers and get their lives working. Through practical support, including training, mentoring and financial assistance, the Prince's Trust helps 14-30 year-olds realise their potential and transform their lives. The trust focuses its efforts on those who've struggled at school, been in care, been in trouble with the law or are long-term unemployed. Most programmes of support are offered in the majority of areas, although there are some variations. The 0800 number will connect individuals directly to their local Prince's Trust office.

Development Awards help 14-25 year-olds get into training, education and work. Individuals are offered grants of between £50 and £500 and support to help set goals, make decisions and find other programmes of support. Young people interested in a career in film/media could use the grant for courses and training in this field. Development Awards can not be used to pay for NVQ, level 4, HNC, HND, degree, post graduate course or courses of equivalent level. Development Awards are not currently available in the South East or London regions or in Wales.

The Trust offers Group Awards to help groups of young people who want to help their communities. In the last three years, 84 community projects across the UK have received Group Awards, for everything from creating drop-in centres to running drug awareness workshops. Groups proposing film and video projects designed to help their communities would be considered. Groups of 3-12 UK residents, aged 14-25 years, are eligible to apply; the size of the award depending on the size of the group and cost of the project. Currently, some regions are not providing Group Awards; check with the local Prince's Trust office.

The Prince's Trust Business Programme offers funding and support to help 18-30 year-olds to start up their own businesses. Support can include a low interest loan of up to 4,000 for a sole trader; up to 5,000 for a partnership (the average loan is between 2,000 and 3,000, but varies regionally); a grant of up to 1,500 in special circumstances; and a test marketing grant of up to 250. The Prince's Trust also offers ongoing business support and specialist advice, such as their free legal helpline and access to a wide range of products or services, for free or at discounted rates.

The Wellcome Trust

✉ London, NW1 2BE

☏ 020 7611 8888

🖳 contact@wellcome.ac.uk
www.wellcome.ac.uk

The Wellcome Trust is an independent charity funding medical, social, cultural and scientific research that improves human and animal health. Established in 1936 with a private endowment from Sir Henry Wellcome, it is the UK's largest non-governmental source of funds for biomedical research. The fund aims to improve understanding of the ways in which science and medicine have developed, and how research affects people and society today.

People Awards of up to £30,000 are a fast-track funding scheme for activities that: communicate biomedical science to the public; stimulate thought and debate about biomedical science; and improve understanding of the powers and limitations of science. Projects must be in the area of biomedical science and span either historical, social, ethical, cultural or contemporary issues.

Society Awards of above £50,000 are available to support academic research or larger-scale activities that aim to make a significant impact - ideally of nationwide importance - on public engagement with science and its related issues.

Projects are funded for a maximum of three years and might include: workshops and discussions; drama and art projects for a variety of different audiences and age groups; education resources; conferences, seminars, or academic research.

Both these schemes are overseen by Dr Veronica McCabe, tel. 020 7611 8415, email: engagingscience@wellcome.ac.uk

SCIART Awards

The SCIART Programme offers £500,000 per year to support arts projects (including film and digital media) that interact with biomedical science in critical, fresh and exciting ways. Projects should aim to explore new modes of enquiry and stimulate fresh thinking and debate in both disciplines. Projects should also be accessible to diverse audiences and should attempt to engage the public in the philosophical and ethical issues that surround contemporary biomedical science. The trust has funded several documentary films since the programme's beginnings in 1997and has a preference for projects of an experimental nature. There are two forms of SCIART awards available:

Filmmaker Roz Mortimer received funding from the Wellcome Trust to make 'Gender Trouble', a documentary exploring the human consequences of the way intersex people have been treated by the medical profession and society. The film has been screened internationally at film festivals and at medical conferences.

The Wellcome Trust also funded the making of 'The Bone Orchestra', an experimental documentary about the nature of bone and the impact of osteoporosis on people lives. Filmmakers Polly Nash and Jocelyn Cammack worked on the film in collaboration with a medical specialist and it has been screened in a variety of public spaces, hospitals, galleries and libraries.

Research and Development Awards:
These awards of between £5,000 and £15,000 aim to support the further development of an idea in its formative stages. Artists and scientists can either work in a collaborative partnership or named scientists can take an advisory role in an arts project. The Research award could have two possible outcomes: either 'blue sky' research (anticipating how to achieve a certain outcome a long way down the line), or small-scale productions, which could include prototypes, artworks, performances, broadcast proposals or digital media. The awards are aimed at arts and science practitioners, as well as mediators, academics and health workers.

Production Awards:
Production awards of £15,000 upwards are awarded to substantial projects likely to make a significant impact on the public's engagement with science. They are aimed at arts, science and broadcast organisations and can be used to fund major activities such as exhibitions, art projects, programmes for TV and radio, theatre, time-based media, and public performance or events programmes. Individuals are eligible to apply provided they are attached to, or associated with, a recognised organisation and can demonstrate a clear strategy for public presentation and associated outcomes.

In 2005, there was an April deadline for both SCIART Awards. Applicants should be based in the UK and the eventual outcome should first be disseminated in the UK. Applications should be accompanied by up-to-date, high quality examples of visual and contextual material. With queries on SCIART, contact tel: 020 7611 8332 or email sciart@wellcome.ac.uk

The Winston Churchill Memorial Trust

 15 Queen's Gate Terrace,
London, SW7 5PR

📞 020 7584 9315

✉ office@wcmt.org.uk
www.wcmt.org.uk

The Winston Churchill Memorial Trust offers fellowships to men and women from all walks of life and from across the United Kingdom to acquire knowledge and experience abroad. Churchill Fellows can be of any age and in any occupation. Every application is judged on the worth of the individual and the merit of the project. In June each year, the trust announces the categories of funding it will offer for the following year. These annual categories are selected from the following fields:

Agriculture and Horticulture
Business, Industry and Commerce
Conservation and the Environment
The Professional and Public Services
Sport, recreation and adventure
The Citizen and Society
Special Awards
Animal Welfare
Arts and Crafts
Education and Training
Medical and Health
Open and general subjects
Science and Technology

In June 2004, the trust announced a specific category of Funding for Photography and Documentary Filmmaking for 2005, with an application deadline of October, 2004. One 2005 award, for example, was for a documentary on the street children of Nepal and Kenya. The trust has not previously funded any documentary filmmaking projects, and it is unlikely that it will be re-selected in 2006. However, documentary projects that are related to other selected categories of funding in a chosen year (for example, conservation and the environment, young people, science and technology) would be eligible for consideration. Categories are announced in June each year, for an October application deadline.

Successful applicants will receive a grant for their project abroad, which will cover all their expenses: return air fare, daily living, travel within the countries being visited and, in exceptional cases, certain home expenses. Fellows will also be insured against accident, medical expenses and loss of baggage while they are away. Grants usually cover a stay overseas of four to eight weeks. Applicants need to demonstrate that their project is worthwhile, and of benefit to the United Kingdom. If selected, individuals are expected to make their own plans and arrangements to achieve their objectives within the scope of the grant awarded and to disseminate the results and findings of their overseas project as widely as possible.

Applicants must be British Citizens who are resident in the UK. Formal educational or professional qualifications are not required and applications are considered for individual projects only; joint or group applications will not be accepted. The trust cannot award grants for attending courses or academic studies, and generally prefers to award fellowships to people unlikely to obtain funding from other sources. In particular, the trust is looking for those to whom the opportunity represents the chance of a lifetime.

The UK Jewish Film Festival Short Film Fund

 UK Jewish Film Festival
11a Jew Street
Brighton BN1 2PN
UK

☎ 01273 735522

✒ info@ukjewishfilmfestival.org.uk
www.ukjewishfilmfestival.org.uk

The UK Jewish Film Festival takes place in London in October and tours the country over the following few months. It offers a grant of up to £15,000 for the production of a short film or video (drama, animation or factual), with a Jewish theme of significance to both Jewish and general public audiences. The scheme is open to filmmakers resident in the UK. The films or videos will need to be of a quality technically acceptable for both broadcast and cinema screenings, with a maximum length of ten minutes.

Applicants must submit a fully developed treatment along with an application form. Short-listed candidates will then need to submit a budget and schedule, a list of talent to be involved, and examples of their previous work. A panel of judges drawn from across the British film and television industry will select the winning application.

Supported by an anonymous donor, the Fund will run until 2007. Application deadlines are in January, with the winner announced in March, and there is an obligation to complete the project by August so that it can be included in the Festival in October. Films that are already part-funded will not be ruled out, nor are there any restrictions on finding additional funds elsewhere if necessary. The winning applicant will be required to enter into a short agreement with the UK Jewish Film Festival for the provision of the grant.

The Channel 4 British Documentary Film Foundation

✒ www.britdoc.org
info@britdoc.org

Jess Search, Director of the Foundation, explains:

"The Channel 4 British Documentary Film Foundation is a major new initiative to change the future for British independent documentary filmmakers. It is an independent, non-profit organisation funded by Channel 4 and set up by the ex-Independent Film and Video team at the channel, Jess Search and Maxyne Franklin.

The idea is to support independent documentary filmmakers as artists and by providing modest bursaries enable them to complete passion projects. The Foundation will provide not only funding but also editorial support by arranging mentors where required and by giving distribution advice and support where needed.

We hope the Foundation can both help to preserve Britain's traditional documentary excellence and foster new approaches to making documentaries and getting them seen. Television will always be one place to find good documentaries but it shouldn't be the only place.

When is it starting? *The Foundation aims to begin taking applications at the end of June 2005 and plans to make the first awards the next month and thereafter on a rolling basis throughout the year*

What will the Foundation fund? *Everything from shorts to features at every stage of the process from development through production, co-production and completion funding. The Foundation's aim is not to compete or double up with traditional sources of funding but to fund those projects which would otherwise not get made. It would be appropriate for filmmakers to have tried the usual broadcast sources before coming to the Foundation.*

Who is eligible? *Any filmmaker who is either British or living in Britain (applications from Ireland also considered). Filmmakers of all levels of experience and background are eligible but established talent should be aware that the foundation provides art bursaries for projects, not full budgets.*

How much money does the foundation have? *We have at minimum £500,000 for films to be made and we will be seeking additional funds from other partners to grow this pot as we go along. There are no rules about the number of films we would support and at what level but we are unlikely to give more than £80,000 to any one project, and we expect to give a lot of bursaries in the £5,000 - £40,000 range.*

What sorts of films? *Any sort of films, about anything, filmed anywhere in the world.*

Where will the films be shown? *The Foundation will work with filmmakers to enter the films to festivals and then devise the best distribution route for each film completed.*

What rights does the Foundation take? *Channel 4 will have the option of exercising the TV rights to the films as part of their overall support of the Foundation. They cannot guarantee to take all the films and if they do not exercise their option, then filmmakers are free to exploit the UK TV rights elsewhere if they can. The Foundation takes no rights in the work produced but will require a big fat credit on the films.*

How do I apply? *All applications must go through the website – and queries by email. We are a small staff and will get swamped unless filmmakers follow the application procedure. We aim to develop a really brilliant, helpful website and if, after looking at the site, you think it isn't clear or comprehensive enough do email us with your question so we can make sure it keeps getting better."*

Patronage and private funding

There are also less formal ways to get support for your film. Someone can simply give you the money you want to make your film. But this isn't too common, and of course most donors will want to know that you are capable of coming up with the goods. Private donors are most likely to be interested in the content and the possible effect of the film on audiences, whereas private investors will probably be indifferent to the film, which they'll view only as an investment vehicle. You'll be delighted if anyone offers you money, but remember to make sure of what the donor requires in return; if someone is remortgaging their house for you, you'll want to be as sure as humanly possible that your film is actually on track to make money and repay them. If they just want you to make a fine film, make sure you do that. If there are any legal or other written conditions, stick to them.

A word of warning from distributor Josh Braun: *"It always gives me a little pang of anxiety when I get on the phone to a filmmaker and he says, 'Well, I hope you can sell my film because they'll be taking away my house shortly.' And there's a reality check; at that point we'll say to the filmmaker, 'You know that among all the possibilities one is that it doesn't sell.' The cardinal rule is: don't spend your own money, but that's not always possible, but at least get your rich orthodontist uncle to put up the money."*

We include here a selection of case studies from both the UK and the US, because the principle is the same. The precise mechanisms won't be the same in any two films, so these aren't examples of charities you should go to, but they are success stories to set you thinking about how it could work for your film.

Proving your competence and previous achievements is useful.

Arthur Bradford's progress towards funding began with some big names seeing his personal material:

"In 1998 we made a pilot episode of 'How's Your News?', and we used that to get the funding. We shot in 2000 and finished in 2001. The way the pilot episode was funded was that I had been making short documentary films at the camp that we all worked at and those tapes got passed around and a friend of a friend gave it to the South Park guys, Matt Stone and Trey Parker. They contacted me and said that they liked the material and wanted to give us $10,000 to make whatever we could make for that. That's when we started getting the idea. We always knew we wanted to travel across the country but we knew that $10,000 wasn't enough so we made a short 28min film and that went to festivals, where a few people saw the film. We used that short to show that we were able to make a feature and then things kinda came together pretty quickly, to the point that we were able to make the feature. In July 2000 we started having meetings to get more funding and I got more money from the South Park guys and then we were shooting by October.

I wrote to HBO to see if they would give us money but they weren't really interested. A lot of times we would get the response, 'We're interested to see what you'll come up with but we won't give you any money now,' which I think is a typical response that you get. Then this one guy John Pearson, he had a company called Grainy Pictures and he had a history of investing in projects that other people didn't think would get off the ground – Spike Lee, 'Roger and Me', 'Blair Witch Project' – he was interested in 'How's Your News?' and he put up half the money and Matt Stone and Trey Parker put up the other half. In the end the whole film cost about $100,000. Originally we raised $75,000 to shoot and I'd say it cost about $25,000 more to finish it and all that."

Mike Mills had made a number of commercials, music videos and short films, but his first foray into documentary came when a wealthy and well connected friend offered him a private commission with no strings attached. After doing the rounds at a number of festivals, 'Paperboys' was broadcast on the Sundance Channel and secured DVD distribution with Palm Pictures.

"'Paperboys' was a very unusual project, a once in a lifetime opportunity. Many years ago Kate Spade – the designer of women's bags – won a design award and with this particular award you have to have a short film made for the presentation. So I made this short film for Kate Spade and I met Kate and her husband Andy Spade and got along with them very well. They're very nice, gracious and wealthy people, contemporary Medici types. Years later Andy Spade wanted to make a film about paperboys. He had been a paperboy, which is an American thing that's coming to an end and he wanted to document it before it had gone away.

So Andy gave me the idea and he paid for it, but then beyond that I was very fortunate - Andy just wanted it to be about paperboys and that was about it. I explained to him that I'd make a film like a Maysles brothers film. It was my opportunity to do something like 'Salesman' and it was great because we got to shoot it on film. He had a few comments at the end but they were pretty minimal, like make it a little shorter.

The budget was about $70,000 including a print. We shot it in six days and we edited it in three weeks. The whole thing was shot much more as if we were working to a music video schedule. There was another half of that project that we also shot, the paper girl's side. It wasn't as well conceived and to this point it's not finished. So the budget also included five days of shooting these different women in three different cities."

Asking and being in touch with the right people is vital. Sandi DuBowski gained funding for 'Trembling Before G-d' from a wide range of US Foundations, but in addition, *"I threw eight benefit parties - in NYC, Los Angeles, San Francisco, Miami, Jerusalem – where I would serve beverages and sometimes food, show our 12-minute trailer and then pitch the crowd for funding. I formed Benefit Host Committees of people from different communities in each city whose role was to give donations, sell tickets and/or invite people who were in positions to give. These often led to private family foundations and sources of financing that I would not have discovered otherwise. From the inception of the film, I developed groups of people who truly became invested in the film's growth and success. I communicated with people through email updates, face-to-face meetings, and print mailings. Sometimes people who brought in the most donations were not wealthy themselves but were friends or colleagues who knew people in those circles and could invite them to events."*

Producer Nikki Parrott and director Ben Hopkins work mainly on dramas and shorts, but when they were invited by a wealthy friend to make a documentary about cluster bombs, they saw the importance of such a film and accepted his offer. 'Footprints' was a great success and was bought by Storyville and the German channel ARD.

"Hans Geissendoerfer runs a very successful film company called Geissendoerfer Films in Germany. Hans likes to put some of his money back into the community and by chance he met a man called Christopher Horwood who works with the UN and various NGOs to sort out the problems of unexploded cluster bombs and landmines around the world. Hans talked to Chris about wanting to make a film about cluster bombs and then he approached Ben and me about it. Hans met Ben when he was at the Royal College of Art. He gave Ben some money for a film he did called 'The National Achievement Day' - it was one of the most successful shorts in the UK. It was a great collaboration and Hans has gone on to support a number of Ben's projects since. So we all decided that we would like to do something about cluster bombs, because they're so devastating and affect so many people around the world. Tigerlily Films (my production company) produced it and we basically decided to give our services for free on the condition we'd get money back if we sold it.

So Christopher Horwood introduced us to people who we could make the film about and we did a budget and shot it very cheaply on digi-beta. Ben was doing sound and directing, Gary Clarke was shooting it and Christopher was acting as a kind of fixer/location manager. Everyone worked for low rates and we got a reduced rate on the camera hire, but it was easy because it was a charity film and it was important. The budget off-hand was probably about £60-70,000 in the end and that all came from Geissendoerfer."

But sometimes you prove yourself by your commitment to the story, and as you go along.

Franny Armstrong became intrigued by the story of the McLibel two, a postman and gardener who took on McDonalds in an epic courtroom battle. With no budget and no commission, Franny set out with her dad's camera. Seven years on, Franny has two major films under her belt that between them have reached more than 40 million viewers in 28 countries.

"With 'McLibel' I was at a complete standing start – I had a job and I had a little bit of my own money, just a few hundred pounds. When I first heard about the trial there were eight production companies interested in the story, all trying to get a commission for 'McLibel'. But nobody would commission it because of the history with McDonalds and no-one else was willing to make it without a commission. Because I was willing to make it without money, I got it. My dad was a filmmaker and he said he'd lend me his Beta camera and then I basically just started getting people involved.

I knew one camera man, just as a friend, and as soon as I told him the story he immediately said he was up for it. So he shot a lot of it for free just because he liked the story. If I phoned him up and asked if he could shoot the next day and he couldn't, he'd say, 'But I've already told these other five camera men and they're all interested'. So anytime I needed a camera person one would come out of the woodwork for free. They all said it was just because they wanted to work on a decent story for once, and it was the same with sound recordists. Then quite quickly, because it was a big news story and we had the inside angle, international news people began approaching us for footage and we started selling our footage to the news. It was only a few hundred quid per time, but it was often enough, and that pretty much funded the whole thing. By this point I was on the dole because I couldn't continue with the job I was doing anymore.

We asked Ken Loach if he would do the drama reconstructions in the court room. He said he'd work on it for free but because he's a trade unionist, he couldn't ask other people to work for free. So suddenly we had to raise £15,000 to pay the actors, which was hell of a lot of money for us. In the end we did an appeal through email lists and a few rich people came forward and said we'll pay. 'McLibel' was a really big news story and there was a hell of a lot email and internet interest – there was a big network. Funnily enough I'm actually writing an appeal right now to the McLibel fans – there are 6,000 of them across the world who are on the email list and hopefully they'll all donate enough money for us to make the DVD.

So there wasn't a budget for 'McLibel' in the normal sense. We were making bits of money and as soon as it came we spent it. Everybody worked for free but I kept a record of who'd done what. Then when we started making money I sent everybody a cheque in proportion to what they'd worked. I definitely didn't manage to pay people fully for the work they'd done, but everybody got a share."

Franny's approach paid off and 'McLibel' was broadcast on BBC Four in April 2005. It was released in cinemas in USA in May and on DVD worldwide on McDonald's 50th birthday.

When filmmaker Alex Cooke heard that Arnold Schwarzenegger was running for the governorship of California she knew instantly she had to jump on a plane and start filming. When initial interest from the BBC waned, she made the difficult decision to stick with it and fund the film on credit cards. The gamble paid off; the film was bought by numerous countries and Alex had a liberating first-time experience of going it alone.

"The production company Mentorn were going to pitch some ideas at the BBC and one of them was about Arnold Schwarzenegger running for governor. The BBC was interested but on the condition that they could get access and get behind the scenes. Alan Hayling who was then at Mentorn – who's my partner - mentioned it to me. I said 'Oh my God that's an amazing story', so he said, 'Well look, they don't have time to start working on access, would you start working on it?' It was one of those things that I knew instantly that's it, that's the one. So I started working on trying to get access from London. I just thought I've got to get a camera, I've got to get on a plane and everyone was saying no. There was a lot of was he going to run, wasn't he going to run and even the day he was going to announce I spoke to the head of his campaign and he said he's not running. But then of course about eight hours later he was running and I was like fuck, I've got to get on a plane.

So we asked if the BBC would just pay the plane fare and Richard Klein said ok, and Mentorn loaned me a camera just to do some research filming. Basically I had a plane fare and that was it and I went and stayed with a friend. I was still trying to get access, which was really tough because there were about 200 other people also trying. But I realised pretty fast that there was still a film even if I didn't get access to him. Then the BBC started saying, 'We're not interested – this isn't a story, you're not going to be able to do anything that is beyond what's going to go on the news,' because we weren't inside. But because I was there I could see the most amazing situation going on and I was very torn. I didn't know whether to stay or go, but every day I was still going out filming on my own and after about two weeks I thought, 'Well, at this point it's my risk. I haven't got any money but I have got a camera, and my friend's letting me stay and I just don't want to go home.' I decided to take the punt and I basically got through my bank overdraft and then applied for credit cards. I was thinking that this was either absolutely the end of my life and I'd be working like a dog to pay this off forever, or it would be ok.

So I was on my own. I did all the producing, all the research, filming and sound recording, which I hadn't done before. I actually loved it and I got to know a lot of the journalists, so it didn't feel quite so isolating. Then the credit cards – you'd get through one credit card and then you'd have to take out another one. I kept taking out credit cards that had 0% interest for six months, so it was a case of getting as many of those as I could and keeping going. The risk at that point also wasn't so terrible because it was only the cost of what I was filming and being there.

Then when everyone realised that he was going to win suddenly everyone was more interested. The BBC went back to Mentorn and asked whatever had happened to that plane fare? At that point the BBC said they'd come in for a licence, not a co-production fee - for about £30-35,000. It wasn't enough for me to finish the film but it was enough for me to know I was on the way. Then the French producer Patrice Barrat did the French side and me and Alan just went nuts and hit every single international broadcaster we could think of and quickly raised not the full amount but enough to know that we could go into an edit and finish the film.

As people came in they said, 'Ok, we'll take it, but we want it in a month.' I had hours of footage and it was slightly frustrating because as a filmmaker I'd have liked the maximum amount of time to edit. One of the things I'd done when I was in LA was buy myself a laptop with Avid on. I was filming everyday so I'd come back at midnight and start digitising my rushes. Then I'd get up at four and I'd start travelling to film and it was just relentless. By the time I came back home I probably had two thirds of the film digitised. I got off the plane and the editor joined me the next day and we just started editing. We turned my apartment into an edit suite - we had two laptops going at the same time to get through it.

It was an independent production that was on my head. All the time I was never quite sure how everyone was going to get paid and how it would all pan out. Even when the BBC came in they would only pay on delivery so we were still cash-flowing on credit cards the whole time. It was rather scary. The budget was about £130K in the end, mainly because of editing, post-production, archive and music rights. We recouped nearly everything. I still haven't paid myself my full salary for it, but anyone who worked on it has been paid. Patrice's company Article Z in France are distributing it, so they keep trying to make continuous sales and there are little ones that come in now and again. I've also given it to Journeyman who took it on to do footage sales. You have to take a slightly longer view on it and say well, you're not going to make everything up front, but you'll make it back eventually.

I would take that gamble again. Sometimes I think that with the commissioning process you can almost lose the story while you're waiting for people to make a decision. If you are in a position to up and off with the camera without too much risk involved then why not, the technology's there, we can do it, but you have to be that hungry. If you feel strongly about it I think its worth going for it."

Jason Massot's experiences on 'Seafarers' is a reminder that funding can come from other parts of your own activity:

"I saved up about £15K from this TV contract I was working on and then just went and made it. What I decided to do was just put the money in an account and not look at it, because the last thing I wanted to think about was that I was now about to completely bankrupt myself. I own my own kit and I'd managed to get cheap stock, so the only real cost was for the sound gear and for an AP to come out with me. She was in the same position that I was in really - she wanted to do stuff without having to package it for TV, so I trained her to do sound when we were working together at the BBC. I had to pay our expenses, but it was a very, very cheap film to make."

And Morgan Spurlock, director of Super Size Me, provides perhaps the happiest ending to a self-funding story.

"After I graduated from film school at NYU, I worked in the film industry as a PA, a schlep. Then I got hired to be the national spokesman for Sony Electronics, doing a lot of on-camera stuff. Then I started doing work for them in-house, making films about what they do. In 2000 I started the company with some friends, some of whom were tech based and some other creative people. There were six of us. We created a show on the web called 'I Bet You Will' which is the first show in the US ever to go from the web to the television. We sold that show to MTV, and ended up making fifty-three episodes of it for MTV, but then it got cancelled.

At Thanksgiving 2002 I had the idea for the movie. At the time we had about 30 – 40,000 dollars, and the great thing was that we already owned all of our equipment, so we had all the facility available that we needed. So all we would be investing, more than anything, would be our time. That's the great thing: technology has really levelled the playing in a way where, if you have the time and not even a lot of money, just a little bit, you can do something. So we dove right in and started shooting in late January of 2003 and the core amount of shooting took about three and a half months. We shot from the end of January till around mid-May and then we continued to do pick ups all the way through to the end of the year.

And during this whole time I would get hired and go do another job, say presenting sports events for a weekend, which I'd pour all back into the movie, or I'd pay the editor's rent, because nobody was getting paid so we were all trying to still find some other work that would help balance out our lives. One of the bread and butter jobs of my production company is as a web company. But I was doing whatever jobs I could just to keep pouring money in. I'd go and move furniture for $20 an hour, move furniture then come back with groceries for the editors who were still editing. It was unbelievable, when I think back. Luckily for me throughout making the film I had a girlfriend who had a job and that's the reality. When you work in independent film you need to have a circle of people who really are supportive of you and that really matters a lot, because you can't get in a position where there are doubting Thomases surrounding you.

For shooting the film, I was on the diet for the thirty days, and a lot of the travel took place during that period. About half the money that we spent on the movie – because the whole film that got us into Sundance 2004 we made for $65,000, which is about 32,000 pounds. Half of that was probably travel expense – us flying all over the country shooting. That wasn't the cash cost, oh no. Nobody got paid. That's in the can, in the reel to Sundance. But to finish the film, to get the music rights, to do the blow up to 35mm was probably upwards of $300,000.

And to backtrack a bit, when we started the film, I had massive amounts of debt, two year's worth. After September 11th, production in New York City fell apart; there was nothing going on, we weren't making any money at our company. I moved into my office; I was sleeping there in a hammock, but I had great credit at the time so I was getting as many credit cards as I could and using credit cards to pay our rent, to pay employees, to pay their rent, to buy us food. In an eighteen-month period I had amassed about a quarter of a million dollars in credit card debt. About 125,000 pounds I guess. Suddenly I owed massive amounts of money to people and then finally in January 2002 MTV picked up our show, which enabled us to keep our head above water. With this, I was able to get a tiny bit out of the hole, I saw a little light out the tunnel but it was still very, very far away; I still had a couple of hundred thousand dollars of debt. But we did have the $50,000 that was left over after making the MTV series. So I said, 'Let's take this money and make a movie.' Because the thing is, the creditors were calling anyway. So rather than give money to them, I said, 'Let's make a movie.' I said, 'If I am going to declare Chapter 11 at some point, I might as well go down screaming and yelling and going woo-hoo! I got a movie!' So for me that was more important. And we took a risk and it paid off.

As soon as I got accepted into the festival, just after Thanksgiving 2003, I called a friend of mine to get her to give me some money to make sure we could finish the film. So, I borrowed some money from her. I called up my grandmother. She and my grandfather had started an annuity for me years and years ago that was about $45,000. I called them up and said, 'I want to cash this in.' And they're like, 'All right. You know, it's your money.' Because everybody who worked on the film worked for free. I'd told people, 'If we get into Sundance I'm taking all of you to Sundance.' So I took 25 people to Sundance. Yeah. It was awesome. By the time the film got up to its mass, when we were editing and doing all the cartoon animation, there were probably forty *people working on the movie, all of whom were working for nothing. People say, 'How did you get all those people?' and you know what, you talk to them, you have a vision for what you want to accomplish. People don't mind giving you the time so long as they know that what you say, you're going to make it happen. There's two kinds of people in this world, those who do what they say they're going to do and everyone else. So you have to decide, what kind of a person am I in making this project? Well, I'm going to talk to people and I'm not just going to talk to shit, I'm going to be passionate. And that's what people want to hear, they want to know that they're going to devote months of their lives for nothing, to see something at the end. That's been a great thing: through the success of this film and through the people I've met, I suddenly have access to people who have money, which I have never had in my life. Access to people who actually have the funds to pay for films. People have come to us with films that they've shot they couldn't finish that we're now helping to finance, to get done, to get completed, to find distribution. With my next film, I'm not going to pay for it myself because the great advice that's been around for years about filmmaking is, 'If you want to make a movie, don't use your own money, use somebody else's money.' And there's plenty of people out there that have a little money that will give you $5,000, or will give you $10,000. Just piecemeal those people together. For me, that's what I'm going to try and do, just find people. Coming off of this film it'll be a lot easier for me to find somebody that will give me a lot more than $5,000. Somebody who's going to say, 'Great, I'll invest this much money into whatever you're doing,' who will say, 'I'm just buying into you,' but doesn't want to be involved, who doesn't go, '… and I've got a daughter who's an actress.' Those aren't the people I want to work with; I want to work with people who are strictly in it for the business, who are investing in me. That's what the people who are reading this should look for as well."*

Financing as for a feature film

As documentaries become aligned more closely with fiction features in terms of their audiences, distribution and budgets, so too does this route to funding open up. Feature funding treats the sums incurred in making and distributing a film as a business investment that can be used to handle money in a tax-efficient manner. This is why government policy on tax and investment has an impact on filmmaking; the more the tax system makes investment in film a profitable option compared to all the other places an investor could keep their money, the more films will be funded in this way.

There are two important aspects of feature funding to highlight. The first is that this is complex and involves large sums of money. You will need professional advice, from a lawyer and/or financial specialist, and having on board a producer with high-budget international experience will be a boon as well. We list some companies offering these services at the end of the chapter.

The second point is that these tax benefits are open only to films that qualify as British according to the rules of the Department for Culture, Media and Sport (the DCMS). See the website www.culture.gov.uk for further information, updates as policy changes, and for details on how to request forms. See also www.inlandrevenue.gov.uk for information on tax avoidance and tax efficiency with regard to filmmaking, and www.hm-treasury.gov.uk has useful press releases and information on changes in taxation policy.

The British Council's film website www.britfilms.com also has resources, examples and information on tax and financing.

British films

British films, tax and investment section by Shamir Allibhai

Qualifying as a British film has the advantage that you can benefit from tax relief. The DCMS considers applications from each film before awarding a Certificate of British Nature of a Film. This is done after the film's completion; there is no advance clearance, but filmmakers in any doubt about their film's eligibility are advised to contact the DCMS early to discuss. This certification is given to films that either meet the requirements of Schedule 1 of the Films Act 1985 as amended 1999, or satisfy the terms of one of the UK's international co-production treaties.

The requirements for Schedule 1 are:

• The filmmaker must be from the UK, EU, or EEA (European Economic Area).

• 70% of the production costs must be spent in the UK

• 70% of the total labour costs must be spent on citizens or residents of the EU, EEA, or Commonwealth. There is a clause specifying that these labour costs can exclude one star actor not from the specified regions, or that two star actors' costs can be excluded if 75% of the remaining labour is spent on those within the regions. But these details are unlikely to be relevant for docs.

For co-production, a film can be classed as British-qualifying if it is produced under one of the UK's bilateral co-production treaties or the European Convention on Cinematographic Co-production. Feature docs are eligible as long as they are intended for theatrical release. Currently there are bilateral treaties with Australia, Canada, France, Germany, Italy, New Zealand, and Norway, and more co-production treaties, with countries including South Africa, India, China, Jamaica, and Morocco, are planned for roll-out in 2005/6.

For more on the co-production treaties, see also the websites of the relevant competent authorities:

The Australian Film Commission	www.afc.gov.au/
Téléfilm Canada	www.telefilm.gc.ca/
Centre National de la Cinematographie	www.cnc.fr/
Bundesamt für Wirtschaft und Ausfuhrkontrolle (BAFA)	www.bafa.de/
Ministero per i Beni e le Attivita' Culturali	www.cinema.beniculturali.it
New Zealand Film Commission	www.nzfilm.co.nz/
Norwegian Film Fund	www.filmfondet.no/

The European Convention on Cinematographic Co-production is a treaty produced by the Council of Europe (see http://conventions.coe.int). The treaty came into effect in 1994, with the aim of promoting the development of European multilaterial cinematographic co-production, which means it encourages co-productions that involve at least three co-producers in three different countries which are party to the Convention. For a fourth co-producer from a non-signatory country (such as the USA), the Convention can be applied as long as that producer does not contribute more than 30% of the total production costs of the film. The Convention can aso be applied to a situation where there are just two co-producers from different countries, but those countries themselves do not have a bilateral agreement.

A cinematographic work qualifies as European for the Convention if it receives 15 points out of 19 according to a schedule of European elements. Points are awarded for the European status of the director, writer or composer; the main performers; the main technicians in camera, sound, editing and art direction, and the shooting and post-production locations. The competent authorities may also decide that a film reflects a European identity and grant it co-production status even if it receives less than the 15 points.

Applications for co-production status must be made more than four weeks before the start of principal photography, but as with everything to do with financing, ample time should be allowed to follow all steps.

With regard to Certification as a British Film, there are certain aspects of particular relevance to docs. The normal limit on archive, or material that is borrowed from other movies or shows, is 10%, but the DCMS has the discretion to permit an increase to this limit, if appropriate to the subject matter of a documentary.

Normally each film in a series must be certified individually, but a documentary series with a common theme can be certified all together as one work.

Sale and leaseback, Section 48, Section 42

British-qualifying features can benefit from tax breaks by using a mechanism called sale and leaseback.

There are two forms of tax relief applicable in this case, one for smaller budget films which allows for 100% tax write-off in the year the film is made, and one for larger budgets, in which the tax relief is spread over three years. Most usually applicable for documentaries is Section 48, which allows benefits for films with budgets of under £15 million. Ie. if an investor (or group) invests £10 million in a film, under Section 48 they can deduct this sum from their tax liability in that year. Section 42 allows benefits for films with budgets of over £15 million, with the relief spread over three years. So an investment of £21 million would have the benefit to the investor that in the first year, £7 million of this investment would be deducted from their tax liability, with the same again for the next two years.

In March 2005, the UK Government announced that it would extend Section 48 (which was set to expire July 2005) until a new tax credit for lower budget films comes into place in 2006. Currenty, as long as films are in production by 1st April 2006 and completed by 1st January 2007, the tax breaks via sale and leaseback can be applied as they stand now. The new credit replacing Section 48 will apply to films with budgets up to £20 million, and the Treasury states that other key features will include:

20% of production costs will be covered as opposed to the current 15%; for the first time the relief will include an added incentive for the film to be profitable; all production expenditure, not just UK, is covered; maximum relief will rise typically to £4 million, from the current £2.25 million (source: HM Treasury press release 79/04, date 21 September 2004). A similarly-structured tax relief is being planned to replace Section 42 in 2006.

The sale and leaseback mechanism works by the producer or production company selling their film to a UK purchaser. They sell the physical print to the film, and the rights to exploit that print, for a sum equivalent to the film's production costs. This is known also as 'negative pick-up'; the buyer has picked up the film negative, and this is the 'sale' part. The 'leaseback' element is that the purchaser immediately leases back the film to the seller, normally for a period of ten to fifteen years. During this time the producer exploits all the rights to the film, and at the end of this period the film reverts to being the property of the purchaser.

As long as certain transaction criteria are met and the film qualifies under Section 48, the purchaser can write off 100% of the purchase price against tax oweable in the current accounting period's profits, or if this is insufficient, against certain previous years' income. Under Section 42, a third of the purchase price escapes tax in each of three years. This tax relief is not an absolute gain, as tax will be recovered on the rental income that the purchaser receives from the producer over the duration of the leaseback. But the purchaser does gain a sizeable return on the deferral of tax liabilities (an interest-free loan), plus commercial profits on the transaction.

The benefit to the seller (the film producer) is that they gain a large injection of income. Again, this is not an absolute gain, as the seller has to secure the rental payments by way of a bank guarantee; most of the money coming in from the purchaser goes straight back out again into a bank account where it is used to repay the purchaser over the period of the lease. But the difference between this money held in escrow (and the interest it will attract over the 15-year period), and the total price received for the sale of the film, is the seller's net benefit, and is generally around 10% of the film's production costs.

Note that all of this also requires a bank to become involved in the deal, and it requires a sale and leaseback provider to arrange it. The provider makes their money by charging the investor for managing the deal. There are therefore several sets of legal and financial costs to consider, especially if any form of sale and leaseback beyond this very simplified explanation of the process is used. For example, discounted sale and leaseback is a method for investors to provide a cash investment in a film before it is completed, rather than after completion as with a straight sale and leaseback, but this requires the extra assurance for the investor of a completion bond, which ensures that the film will indeed be completed, will gain its Certification, and will be sold to them. The deals become more complex and expensive; we mention this to hammer home the essential message that you should get professional help with your financing.

The investor's point of view

By financing a film, investors are not doing producers a favour; both groups need each other. If there were no projects to invest in, financiers would be out of a job! The goal for the producer should be to find a suitable investor, to get a deal signed which is mutually beneficial to both parties, and to deliver on commitments. For financiers, the questions are: what do they want from the deal? what are the key criteria? will this deal get their capital back plus interest, and what size returns are they looking for?

Asking how much money a film will make back can be like asking the length of a piece of string. It is very difficult to say for sure and what people tend to do is find comparables in the marketplace. For example, by showing what a similar film made, with a similar budget in the same genre, investors can get an idea as to what they might expect to make back and how the market will respond to the proposed film. The end number can still vary vastly from the predicted amount but this is the nature of investing in films. With doc features it will be difficult to find historical returns as this is newer ground, so investors will put more emphasis on their confidence in the producers. Can the producers deliver on their commitments? Do they have a track record and credibility? How good was their oral and written presentation and do they demonstrate an understanding for the business side?

The first step for a producer should be to create a legal company under which to include the production. The second step is to create a film finance package: a set of documents that describe in-depth the business side of the proposed film. It gives the producer an opportunity to formalise their thoughts onto paper and understand the proposition. Who is the target audience? What is the investment required and how will it be spent? Who makes up the key team and what are their backgrounds? What kind of returns can the film expect to make? Thirdly, the producer researches the potential sources of money. This will be done either by approaching wealthy people, or by going through a film financing specialist, such as the ones listed below, who exist to bring investors together with producers.

For choosing investors and financiers, you should screen them as carefully as you would a potential boyfriend or girlfriend before you started going out with them! Taking investment is getting into a relationship; some are fabulous and others disastrous. Unfortunately it often takes getting into a few relationships on a few different projects before you realize what works optimally for you. Investors can bring in 'smart money', where the investor brings not only cash, but skills, experience and contacts. For this, they usually expect a higher percentage of the project, but this may be worthwhile if it helps the film succeed. Other investments are called silent partnerships as the financier takes a very hands-off approach. For filmmakers who prefer to retain control of the project, this may be a better type of partnership. Be careful when going to friends or family for money – it can turn relations sour if the film isn't profitable and expectations aren't managed, or there can be a conflict in mixing business and pleasure. It is harder to walk away from family than from a private investor, and close friends can use friendship as the criteria for investing, rather than following any business logic.

Once a potential investor list has been mapped out, the producer contacts each one to set up meetings to present the project. For each meeting, the producer should adjust the proposal and presentation, based on the research they've done on this investor. A tip is not to see the number one choices first – presentations get better with experience so if you screw up on the first couple, you haven't at least screwed up on your top choices. Importantly, make sure you anticipate questions. Prepare in advance to have confident answers ready for questions you suspect the investors may ask.

At the meeting, a producer should:

1. Instil confidence in the potential investors of the project and team.

2. Demonstrate that the team is capable, well organized and has the experience to meet the targets and deliver.

3. Demonstrate that the project is commercial enough to make back an investment plus a return and that the project will get a distribution deal and maximum exposure.

4. Show familiarity with all aspects of producing including budgeting and distribution, as the investor wants to believe that the producer knows how to responsibly handle any funding and can make the money back.

5. Address any negative aspects of the package. There will always be some but it shows resourcefulness of the producer to deal with them head-on and show how the impact or risk will be minimized. If the investor uncovers negative aspects which the producer did not bring to the forefront, the chances of securing funding are greatly reduced.

And don't take rejection personally as there will be plenty of it along the path from script to screen.

Listings: media law and finance firms

Many of these have offices around the country; this list gives the London or head office.

BAKER TILLY

✉ 2 Bloomsbury Street
London WC1B 3ST

☎ 020 7413 5100

🖱 www.bakertilly.co.uk

BIRD & BIRD

✉ 90 Fetter Lane
London EC4A 1JP

☎ 020 7415 6000

🖱 www.twobirds.com

CMS CAMERON MCKENNA

✉ Mitre House
160 Aldersgate Street
London EC1A 4DD

☎ 020 7367 3000

🖱 www.law-now.com

DENTON WILDE SAPTE

✉ 5 Chancery LaneClifford's Inn
London EC4A 1BU

☎ 020 7242 1212

🖱 www.dentonwildesapte.com

FINERS STEPHENS INNOCENT

✉ Solicitors
179 Great Portland Street
London W1W 5LS

☎ 020 7323 4000

🖱 www.fsilaw.com

HARBOTTLE & LEWIS

✉ 14 Hanover Square
London W1S 1HP

☎ 020 7667 5000

🖱 www.harbottle.com

JAYES & PAGE

✉ Solicitors
Universal House
251 Tottenham Court Road
London W1T 7JY, UK

☎ 020 7291 9111

🖱 www.jayesandpage.com/

LEE & THOMPSON

✉ Solicitors
Greengarden House
15-22 St. Christopher's Place
London W1U 1NL

☎ 020 7935 4665

🖱 www.leeandthompson.com

OLSWANG

✉ 90 High Holborn
London WC1V 6XX

☎ 020 7067 3000

🖱 www.olswang.com

PARK CALEDONIA

✉ Glasgow Office
4 Park Gardens
Glasgow
G3 7YE

☎ 0141 332 9100

🖱 www.parkcaledonia.biz

RICHARDS BUTLER

✉ Solicitors
Beaufort House
15 St Botolph Street
London EC3A 7EE, UK

☎ 020 7247 6555

🖱 www.richardsbutler.com

THE SIMKINS PARTNERSHIP

✉ 45-51 Whitfield Street
London W1T 4HB, UK

☎ 020 7907 3000

🖱 www.simkins.co.uk

SJ BERWIN

✉ 222 Gray's Inn Road
London WC1X 8XF

☎ 020 7533 2222

🖱 www.sjberwin.com

TARLO LYONS

✉ Solicitors
Watchmaker Court
33 St. John's Lane
London EC1M 4DB

☎ 020 7405 2000

🖱 www.tarlolyons.com

WJB CHILTERN

✉ 3 Sheldon Square
London W2 6PS, UK

🖱 www.chilternplc.com

Other resources

PEACEFULFISH

🖱 www.peacefulfish.com

Film financing, corporate finance and digital distribution in the audiovisual industry. Access to website and consultancy services, £63 / year.

SCREEN FINANCE

 www.informamedia.com

Fortnightly online and print newsletter on the film industry. £677 / year.

SCREEN INTERNATIONAL

Weekly publication giving business-critical information and essential market intelligence on the global film business. Shooting People members are eligible for at 25% discount on subscription, reducing the price to £27 quarterly by Direct Debit. Subscription includes free access to ScreenDaily.com (normal price £140), which gives 365-day access to the latest news, plus the World Box Office service covering 25 territories.

PRODUCER'S GUIDE TO UK TAX FUNDS

www.kays.co.uk

By Martin Churchill and Adam Minns. Hard copy book plus monthly updates on new funds as they launch, £150.

Chapter Eight
European funding,
television & events

An introduction to Europe and the documentary

In Europe, the world of documentary is a big arena, and can be hard to make sense of from the outside. Finding a way in, however, is extremely useful - not just because your potential market and audience are massively increased, but also it's a real eye-opener culturally and artistically. Kersti Uibo, director of *'Narrow is the Gate', explains, "For me England is the place I live but it is very soundly in Europe. As soon as England says no then I go to Europe because Brussels and Paris are only two hours away. Once you go to the Amsterdam film festival and attend the Forum you see there is a documentary family; somehow you feel that you are part of a whole. It's very important because I used to find it frustrating that you could be so isolated, because there are only a few doors in Britain to knock on. You have just a few commissioning editors and even if there are ten it's still a small number. Somehow it's very important to see that there is a much bigger world out there, that you are not on your own."*

The schema of this book is that we've split the processes of funding and distribution, but the divide isn't always so pronounced, particularly in a European environment. Often funding is a process of piecing together small sums of money from different investors at both the development stage and at acquisition. So this chapter includes all elements of Europe and your documentary, apart from companies that exclusively do distribution, which you'll find in Chapter 14, high end distribution. We start with a description of two organisations, MEDIA and EDN, which are the vital first points of call if you're thinking about working non-domestically. Then we outline the state of television in Europe, before guiding you through the most useful events in the Euro documentary year. Festivals in Europe are found in Chapter 12, Festivals and markets.

What is international co-production? At the expensive end of the market, international co-financing is a way to increase investment in your film, and to benefit from 'soft money' or tax breaks and investment incentives in more than one country. See Chapter 7, Private funding, for a reminder of how soft money can help your film. If you qualify as an international co-production according to the rules of more than one country, you ▶

Marc Isaacs, director:
"I'm getting really interested in the idea of co-production. Through 'Lift' and 'Calais' I've been able to build some connections in France and I just feel that if I had more time and money I would exploit that much more. At the moment I'm trying to organise a trip to Paris where I meet up with five or six different people and start to build up some connections. I'd love to be able to go to Storyville or whatever and say, "Look, I've got 20K from France, all I need from you is 40K - I'll make a cheap film, I don't mind." I'm in a position to be able to do that in Germany; people know my work there through different festivals, and in Holland. It's hard when you just email people and they don't know who you are, because it's a strange world, people don't know anything about you. If you've got something recognisable to them, some means of presenting yourself to them, then it really helps.
When I was in Sweden with 'Calais' I met a commissioning editor who was running a new strand and he needed a film. He was a Swedish commissioning editor from Swedish television and he was saying maybe we're interested in buying it in. In the end he didn't want to buy it but it's just an example of how you can get to meet people and access somebody quite directly just like you do in England. It's a slightly different ball game doing it abroad and introducing yourself and your work."
A vital point to remember about working in Europe is that you're not completely alone. The European Union invests in film, both as an industry and as a part of our cultural heritage, through the MEDIA scheme, while there are a range of organisations offering training, help and support. In this chapter we also include a large number of interviews and comments from filmmakers who've already dipped a toe in European waters, so you can take advantage of their hard-won knowledge.

can get these breaks in as many countries as you qualify. Some regions offer financial incentives for films that spend money and/or create employment in their locality. We're not going fully into that here; if you are on a documentary with that sort of budget, get some proper, international financial advice (see Chapter 7, Private funding, for a list of financial advisors).

At the level of independent docs, though, the more common method of international co-operation is to get funding for your film from one of the European broadcasters, either as production funding or as an acquisition. This could involve you making your film entirely off your own bat, then as a British filmmaker, selling it to a foreign broadcaster. Sometimes, however, and more interestingly, co-production involves working closely with a foreign production company or filmmaker as a partner, or with the input of a foreign broadcaster.

André Singer is CEO of Café Productions and has a long history of looking beyond the UK, from his work on the 1980s series 'Disappearing World' to his current work in Europe, which includes producing Werner Herzog's latest documentary fantasy 'Galileo'; producing single documentaries for National Geographic Channels International, History Channel (US, UK and Canada), Five, FR2, and BBC; and working with Reader's Digest on new video production. He says, *"I am developing special relationships with one or two select companies in France and Germany with a view to jointly develop and produce in the long-term."*

Q. How has the UK historically differed from other European countries in documentary?

We have always in the UK had a reputation (often deserved) for approaching the documentary in an insular and arrogant manner. We have not wanted to compromise for the sake of additional foreign finance and so were not always welcomed as partners in Europe. That has changed with the need from both the UK and Germany to co-finance projects and more and more to properly co-produce them (i.e. to share production roles and to make narratives work across borders).

Q. How have UK filmmakers', viewers' and commissioners' attitudes changed towards the world outside?

Broadcasters (and thus commissioners) have always believed domestic subjects are more popular in the schedules than international ones – natural history excepted. And of course they are cheaper. I don't think those attitudes have changed much, although the squeeze year on year of budgets has meant that for those of us interested in international stories, the need for co-production partnerships and finance has become essential. The ability for UK commissioners to fully fund international stories is distinctly less today than in the past.

Q. Could you give an overview of the most important European countries for independent documentary makers? Who's most amenable for British filmmakers to work with?

Germany has become extremely important for UK producers. Not only is it the largest European market (second only to the US in the global market-place) but culturally it is the closest to UK tastes. Germany in the past was even more self-sufficient than the UK. But their money has run out and partnerships are now growing. France has a long and more relaxed tradition of co-production but it does entail understanding and complying with the unique French subsidy system (CNC, Procireps, etc) which can bring considerable financial advantages but needs substantial production work to be done in France or with French production teams. Company to company relationships is the best method for working with this. Various other links are worth-while (the Nordic Group and Spain in particular). The European Documentary Network in Copenhagen is an essential first port of call for European co-prduction. Eastern European accession has the potential to provide more opportunities for British filmmakers to co-produce and collaborate, but realistic finance for collaboration with eastern Europe is still some way away.

Q. What's most often misunderstood about international co-production; what are the vital questions for a UK-based filmmaker to consider when taking the first steps to international co-production?

Some producers still believe co-production means "you give me your money, and I will make and provide you with a finished film". Most international broadcasters and producers, understandably resent this and ▸

want co-production to be genuine partnerships. We also often forget that even though communications are so extensive and global; culturally we still need different things. It is not too often that the identical product works everywhere without re-versioning.

Q. To some minds, British broadcasting has experienced a narrowing of the range of options for documentary. Where do you see the best opportunities for independent and original doc filmmakers at the moment?

The options are narrowing too for the independent filmmakers. Consolidation has clearly begun for bulk and formulae production with broadcasters finding it easier to block-commission and do output deals. That will inevitably continue and put a squeeze on the smaller idiosyncratic independent producer. Their survival will depend on originality, quality and more and more on the international partnerships they can bring to the table. The feature or cinematic documentary is also still likely to be a growth area for the smaller independent.

Support for you in Europe

The EU's MEDIA Plus Programme

The MEDIA Programme is the European Union's scheme to support the audio-visual industry. MEDIA Plus is the name of the third and current incarnation of the programme, which runs until December 2006. The budget for the five-year period of MEDIA Plus is €513 million. 2004 spending in the UK was in the region of €7 million, from the total of over €70 million.

The Programme covers more than the 25 members of the EU. Participating countries are:

Belgium, Denmark, Germany, Greece, Spain, France, Ireland, Italy, Lichtenstein, Luxembourg, Netherlands, Austria, Portugal, Finland, Sweden, UK, Island, Norway, Cyprus, Czech Republic, Estonia, Latvia, Lithuania, Poland, Slovakia, Slovenia, Malta, Hungary and Bulgaria, with Switzerland to join on 1st January, 2006.

The MEDIA Programme has three stated aims:
• To strengthen the competitiveness of the European film, TV and new media industries;
• To increase international circulation of European audiovisual product; and
• To preserve and enhance European cultural diversity.

MEDIA has a national office, known as a Desk, Antenna or Service, in each participating country, jointly supported by the EU and the relevant national film body. The Desk has the role of disseminating information, helping with queries, and encouraging filmmakers in that country to take advantage of the various funding available through the programme. MEDIA Desks do not distribute funding; this is controlled through the Brussels central office of the programme, and must be applied for through the central system.

UK MEDIA DESK

✉ Agnieszka Moody
c/o UK Film Council
10 Little Portland Street
London W1W 7JG

☎ 020 7861 7511

✎ england@mediadesk.co.uk
www.mediadesk.co.uk/england

MEDIA ANTENNA WALES

✉ Gwion Owain
c/o SGRIN, 10 Mount Stuart Square
Cardiff Bay
Cardiff CF10 5EE

☎ 02920 333 304

✎ wales@mediadesk.co.uk
www.mediadesk.co.uk/wales

MEDIA ANTENNA SCOTLAND

✉ Emma Valentine
249 West George Street
Glasgow G2 4QE

☎ 0141 302 1776/7

✎ scotland@mediadesk.co.uk
www.mediadesk.co.uk/scotland

MEDIA SERVICES NORTHERN IRELAND

✉ Cian Smyth
c/o Northern Ireland Film Commission
Third Floor, Alfred House
21 Alfred Street
Belfast BT2 8ED

☎ 02890 232 444

✎ media@niftc.co.uk
www.mediadesk.co.uk/northernireland

There are constantly new schemes, new deadlines and tweaking of eligibility criteria, so do check for the latest state of play.

Like the UK Film Council, the MEDIA Programme has examined the filmmaking terrain and decided what areas need particular support. Its decision is that production is the part of the filmmaking process that needs the least stimulation, and can best be left to national governments to support. The programme also defers to the national level when it comes to supporting beginners, preferring to concentrate on helping filmmakers only when they have reached a point when they are ready to expand beyond the domestic sphere. See below for details on the levels of experience needed in order to apply to MEDIA schemes. With this exclusion of production, MEDIA's support is concentrated on the four priority areas of training, development, distribution and promotion, with a fifth strand of support for new initiatives. We mention more on their support for distribution in Chapter 12, Festivals and markets, while the training schemes that incorporate elements of pitching and funding are listed below. Among the pilot projects in the €17 million New Initiatives was the European DocuZone project, now renamed CinemaNet Europe; for an interview with Amy Hardie, Director or CinemaNet Europe, see Chapter 15, DIY distribution.

In this section we describe how direct funding from the MEDIA Programme can go towards getting your documentary funded and seen. In the following section we cover MEDIA-supported events that help with development and funding. Direct funding is available through two schemes: Development funding and TV Broadcasting funding.

MEDIA Development Funding

What: Only 'creative documentaries' of over 25 minutes are eligible: they must be scripted, authored, point-of-view films, not current affairs or reportage (there is some debate within the programme on the status of wildlife documentaries and the changing boundaries between documentary and other formats). The funding is for development costs, which include: writer's fees (as documentaries must be scripted), research, travel, scheduling, developing the budget, and arranging finance. No production or filming is included in this development stage, apart from making a video treatment as a taster.

Funding for up to 50% of the development budget, capped at €30,000, is the maximum that MEDIA offers for single project funding, except for projects that exploit or reflect European cultural diversity, which could be eligible for up to 60% of development funding.

Who: Production companies, not directors, apply for the funding. Applications can be made for either a single film or a slate of projects. For a single film, the applying company needs a track record of having produced and broadcast at least one documentary in the preceding eighteen months. For first-time applicants, national broadcast of the qualifying film is sufficient; for seasoned applicants, international broadcast is required. A company needs to have been registered (as a legal entity) for at least one year, and it must be the majority producer of the qualifying film. Slate funding has slightly tighter rules: a company must have been registered for three years, and up to €90,000 is available for development of a slate of three to six films.

How: There are two deadlines per year for single film funding, usually in February and May, but check with your MEDIA Desk for changes. Each company can put in only one application per year.

Each application goes through a basic eligibility assessment, then is assessed by industry experts, usually one who is local to the project, who can check that details such as budgets for the project are accurate, and one foreign expert. The grounds for a decision are whether the film has international potential within Europe, whether there will be investors and an audience, either for theatrical or broadcast distribution. The results are published three to four months after the deadline.

Comments: Numbers of applicants varies, but as an indication, in 2003 roughly forty UK production companies obtained single and slate development funding.

The aim is to strike a balance between genres so that the four categories of fiction, documentary, animation and multimedia are all represented healthily. In 2004, €2.2 million were distributed among between 20 to 30 companies, out of the €17 million total European funding.

Scottish production company Autonomi received €20,000 of MEDIA funding in the 2003 call for development, for the project 'Peshmarga: Those Who Die First'.

The success rate is roughly a third of companies applying to obtaining funding.

If you're thinking of applying for development funding, your MEDIA Desk is there to help you in the application process.

Development funding takes the form of a grant with obligation to reinvest. This means that in a case where the maximum €30,000 has been given for development, when film goes to production, the producer must find €30,000 in the production budget, that can either be repaid to MEDIA, or that must be reinvested in the producer's next project. In the next project, this €30,000 sum must be matched by their own funding, and at this point it becomes non-repayable grant money.

New Talent Funding

What: This is further development support, along the lines of development funding for single projects, but it is only available for producers who have already participated in MEDIA-supported training activities in the 24 months preceding the application. Fifty percent (60% for projects highlighting cultural diversity) of the development costs are available. Depending on the type of project submitted, you must request an amount between €10,000 and €30,000.

TV Broadcasting

What: This is the only MEDIA funding that touches on production, but it's really an aid to distribution, maximising the international potential of a project and helping suitable films to travel across European borders.

Who: Established production companies who have a television project due for production within six months of the date of application to MEDIA can apply for up to 500,000 euros, up to a cap of 20% of the production budget for a documentary, or up to 12.5% for drama and animation. Application can only be made after 50% of the budget is already in place, and the project must be 50% financed from European sources. A project must involve at least two broadcasters from MEDIA countries in two different language zones. Rights must revert from the broadcaster to the producer within seven years if the project is a pre-sale, or ten years for a co-production.

How: Eligibility is decided on a points system, with merit given for the number of European broadcasters, then non-European, involved. Securing international distribution helps, as does your international sales track record, to a lesser extent. Funding is awarded on a rolling basis with deadlines in approximately February, May and September; again, check with your MEDIA desk. The funding is in the form of a non-refundable grant.

Comments: TV Broadcasting funding goes to larger projects of international appeal, and is often used to help with versioning the film for broadcast in different countries.

For example, in 2004, the three UK documentary beneficiaries were Brook Lapping, awarded €365,000 for their three-hour series on Israeli-Palestinian relations, made for BBC Two, PBS and other broadcasters; Zef Productions, awarded €79,000 for 'Ditchling', their anthropological documentary mini-series about director Luke Holland's Sussex hometown, for BBC Four's Storyville; and Seventh Art Productions, awarded 110,000 euros for 'In Search of Mozart', a 100 minute feature documentary from Phil Grabsky (director of 'The Boy who Plays on the Buddhas of Bamiyan'), following the composer's journeys through Europe and investigating his genius.

Agnieszka Moody, director of the UK MEDIA Desk, comments that European broadcasters and producers are much more savvy when it comes to applying for this MEDIA funding, and it's taken for granted that MEDIA money should form part of the budget for any film with the right sort of content. *"In the UK we suffer from the curse of affluence, as the relatively high levels of broadcaster funding have meant that UK producers have had no need to turn to co-production and European money. For creative documentaries, there's a fixed pool of European commissioning editors that a producer-director can go to. It's a limited pool, but not too small. The problem can lie in knowing who to go to, especially because more of these editors are outside the UK than inside, and that's what the MEDIA Programme can help with." For members of EDN the website gives access to profiles of members, industry guides and the option of initiating co-productions."*

EDN - European Documentary Network

✉ Vognmagergade 10, 1
   DK 1120 Copenhagen K
   Denmark

☎ +45 3313 1122

✉ edn@edn.dk
   www.edn.dk
   UK contact:Lucinda Broadbent mail@lucinda.org.uk

Started when the MEDIA Programme spun off its documentary department in 1996, EDN has grown into what producer Andre Singer calls "an essential first port of call for European co-production." With head offices in Copenhagen and national contact people all round Europe, EDN works to be the central meeting point for professionals within the documentary sector in Europe, including filmmakers, producers, production companies, distributors, associations, film institutions and boards, universities, festivals, broadcasters et al. EDN publishes both the EDN TV Guide (see below) and DOX magazine, a magazine both practical and discursive that comes out six times a year.

EDN's primary function is to create and support networks for its 700+ members, with annual membership costing €110 for individuals and €750 for institutions

(Shooting People members get a 30% discount, bringing membership down to €77. Sign in at www.shootingpeople.org and follow the EDN subscriptions instructions).

To members, EDN offers individual consultancy and the opportunity to initiate co-productions with other members. For non-members also, it organises a range of workshops, seminars and conferences all over Europe throughout the year, often in partnership with local organisations. The most important of these are the pitching and development forums, which help newer filmmakers in honing their projects and improving their skills, give the chance to pitch to commissioning editors, and encourage interaction and partnership between filmmakers from diverse backgrounds. We list the main ones below.

Director Kersti Uibo explains EDN's appeal as, *"British TV has the monopoly in England but as a member of EDN I have moved closer towards a more European way of seeing things. I don't like monopolies and that's why I go to other countries where TV doesn't have this monopoly. EDN has given me a lot of strength and solidarity; I've seen a lot of good films through EDN that have inspired me and given me the feeling that it's possible to make very strong and different films that are not funded by TV."*

Cecilia Lidn, EDN Event Co-ordinator, explains:

"Not so long ago when the word co-production was not common knowledge and there were no pitching forums, a few lucky souls in countries with Film Institutes got their films fully financed. Those days are over! Even in countries with a strong tradition of support it is more the rule than the exception that the credits of the films are getting longer and longer. EDN grew out of this situation. The change of the documentary landscape in Europe was very much connected to the creation of the EU MEDIA Programme, set up to stimulate cross-border activity in film distribution and production through loans given to independent producers. To do so for documentaries, the office DOCUMENTARY was set up in Copenhagen, financed partly by the EU, and partly by the Danish Ministry of Culture. DOCUMENTARY initiated the Forum in Amsterdam together with IDFA. It started the publication of the DOX Magazine. It made European documentary filmmakers feel like brothers and sisters. Most important, however, was the implementation of a new culture for sharing information and getting into the open with projects.

When the office was closed down in 1996 due to another EU restructuring, a need for some kind of continuity was evident. A visionary board of DOCUMENTARY laid the foundation stones for a European Documentary Network and the Danes convinced their ministry to give seed money for the building of an independent pan-European association.

In the fall of 1996 Tue Steen Müller (previously of the National Film Board of Denmark) was appointed director and Anita Reher (previously of DOCUMENTARY), network manager. Now, eight years, seven hundred members and hundreds of workshops later, EDN has a staff of six and is based in the Film House in central Copenhagen.

EDN is a pan-European organisation, and we are dedicated to strengthening and enhancing the documentary community both in and outside of Europe. That is done through the organisation and co-organisation of numerous events each year, bringing the filmmakers, producers and financiers together. The aim is either to search for co-production and financing; or to focus on the genre and the history of the documentary film;

or to celebrate the creative documentary and the dedicated filmmakers that make them. EDN specialises in tailor-making seminars and events so that they suit the region in which they are held.

From the very beginning EDN has put a strong focus on Southern Europe. This has resulted in the creation of national documentary associations, and DocsBarcelona (held every year at the beginning of November) now includes the second-most important forum after IDFA. In the Nordic countries we have a two-part co-production workshop for young filmmakers. Through this workshop, young, inexperienced filmmakers have created a network of colleagues, that has resulted in Nordic co-productions, that have ended up as brilliant films! The Finnish film 'Screaming Men' took its baby-steps as a project at this workshop Twelve for the Future and three years later it was selected to Sundance and got its thirty seconds off fame on CNN! EDN works to matchmake documentarians from Eastern Europe, from Estonia down to Thessaloniki in Greece, where producers from the Balkans get their chance to meet financiers from the West.

EDN publishes the EDN TV Guide, which is a directory of all the TV channels in Europe. From November 2004 this guide is also available in an electronic version for EDN members. The EDN TV Guide is updated annually. DOX Magazine is also a publication of EDN, and as EDN members you receive the TV-Guide and DOX Magazine six times a year. Furthermore, as member of EDN you have access to the members area of the EDN web site, where it is possible, among other things, to find the profiles of all the EDN members. All members can send in their projects to the office for evaluation in terms of financing or writing, or send in their films to get a hint on where to take them. If the office staff cannot answer the requests, the network is used. There is always someone to go to for help in the modern co-production jungle of documentaries!"

European television

"When I first met all the European broadcasters it was a bit like joining a completely new and very noisy school and thinking that I was never going to remember who everyone was, and definitely wouldn't be able to find the right classroom. It got better." – Jess Search

Bear in mind that the questions we set out in Chapter 2 – is your film suitable for TV, how would you go to broadcasters, are you offering something that anyone wants to buy or invest in? – are equally applicable in Europe, and you have the added question of needing to find out if this is the sort of doc that goes down well in that country, which is often harder to know than about your own. The positive side of this is that there's more scope, and a broader range of acceptable filmmaking; you just have to track down where your film might fit.

Jo Lapping, Strand Executive for Storyville, the height of cosmopolitanism on UK TV, says this about working in Europe:

"There are fewer British producers active on the international market than most other Europeans; I suspect it's because there has always been quite good funding from terrestrial TV stations in this country for a documentary film. When British producers come and talk to Storyville, they're always quite surprised how long it takes to get the money together. I'd always reckon at least nine months to raise money for these kinds of films. It is a lot of legwork, and, if you're dealing with other European broadcasters, a lot of trying to get hold of people and chase them up. Getting personal relationships or knowing the commissioning editors, knowing who likes programming what, is very valuable information to have. It's worth looking at what the EDN offers, looking at their guides, and going to those various events that the commissioning editors all show up at.

A lot of it boils down to getting experience. Guides like Shooting People's are helpful in pointing people in the right direction, but having face time with all the various characters involved is good: get out there, get to know people, get to know what they want to do. It's quite a small world, in terms of broadcasting these kinds of films, so you do tend to see the same commissioning editors pop up at all the various international events; there's a gaggle of them that go round. Most of the broadcasters know what each other are up to, so if people do get a foot in the door with one broadcaster, it's always worth asking them who they normally work with or who you could try. The festival circuit is one way of doing that, and probably the easiest and most interesting way. And there seem to be more and more British people going. When I started going to these things about six years ago, there were very few, but I've certainly seen it increase. Maybe it was the downturn in financing available at home that has made people branch out a bit."

EDN TV Guide

The vital handbook to know who's who in European documentary, the EDN TV Guide gives channel profiles, details of their documentary output, and details on all strands, commissioners and contacts for broadcasters throughout Europe.

European Broadcasters

ARTE France

 Documentary Unit of ARTE France,
8, Rue Marceau
F-92785 Issy-les-Moulineaux
Cedex 9

☎ +33 1 55 00 77 77
fax: +33 1 55 00 77 00

No English website but extensive information on the commissioning process in French via www.artepro. com , including searchable database of every filmmaking individual and organisation in Europe with whom ARTE France has worked, and submission guidelines.

ARTE France is the French half of ARTE G.E.I.E., the European channel jointly owned by ARTE France and ARTE Deutschland, whose aim is to create and broadcast television of a broadly international and cultural nature that will aid mutual understanding between Europeans. ARTE France co-produces and acquires foreign documentaries, ranging from 26-minute docu-soaps to 150-minute themed culture strands.

ZDF German Television

 55100 Mainz
Germany

☎ +49 61 31 70 59 00 / 61 31 70 1
fax: +49 61 31 70 59 09

🖱 www.zdf.de

✉ ZDF London Bureau
30 Old Queen Street
London SW1H 9HP

 020 72 33 41 00

 StudioLondon@zdf.de

ZDF (Zweites Deutsches Fernsehen) is Germany's national public television broadcaster. It is an independent nonprofit corporation under the authority of the Länder, the sixteen states making up the Federal Republic of Germany. Factual and documentary programming make up roughly a quarter of its output. ZDF is the home of operations for German-language satellite broadcaster 3Sat, and is a 25% shareholder in ARTE. ZDF co-produces, commissions and acquires documentaries ranging from 30-minute foreign affairs pieces to 40-plus minute authored docs.

Euro commissioners' profiles

Profile of Leena Pasanen

Head of Programmes
YLE Teema
Finland

✉ Box 88
FIN-00024 YLE
Finland

☎ +358 9 1480 2680
Fax. +358 9 1480 2421

🖰 www.yle.fi/teema

"YLE is Finland's national broadcasting company. Foreign documentaries are co-produced, acquired and pre-bought, in slots ranging from 30-minute acquired nature docs to 60-minute docs of all types, and there are open-ended slots.

As a commissioner for YLE Teema, a digital-only channel for culture, science and education, I commission around 50-60 international co-productions/pre-buys a year. In theory I'm looking for creative documentary films (also feature length) on arts, but recently I have noticed, that I just take whatever I cannot resist. Any cinematic, poetic even experimental film, that I cannot ignore, often ends up on my channel.

My colleagues in documentary are Riitta Pihlajamäki, commissioner for the main channel YLE TV1; Erkki Astala, head of co-productions and Iikka Vehkalahti, who's commissioning for YLE TV2. It's a bit of a tricky system, but Riitta and I are heads of factual programmes (I'm commissioning fiction as well) and we order the whole programming (documentaries, reportages, discussion programmes, current affairs etc) for our channels. Erkki is head of the department dealing with co-productions and Iikka is working on that department as a producer. So, Riitta and I are doing a lot of ourselves, but also commissioning strands or single programmes from Erkki's department. (I guess it's even more complicated than the system at Arte).

When it comes to approaching me: if I know nothing about you, I need to see your previous films, or need to know your producer or British commissioning editor and have them recommending you. The average amount I give is between €5,000 to €10,000. For series (like docu-soaps or art series) it can be up to €30,000.

For docs that epitomise my style, if you've seen The Dreamland by Latvian filmmaker Laila Pakalnina, you know what I'm looking for. And as a case study:

'Tuvalu - Before the Flood', director Paul Lindsay, producer Mike Chamberlain from Stampede. Mike pitched it in EDN workshop, Thessaloniki. I guess I was the first one to step in, and only because I loved the

subject: imagine if your country would be sinking and you'd have to find a new one to live in! A great way to tackle greenhouse effect and globalisation. A bit later on Nick Fraser stepped in and gave the research money. With my money Paul could barely buy the flight ticket to Tuvalu, but I helped them to pitch it in Amsterdam and we managed to get this project going.

Another example is 'The Art Safari' by Ben Lewis. This project was already very much alive and kicking when I stepped in. They already had most of the budget in place and were only looking for some smaller pre-sales. I got to know this one from Mette Hoffmann-Meyer from Danish TV2."

Profile of Mette Hoffman Meyer

Mette Hoffmann Meyer
Commissioning Editor
TV 2/Danmark
Denmark

✉ TV 2/DANMARK
Sortedam Dossering 55 A
2100 København Ø

☎ + 45 35 37 22 00
fax + 45 65 91 33 22

"TV 2/Danmark is the market leader and one of Denmark's two public service channels. Foreign documentaries are commissioned, co-produced and acquired, for slots ranging from 40-minute weekday factual programming, to 90-minute docs both weekly and throughout the year. Within the channel's output, my particular area of documentary is human interest stories, political and social issues stories, current affairs as well as crime. For programmes not originating in Denmark we would not enter into co-productions or pre-buys unless there is a long successful track record or a broadcaster from the country of origin involved.

Docs can be any price. A programme that I'm proud of is 'The Liberace of Baghdad'. I had given some developing money to Team Production, a Danish company to develop a certain story in Baghdad. We agreed to send Sean McCallister and off he went. This specific story did not develop, but Sean called and said he had found this other story he would like to pursue. I then commissioned the film and so did Storyville at BBC. The film won special Jury Award at Sundance Film festival 2005 and it was the first time for a Danish production with a British director."

Profile of Bert Janssens

Bert Janssens
Managing Director / Head of Programming
Humanistische Omroep (Humanist Broadcasting Foundation)
The Netherlands

Borneolaan 17
1217 GX Hilversum
tel: +31 35 6722020
fax: +31 35 6722025
www.humanistischeomroep.nl
www.donderdagdocumentaire.nl

"Humanistische Omroep is a small public service broadcaster going out over the Nederland 1 and Nederland 3 channels. Realising the humanist tradition and values within the context of present cultural, social and political developments is the main characteristic of our TV, radio and internet programming. We transmit roughly twenty hours a year of documentary, some of which is acquired and co-produced. We look for docs of 50 minutes (unless they really need to be longer....). We are looking for documentary filmmakers who marry cinematographic talents with the ambition to use their films to intervene in the debate on current issues.

If a documentary does not originate in the Netherlands it is important that it comes from a director with an interesting track-record, working with a well-established production company. It is recommened that the production has the commitment of a broadcaster in its own country. The quality of the commissioning editor that supports the project is an important factor for us. There is no standard budget: the content of each documentary determines the budget. Our maximum participation for Dutch documentaries is €40,000, for co-production €17,500, for pre-buys and acquisition €10,000.

A good documentary is an exercise in discovery, for the filmmaker as well as for the audience. That's why we are proud of having been part of international co-productions like 'Nadav's Peace', 'Liberace of Baghdad', 'A Decent Factory', 'Georgi and the Butterflies'. All had co-funders from different European broadcasters. In different ways these documentaries gave a look from the outside onto issues our society is dealing with. We got involved with them in different stages of productions, mostly when they were presented during international pitching sessions (EDN, Discovery Masterschool, Forum etc.). Generally speaking: the earlier we get involved the better it works for the establishment of a good relationship. And what doesn't work is when someone that pitches or sends us a proposal did not do his homework: checking the EDN-guide, our website etc. Know who you are talking to!"

International funding case studies

'Hidden Gifts'

Glasgow-based director Nick Higgins looked to Europe for 'Hidden Gifts: the story of Angus MacPhee', a documentary for which he was nominated for a 2005 Royal Television Society award.

"Initially I submitted the idea to two of Scotland's new talent documentary schemes. Both times I was short-listed and in the end rejected, but this only made me more determined and seeing little potential within Scotland I took the idea to Europe. YLE (the Finnish broadcaster) liked it and offered a small amount of money towards the budget, so with this in hand I then went to other European broadcasters and after various knockbacks eventually raised finance from Sweden, the Netherlands and Germany which eventually led to Scottish Screen and Grampian Television coming on board. So from having the initial idea rejected, I was forced into creating my own production company, brokering a European co-production and most recently being nominated for a Royal Television Society award.

The film's been shown both on Grampian and Scottish Television and we have had several screenings at art schools where the film seems to strike a particular chord. It has still to be broadcast in Finland, Germany, the Netherlands and Sweden, leaving us a small window in which to try and realise some festival screenings. But I must admit I find the process of entering the film into festivals incredibly tedious and would rather try and raise money for the next project. The good news, though, is that the film was picked up in Amsterdam by the doc distributor Marfilmes of Portugal, and so we may yet see some more broadcast sales.

I say all this not as a boast but as a form of encouragement to any filmmakers out there who have had rejections: whatever happens don't buckle under and find a way!"

On leaving film school in 1998, Rodrigo Vazquez had the idea for 'Condor: Axis of Evil', about Western governments' complicity in the repression in Chile during the 1970s. He worked with French production company Article Z.

"I made a film off my own back about my mentor, filmmaker David Monroe who died of brain cancer, and I showed the film at the Sheffield festival in 2000. Around the same time I was working on shows like 'Holiday Airport' and 'Prickly Heat' and reading Nietzsche just to compensate. At Sheffield I met this French producer called Patrice Barrat. Patrice runs an NGO and is very much involved in the anti-globalisation movement in France. He has a very small production company called Article Z – the name of the company is a homage to Costa-Gavras' film 'Z'. He's a left wing, Christian producer: an odd cocktail. When I told him I had exclusive access to these people and had shot some footage of the Chilean executioners, he was interested in producing or in trying to raise some money for 'Condor'. I said to him we could try and get a commission because nobody else has this footage and this access, and he said alright.

So I wrote the script and Patrice sent it to many, many places but they all turned us down, all but one. This was in France. I had forgotten about Britain - I sent it to every single commissioning editor in the UK in the year 2000/2001 and everybody turned me down. They don't even really explain why – it's not for us, or not what we want or it's too political. But Patrice has a very small company and nothing to lose. Also France is a country where the TV industry is more liberal-minded. They are open to commissioning films that don't need to be dubbed or don't need a white journalist to present them and they can be subtitled. They're more open in that sense to third world film and I always wanted to make a film in France anyway. So Patrice sent it to many places and they all turned us down for one reason or another and then we were lucky because the commissioning editor of France 5, which is a daytime Arte channel, got ill and left the job temporarily and his replacement was this guy who makes films about fish, boats and that sort of thing – completely left-field. I showed him some footage; they invite you for lunch and you have red wine. Patrice has a good reputation as a left-wing producer and the France 5 guy – I think his wife is Chilean and he has friends who are Chilean exiles so he could relate to it – said why not, for just €40,000. We couldn't really make the film with the money he was giving us, but that's why I say I was lucky, because the most difficult thing is to get that first commitment from someone. Once you get the first commitment then it's easier to get the rest. But at times it looks like it's impossible, especially when you are starting and you are nobody and you may have a great idea or exclusive access and exclusive footage and they still don't commission you because they don't know you. You have to get someone with experience to work with you and to open doors and still you may not get in, you may not get through.

I'd encourage filmmakers to make their own alliances in each country. France and Germany are two places to look for funding. It just depends on personal contacts really; there's no recipe. If you get along with a producer who happens to have a French production company or German production company and you can pitch your project through them, its great. The problem with British television is that it's very parochial. For certain films you have to go abroad and look for money elsewhere and then maybe come back and sell it or maybe re-cut it for British television. I think somehow French and German television are more open. Forget about American television; that's like Nazi Germany at the moment. Some projects need you to forget about getting money in the UK; for me it was impossible, nobody was interested, everybody was chasing the next Big Brother. So just go somewhere else and then come back with it.

'Condor' took from 1998 to 2003, so that's five years. It usually takes three to four I think. All the films that you personally pay for will take at least a year, but five years, God, I hope the next one doesn't take that long."

Things to look out for:

Jo Lapping advises:

"There is something to be said about not being too precious, and being prepared to version your film. Do have a director's cut, have a festival cut, but if needs must, embrace the fact that you may have to make more than one version of something, for different broadcasters. People have different length slots, they have different audience profiles, different needs. I'd encourage people to look kindly on that. And to think about it at the budgeting stage. A lot of productions get caught out. They've got four or five different broadcasters involved in something, and they get to fine cut stage and they're suddenly getting very mixed messages coming back about what each investor wants. If you've made contingency in your budget, at that stage you can say, okay, we're just going to have to do a version for France, a version for the UK, a version for the US, and we'll have our festival cut.

If people can think in those terms from the outset, thinking this may well be what's required, that's good. It gets easier the more established you get, as well, and the better your relationships get with the commissioning editors. These things do get easier. Most of the filmmakers we work with do end up making at least two versions of their films, if not three. That's becoming common practice now."

Public funding in Europe

Europe's not just about the television, though; there are a range of ways to find money from private sources, including foundations and trusts. The possibilities here are too disparate to list, but we offer this case study as an example of how you need to think laterally with your subject matter in order to reach contributors, potential funders, and, eventually, audiences.

Kersti Uibo's last film 'Narrow is the Gate' was funded by the Catholic Church of Germany. It has been broadcast in Eastern Europe and has shown at festivals and art house screenings around the world.

"I wanted to make a film about Balkan people and what it's like to live in a country which has so many conflicts. I did a lot of research and found a story about a cyber monk that I was really attracted to. I pitched the idea at a pitching session in Denmark arranged by the European Documentary Network. I had a Canadian producer with me who I met through a previous EDN workshop. Many of the commissioning editors were interested and I was promised development money from Canadian TV. British TV weren't interested because they saw it as a religious subject. But you may be promised money and it may be a good pitching session, but that doesn't mean the money will actually arrive, and in my case it didn't. I think this was because every country wants to work with their own directors so they support their own industry. So in the end the money from Canada didn't come through and my Canadian producer said you'll have to carry on without me. At that point I realised I was on my own but I knew I needed to make the film. It meant lots and lots of phone calls, emails and meetings, but in the end my conviction in my idea was so strong that finally after a year I did find funding. The money came eventually from the Catholic Church of Germany - their reconciliation fund - but the route was so complicated that I couldn't even begin to describe it.

Once I was in Kosovo I met the cyber monk, but I then realised that he wasn't a good character for a documentary. It had taken me a year to get the funding to get there, and with a TV commission I would have had to do that film, but I would have lost interest and the film wouldn't have been very good. So I decided to search for a new story and after about a month I found a new character - another monk, a Serbian who was distributing food through Kosovo. It sounded like a good subject. I came back and wrote a synopsis, made a website and then started asking for money for this new story. A website helps if you are asking for money - you just put your film idea, synopsis and clips of the rushes onto it. It's better than a synopsis on a piece of paper and a photograph.

I arrived in Kosovo the second year to find that the monk was dying and too ill to be in the film. So once again the film idea I was raising money for suddenly disappeared. After two years of focusing on that project the second film idea was gone, but I knew there was no need to panic. It obviously helped again that there was no commission to tie me. By that time TV would have said there's no way, this is unprofessional – but with documentary, people die sometimes, that's life, things change. The third character, who is the one in the film, was a nun who found me. We were filming a beautiful sunset at the monastery gate and this nun just walked into the frame whilst I was filming. I'd done a lot of research, I'd met Balkan specialists and yet in the end the film is just about an old woman. The cost of a camera and the initial month long research trip came to about £6,000. This also included a bodyguard, because the foundation who funded me wanted me to get a bodyguard because if I were to be killed they felt it would be their responsibility. I actually trained him as a sound person but as it turned out I didn't use him at all because I felt that it would have interfered too much with the filming. It's ended up as a 65 minute film and I can't remember now the cost of the two 35m prints.

I always kept my options open with regards to a television commission. I even went to two big production companies with my pilot. There was initial interest but they thought that it would be too religious, whereas the film is actually not about religion in that way at all, it's a human story. The production companies got interviews straight away with the British commissioning editors but nothing came of these meetings. I also sent the film to a number of other European Commissioning editors. I got quite positive letters saying that it's a very good film, a good human story but they didn't want it. I think that if you don't get money from them for production then they're very unlikely to buy it unless it is a major festival winner; then they'll buy it. For me it was very important that Yugoslavian TV bought the film. That was a big struggle to achieve because it's a controversial film. There was a great couple who left TV during the Milosevic era in protest and set up a little film school at their home in Belgrade. They believed my film needed to be shown on Yugoslavian TV and it so happened that the commissioning editor of documentaries for Yugoslavia TV had also made a film in a Kosovan monastery. With this commissioning editor and my friend's constantly putting pressure on Yugoslavian TV my film was eventually shown on Yugoslavian TV in 2004.

Estonian TV have also shown it because of the Parnu International Festival. During the festival 12 films are shown on Estonian TV and the viewers vote to chose the Grand Prix. The TV audience chose my film as the winner and Estonian TV buys the winning film. As it's my home country and it is about Yugoslavian and Serbian people's history, I'm really pleased about it. From Yugoslavian TV I got about $400 and from Estonian TV the same so that shows how much money you get for a 65 minute film. But it's not about money, you're just so happy that it's shown. I'm not thinking of it as a failure because it hasn't been shown on British TV. Once you are liberated from the idea that TV is the only source of funding or place to show, then you are free. It's not that I'm against TV; I think basically try everything and see what works.

There are lots of different funding organisations, it depends on your theme. I had a lot to do with reconciliation networks, NGOs and people I met there. You don't get necessarily get money from NGOs but they might give you contacts. It is very much dependent on your subject matter. If you go to the middle east, for instance, there would be funding organisations that are supporting that area, or if it is homeless people in Britain then you try to start meeting people who are in that network. You have to be very flexible, do a lot of research, and ask around. Somehow by reading a lot, by meeting people, you start finding your way. Foundations that normally wouldn't fund a film can make exceptions. The foundation I received money from had never funded a documentary before and they probably never will again, but as a one-off they decided to do it. Because they somehow see that you have the conviction and think, ok then let's do it, let's try it. I had complete freedom, absolutely no conditions and they also gave me the money for a print. In the end they have found it a controversial film - they didn't expect a film like that. I've been letting them know that the film has been winning prizes and they thank me for that but they haven't used it in anyway at all. But that's their problem not mine, I can only keep them informed. It's a complicated route to take but somehow you will find these people who will let you make your film, but it took me two years to find these people."

Euro Events

As described above, two places to start when thinking about expanding into Europe are EDN and the MEDIA Programme. Both of these work with national organisations and educational institutes to support a wide and continually-changing programme of events, training and festivals, so it's worth checking their websites for forthcoming events and latest news. Also included here are Discovery Campus and the IDFA Pitching Forum.

If the deadline for the next event has not yet been announced at the time of going to press, we've given details of the most recent course, to indicate probable times and dates; look to the websites given for the latest details.

The events included in this section are mainly pitching forums and training sessions that expand into giving trainees the opportunity to pitch to commissioning editors, sometimes for practice, sometimes for real. For some filmmakers, attending a course of this sort will help bring the film along and provide comradeship and advice that will prove valuable in later stages of the film's life; in some cases, attending a course can result in international co-financing being made available there and then. Some pitching forums require you to have a proportion of funding already in place, or at least to have an expression of interest from your domestic broadcaster.

Giving your film the time and attention of thirty-odd other filmmakers and a dozen experts, and offering yourself a new perspective, can be just the boost it needs. There's the opportunity at pitching and development sessions to learn from what the other attendants are doing, and you get input, sometimes in the form of individual coaching, from just the industry linchpins whom you might spend months trying to access through the normal methods. You have concentrated access to filmmakers and commissioners from around Europe, so you can learn much more quickly both where your film might find a home, and, conversely, how to think in a way that's better suited to a European arena.

Another benefit of such sessions is that many offer structured follow-up, while the informal networking and mind-broadening experiences can be just as effective. And if you take your project through certain long-term, MEDIA-supported courses, you are eligible for New Talent development funding.

Jo Lapping's advice on events for British filmmakers:
"There's such a world of difference between being good at pitching and being good at filmmaking. You need to have a broadcaster attached to your project to get through to a pitching forum. They can be very useful. You have seven minutes to put your case to a roomful of people, and some projects more easily lend themselves to that. It has been known for people to get themselves financed in a heartbeat, but for something that's a personal vision, it can be difficult to communicate it. If you do go in for pitching, it's always essential to have footage to show, especially when you're pitching to a lot of people, and English isn't their first language; it really saves you time. And it's another way of getting your face known, getting people aware of who you are and what you're doing.
As to recommending particular events, it depends what you're trying to do. If it's just a general get-to-know-you, Marseilles is the best talking shop which is specific to documentary. Sunny Side of the Doc is the market; it comes just before the Marseilles International Documentary Film Festival. For festivals, Amsterdam is the most high-profile documentary festival, and that's the one European event in the year that gets a big international draw, with the Forum running at the same time. That's less easy though, less intimate. Marseilles is quite intimate, everyone sits around on the terrace drinking coffee and cocktails and chatting, so it's much easier to find people. It's a bit more approachable, more relaxed.
The Discovery Campus Masterschool is great. Storyville has had a couple of things that have come out of

that, including Alexandru Solomon's film 'The Great Communist Bank Robbery'. Because they take about fourteen, fifteen people on a year, and they normally like to get people with some experience of filmmaking, and because you get to spend time with them, there's actually a chance to develop relationships, almost as much as to get your film developed and sold. It's really valuable in that sense. It's not like you've just got that fifteen minutes to get in there and feed someone a pitch or an idea, you've actually got time to talk to them and find out what people like or don't like. It's much more constructive in that sense. It's less aggressive, it takes that edge off it, which is why I like it."

Documentary in Europe (Bardonecchia, Italy)

 Documentary in Europe
Via C. Lombroso 26
10125 Torino

✆ 011 6694924

✒ documentary@docineurope.org

Dates: 6 –9th July 2005, Bardonecchia
Number of attendants: up to 15
Cost: individual €95
EDN members: 20% reduction
Students and under-25s: 50% reduction
Language: English with Italian translation

The non-profit Documentary in Europe association endeavors to advance documentary culture. It organises an annual pitching forum of three days of preparation followed by presentation and follow-up discussion with a panel of commissioning editors from international broadcasters. There is also matchmaking between directors and European independent producers, which allows ten authors and directors, coached by commissioning editors, to introduce themselves and a new proposal to European producers. Screenings and debate round off the Forum.

Producers present in 2004 included: Philippe Van Meerbeck, VRT, Belgium; Wolter Braamhorst, AVRO, Netherlands; Arte Kathrin Brinkmann, ZDF, Germany; Carmen Cobos, Cobos Film , Netherlands; Robin MacPherson, Asylum Pictures, Scotland; Leena Pasanen, YLE TV, Finland; Rudy Buttignol, TV Ontario, Canada; Ronnie Griens, RVU, Netherlands; Christiane Hinz, NDR/ Arte, Germany; Eva Stefani, Greece; Esther Van Messel, First Hand Films, Switzerland.

Daniela Zanzotto took her film Battaglia to Documentary in Europe.

"My third film, 'Battaglia', I also started to shoot without official funding. I always knew it would be a tough sell for the UK market as it was in Italian and would have lots of subtitles. So I wanted to aim for the European market but didn't know how to go about it. I started checking the European Documentary Network website regularly and saw an announcement for the Documentary in Europe pitching workshop and forum in Bardonecchia, Italy. I'd heard horror stories about the pitching forum in Amsterdam and hated the idea of having to 'pitch' in public, but I thought at least with a preparation workshop beforehand I might stand a chance. It turned out to be fantastic. There were three days of intense pitch preparation with tutors. There were about fifteen of us, from various European countries. And although we were all pitching for very few slots, there was a real sense of support and helping each other out, and the best thing was not feeling alone. And then on the fourth day we had to pitch to the panel of commissioning editors and an audience. I showed a trailer during the pitch which was really helpful. I think I really lucked out with the commissioners and what they were after, and two came on board there and then, as well as a sales agent. It's not always the case that during a pitch there will be commissioners who have a slot for your film, so it does depend on who's at the event.

About four months later I got into the Amsterdam pitching forum. A much more intimidating event, and luckily I'd had the practice at the friendly and more managable Bardonecchia event. In any case, I got one more commissioner on board there. And the fourth one subsequent to that, thanks to the sales agent. The experience I've had of co-producing has been great. The commissioners only requested to see a rough cut, gave their suggestions and then it was up to me to finish the film as I saw fit. On the whole, they've been very open and supportive. The other good thing about having several co-producers is that you keep greater creative control because people are bound to have differing opinions but you can't obviously take everyone's opinion on board, so you get to choose what you listen to.

The only drawback I've found is that the funds are slow in coming through. Some of them will only pay on delivery, but by that time all kinds of bills have had to be paid, so it's really difficult from a cashflow point of view."

Docs Barcelona

Dates: 3 – 5th November 2005
www.docsbarcelona.com
EDN contact: anita@edn.dk
Number: 25
Cost: with project: €150
Observer: €135
Pitching workshops, pitching, follow-up sessions with industry experts, aimed at obtaining financing from TV networks. Projects do not need financing already in place.

Lisbon Docs

Dates: 19- 22nd October 2005
Deadline: 1st September
www.apordoc.ubi.pt/
Contact: anita@edn.dk
Telephone: +45 33 13 11 22

Takes place within the framework of the DocLisboa festival. Seven commissioning editors work with attending filmmakers to develop projects and plot future collaboration. Organised in conjunction with Portuguese non-profit docs body AporDoc.

Docs in Thessaloniki Pitching Forum

Dates: 6th - 10th April.2005
Deadline: 18th Feb
EDN runs the selection process for this forum:
EDN contact: anita@edn.dk
Telephone: +45 33 13 11 22
www.filmfestival.gr/docfestival/uk/pitching.html
Cost: producer/director with a project: €250 including four lunches and festival pass.
Participation for a second person connected to a project: €150 including four lunches and festival pass.
Participation for observers without a project: €150 including four lunches and festival pass

Docs in Thessaloniki is run by the European Documentary Network as a pitching event during the Thessaloniki festival. Forum participants gain access to screenings and market events as well. There's an emphasis on South European and South East European interests. The Forum lasts for five days: an overview of the market situation for docs in Western Europe; group work, in which experts help producers improve, target and pitch their projects; two days of public pitching to various commissioning editors, with individual meetings in the afternoons.

Archidoc at La Femis

✉ 6 rue Francoeur
Paris 75018
France

✆ +33 1 53 41 21 40
fax: +33 1 53 41 02 80

🖰 format.continue@femis.fr
www.femis.fr

2004 dates: 6th – 10th December and a weekend in January 2005, deadline 22nd Nov
Cost: €1,500, including travel and expenses; some grants available.

The French film school La Fémis organises this course for ten filmmakers with archive-based documentary projects in development, examining the role of archive in documentary and considering both practical and artistic questions that its use raises. Moderated by tutors - EDN director Tue Steen Müller and Belgian producer Paul Pauwels. The training involves working on filmmakers' own projects, sessions with established filmmakers such as Peter Forgacs, director of 'El Perro Negro', and it ends with an opportunity to pitch to European broadcasters.

La Femis also runs an eight-part course on similar topics from May to November, 2005. Three hundred hours of training over this period, at a cost of €5,536 inc. VAT, deadline April 2005.

EURODOC

✉ Head of Programme: Anne-Marie Luccioni
4 rue Astruc
BP 2060
Montpellier Cedex 1
F 34025
France

☎ +33 4 67 60 23 30

🖱 eurodoc@wanadoo.fr
www.eurodoc.asso.fr

Cost: €2,000, excluding travel and accommodation.
Course languages: English and French

The **Eurodoc Production** course offers three sets of five-day intensive workshops on development and financing of documentary projects for the international market, to thirty producers and filmmakers who are working on a specific project of international potential, and who are at the stage where they have a financial and development strategy. In 2004, Eurodoc's sixth round, the deadline for applications was July, with sessions in September, December and March 2005. The first session covers development of the films and work on legal and marketing issues, the second session is to finalise and package the projects, and in the third session the filmmakers have individual meetings with commissioning editors to pitch their work.

For previous Eurodoc attendants there is also the option to participate in the follow-up Eurodoc Screening event. In May 2005, this was held in Lisbon, with a January application deadline. Projects from the Eurodoc course, or a new idea, can be worked on with coaching from experts, resulting in a screening at the event in May, followed by workshopping and analysis of the film. The screenings and discussion sessions are also open to filmmakers who want to bring a project but forgo the specialised coaching (deadline: March), and to observers.

Eurodoc also offer the **Eurodoc Script** programme, for writers and filmmakers who are developing documentary projects with international potential. The programme involves two five-day sessions over a three-month period, with support between the sessions.

Director Nick Higgins is a connoisseur of European courses, having attended both Eurodoc and Eurodoc Script, and Archidoc.
"I went to Eurodoc production in 2001/2002 with a project on Mexico. I had no real idea about the European scene then and it was incredibly refreshing and inspiring to meet all these documentary fanatics. I think it's a brilliant scheme that introduces producers to the world of European co-production. Its founder Jacques Bidou has a very simple saying that I always try to remember: "Find an economy to make your films and don't make films for the economy."
It was Jacques who asked why I wasn't directing, seeing how I was there with my own project. As a result of that question I also ended up on the first ever Eurodoc script in 2002/3. Which was also fantastic and gave me the opportunity to work with Patricio Guzman. He is a such a maestro and we conducted all our session in Spanish. I think I'm the only person in Europe to have done both courses and I consider Eurodoc in many ways to have been my film school. So I suppose it was thanks to Eurodoc that I even scraped together my Euros for 'Hidden Gifts' and now let's see if we can continue..."

*Note: the MEDIA Programme is not funding Eurodoc in 2005; check the Eurodoc website for future programmes.

European Films Crossing Borders

 Co-ordinator: Sonia Ziade Trives or Brigitte Veyne bveyne@sgae.es
Spanish Copyright Management Society (SGAE)
c/o Barbara de Braganza, 7
Madrid 28004
Spain

☎ +34 915 036894 / 50

✆ sziadi@sgae.es
www.eufilmscrossingborders.com

Number of attendants: 25
Cost (for Karlovy Vary, July 1st – 3rd 2005):
€684 (€570 early booking rate) for four nights including accommodation
Deadlines: (for July 05) application deadline May 27th, final selection 10th June.

European Films Crossing Borders is a series of three-day workshops that take place during major European film festivals. Locations include: in 2003, Cannes and San Sebastián; 2004, Berlin, Cannes, Karlovy Vary; 2005, Berlin, Cannes, Karlovy Vary; 2006, Berlin. The aim is to encourage and strengthen newer producers in their engagement with the international markets, within the stimulating setting of the large festivals.

Past tutors: Vincent Maraval, Wild Bunch; Hengameh Panahi, Celluloid Dreams; Frédéric Sichler from Studiocanal; Claudia Landsberger, Holland Films and European Film Promotion; John Hopewell, Variety; Renate Roginas, Eurimages.

See also:
The Maurits Binger Film Institute's Documentary Directors' Coaching Programme
www.binger.nl
European Social Documentary, a course from the ZeLIG School for Documentary, Television and New Media, in Bolzano, Italy
www.esodoc.com

Discovery Campus

 Discovery Campus e.V.
Einsteinstrasse 28
D-81675 München
Germany

☎ +49-89-410 739-30

✆ info@discovery-campus.de
www.discovery-campus.de

Discovery Campus is a training initiative aimed at encouraging high-quality international co-productions for a large audience. Its aims are:

• To familarise European filmmakers, distributors, commissioning editors with the international market

• To stimulate the economic and creative competitiveness of doc professionals and strengthen the European audio-visual sector
• To link independent filmmakers with the industry and open up work opportunities
• To encourage variety in films, thereby developing documentary
• To foster international networking.

It pursues these aims through symposia and the Masterschool
Four symposia or weekend-long Open Training Sessions take place every year, in cities around Europe. They're open to all, and usually consist of a wide selection of commissioning editors explaining to participants what the state of play is around Europe, although some symposia take a particular topic to investigate as well. Past subjects have included: CGI and visual effects in documentary; natural history films; Eastern Europe and new horizons.

The July 2005 symposium in Vienna is on Big Budgets for Small Countries, and looks at how to enter the international market with ambitious documentaries from smaller countries; guerilla tactics and clever strategies for newcomers; case studies and discussions on international co-productions and insights into current trends in science, history and arts programming.

Details for the second Open Training Session 2005:
Munich 6-8th May 2005
Application deadline: 2nd May
Subject: the business side of docs
Cost: €150 (incl. catering)
Students and East Europeans: €90

The first Open Training Session:
Belfast 4th –6th March 2005, deadline 23rd Feb
Cost: €140 or £100
Students and East Europeans: €90, or £60

Commissioning editors pitch their documentary slots and programming needs to producers and filmmakers. Each one has seven minutes by the stopwatch, and the best presentation wins a prize. They reveal: what's going on in Britain; which broadcasters are open to proposals from independents; what's currently happening inside the BBC; and how will the British documentary market change in due course?

Discovery Campus' other, more exclusive event is the Masterschool, or European Masterclass for Project Development of Documentary Films for an International Audience.

Jess Search has attended the Campus as a commissioning editor, and says, *"The Campus is one of those rare things: a great initiative on paper which is actually even better when you get there. They bring together a cohort of really interesting emerging filmmakers from all over Europe and pull fantastic mentors from international broadcasters and everyone gets a lot out of it."*

Discovery Campus Masterschool

✉ Masterschool director: Donata von Perfall
Einsteinstrasse 28
Munich
D-81675
Germany

✆ +49 89 410 739 30

 www.discovery-campus.de

Dates: deadline 15th Oct 2004, for the 2005 sessions in February, May, July and October.
Number: 15
Location: various cities throughout Europe
Costs: free to participants (see details below)

The Masterschool takes on 15 filmmakers a year, chosen from different countries. Participants should be experienced in their own national market, but in need of a boost to join the international scene, and they have one project that they develop through the Masterschool. Exceptional un-broadcast talents with filmmaking experience can be accepted. This is what Discovery says about the type of project that's eligible:

• The topics should require research and be suitable for intensive script development.
• Projects should have a strong storyline that does not only appeal to a small, special-interest audience but might attract viewers with varied backgrounds from different cultures and countries. Please bear in mind that a project does not get "international" by simply setting it in several countries.
• The range of genres to be developed in the Masterschool encompasses all kinds of creative documentaries dealing with history, portrait, science, politics, nature, wildlife, foreign worlds, etc.
• All non-fiction formats that are internationally distributed are eligible. The projects should be suitable for broadcasters in more than one country.
• The applicant has to hold the author's rights of the entered project(s).

Participants attend four five-day workshops over the course of the year, during which they look at story development and scripting; production and financing; distribution and marketing; and in the final session they do project presentation and pitching, in front of the public and to distinguished international decision-makers. Two mentors are assigned to each project, one a production or distribution expert, the other an experienced commissioning editor. Tutors come from broadcasters including: AAC Fact, ARD, ARTE, AVRO, BBC, Channel 4, Discovery, HBO, Les Films d-Ici, ORF, Scandinature, Spiegel TV, TVOntario, YLE, and ZDF.

The Masterschool also arranges an optional internship with a production or distribution company in the participant's field of interest, during which they get involved in current productions, obtain an insight into the multinational strategies of enterprises, visit programme fairs and pick up practical experience.

By the end of the Masterschool, the documentary projects for TV or theatrical distribution should be ready for production with co-operating TV channels, production companies and distributors. The participants have also gained vital contacts with executives, and forged links with fellow filmmakers.

The Masterschool is free. Participants pay for travel and accommodation for the four workshops, and grants and bursaries are available. When a project goes into production, Masterschool fees of up to €15,000 are repaid from the production budget.

In 2005, the UK participant in the Masterschool was Emeka Onono of October Films, with his project 'God's Tree', about an ancient African cult that believes that the powerful psychedelic substance contained in a special tree - God's tree - takes the soul on a journey to the land of the dead, from which you return purified. The film depicts the director's own 'death journey' and his struggling to come to terms with an experience that changed his life forever.

In 2004, the UK participant was Nikki Parrot with 'Migration - 47 Uses of a Dead Sheep'.
"I went to the Discovery Campus and it's fantastic, I love it. If anyone wants to do documentaries they should go on this course, because you just meet everybody - you meet the head of ARTE, you have drinks with ZDF people, and they give you a mentor. My mentor is Christophe Jörg at ARTE and I'm going to see him next week to talk about this particular project again. It was Nick Fraser who said, 'You should do this; if you want to be an international documentary-maker, go on this course'. At first I didn't want to be there but after a couple of days I got into it. It teaches you about Germany and France and basically about how to enter into the international world of documentary.

In Europe people are much more open to documentaries and different ways of making them. This is particularly true in France where there's such an amazing range of documentaries on the TV all the time. So it's important to try and make contacts with the Europeans through festivals and to talk to people there about your project. If it's a unique and slightly different project then that's good; you have to explore and emphasise the uniqueness of it. You won't make as much money, of course, making films in this way, but if you want an interesting life and want to go to interesting places ...."

National Film School graduate Sasha Snow was having difficulties raising interest in 'Conflict Tiger', a film he wanted to make about Siberian hunters. Then he got onto the Discovery Campus where he was provided with expert guidance on the international co-production scene. Sasha quickly raised the money to make his film, but learnt the hard way that the co-production route has pitfalls of its own.

"Discovery Campus takes films on the basis of the idea being internationally marketable. They're interested in the filmmaker but it's the idea that comes first. And they have a much broader definition of what constitutes an interesting and marketable documentary than we do here. It's a lot more cultural and artistic, and they'll consider anything, no matter how unlikely. It runs for a year, during which they take you through a series of four week-long residential programs, each in a different European city. The tutors and panelists are producers and commissioning editors from all over the world. On these residential programmes they look at the idea itself in terms of structure and storytelling, at marketing and distribution plans and the legal aspects of co-production. In between those times you're developing the idea back in your own country in liaison with the two tutors that have been assigned to you. Then in the last week you have a pitching session to a panel of broadcasters and members of the public in a cinema. As a result of that I got Richard Klein at the BBC and Arte to come in with the rest of the money.

The best thing about the campus is that they teach you how to pitch. And rather than just teaching you, you have an idea that you've been working on for a year to practice on. In the end you have to pitch it in front of a live audience and although it's scary at the time you come out understanding what pitching means. All you need to know is what people want to hear; if someone's wanting to take a risk on a filmmaker and a film what reassurances do they need.

The advantage of a pitch to a panel is that you have commissioning editors sitting next to each other, being influenced by each other. When you're just one to one with a commissioner they can easily dismiss you, but if they've got someone sitting next to them going, 'That sounds interesting, tell me more,' they sit up as well. And if someone says, 'Oh, I'll buy that, that sounds great,' you get a snowballing effect and they all get carried away and start throwing their wallets on the table. Whether they actually come up with the money after that is another matter. But I think ten out of fifteen of the films that were pitched there all had money committed on the spot, not necessarily enough money to get the films made but enough to get started. The BBC expressed interest at the pitch but they didn't come through with the money until two or three months later. Arte and Discovery had come on board even before the pitch and there were various other channels who said when the film was made they'd buy it – Poland, Scandinavia and Germany, various other places. So it gave the producer confidence to go ahead with the risk because he knew there was a market for it.

We shot the film on digi in February of 2004 with a five person crew and we had a great time. Then I came back and I got my fingers burnt by the whole multiple broadcasters situation and I learnt that the international co-production scene is no bed of roses. Working with three different broadcasters is tricky, particularly when you have an American broadcaster involved. Their needs are completely different from a European broadcaster and usually their needs are dominant. So what ended up happening is that we made a very Americanised, over-explanatory film that was then slightly tweaked for the rest of the world. It wasn't what I wanted at all. It's a long and slightly bitter story and at this stage I can't say much about it because I'm still in the middle of it. But within the contract I had an option to make my own cut for theatrical release which is what I'm doing now, so it's a kind of compensation."

Forum for co-financing and co-production, International Documentary Film Festival Amsterdam (the IDFA Forum)

 Managing director: Fleur Knopperts
Kleine-Gartmanplantsoen 10
1017 RR Amsterdam
The Netherlands

 +31 20 627 3329

theforum@idfa.nl
www.theforum.nl

Dates: 28th – 30th November 2005
Deadline: 1st Sept 2005, applicants informed by 5th October.
Cost: registration fee is €550 inc. VAT for each project included in the catalogue and an additional €25 to place the project on the Virtual Forum.
Eligibility: Independent production companies with a project in development. A project needs to have the commitment of at least one broadcaster, film board or film institute. At least 25% (but not more than 75%) of the financing has to be in place (financing is defined as real, market money and excludes personal investment and investments by other production companies or producers). Up to 15% of projects can come from non-MEDIA countries. Two people can attend from each successful production company, and the commissioning editor supporting them.
Observers: Producers with no project in the Forum may attend as observers, limited to one per production company. There is a selection process to be an observer, to apportion observer status among countries. The observer application deadline is 12th October 2005. Producers whose entry to the Forum was unsuccessful have priority for observer status.
Deadline for observer applications: 12th October 2005, applicants informed 4th November.
Cost: €300, which includes access to the Forum, lunches and receptions, the Forum catalogue, the programme guide and the EDN Television Programming Guide.

IDFA is one of the big events in the documentary calendar, and as well as the festival itself there is both the market Docs for Sale (see below in Chapter 12, Festivals and Markets) and the Forum.

It's a big deal to win a place at the IDFA Forum. Co-organised by EDN, it is Europe's largest gathering of television commissioning editors and independent documentary producers. Its aim is to stimulate co-financing and co-production of new documentaries by enabling producers to pitch their projects to the assembled commissioning editors and other professionals, and follow up with individual meetings. It also provides an opportunity to feel the pulse of the European documentary market, to get to know other players and to strengthen the network of documentary producers and broadcasters throughout Europe.

Producers submit a project that has in place a proportion of funding and a supporting broadcaster. The producer and/or director has seven minutes to pitch their idea, followed by an eight-minute question-and-answer session in which the commissioning editors discuss the project with the producer and the broadcaster committed to the film. Two moderators monitor the schedule and stimulate post-pitch discussion to advance financing.

In the three days preceding the Forum a pitch workshop is organised, in particular to help newcomers to prepare their pitches. There is an introductory session introducing key Forum players and their profiles, then participants are recorded on video as they practise pitching. Commissioning editors and special trainers give feedback, and advise on general pitching principles and techniques.

Participants can also have formal, individual meetings with specially invited experts, who can answer specific questions about subjects like distribution/sales, marketing and promotion, use of archives, etc. in detail. These meetings are arranged through the Forum Desk, which coordinates everything for participants. The Desk includes two matchmakers, who facilitate networking and help set up meetings.

Participants all receive, and are all included in, the Project Catalogue, which gives for each project: a one-page synopsis, a two-page treatment, a detailed budget and a profile of the producer, director, and production company. The commissioning editors each receive the catalogue before the Forum.

The Forum also publishes the Programme & Participants Guide, which contains the pitch schedule, profiles of the moderators, consultants (including the kind of projects each commissioning editor attending is looking for) and matchmakers, and lists all participants. All participants will also receive a copy of the latest EDN TV Guide.

UK 2004 participants:
Faction Films – 'Going Nuclear'
Mosaic Films Ltd. – 'A Year in Tibet'
October Films – 'God's Tree'
Picture Palace North – 'Attercliffe Road'
VeryMuchSo Productions – 'Crossing the Line'

UK 2003 participants:
Bergmann Pictures – 'The Communist Joke Book'
Brook Lapping Productions – 'The Lie that Will Not Die'
Disruptive Element Films – 'Chiaroscuro – Shadow and Light'*
Illuminations Films – 'Unrequited Love'
Tigerlily Productions – 'The Flying Tribe of Afghanistan'

*(This is Daniela Zanzotto's film 'Batagglia'; see interview above.)

Fleur Knopperts is Managing Director of the Forum. She gave these tips on it:

"The average budget for films in to the FORUM in 2004 was 400,000 Euros, but this includes some series and also some of the projects have both an international version and a feature length one. The budgets vary depending on the country of production. Projects from South Africa, Eastern Europe or Israel, for example, usually have a much lower budget.

To be selected, projects need to have at least 25% of their financing secured and no more than 75%. This means that we never have projects in early development stage or projects needing gap financing. The length of time the producer has been developing the project varies greatly. How long it takes them after the FORUM to finish the film, varies from one to three years. Of the projects selected for the 2001 FORUM 93% are finished. Of those pitched in 2002, 84% are finished (and broadcast).

For the ratio of films submitted to films selected, in 2004 we received:

189 projects in total from 34 different countries. Of those, 152 projects met the regulations of which we selected 43 projects, which came from 22 countries. There were 63 television channels represented; 120 commissioning editors of which 29 were non-EU; 49 financiers, 143 observers and 87 producers with a project.

In 2003 those figures were 177 submitted : 152 eligible : 43 selected, and in 2002, 162 submitted : 127 eligible: 44 selected.

That's a common mistake, not sending all the necessary information.

To select, first of all we look at the quality of the project and the chances we think it will have to find financing at the forum, meaning that we take into consideration the financiers attending the forum. Besides this, we also try to have a balanced cross-section of different countries and broadcasters. Every year, there are subjects about which we receive more than one project, but the only trend I've seen so far is that after September 11th, the number of projects about international politics we received, as well as projects directly related to this event, increased.

Not all producers have a clear idea of what kind of projects and subjects work on the international market. One way to work on that is to attend the FORUM (and other markets) as an observer, but especially the FORUM, because it's a public event which makes it the perfect place to find out which projects are successful and why. And it's a good place to feel the pulse of the market. I don't think you could say that the observer status at the FORUM is particularly suitable for one type of producer. There are very experienced producers, who have been attending the FORUM for years, that attend as observer, either because they don't have a project that's at the right stage to pitch, or because they have their contacts and feel they don't need to pitch, or simply because they dislike presenting in public. For a producer with less or little experience in the international market, it might be advisable to first attend as observer to see how it works and the next year come with a project to be well-prepared and make the most of it.

To make the most out of pitching in Amsterdam, first of all you have to be well-prepared, do a great pitch, draw people's attention, but just show is not enough. In general, the commissioners around the table prefer to see visual material with the pitch. But what's equally important is the follow-up after the FORUM. You have to make sure you maintain the interest you have raised here for the project.

As well as the pitching forum, participants can have individual meetings with our experts or consultants, who are there to give producers advice on who to approach with a specific project. There are so many people attending the FORUM. Many producers, especially the less-experienced ones, tend to go for the usual suspects when in many cases they might be more successful with other commissioning editors. The consultants, because of their long experience in the international market, can help determine who are the best broadcasters/commissioning editors to approach for that project. Producers need to do their research before they come over, but at the same time it is very helpful that the consultants are there to share their market knowledge, also because they often have very up-to-date information on which commissioning editor is looking for what. (We also have two matchmakers on our team that help producers with introductions.) The experts/consultants are usually experienced producers or distributors/sales agents. For example, Steve Seidenberg (former head of development at Café Productions), Heino Deckert (sales agent and producer) Alan Hayling (head of documentaries BBC), Esther van Messel (sales agent), Tue Steen Müller (director European Documentary Network) are or have been working for the FORUM as consultants.

Since the start of the FORUM the focus has shifted. The first years, the project pitches were most important. Back then, the number of selected projects was a lot higher (the first year almost 80 projects were pitched in three days). Three years ago we decided to lower the maximum amount of selected projects to 45, leaving more room for networking and meetings. Now the FORUM focuses on pitching as much as on networking. In line with this, we decided last year to make the pitch schedule more compact leaving the afternoon free for networking and meetings. The FORUM was set up because commissioning editors and producers around Europe didn't know each other, or at least didn't meet on a regular basis. This has changed significantly since then. The international market has become and will still become more professional. Producers know a lot better what broadcasters are looking for and broadcasters expect producers to know this. The FORUM has to continue to be the place for both projects that are relatively easy to finance and for the smaller projects that are harder to sell, because of subject or, for example, because of the country of origin."

Chapter Nine
North America

With research by Vibeke Bryld

Introduction

American television plays a different role in American life from British television's role in British life. In some aspects, we follow them and in some we have completely different expectations. Technologically, the US often leads the way, but in culture and content the UK and Europe come from a very different background.

Developments coming from the US include: a choice of channels on terrestrial TV; cable, then satellite multi-channel; 'narrowcasting' or the provision of programming for a smaller and smaller segment of the viewing population; the aggregation of distinct parts of the entertainment industry into multi-sector empires.

In the USA, there are three major free networks: NBC, CBS and ABC, each of which groups together a large number of local television stations. Local stations do their own programming, and they show network television as distributed by the networks. Advertising brings in their revenue. In addition, there are a vast number of pay-TV channels, delivered by cable or satellite, including those that are special-interest.

There are also 350 public service broadcasters, which are autonomous stations based in local communities. They are linked by affiliation to PBS, the Public Broadcasting Service, which itself commissions, distributes and promotes programmes that then appear on local stations. Public service stations receive roughly 15% of their funding from the federal government, and the rest from corporations, foundations and other sources. PBS does not answer to advertisers (sponsors) nor, to as great an extent, to financial backers and political interests. In that sense it has the opportunity to show non-mainstream programming with an international or more investigative slant.

Canada has both a national broadcaster and independent broadcasters. Also useful could be the strong documentary section of the National Film Board of Canada, which, although set up for Canadian filmmakers, has an International Co-production Unit (ICU), aimed at assisting large-scale, innovative projects in a variety of ways. The ICU also develops agreements and partnerships with international production and distribution companies and institutions. The executive producer is Éric Michel.

The Toronto Documentary Forum

Based on the IDFA Pitching Forum, the TDF does the same but at Hot Docs, the annual international documentary festival held in Toronto in spring each year.

Michaelle McLean is the director of the Toronto Documentary Forum.

"We get about 120 submissions a year, and it's stayed about the same. The first year we got a hundred and then the subsequent four years it's stayed at about 120. The jury is a team of three and I usually have one American, one Canadian and one International. They are different each year. They are always buyers, broadcasters or distributors because they know the market. With my jury we pick up to thirty-six films, and the producers get an opportunity to pitch and to network with all of these Commissioners and Broadcasters from around the world. It's more than just their fifteen minute pitch in that sense. In fact, if a producer doesn't work the room over the two days and follow up over the subsequent months they're not making the most of the situation.

Every project has to have a broadcaster on board whether that's a licence, commission or co-production. We have also allowed a project where the broadcaster's committment is only verbal so far, but they are willing to say in front of their colleagues from around the world, "We are on board." People always ask me why I make this a rule because surely securing funding is the hardest part, but it's a way to get people from the market to the table. They've already got a vested interest in making it work and ideally there is a sense of reciprocity. Commissioners come to TDF with the project they are supporting and they might be interested in another commissioner's project too and that's why this kind of market works.

The mandate I give the selection crew is: do you like the idea and do you think it will fly at the TDF given the people that I can pull round the table? And, if you think it's a great idea and the market should be hungry for it, who should I bring to the table to fit those ideas? I initially invite a whole load of people and after we've made the pitch selections I do a whole other round to fit the projects. For example, this year we had an awful lot of arts projects, more than we've ever had before, so I tried to get more arts commissioners round the table. The second thing that matters is the filmmaker because a broadcaster is less likely to risk a great idea on an unknown filmmaker rather than on someone they know, that's just human nature. So it does become a combination of factors but the main focus is on the idea and whether the jury thinks it will work in today's market. Having said that, of course we do always end up with a certain percentage of young filmmakers and emerging producers because – to be eligible for the TDF – at least one broadcaster is already taking a risk on them and they have a great-sounding project.

Not everyone wants to pitch and some people choose not to. It is an unusual format and it is to some extent an artificial format because some people who are good programme makers are not good public speakers. But it's incredibly efficient because you are pitching to eighty commissioners from around the world all at once. So yes, the format does intimidate some people and it does take a certain frame of mind to be able to do it and do it effectively but it works for people raising money. Mark Achbar, who did the Corporation, pitched it at TDF first and he said he just used drugs. He got some beta blockers and said we should pass them out to everyone! Whatever works for you.

The most valuable thing for most of the delegates is that they get to hear the commissioning editors talk and give their feedback on the pitches. And the broadcasters as much as the producers say the same thing. Half the broadcasters come to hear about what the other broadcasters are doing so it's not just for producers, it's a two way street in that regard.

You know that there are a certain number of people around the table who always work together. People like Cristophe Jorg at Arte, Nick Fraser at the BBC, Mette Hoffmann at TV2 and Tom Koch of PBS-WGBH in Boston have formal and informal deals between them. The broadcasters are increasingly working together through relationships that they have cultivated at places like the TDF and IDFA in Amsterdam. Again, that's part of the evolution of the Forum. When IDFA was founded a lot of the commissioning editors had not met before and now they know each other really well and at TDF the European broadcasters have met more North American contacts and vice-versa.

Something I've noticed in the five years that we've been running is that more and more channels means lower and lower licences because the advertisers now have more outlets and those dollars are spread further. As a result you need more co-producers to make it add up. We're beginning to see other countries coming into the international market such as Germany. The big foreign markets like France, America and the UK that have traditionally been very insular are having to nurture international relationships for co-productions. It's the smaller countries like Canada who are geniuses at co-production because historically we've had to be. At filmmaker organisations like Hot Docs we've been doing producer exchanges to other territories for 15 years to facilitate introductions, market intelligence and encourage international partnerships."

Canadian Broadcasters

CBC

www.cbc.ca/documentaries/staff.html

In Canada, CBC or the Canadian Broadcasting Corporation is the national public broadcaster

Rough Cuts is a weekly strand of new documentaries, of approximately 40 minutes, about social and political issues that have not been sufficiently covered by mainstream news, and are of interest to all Canadians. First, submit a brief outline of proposal; a phone enquiry is acceptable also at this stage. If the proposal prompts interest, there will then be required: submission of a project summary, development plan, budget and financing scenario for the development phase, and identification of the key creative participants. After development, the producer needs to deliver a full treatment, production budget, production plan and financing plan along with confirmation of key creative participants. This material will be assessed for a potential Rough Cuts commission.

Commissioning editor:
Andrew Johnson
Tel. 416 205-6643.
Fax. 416 205-8842.
Online contact via: www.cbc.ca/roughcuts/producers.html

The Passionate Eye is for provocative, character-driven stories on contemporary political or social issues made with a strong point-of-view from either the filmmaker or the characters. Examples: 'Control Room', 'The World According to Bush', 'The Staircase', 'Bowling for Columbine', 'Born into Brothels', 'Liberace of Baghdad', 'Mission Accomplished', 'The Boy Whose Skin Fell Off'. 'Aileen: the Life and Death of a Serial Killer', 'Army of One'.

Short proposals for a one-hour documentary, with details of story, style, access, track record and key personnel, should be emailed to a unit member. Proposals can be made all year round. Proposals that prompt interest will be further developed.

Proposals to:
Catherine Olsen, Series Producer, The Passionate Eye: catherine_olsen@cbc.ca
Charlotte Odele, Commissioning Editor: charlotte_odele@cbc.ca
Diane Rotteau, Commissioning Editor: diane_rotteau@cbc.ca

The Passionate Eye
205 Wellington St. West
Suite 5A300
Toronto, Ont. M5V 3G7
Tel 416-205-2301
Fax 416-205-8842

Saskatchewan Communications Network

 SCN
2440 Broad Street, 3rd Floor
Regina, SK
S4P 3V7

 (306) 787 0490

 www.scn.ca

Regional public broadcaster for the Saskatchewan and Manitoba provinces. Programming includes social and political docs on non-Canadian international topics, eg. Slovakian Gypsies. Licensing and acquisitions are considered. Submissions can be made throughout the year.

For acquisitions, send one-sheet outlines to:
Rhyse Cardinal
2440 Broad Street, 3rd Floor
Regina, SK
S4P 3V7
rcardinal@scn.ca

TVOntario

 TVOntario
Box 200, Station Q
Toronto, Ontario
Canada, M4T 2T1

www.tvontario.org

TVOntario commissions mainly Canadian programming for some of its strands and acquires other international programming, generally high-budget productions made for broadcasters in other countries.

Human Edge A prime time series of provocative social-issue documentaries acquired from around the world, from auteurs including Victor Kossakovsky, Barbara Kopple, the Maysles. Commercial rights offered vary according to competitive market conditions. Licence fees for works in progress may be advanced at the discretion of the Creative Head of Network Programming.

Masterworks A prime time documentary series, Canadian and international in scope, exploring the life, work, and creative process of influential artists from all fields. Eg. the BBC series 'The Private Life of a Masterpiece'. Limited commissions are available for Canadian productions, although most are acquisitions and some are pre-buys. Commercial rights vary according to competitive market conditions.

History Hour-long documentaries that examine historical events of national and international significance, such as Channel 4's 'First World War' and the BBC's 'Horror in the East'. While acquisitions dominate the strand, a limited number of pre-buys and Canadian co-productions are funded each year.

Naomi Boxer
Acquisitions, Network Programming
Masterworks, Human Edge, Natural History, Science and Technology, Nature
Tel: 416.484.2600, ext. 2471
Fax: 416.484.7410

The View from Here TVO's signature series of advert-free one-hour and feature-length creative documentaries on social and 'human condition' issues, of direct relevance to Canadian audiences. Also limited-length series, eg. 'The Corporation'. Commissions are only given to Canadian independent producers, preferably from Ontario, and to official International Co-productions.

Budgets for hour-long and feature-length documentaries are in the range of C$100,000 to 400,000. Licence fees range from C$15,000 to C$75,000. Development funds of up to C$10,000 may be advanced. Proposals of one to three pages in length may be submitted at any time, preferably by conventional mail, and allowing at least six weeks for response. Supporting documentation should include an outline, treatment or script, and a summary of the project's budget, financing, and key personnel.

Submissions to:
Rudy Buttignol
Creative Head, Network Programming
Tel: 416.484.2972
Fax: 416.484.7410

The Documentary Channel

 64 Jefferson Ave., Unit 18
Toronto, Ontario
M6K 3H4

✆ 416 534-1191

✍ docs@corusent.com
www.documentarychannel.ca

This digital channel screens films already in the libraries of the CBC and the NFB and commissions original work of Canadian interest. Development finance and co-financing are available. Submissions of a one-page synopsis, treatment and access should be made online. Examples: 'Liberia: an Uncivil War', 'Dig!', 'The Fog of War', 'Outfoxed'.

United States broadcasters

PBS

PBS has several documentary strands, most with a strong American focus, but some that are more open to international commissioning and acquisition.
There is clear and thorough information for producers at www.pbs.org/producers/faqs.html.

P.O.V.

 American Documentary, Inc
32 Broadway, 14th Floor
New York, New York 10004

✍ www.pbs.org/pov

This major independent documentary strand presents 12-16 non-fiction films per year to an audience of two to four million, with extensive promotion and website and educational tie-in. Previous POV films include 'Gates of Heaven', 'Roger and Me', 'The Education of Shelby Knox', 'Wattstax'.

Films must be: strictly non-fiction; made by independent filmmakers who retain complete editorial control; released within the preceding four years; complete or nearly complete. Works of any length are considered and short pieces of under twenty minutes are encouraged.

The filmmaker must be a US citizen or have resided in the US during the production of the program, except that the strand Executive Director may solicit works from foreign producers on topics of international significance. Submitted projects by non-US citizens produced outside the US will NOT be considered for broadcast without prior approval.

The window for submissions is between April and July; see www.pbs.org/pov/utils/forproducers.html for details.

In the Works
You can also contact POV with a non-fiction project that is not at the submission stage, sending a brief biography, budget and schedule to intheworks@pov.org . There is no deadline for this.

Frontline

attn. Series Editor
125 Western Avenue
Boston, MA 02134

617 300-3500

www.pbs.org/frontline

Twenty years old, PBS's flagship public affairs series airs at 9pm on Tuesday nights, with "incisive documentaries covering the scope and complexity of the human experience". Roughly 18 programmes are made each season from six hundred suggestions and proposals. Eg. 'Blair's War' (2003), a co-production between Frontline and British production company Mentorn. Story ideas should be sent to the postal address above.

Wide Angle

Stephen Segaller, Director, News & Public Affairs
Pamela Hogan, Series Producer
Andy Halper, Senior Producer

450 West 33rd Street
New York, NY 10001-2605

212.560.3004
Fax: 212.560.8279

WideAngle@thirteen.org
www.pbs.org/wideangle

The international public affairs documentary series Wide Angle screens at 9pm on Tuesday nights over the summer, 'providing American audiences with insight into the economic, cultural and political factors shaping the world today. Each program focuses on a single subject, with character-driven narratives revealing the humanity behind the headlines of international events and issues'. Each 45-minute programme is accompanied by contextual interviews, web resources and educational material. Wide Angle is produced by local station 13 / WNET, which separately acquires completed programming for local rather than network transmission.

Subjects should be: current; examining neglected stories behind the headlines; concern the global economy, social and economic impact, and US influence; connect viewers to the world; personal stories illuminating a bigger picture.

Proposals are reviewed on an ongoing basis from December through June. Most films are commissioned from international independent producers, who are encouraged to partner with filmmakers in countries where their stories originate. Filmmakers from developing countries are encouraged. One or two acquisitions are included in each season.

To pitch a proposal, send a brief description of the subject, the narrative, and your production credits to the addresses above.

Notes:

Wide Angle is primarily interested in character-driven narratives that reveal larger geopolitical issues. The stories should be international with little or no American content.

Wide Angle films do not use correspondents or interview think-tank analysts, academics or journalists.

Wide Angle budgets allow about four weeks of shooting and six to eight weeks of post-production.

Wide Angle re-narrates the film and voices over the foreign dialogue.

The primary deliverables are a textless, 45-minute master and backup and a DA88 or OMF.

Wide Angle requires material to be shot in wide screen.

Program budgets range from $200,000 - $300,000 depending on subject and travel.

In its first three seasons, Wide Angle has reported on subjects including: the forgotten conflict in Western Sahara; Muslims and the veil controversy in France; the Argentine economic crisis; the war in Chechnya; AIDS and the Angolan military; women rebuilding Rwanda; global access to primary education.

Programmes from UK-based filmmakers include: 'A State of Mind'; 'The Russian Newspaper Murders'; 'The Rock Star and the Mullahs'.

The Independent Television Service (ITVS)

 Independent Television Service (ITVS)
501 York Street
San Francisco, CA 94110

 415 356 8383
Fax: 415 356 8391

itvs@itvs.org

An organisation dedicated to freedom of expression, civil and open society and minority participation, ITVS works between producers and public television to fund, develop and launch independent filmmaking.

Only US citizens or legal residents are eligible for its funding.

Open Call deadlines for variable funding are twice yearly in February and August, for projects needing completion funding at the production and post-production stages.

With PBS, ITVS co-curates the Independent Lens series, which runs yearly from October to June, with a submissions window from April to September for broadcast in the following year's season (eg. September 2004 is deadline for an October 2005 screening). Acquisitions only, of almost complete and completed works, primarily non-fiction. All lengths are accepted but most successful submissions likely to be sixty minutes. Programmes must be 'compelling, pro-social stories, well told, with elements suited to attracting a national audience; innovative, character-driven, well crafted.' They must be solely produced and authored by individuals not acting under the employment of a television station or major production and/or distribution studio. Accepted programmes receive a licence fee, which is variable but standard acquisition

For submission, two copies of the programme and programme information as on website www.pbs.org/producers/release_form.pdf should be sent to:

Cheryl A. Jones
PBS — INDEPENDENT LENS
1320 Braddock Place
Alexandria, VA 22314

International Media Development Fund

Claire Aguilar is Director of Programming at ITVS, and she tells Shooting People about a brand new fund that's just starting up, eligible for non-US producers.

"The Independent Television Service (ITVS) - the leading funder of American independent programming for US public television - is reaching out to non-US producers for the first time with a new five-year production initiative. Through the International Media Development Fund (IMDF), ITVS will:

• *Fund international producers to make documentaries*

• *Manage programs to completion*

• *Distribute programs to national US audiences*

• *Promote programs to the press and the public*

• *Engage communities through outreach and education*

The IMDF seeks out programs that present people, cultures and points of view seldom seen on US television. Guidelines for the 2006 open call will be available in late 2005. For more information about ITVS international and IMDF, visit www.itvs.org.

The IMDF is a project of ITVS and is funded by the William and Flora Hewlett Foundation, the Ford Foundation and the John D. and Catherine T. MacArthur Foundation."

Beyond US Television

US foundation funding for film: a roadmap

By Kathy Leichter and Mitch Teplitsky, with research by Ava Fedorov, and special thanks to Gail Silva, President of the Film Arts Foundation in San Francisco, CA.

Seeking US money for your documentary film outside of television sources? There are four options: foundations, individual donors, government agencies and corporate sponsorship. We are proponents of developing fundraising strategies that incorporate at least the first three methods (because not every film will be attractive for corporate funding). Actually, individual donors are by far the biggest source of charitable donations in the US (just under 75% in 2003, according to Giving USA, www.givingusa.org), and we think more filmmakers should pursue that route. But plenty of guides on individual fundraising and sponsorship already exist. For the purposes of this chapter, we've focused on compiling a roadmap to US foundation funding for film. What follows is an overview supplemented by comments from top American filmmakers and fundraisers, useful resources and a list of US foundations that fund film.

The role of foundation funding for documentaries in the US has changed enormously over the past twenty years. Foundation and government monies used to be the bread and butter of a film's path to completion. They were a critical source for funding and also an important stamp of approval – if you had a grant from, say, the MacArthur Foundation, you were well on your way to success. Though this continues to be true, the lay of the funding landscape has changed.

US government funding for film decreased during the Reagan Administration in the 1980s. Private foundations such as the Ford and MacArthur Foundations and smaller private and family foundations were able to fill some of the gap. A major new funding source was added in 1991; the Independent Television Service (ITVS) was established to distribute about $6 million Corporation of Public Broadcasting dollars annually to independent producers. This was a big help, though this may have left foundations feeling like their own grants were less necessary. In the late 1990s, raising money got even tougher – when the stock market fell, many foundations that were still giving money to media cut back on the number of grants and on grant amounts.

That's the supply side, but then there's the other side of the equation: demand. The emergence of affordable digital cameras and editing equipment has enabled more people to make films. There's a lot to be said for access – but it's also meant many more filmmakers competing for fewer dollars. For example, in its first year of giving, the Anthony Radziwill Documentary Fund received over eight hundred applications for a projected ten development grants. The Sundance Documentary Fund recently announced its first round of funding for 2005. Grants were awarded to fourteen projects, chosen from 450 applications submitted from around the world.

But don't be discouraged. There are a handful of foundations that fund film and, depending on several key variables, you may have a shot at getting some money. Those key variables are:

1) If your film fits into the foundation's guidelines (eg. issue-focused stories like human rights or the environment, or films made by or about under-represented ethnic groups);

2) You're at the correct stage of production for that funder's interests (development, production, post or distribution);

3) You submit a well-written, concise proposal, which must include an excellent discussion of audience and distribution: who will see the film and how;

4) You have a really compelling work sample or trailer

Not all US foundations are open to British filmmakers. In fact, many require that a US citizen apply, even if the story is an international one. That shouldn't stop you, however. Some foundations will let a British filmmaker apply if there is an American co-director, co-producer or an executive producer attached to the project. And since doing the legwork of getting a grant can be difficult if one is overseas, having a US partner on your project can be critical.

One vital rule is to know your funder. Research the potential foundation online, find out what kind of films they fund, who they give to, how much they give, when, and why. Contact other filmmakers who received money from that foundation and ask them about their application and their experience with the funder. Another recommendation is to build a relationship with the Programme Officer. Many are surprisingly accessible. Personal contact is always best. If possible, go hear them speak on a panel, introduce yourself afterwards, mention your film and send a follow-up email. If a personal encounter is not an option, build a relationship via the phone and email – whatever works. The Programme Officer may save you time and energy by letting you know early in the game whether your project is worth submitting or not.

Fortunately and unfortunately, it's not too hard to know your funder: there just aren't that many. Here's the lay of the land. Basically there are three categories of institutional funders to consider:

First, there are the government-funded national entities such as the National Endowment for the Arts (NEA), the National Endowment for the Humanities (NEH), and the National Science Foundation (NSF), whose grants are heavily competed for, whose names lend great legitimacy to a project, and whose applications are lengthy and require in-depth scholarship. There are also government-funded state and local humanities and arts councils such as the California Council for the Humanities and the New York State Council for the Arts.

The second category is entities such as the Independent Television Service (ITVS), The National Black Programming Consortium (NBPC), Native American Public Telecommunications (NAPT), Latino Public Broadcasting (LPB), and the National Asian-American Telecommunications Association (NAATA). Basically, the money that comes from these organisations buys the PBS television licence for US broadcast, and – in the case of all but ITVS – is earmarked for films made by or about specific ethnic groups.

The third category is private foundations. There's a first tier of big-hitters that fund film: the MacArthur Foundation, the Ford Foundation, and the Sundance Documentary Fund (formerly the Soros Documentary Fund).

Beyond these are a slew of other foundations that either have very specific guidelines (such as being regional funders) or provide less money, but remain well-respected sources that can help a film get noticed by the aforementioned big four. Some of the better known ones are:

- The Arthur Vining Davis Foundation, which funds educational projects with a promise of PBS broadcast.

- The Paul Robeson Fund for Independent Media, which supports media activism and grassroots organising by funding the pre-production and distribution of social issue film and video projects.

- The Roy W. Dean grant, which provides goods and services as opposed to money.

- The National Fund for Jewish Documentary, which funds films and videos that promote thoughtful consideration of Jewish history, culture, identity, and contemporary issues.

- The North Star Fund, which funds progressive films that are part of organising efforts in New York City

- Creative Capital Foundation, which funds individual artists for specific projects, with an emphasis on experimental work.

- The Lucius and Eva Eastman Fund, which funds films about social issues.

In addition, there are literally hundreds of smaller private or family foundations in the US that are issue-based (rather than media-based). Your job is to research and seek out the ones that may have an interest in supporting your project – not because you are making a film, but because you are addressing a topic of vital interest to that funder.

How do you find the right foundation for your film? The web is a terrific resource. Start with The Foundation Center (www.fdcenter.org) - an indispensable resource with an online database of more than 5,000 foundations that fund artists and other individual grant seekers, accessible for modest subscription fees. The New York Foundation for the Arts is another portal into the foundation world (www.nyfa.org). Its search engine even lets you submit searches for programs open to applicants outside the US. So too does the Council on Foundations at www.cof.org and the Chronicle of Philanthropy at www.philanthropy.com. Another great way is to look at who has funded other films on a similar topic to yours. As Executive Director of Women Make Movies, Debra Zimmerman says, "My favorite tip to give filmmakers is to look at the end credits of documentaries of films on similar subjects and contact the filmmakers of those films. Most filmmakers only make one film on a particular subject and sometimes are willing to share their contacts!"

If you are lucky enough to receive money from any one of these foundations, the process of receiving funds is fairly consistent. Most funders will require that you have a fiscal sponsor - a 501(c)3 charitable foundation that will receive and distribute your grant monies for a percentage, typically 5-8%. There are several US fiscal sponsors that focus on serving filmmakers (see list below) and filmmakers can apply to several and then choose one. In addition to a fiscal sponsor, most foundations require a financial and narrative report either annually or once all monies have been spent. And virtually all will ask for a finished copy of the film and to be properly credited in the film and in marketing and publicity materials. Good FAQs about the fiscal sponsorship process are posted on the websites of two of the leading sponsors – Documentary Education Resources (www.der.org) and Film Arts Foundation (www.filmarts.org).

One of the plusses of foundation money is that - as opposed to money from corporate or individual donors - there are usually no strings attached in terms of content. You retain complete creative control, as long as you make a film within the range of what you proposed in your application. And unlike broadcasters such as HBO, PBS, The Discovery Channel, A & E, and National Geographic, the private and government-funded foundations do not purchase any rights to your film, although ITVS and the other PBS-funded entities do.

So do your research, stay positive and have fun. Raising money for your film is a great way to hone your project and meet interesting people along the way. Good luck!

Comments from American filmmakers and fundraisers

On foundations:

"Thoroughly research the foundation, so that you can see if your film really fits with their mission guidelines. Remember that this process of giving grants and making films is a two way street and each partner should be mutually supportive and respectful of the other."

Pamela Yates
Director of 'Presumed Guilty' and 'State of Fear', President, Skylight Pictures, www.skylightpictures.com

"Foundations remain vital to independent documentary filmmaking today. Because most are focused on the importance of a topic, not just the appetite of the marketplace, foundations are able to support projects about issues often before the general public even has enough exposure to be interested.

Foundations also place an importance on the full lifespan of the film (research, production, post production, outreach and distribution), not just the end product. It's the difference between supporting a farmer over several seasons and buying someone lunch one day."

Dallas Brennan Rexer
Producer of 'Deadline', Big Mouth Productions and Arts Engine, Inc., www.bigmouthproductions.com

"A good trailer is a must. The first few minutes are critical - they condition the rest of the viewing and in many cases that's all that will get watched. Major funders receive huge amount of trailers and usually don't have time to watch more than the very beginning."

Fernanda Rossi
Story consultant and author of 'Trailer Mechanics: A Guide to Making Your Documentary Fundraising Trailer', www.documentarydoctor.com

"My best advice is to move to the US and/or hook up with some US filmmakers! There are only a handful of foundations that will support "foreign" projects - US generated programs shooting abroad, or foreign generated programs shooting in the US. At the very least the UK filmmaker who wants US foundation support will need someone "on the ground" in the US because personal contact and ease of communication are so central to the successful foundation approach. Also, spend lots of time upfront doing basic research - much of which can be handled over the Internet since many foundations maintain their own websites."

Morrie Warshawski
(www.warshawski.com, author of 'Shaking the Money Tree: How to Get Grants and Donations for Film and Television - 2nd Edition' (Wiese Books).

"Look at the prior winners of the foundation you are interested in and see if you find any that had the same executive producer or producer on board. I sometimes find the major US institutions tend to give money to people they have funded before, so you might want to do a co-production with a prior winner. I also suggest you keep entering because funders like to get to know you, and to know you are steadfast. In year two come back to the grantor with the changes suggested - and year 3 again!"

Carole Dean, author, 'The Art of Funding Your Film', www.fromtheheartproductions.com

"Personal relationships are always important, never more so than in the foundation world. So is legitimacy- -having someone with credibility and authority endorse you, vouch for you, drop a reference to you into an article or discussion. Foundations are increasingly interested in accountability--showing that you get the results you claim. They are interested in your metrics—hard measures that show success. Program officers may even ask for proofs of effectiveness that are unrealistic to expect from a film. (Did your film increase AIDS awareness by more than 7 percent in Des Moines?) But they certainly deserve as much evidence as you can give them that their money was or would be well-spent. Filmmakers need to think strategically about their project design from the start, to create opportunities for funders, both nonprofits and foundations,

to join with them in making their work connect with as many audiences as is possible, as effectively as is possible."

Pat Aufderheide
Professor and Director, Center for Social Media, School of Communication, American University,
aufder@american.edu

"My advice for putting together pieces for fundraising is to research the foundations you are applying to. Once you know their focus, you can tailor your treatment and trailer to their interests, as much as possible given the limits of your project. Above all, your video material should have high production value and should grab funders' attention quickly -- they have a lot to evaluate and are eager to find reasons to reject projects."

Aaron Matthews
Director, 'My American Girls' and 'A Panther in Africa'

"Remember, you rarely receive all required money from one source or fund. Do your research carefully and tailor your 'ask' to an amount that fits the grantor's grant range. If their average grant amount is $5,000, find a few things in your budget that they can pay for; otherwise, a nonspecific ask of $5,000 in a budget of $95,000, could make the grantor feel that their small amount can't make a difference."

Gail Silva
President, Film Arts Foundation

On other funding sources:

"I also recommend approaching individual donors. Many are interested in supporting documentaries shot abroad if the cause is close to their heart. Fortunately the latest internet bubble left a fair amount of people with spare cash.
Needless to say all of the above is much easier if the filmmakers partner with an American filmmaker. In that way they can qualify to attend certain markets and apply to foundations that require residency."

Fernanda Rossi

"I tell all my clients that they should pursue a diverse set of funding options and strategies. Foundations represent only a small portion of the total funding pie in the US. The most important of these is asking individuals. For a UK filmmaker with a film that has a strong social-issue message, a good option is having a group of US volunteers/supporters throw fundraising house parties in a number of communities."

Morrie Warshawski

"I would definitely go after individuals first because the statistics say most docs get most of their money from individuals.I love fundraising house parties. And I promote asking local corporations for goods and services - food, water, phones, etc. Outlined in "the Art of Funding Your Film" is a one page proposal for free goods and services. I believe the pitch is the foundation of the film. You need a 20-second pitch, a 1-minute pitch and a 2-minute pitch depending on who you're talking to. People make decisions on you in less than 60 seconds, so that old adage "Gone in 60 Seconds" can work against documentary filmmakers who are not succinct."

Carole Dean

"Not only do individuals increasingly give to documentary film projects, their money can be what keeps you going between government or larger foundation gifts. Each time you have to stop production and fundraise, the project will cost more and take a longer time to finish."

Gail Silva

Resources

Online grant databases

The Foundation Center   www.fdcenter.org
The New York Foundation for the Arts   www.nyfa.org
The Center for Social Media   www.centerforsocialmedia.org/res_fundingsocial.html

Online communities for US filmmakers

www.doculink.org   (More West Coast oriented)
www.shootingpeople.org   (New York chapter)
www.d-word.com   (National and International)

Free e-zines

Don Griesmann's Grant Opportunities
Sign up at http://charitychannel.com
A terrific online guide to grant opportunities, available on the website and/or via email delivery. Headlines, brief descriptions of articles, and links to articles.

'Splice' – published by the Independent Video and Filmmakers (AIVF)
Subscribe at http://www.aivf.org
AIVF's e-zine is one of the best monthly guides to U.S. grant opportunities, festivals, screenings and other news

'Beyond the Box' - published by Independent Television Service (ITVS)
Subscribe at http://www.itvs.org
Complete List of Opportunities. The latest ITVS News, including funding applications, guidelines and broadcasts.

Fiscal sponsors

Center for Independent Documentaries   www.documentaries.org
Documentary Education Resources   www.der.org
Film Arts Foundation   www.filmarts.org
Film Video Arts   www.fva.com
Fractured Atlas   www.fracturedatlas.org
International Documentary Association   www.documentary.org/
New York Foundation for the Arts   www.nyfa.org
Third World Newsreel   www.twn.org
Women Make Movies   www.wmm.com

Books

'The Art of Funding Your Film', Carole Dean, www.fromtheheartproductions.com

'Shaking the Money Tree: How to Get Grants and Donations for Film and Television - 2nd Edition' (Wiese Books), Morrie Warshawski, www.warshawski.com

'Trailer Mechanics: A Guide to Making Your Documentary Fundraising Trailer', Fernanda Rossi www.documentarydoctor.com

US Foundations that fund film (alphabetically by name)

1. A. J. MUSTE INSTITUTE

Jane Guskin, Programme Associate
A. J. Muste Institute
339 Lafayette Street
New York, NY 10012

Phone: 212 533 4335
Fax: 212 228 6193

info@ajmuste.org
www.ajmuste.org

Guidelines: Funds film/video ONLY as part of projects organising for social change. Supports non-violence training projects outside the United States, and within Native nations in the US. Projects eligible for support include those which build capacity and leadership among people engaged in non-violent struggles; those which prepare participants for specific non-violent actions or campaigns; and those geared to 'training the trainers', in order to expand and multiply non-violence training throughout a targeted community.

Grants: The maximum amount is US$3,000

Deadline: Proposals can be submitted at any time. The review and decision process takes approximately eight to ten weeks.

British Filmmakers: The grant-making programme has no geographic restrictions and British filmmakers may apply.

Recent Grants/Projects: $1,000 to Lioness Media Arts of New York City for post-production expenses of 'Race to Execution', a documentary about racial bias and the death penalty.

2. THE ANTHONY RADZIWILL DOCUMENTARY FUND

Anthony Radziwill Documentary Fund
IFP/New York
104 West 29th Street, 12th Floor
New York, NY 10001

Phone: 212 465 8200 x 830

docfund@ifp.org
www.ifp.org/docfund

Guidelines: Grants to emerging and established documentary filmmakers in the form of development funds for specific new projects. Administered by IFP/New York, the fund seeks to provide an additional much-needed source of funding for independent non-fiction filmmakers at the earliest stage of new work, traditionally a difficult point at which to secure funding. The fund is named in memory of the late Anthony Radziwill, an Emmy Award-winning documentary producer. The average number of applications that received is 300-400. The number of awards given is a maximum of 10 per year.

Grants: $10,000 Development grant

Deadline: March 1, 2005 & September 1, 2005, website will be updated in January 2005.

British Filmmakers: British directors cannot apply alone. They need to be working together with an American producer in order to qualify for the award.

Recent Grants/Projects: There are no examples of films made because this is a new award.

3. ARTHUR VINING DAVIS FOUNDATIONS

Arthur Vining Davis Foundations
225 Water Street, Suite 1510
Jacksonville, FL 32202

Phone: 904 359 0670

arthurvining@bellsouth.net
http:// jvm.com/davis

Guidelines: Grants provide partial support for major educational series assured of airing nationally by PBS. Consideration is given from time-to-time to single stand-alone programmes.

Grants: to $400,000, average $125,000

Deadline: Rolling admission, but the board meets three times a year and their approval is required for any award.

British Filmmakers: British directors can apply only if their project will be aired on primetime PBS; it can air in other places as well. A couple of hundred applications are received each year and of those a few (maximum of eight) are awarded grants.

4. CHICAGO UNDERGROUND FILM FUND

Chicago Underground Film Festival
3109 North Western Ave.
Chicago, IL 60618

Phone: UNAVAILABLE
Fax: 773 327 3464

info@cuff.org
www.cuff.org

Guidelines: Grants awarded to selected film or video makers for post-production on works-in-progress that are in keeping with the festival's mission to promote works that push boundaries, defy commercial expectations and transcend the mainstream of independent filmmaking.

Grants: between $500 and $2,000

5. CREATIVE CAPITAL FOUNDATION

Creative Capital
65 Bleeker St 7th floor
New York NY 10012

Phone: 212 598 9900

Fax: 212 598 4934

info@creative-capital.org
www.creative-capital.org

Guidelines: Provides grants to individual artists for specific projects, with an emphasis on experimental work. Disciplines rotate, meaning that media grants are given every other year.

Grants: up to $20,000

6. CROSSPOINT FOUNDATION

C.G Zarbock
The Crosspoint Foundation, Inc.
12322 W. 64th, PMB #118
Arvada, CO 80004

Phone 303 902 2072
FAX 603 737 3388

info@crosspointfoundation.org
http://crosspointfoundation.org/

Guidelines: The Crosspoint Foundation specifically supports projects in the areas of: education, the arts, societal concerns, indigenous issues, intellectual property rights, religion, family, general cultural issues. Supporting the production and dissemination of documentary film, dramatic works, CDs or other media; supporting public film, arts, and cultural festivals; facilitating public discussion and debate; encouraging and supporting educational activities; encouraging and supporting domestic and international exchanges. Last year 60 applications were received and two to three awards were made.

Grants: range from $500 - $1,500.

Deadline: Second quarter of every year, but they will be taking a break until 2006 to regroup.

British Filmmakers: British directors will be welcome to apply. No British director has ever won an award

Recent Grants/Projects: 'Darwin in the Dreamtime' — Multi-media theatrical production by Laura-Lee Cannon (Boulder, CO).

'What Big Teeth' — 35mm short film by Rebecca Foster (Brooklyn, NY).

7. DANCE FILM ASSOCIATION, INC.

Deirdre Towers
Dance Film Association, Inc.
48 West 21st Street, #907
New York, NY 10010

(phone/fax) 212 727 0764

fda5@earthlink.net
www.dancefilmsassn.org

Guidelines: Supports dance and dance-relevant subjects documented in film.

Grants: $500-$2,500

Deadline: application due by May 30th of each year

British Filmmakers: may apply if they are members of the Dance Film Association.

8. FORD FOUNDATION

Ford Foundation
320 East 43 Street
New York, N.Y. 10017

Phone: 212 573 5000
Fax: 212 599 4584

office-secretary@fordfound.org
www.fordfound.org/

Guidelines: Supports the development of media, information and technology resources to advance social change, human achievement and understanding. Grant making includes both infrastructure and access issues and independent production. In 2003 the Foundation received about 40,000 grant requests and made 2,510 grants. Of that number, 22% were first-time grant recipients.

Deadlines: Applications are considered throughout the year.

British Filmmakers: are welcome to apply, however the project must be charitable, educational or scientific, as defined under the appropriate provisions of the US Internal Revenue Code and Treasury Regulations.

Recent Grants/Projects: $75, 000 to Fuse Films, Limited, for the production of 'The Widows of the Other September 11th', a documentary film recounting the stories of four women widowed in the September 1973 ousting of the Allende government in Chile, England (UK), 2004.

9. GUGGENHEIM FOUNDATION

John Simon Guggenheim Memorial Foundation
90 Park Avenue
New York, NY 10016

Phone: 212 687 4470
Fax: 212 697 3248

fellowships@gf.org

Guidelines: The Foundation only supports individuals and offers Fellowships to further the development of scholars and artists by assisting them to engage in research in any field of knowledge and creation in any of the arts, under the freest possible conditions and irrespective of race, color, or creed.

Grants: The average amount of a Fellowship grant in 2004 was $36,652

Fellowships are awarded through two annual competitions:

• Open to citizens and permanent residents of the United States and Canada, only. Deadline: completed applications must be submitted by the candidates themselves no later than October 1

• Open to citizens and permanent residents of Latin America and the Caribbean, only. Deadline: completed applications must be submitted by the candidates themselves no later than December 1

British Filmmakers: Only citizens and permanent residents of the US, Canada, Latin America and the Caribbean may apply.

Recent Grant/Project: Linda Goode Bryant, Filmmaker, New York City, New York.

10. THE JEROME FOUNDATION

Cynthia Gehrig, President
125 Park Square Court
400 Sibley Street
St. Paul, MN 55101-1928

Phone: 651 224 9431
Fax: 651 224-3439

info@jeromefdn.org

Guidelines: The Jerome Foundation provides funding for emerging artists and non-profit arts organisations in Minnesota and New York City. By focusing on emerging artists, the foundation encourages artistic innovation and excellence, and it welcomes work that embodies a celebration of and respect for diverse cultural perspectives.

11. JOHN D. & CATHERINE T. MACARTHUR FOUNDATION

John D. & Catherine T. MacArthur Foundation
149 S. Dearborn St., Suite 1100
Chicago, IL 60603

Phone: 312 726 8000

media@macfound.org (information)
loi@macfound.org (letter of inquiry)
www.macfound.org

Guidelines: Grants support public interest media projects, including independent documentary film, that advance the broad purposes of the Foundation: Human and Community Development and Global Security and Sustainability. Only documentary films on important social issues that are intended for US television broadcast are supported by the Foundation. The Media Programme funds both series and one-hour documentary films.

Grants: from $50,000 to $300,000 for production, and provide partial support for documentary series and individual independent films

British filmmakers: may apply, but must have a US non-profit fiscal agent through which the grant can be made.

Recent Grants/Projects: Center for Investigative Reporting, San Francisco, California, $250,000 in support of the documentary film 'No Place to Hide: Stories from a Surveillance Society' (2004); OneWorld International Foundation, London, United Kingdom. $250,000 in support of the OneWorld Network, including oneworld.net, tv.oneworld.net, and us.oneworld.net (over two years) (2004).

12. LATINO PUBLIC BROADCASTING

6777 Hollywood Boulevard, Suite 500
Los Angeles, CA 90028

Phone: 323 466-7110
Fax: 323 466-7521

info@lpbp.org
www.lpbp.org

Guidelines: Supports the development, production, acquisition and distribution of non-commercial educational and cultural television programming that is representative of Latino people, or addresses issues of particular interest to Latino Americans. LPB funds television programs including dramas, documentaries, comedies, satire or animation. These may be single programs or limited series, new productions or works-in-progress.

Grants: between $5,000 and $100,000

British Filmmakers: Applicants must be citizens or legal residents of the United States or its territories. Producers or production entities that are foreign-based, owned or controlled are not eligible.

13. THE LUCIUS & EVA EASTMAN FUND

The Lucius & Eva Eastman Fund
Jennifer Eastman, Attorney at Law
48 Lakeshore Dr.
Westwood, MA 02090

Phone: 781-326-7922

Lucius R. Eastman, President
5926 Fiddletown Pl.
San Jose, CA 95120

Phone: 408 268 2083
Fax: 408 268 2083

Guidelines: Focused on filmmakers and organisations geared for film based in the NYC area. The fund mainly provides grants for completion for a variety of documentary and narrative projects. No specific criteria for selection. Rarely provides development funds.

Deadline: 1st of January, May, and September

British Filmmakers: may apply with a US fiscal sponsor, as long as the project is consistent with the Foundation's guidelines.

14. THE LYN BLUMENTHAL MEMORIAL FUND FOR INDEPENDENT VIDEO

The Lyn Blumenthal Memorial Fund
For Independent Video
P.O. Box 3514
Church St. Station

New York, NY 10007

www.lbmf.org/about.html

Guidelines: Awards grants for criticism and production.

15. THE PUFFIN FOUNDATION

The Puffin Foundation
20 East Oakdene Avenue
Teaneck, NJ 07666-4198

Phone: 201 836 8923
Fax: 201 836 1734

puffingrant@mindspring.com
www.puffinfoundation.org

Guidelines: Grants that encourage emerging artists whose works, due to their genre and/or social philosophy, might have difficulty being aired.

Grants: up to $2,500

British filmmakers: Only a US citizen with a valid social security number can apply. The funded film can be produced abroad as long as the applicant is a citizen of the US.

16. THE NATHAN CUMMINGS FOUNDATION

475 10th Ave. 14th Fl.
New York, NY 10018

Phone:212-787-7300
Fax: 212-787-7377

arts@nathancummings.org

Guidelines: Funds projects that encourage cross-cultural and multidisciplinary collaborations, and give voice to the issues and experiences of under-represented communities, in order to build a stronger society.

17. NATIONAL ASIAN AMERICAN TELECOMMUNICATIONS ASSOCIATION (NAATA)

145 Ninth Street, Suite 350
San Francisco, CA 94103

Phone: 415 863 0814
Fax: 415 863 7428

mediafund@naatanet.org
www.naatanet.org

Guidelines: Funds projects working to increase the visibility of Asian-American programmes on public television and impacting the way in which Asian Americans are perceived and understood. Project may be very specific or unique in its subject, but should have deep universal meaning.

Grants: $20,000 to $50,000 for projects in production and/or post-production phases.

Deadline: April 22

Open Door Completion Fund:

Grants: average $20,000 for public television projects in the final post-production phase. A full-length rough cut must be submitted.

Deadline: No deadline. Applications will be accepted on a rolling basis.

British Filmmakers: Must be an American citizen or legal resident to apply and have a US fiscal sponsor.

18. NATIONAL BLACK PROGRAMMING CONSORTIUM (NBPC)

145 East 125th Street, Suite 3R
New York, NY 10035

Phone: 212 234-8200; 212 828 7930

info@nbpc.tv
www.nbpc.tv

Guidelines: Funds, commissions, acquires and awards talented makers of quality African-American and African Diaspora film and video projects. Selected programs reflect a variety of subjects and production styles. NBPC funds every phase of the production process – research and development, production, post-production, and outreach. Funding in two forms:

Annual Open Solicitation or Request for Proposals (RFP):

Grants: Funding awards range from $1,000 to $80,000.

Funds to begin or complete projects. The programme is open to all producers and directors who are creating work about the African-American and African Diaspora Experience.

Discretionary Funding:

Grants: Funding awards range from $1,000 to $3,000.

NBPC will consider funding support outside of its annual Open Solicitation for: 1) Programs and/or subject matters and issues of urgency and timeliness which cannot wait until the next Open Solicitation; 2) Programmes that have a PBS broadcast commitment and are seeking minimal completion funding; 3) Documentation of one-time events or happenings that are pertinent to the project's development; 4) Small Projects or ideas from Emerging Producer Directors that show major potential but which may get lost in the RFP competition.

British Filmmakers: Applicant must be a US citizen, but British filmmakers may apply with a co-producer or prominent member of the production who is a US citizen.

Recent Grants/Projects: $30,000.00 production support to Globalvision, Inc for the documentary 'Speak Up Young Africa: African Youth Confront the AIDS Epidemic'.

19. NATIONAL ENDOWMENT FOR THE ARTS

National Endowment for the Arts (NEA)
1100 Pennsylvania Avenue NW
Washington, DC 20506

Phone: 202 682 5400
Fax: 202 682 5721

webmgr@arts.endow.gov
http://arts.endow.gov

Guidelines: Provides grants to organisations for the production, public exhibition, distribution, and preservation of film, video, and audio works as art forms themselves. Media Arts organisations also receive funds for services to media artists, media literacy programs, publications, and professional training.

Grants: From $25,000 to $50,000 for single documentaries and up to $200,000 for multi-part series.

Deadline: September 10th

British Filmmakers: Applications may be submitted by US fiscal agents that are willing to assume full responsibility for the grant.

Recent Grants/Projects:

$40,000 to support the production of a documentary film 'Good Work' about contemporary building artisans from a variety of traditions that contribute to America's architectural heritage, intended for national PBS broadcast. American Focus, Inc., Charlottesville, VA.

20. NATIONAL ENDOWMENT FOR THE HUMANITIES (NEH)

National Endowment for the Humanities
1100 Pennsylvania Ave, N.W.
Washington, DC 20506

Phone: 1-800-NEH-1121
Fax: 202 606 8400
TDD: 202 606 8282

info@neh.gov
www.neh.gov

Guidelines: Offers grants for independent filmmakers and digital media producers whose work: addresses significant subjects in the humanities; reaches broad public audiences; grows out of sound scholarship; and uses imaginative, engaging formats. The number of applications for the last two years ranges from 130 -145. From those applications, 18-20 grants were awarded.

Grants: Planning (max $30,000) Scripting (max $60,000) Production ($400,000 - $800,000)

Deadline: 03/11/2005 (Planning/Scripting/Production) 22/03/2005 (Consultation)

British Directors: cannot apply, but can be a member of the team, if they are not the main director and the team is comprised primarily of Americans..

Recent Grants/Projects: 'The Civil War', 'The Great Depression', and 'FDR', as well as such family programming as 'Long Ago and Far Away' and 'Booker'.

21. NATIONAL FUND FOR JEWISH DOCUMENTARY

Phone: 212 629 0500
Fax: 212 629 0508;

nfjc@jewishculture.org
Grants@JewishCulture.org

Guidelines: The fund is designed to support the creation of original documentary films and videos that promote thoughtful consideration of Jewish history, culture, identity, and contemporary issues among diverse public audiences.

Grants: maximum $50,000 or 50% of the total project budget, whichever is less. Most grant awards are expected to fall in the $20,000-30,000 range. They prefer to be last monies in.

Deadline: March 10, by 4pm

British Filmmakers: Applicant must be a US citizen or permanent resident.

Recent Grantee: 'The Sky Socialist', by Ken Jacobs, documents "a deeply loved pocket of Manhattan, just below the Brooklyn Bridge" during the early Sixties, and the frame of mind through which he experienced this corner of the world—as an artist, a Jew, a young man moving toward marriage and an activist (2003).

22. NATIVE AMERICAN PUBLIC TELECOMMUNICATIONS (NAPT)

1800 No 33 St
Lincoln, NE 68583

PO Box 83111
Lincoln, NE 68501

Phone:(402) 472-3522

visionmaker@unl.edu
www.nativetelecom.org/

Guidelines: Proposals are requested for programs in many genres including documentary, performance, cultural/public affairs, children's and animation. Projects submitted to this solicitation must be intended for national public television broadcast. Must have relevance to/for Native Americans and/or have Native Americans on the production team.

Grants: $25,000 maximum

Deadline: May 14th

British Filmmakers: Applicants required to be US citizens or legal residents of the United States or its territories and have a fiscal sponsor. Producers or production entities that are foreign-based, owned or controlled are not eligible.

23. THE NEW YORK STATE COUNCIL ON THE ARTS

Richard J. Schwartz, Chairman
Debra R. Black, Vice-Chairman
175 Varick Street
New York, NY 10014-4604

General Information (212) 627-4455
TDD 1-800-895-9838

helpdesk@nysca.org

www.nysca.org/public/

Guidelines: The programme supports a variety of activities that assist diverse constituents in the development and realisation of film, video, sound art and new media programmes and opportunities.

Grants: $2,500 to $25,000. General Operating Support grants will be no less than $5,000, and will rarely exceed 25% of an organisation's budget. GOS support is awarded on a multi-year basis.

Deadline: March 1, 2004 is the registration deadline for submission of grant requests

British Filmmakers: Artists apply through the fiscal sponsorship of a New York State non-profit organisation in the Individual Artist category. Funding is awarded on a single-year basis.

24. THE NORTH STAR FUND

305 Seventh Avenue, 5th Floor
New York, NY 10001-6008

Phone: 212-620-9110
Fax: 212-620-8178

info@northstarfund.org

Guidelines: The foundation supports grassroots social change organisations in New York City only.

Grants $5,000 and $10,000

Deadline: Fall and Spring grant cycles, dates vary year to year. Check website for specific deadlines.

Recent Grantee: ($2,130) 'Silent Choices', a documentary about African-American women and racist myths of abortion, by Organized Chaos Mediaworks.

25. OPEN MEADOWS FOUNDATION

Open Meadows Foundation
PO Box 150-607
Van Brunt Station
Brooklyn, NY 11215-0150

Phone: 718-768-4015

openmeadows@igc.apc.org
www.openmeadows.org

Guidelines: Projects that have limited financial access, which reflect the cultural and ethnic diversity of our society and promote the empowerment of women and girls; projects for social change that have encountered obstacles in their search for funding.

Grants: up to $2,000

Deadline: Proposals are due August 15th and February 15th of every year.

British filmmakers: may apply but must have tax exempt status or a fiscal sponsor that is tax exempt under 501(c)3 of the Internal Revenue Code (IRC)

Recent Grants/Projects: 'The Lydia Pink Project', Providence, Rhode Island - $1000. Funding will go towards submitting two short movies about young queer women of colour to film festivals and distribution to queer- and diversity- themed groups in high schools and youth-focused non-profit organisations.

26. PACIFIC PIONEER FUND

Print out an application from their website — www.pacificpioneerfund.com--and send it, along with a VHS tape of up to 10 minutes of edited footage from the project for which support is sought, to P.O. Box 20504, Stanford, CA 94309. If you have questions, email Armin Rosencranz: armin@stanford.edu

Guidelines: To support emerging documentary filmmakers or videographers who live and work in California, Oregon and Washington.

Grant Range: $ 1,000-$ 10,000

Deadlines: The board meets three times a year. Applications are accepted on an ongoing basis. Application deadlines in 2004-05 are 9/1/04, 1/1/05, 1/05/05 and 1/09/05. Rejected applicants must wait one year to reapply.

27. PAUL ROBESON FUND FOR INDEPENDENT MEDIA

Paul Robeson Fund for Independent Media
The Funding Exchange
666 Broadway, Suite 500
New York, NY 10012

Phone: 212 529 5300
Fax: 212 982 9272

trinh.duong@fex.org
www.fex.org/2.3grantmakingindex.html

Guidelines: Film/video projects that will reach a broad audience with an organising component and can demonstrate that the production will be used for social change organising.

Grants: Up to $15,000; most $3,000-$6,000

28. P.O.V.

P.O.V./American Documentary, Inc.
32 Broadway, 14th Floor
New York, NY 10004

Phone: 212 989 8121
Fax: 212 989 8230

programming@cpb.org
www.pbs.org/pov

Guidelines: There is no standard application process for the Program Challenge Fund, and producers should submit projects according to the general PBS submission guidelines. In addition to supporting limited series and specials, the Challenge Fund will also consider proposals to launch new continuing series (the fund, however, will not sustain series beyond their first year of broadcast).

Deadline: CPB reviews proposals on an ongoing basis.

British Filmmakers: are welcome to apply, if their project is intended for national broadcast in the US on PBS channel.

Recent Grantee: 'The Commanding Heights', which documented the emergence of a global economy, and 'American Family', the first broadcast drama to focus on a Latino family.

29. THE PLAYBOY FOUNDATION

The Playboy Foundation
680 N. Lake Shore Drive
Chicago, IL 60611

Phone: 312 751 8000

www.playboyenterprises.com

Guidelines: The foundation supports projects of national impact and scope involved in: fostering open communication about, and research into, human sexuality, reproductive health and rights; protecting and fostering civil rights and civil liberties in the United States for all people, including women, people affected and impacted by HIV/AIDS, gays and lesbians, racial minorities, the poor and the disadvantaged; and eliminating censorship and protecting freedom of expression. Special preference is given to projects where a small grant can make a difference. Grants: $5000-$10,000

Deadlines: The Foundation accepts grant proposals throughout the year. The Board of Directors generally meets in the fall to consider proposals.

British filmmakers: are welcome to apply with a US fiscal sponsor.

Recent Grants/Projects: Thomas Allen Harris' film, 'E Minha Cara/That's My Face', exploring black identity issues in the US, Brazil and Africa.

30. THE ROCKEFELLER FOUNDATION

MULTI-ARTS PRODUCTION FUND
The MAP Fund at Creative Capital
73 Spring Street, Suite 401
New York, NY 10012

mapinfo@mapfund.org
www.mapfund.org

Guidelines: MAP funds all stages of the creation of a work, from early development to the world premiere production. Does not fund filmmaking/documentary production. It's for multimedia and performance art. MAP awards approximately 40 grants per year, which is approximately 7% of the total number of applications received annually.

Grants: average $22,000

Deadline: February

British Filmmakers: Applications accepted from US-based organisations with a tax-exempt 501(c)3 tax status. Individual artists may apply for a MAP grant if they are partnering with a US-based 501(c)3 organisation.

Rent Grantee: Gametophyte, Inc., New York, NY $20,000 to support the development and production of a mutlimedia performance installation by choreographer and videographer Dean Moss and visual artist Laylah Ali.

31. THE ROY W. DEAN GRANT

From the Heart Productions
Attn. Roy W. Dean Film Grant
1455 Mandalay Beach Rd.
Oxnard, CA 93035

Phone/Fax: 866 689 5150

caroleedean@worldnet.att.net
www.fromtheheartproductions.com

Guidelines: Grants offer awards annually to short films, documentaries and other projects that are unique and benefit society. There are approximately 100 applications for each of the 5 grants and they are open to anyone, anywhere, but the 3 NY & LA grants are goods and service grants, so the services can only be received in either NY or LA.

Grant: The goods and service grants for NY & LA range from $40,000 - $50,000.

Deadline: 28/02/2005 – Writing, 30/09/2005 – Editing, NY Film/Video, LA Film, LA Video (no deadline posted)

British Filmmakers: There has never been a British winner in any of the grant categories, but there was recently a finalist, who received $500 in Kodak film.

32. THE SISTER FUND

116 East 16th St., 7th Floor
New York, NY 10003

Phone: 212-260-4446
Fax: 212 260-4633

sisterfund@aol.com
www.sisterfund.org

Guidelines: Support for programming that fosters the economic, social, political, and spiritual lives of women and girls, with a primary emphasis on national advocacy and media strategies to heighten public consciousness around issues affecting women and girls.

Grants: $5,000 - $30,000

Deadline: Letters of inquiry must be postmarked by December 1st or July 1st

British filmmaker: are welcome to apply as long as their work is local to New York City, National (to the US) or international in scope. They must have their own 501(c)3 or a US fiscal sponsor with 501(c)3 IRS tax determination.

Recent Grantee: Aubin Pictures: $10,000 for a documentary, entitled 'Dangerous Journey', a film about maternal mortality in post-Taliban Afghanistan.

33. THE UNITARIAN UNIVERSALIST FUNDING PROGRAM/FUND FOR A JUST SOCIETY

Hilary Goodridge, director
P.O. Box 1149

Jamaica Plain, MA 02130

Phone: 617 971 9600
Fax: 617 971 0029

uufp@aol.com
www.uua.org/uufp/

Guidelines: Funds granted mainly for distribution support, as long as the project is an integral part of a strategy of collective action for social change on a grassroots level and is intended for audiences in the United Sates and/or Canada.

Grants: The maximum grant is $15,000. Most grants are between $6,000 and $8,000

Deadline: Completed applications must be postmarked no later than:

Spring Cycle: March 15 and Fall Cycle: September 15

British filmmakers: are welcome to apply with US fiscal sponsorship.

Recent Grants/Projects: 'Deadline', a film about the death penalty.

The Sundance Institute

Sundance Documentary Fund
Formerly the Soros Documentary Fund of the Open Society Institute

 Sundance Documentary Fund
Sundance Institute
8857 West Olympic Blvd.
Beverly Hills, CA 90211

 310 360-1981

 sdf@sundance.org
www.sundance.org

Guidelines: the Sundance Documentary Fund supports international documentary films and videos focused on current and significant issues and movements in contemporary human rights, freedom of expression, social justice, and civil liberties. In supporting such works, the Sundance Documentary Fund hopes to give voice to the diverse exchange of ideas crucial to developing an open society, raise the public consciousness about human rights abuses and restrictions of civil liberties, and engage citizens in a lively, ongoing debate about these issues. The fund only accepts projects dealing with contemporary issues, and does not accept historical projects, biographies, or series.

Grants: Development funds up to $15,000 and Production/Post-Production to $75,000, though most will range from $20,000 to $50,000.

Deadline: Rolling submissions, no deadline. Guidelines and application form on the website.

British Filmmakers: may apply with documentary film or video projects that range in length from full hour broadcast to long format feature. Applicants must have creative and budgetary control over the proposed documentary.

Nick Francis and his brother Marc Francis received a Sundance grant for 'Black Gold', a timely feature-length documentary about international trade and how the profits from the two billion cups of coffee we drink everyday are kept away from the people who produce it.

"Some time ago we had heard about how the documentary fund at the Sundance Institute is one of the best places to apply for funding for international documentary films that tend to deal with serious issues around human rights, social justice, and freedom of expression. By the time we applied to Sundance, we had already been over a year into the production and we had received funding and support from international development organisations, foundations, and the Screen South/UK film council. We had already shot in several locations around the world and had also produced a rough cut.

We then applied to the Sundance 'work in progress' strand for completion funding to finish filming some key scenes in the US, Italy and Ethiopia and also edit the final cut. Other than the rough cut, Sundance required various supporting material such as; director show reels, production crew CVs, treatments, director's notes, budget forecasts, company accounts, distribution and marketing strategies. The rough cut was also used to enlist initial interest from international broadcasters and distribution companies and it helped us earn a place on Screen South's filmmaker's trade mission to LA where we met with US distribution companies behind releases such as: 'Fahrenheit 9/11', 'Touching the Void', 'Capturing the Friedmans', and 'Super Size Me'.

Do we hope to continue our relationship with the Sundance Institute? Yeah, we do! Apart from giving the grant, Sundance is also keen to support the film right the way through to setting up distribution opportunities. They also have these story and editing lab workshops and that's something we're looking into now. As to what we could pass on to other independent filmmakers, it's difficult to say right now! I think we'd probably be better placed to answer that question once when our film is finished and it starts finding its audience. Watch this space!"

The Sundance Documentary Film Editing and Story Lab

Admission for the Lab is extremely limited. For British filmmakers it would be by invitation only, but the emphasis is on international Fellows from the Middle East, Africa, and Central Asia only. The Lab is a five-day programme for fellows who have previously been supported by funding from the SDI Fund. The Lab provides the filmmakers with the opportunity to collaborate with established and award-winning editors and directors as they work on the editing phase of their documentary works-in-progress.

2004 participants:

Mercedes Moncada, director and Viviana Garcia-Berne, editor of 'The Immortal', (Nicaragua/Spain). Moncada tells the story of twin brothers from Nicaragua who fought on opposite sides of the Contra war during the 1980s, and their present day attempt to reconcile with each other in a divided and devastated country.

Shiri Tsur, director and Avi Banon, producer of 'On the Objection Front: a Personal Journey' (Israel). The filmmaker presents the stories of high-ranking officers in elite units in the Israeli military who refuse to serve in the Occupied Territories and are willing to voice their objections.

Mark Becker, director/editor, 'Romantico' (USA). 'Romantico' is an intimate portrayal of undocumented immigrants in the US through two Mexican musicians who play romantica music for tips to support their families in Mexico. The film exposes their struggles as they repeatedly cross the border in both directions in hopes of a better future

Hank Rogerson, director and Victor Livingston, editor of 'Shakespeare Behind Bars' (USA). An all-male Shakespeare company at a prison in Kentucky confront their pasts and futures as convicts while they rehearse and perform a full production of 'The Tempest'.

The Fellows worked with an acclaimed and award-winning group of editors and directors including: Alex Cooke ('How Arnold Won the West'), Jean-Philippe Boucicaut ('Citizen King'), Kate Amend ('Beah: a Black Woman Speaks' and 'Into the Arms of Strangers: Stories of the Kindertransport'), Richard Hankin ('Capturing the Friedmans'), director Robb Moss ('Same River Twice'), and producer/director Vikram Jayanti ('Game Over: Kasparov and the Machine' and 'When We Were Kings').

Documentary Composers Laboratory

The Documentary Composers Laboratory offers creative support to Sundance Documentary Fund filmmakers, by providing them with an intensive four-day laboratory experience focusing on musical composition and non-fiction filmmaking. Six composers from the Sundance Composers Laboratory are paired with four documentary projects to explore the works-in-progress in relation to musical score. The laboratory is designed to offer documentary filmmakers and emerging composers the creative opportunity to work together and concentrate on an important and under-developed component of documentary storytelling under the mentorship of veteran composers and documentary filmmakers.

Diane Weyermann is director of the Sundance Institute Documentary Film Programme. She gave an inside view of Sundance to Shooting People:

"In this year's Sundance festival (2004), we initiated a World Documentary competition section. We programmed twelve films in competition, and two of the twelve were British. We started a World Documentary section (non-competitive) in 2003. That year one of the ten films was from the U.K.

I think that the rise of the documentary is attributable to a combination of factors. 9/11 is one of them, or speaking in a broader context, the pervasive sense that the world is smaller coupled with the apprehension of an uncertain, potentially ominous future. But the interest in documentary is not only attributable to the political situation. I strongly believe that documentaries have gained greater prominence in the marketplace because of the quality of the storytelling and the cinematic appeal of the work. There's terrific filmmaking, stories and artistry in much of the work that is breaking out.

For the role of the Sundance Documentary Fund in the bigger international picture for documentaries, the Fund (formerly the Soros Documentary Fund) has been supporting international documentaries dealing with contemporary human rights, social justice, civil liberties, and freedom of expression since 1996. We've been able to identify tough, risky projects about extremely important issues and stories that might not have been made without our assistance. Our role continues to be to support work and artists that are committed to tell stories that might be unpopular, difficult to fund and produce, but which absolutely should be made, discussed, debated and seen by as many people around the world as possible. And we also want to support artistic work with the potential for theatrical distribution, which in some cases might be hard to fund through the broadcast system.

Each year (since 1996) the fund has distributed approximately one million U.S. dollars to filmmakers, with a maximum grant of $75,000. With submissions, we get too many films that I would more accurately term "news magazines." We're looking specifically for feature length documentaries that are both cinematic and have a compelling narrative. And we get too little of work that really pushes the limits in its aesthetic approach. The most common mistake that applicants to the Fund make is not reading our mandate and guidelines carefully. I always encourage potential applicants to go over our website, including the "frequently asked questions" section, because it makes no sense to apply if the project falls outside of our mandate.

For first-time directors, it's never easy to get funding, but having said that we do fund first-time filmmakers, sometimes very successfully. I think it's important to take risks, particularly when there's something unique or compelling about the story and the filmmaker's passion and connection to the work. Some of the best and most successful films we're supported have been directed by first-timers.

The Fund remit is not very narrow; we're quite open. Our mandate is broadly defined, and if anything we're moving in the direction to open it even further to include creative storytelling that might not fit within a human rights context. The grant-making committee meets twice a year and is comprised from a pool of filmmakers, curators, critics, human rights experts, etc.

We've had a decent number of proposals from the U.K. and have funded a number of them, including these:

'A Cry From the Grave' (Leslie Woodhead)
'Coconut Revolution' (Dom Rotheroe)
'I Was A Slave Labourer' (Luke Holland)
'Injustice' (Ken Fero)
'Next Year in Lerin' (Jill Daniels)
'One Day in September' (Kevin Macdonald)
'A Pig's Tale' (Anne Parisio)
'Solitary Confinement' (Gabriella Polletta)
'Somewhere Better' (Mira Erdevicki)
'Black and White in Colour' (Mira Erdivicki)
'Wanted' (Kim Hopkins)
'Black Gold' (Marc and Nick Francis)
'An American Martyr' (Rodrigo Vazquez)
'The Boy Who Plays on the Buddhas of Bamiyan' (Phil Grabsky)
'To Be Gay in China' (Julian Ozanne / Eric Ransdell)

As well as the Fund, we have two documentary labs: the Editing and Storytelling Lab and the Documentary Composers' Lab. They are both by invitation only and currently are open only to projects and filmmakers we're already identified and supported through the Fund. There's such limited space (only four projects each year) that it makes no sense to open the participate to the filmmaking community at large. We simply cannot accommodate the demand."

US production and funding services

For filmmakers who aren't themselves based in North America, a world of trouble can be saved by getting on board with a production or funding company who is familiar with the different international cultures.

CACTUS 3

 451 Greenwich Street, 7th Floor
New York
NY 10013

 212 905 2340

cactusjg@yahoo.com

Cactus 3 is a production and funding company based in New York. It's run by Krysanne Katsoolis, Julie Goldman and Caroline Stevens, whose background expertise ranges from hands-on production for TV, music videos, commercials, live TV and feature films, through distribution and sales to legal and acquisitions. Projects include 'The American Working Class', a 'social issue doc with musical numbers'; John Landis' first documentary 'Slasher'; and a ten-part Sunday night series on HBO, a "real non-fiction series following a family of bounty hunters/ bail bondsmen, kind of like 'Sopranos' meets 'Midnight Run' meets 'The Osbournes'."

In a combined interview, Katsoolis, Goldman and Stevens say,

"We formed Cactus 3 over a year ago because we realised there was a need in the market place to help filmmakers, producers and directors to raise money for their projects. We do this by going to the international and domestic community to get financing, from a variety of sources, which are appropriate to the project. So some films we set up as a feature film documentary and other films may be straight to broadcast but we're working with broadcasters domestically and internationally; we're working with video and DVD distributors and international sales agents; and with sources of tax-exempt funding and private equity sources. Unusually for an American company, what we've specialised in is the international dimension, so the funding we draw on is primarily international, from the UK, France, Germany, the Netherlands, Australia, Japan. We try to only bring in two or three or maximum four partners for co-production, because for the filmmakers it's hard to answer to four different end-users. We also work as the liaison between the different partners so the filmmaker doesn't feel overwhelmed with that part of production, and can really focus on the film.

We should stress that we market ourselves as creative executive producers which means that we're involved creatively with the project, in order to take it to the highest possible level for revenue raising. But we're also about creative financing, so we work on both sides. On any project we're likely to get involved with developing the treatment, working on the budgets… The good thing is we don't have a template, we look at each project as a blank slate and figure out what will work best for it. So if it's something that needs a lot of creative or production input we can do that, but if they feel like they're all set with that then we don't have to do that; we can really work at different levels.

Once the film is done we're also involved with structuring a festival run. We stay involved with every aspect of the film and if we're dealing with a commissioning editor or a sales company from another country or from here we are very much answerable to them so we make sure we look after a project on their behalf as much as we're looking after it for the producer and director. If a filmmaker approached us an an individual, we could give help in assembling a production team, but more often than not the filmmaker comes with a production team. And it's a production team that wants to make films, not spend their time raising financing.

The one thing we're not is an international sales agent, in as much as we don't usually take a finished film and sell it. Occasionally, if someone has, say, a film from Europe that for some reason hasn't been sold and we fall in love with it, then we'll try to sell it in the US for them. But usually we're involved with finding the most appropriate partner for that film. So if a film is finished we may recommend a sales agent, and we have relationships with a number of different sales companies all around the world. In the same way we have relationships with video and DVD distributors both in the UK, the US and around the world, so we can go back into the DVD or theatrical world for our own projects if we need to. We were in distribution for many years so we know the distribution circuit very well and we're able to help position a film in a theatre. We basically position the whole strategy of distribution, even though we're not a distributor.

The films we're looking for don't have to be based in any particular country. Really we're looking for great stories that are going to transcend territorial barriers. Ideally they'd be something that's new; it's always exciting when you get something that you feel you haven't seen before, because most of the time people pitch something and you're like, 'Oh yeah, I've been pitched that 12 times,' so it really is wonderful to find these projects and then to work on them. We have a diverse slate of projects, with a lot of music, arts and cultural projects.

Sometimes a filmmaker brings some private funding with them but in addition we've lined up a couple of individuals who are interested in investing in documentaries and we're working with them to develop a slate of programming. If you have a film, ideally you want to find investors who have an affinity with that topic. But we're also working with traditional UK financing sources.

For one of our films, 'Once in a Lifetime' which John Battsek at Passion Pictures is producing, we brought in the US international sales company Green Street Films. That's an example of creatively using what's out there, because this is a company known for fiction feature films like 'In the Bedroom' and 'Uptown Girls'.

We convinced them that a feature doc would be great in their line-up and they put a substantial amount of financing into the film. We're also using UK sale and leaseback funding which is traditionally used for feature films in the UK, so this is a documentary positioned as a feature film, it will have sale and leaseback funding, and will have theatrical release in the UK. We did a co-production deal with the BBC and then with Green Street Films who will be selling it internationally. They attend all the festivals so in the last Cannes they were promoting a trailer of the film. It's about the New York Cosmo soccer team, New York in the '70s, the Boogie Nights of football.

If someone wants to contact us with an idea, they should email Krysanne, or call us to talk through the idea. If we feel like we want to pursue it then we'll ask them to send us some more information on it and develop a treatment with them. People shouldn't send tapes but should get in touch first. In a five-minute conversation we can get a pretty good idea on whether we can move on it, because there's some projects that we're better at raising finance for than others.

One thing that's really different between the US and the UK is that a lot of people who are putting money into projects here in the US want to see a lot of commitment already. We find a lot of UK filmmakers will bring treatments, whereas here the filmmaker will have gone out and spent months or years with a subject and they've moved it along to that next step. That does help us a lot, but on the other hand we also tell filmmakers to give us a certain amount of time to see if we can raise the financing rather than spending your life savings. We can tell you very quickly or at least within a three- to six-month period if we feel like we can raise money on it for you.

With filmmakers, if they get something away with us, they don't just take their cut out of the budget. We're very wary of the fact that people spend some of the best years of their lives making these, and we try and cut the best deal for them and retain for them as much out of the back end as possible. We deal with distributors as well on their behalf; we paper the deals, we lawyer the deals for them. We do the best we can by the filmmaker. We take a percentage of the budget is how we take our fees, usually between 10 and 15% depending on the timing and when we get involved."

Part Two: Distribution

Chapter Ten
Introduction to distribution

By Jess Search

The reality

Once you've made the film, you've only done half the work. I think I should say that again: once you've made the film, you've done half the work. Too many directors and producers think that once they've finished post-production, their job is almost over and they start concentrating on their next project. The truth is that you now need to employ just as much energy, determination, networking and lateral thinking into getting your film seen as you did getting the thing made. It's not unusual for a doc feature filmmaker to spend the best part of a year just travelling to festivals, selling the film, promoting the openings, and doing the press for their last venture. All this is going to cost money too, and it's vital that you budget for distribution at the outset: you'll need to pay entry fees for festivals, make and send press copies, and travel around meeting possible international partners. It ain't cheap and any money you do make will only come later.

What is distribution?

Distribution is any way your film can reach an audience and by doing so, hopefully make money. So it is both a matter of big love (getting your lovely film seen) and cold business (making money back for the investors in the film, whether that is just you, or not).

These are the main distribution outlets:
Film festivals
Theatrical release
DVD rental
DVD sales
TV screening
Other screenings – local, specialised, clubs, galleries, etc.
Airlines
Online/mobile

Some films will be distributed in almost all the above, others just one or two. This distribution section of the book will go into detail about the key areas, telling you how to go about trying to get a distributor / sales agent, or how to go it alone if your film doesn't attract their interest, either because it isn't commercial enough or because they just don't understand your film.

The state of distribution

The past ten years has seen unbelievable changes in the means of film production and it is now much, much easier to make a film than ever before. Distribution, however, has not changed so fast, so it is much, much harder to get a good film seen than made. Market forces have actually made it much harder for an independent film to 'break through' and become a success now than it was fifteen years ago. This is because there are more films competing for cinema screens, there are fewer independent cinemas and, crucially, the amount of press and marketing money needed for any one film to be visible in such a busy, over-saturated culture has gone through the roof. Most distributors operate on a model of opening a film on several screens simultaneously (to coincide with their marketing spend). The cinemas agree to hold it for a week, judging the success based on the first weekend's takings and then deciding whether it stays a second week. Without a really big marketing campaign, it's very hard to make this work – it doesn't leave room for a slow word-of-mouth build, and there are so many films queuing up behind to take their place on the screen.

Some great schemes exist to try to make it easier for small, foreign, specialised films and documentaries to get into cinemas. The Film Council is investing in lots of digital screens, which increases the possibility of recouping outlay and opens up the chance for a filmmaker to gain reputation in cinemas and then capitalise on direct DVD. The Film Council also has a p&a fund which is designed to give a leg-up to 'specialised' films that can't otherwise raise enough money to release widely enough to compete with Hollywood.

The MEDIA Programme helps to get European films into our cinemas (and on DVDs in our shops) and conversely encourages our films into European cinemas, through a scheme which pays distributors a bonus on every ticket or unit sold.

And with direct DVD sales, new distributors like WARP are springing up, interested in taking on good films which couldn't get a theatrical release. Some filmmakers are distributing through their own websites, as opposed to the traditional sales through dealers such as HMV, which take a larger percentage of the potential income. Plus the very passionate people at DocSpace (led by Amy Hardie) are part of a Europe-wide iniative which has put documentary digital screens in Britain (read more in Chapter 15, DIY distribution). I take my hat off also to Elizabeth Wood at DocHouse for running a fantastic dedicated documentary cinema programme (see too Chapter 15).

The best strategy for independents

Despite the imminent arrival of many more digital screens, my conclusion is that it only suits a very small number of documentaries to play the grown-ups at their own game in the distribution arena. For the rest of us it's all about seizing opportunities to re-invent the rules so that they work better for independents. You don't have to try to get your film released in a traditional way for the distribution to be a success. Go straight to DVD, show your film in art galleries, ring your local cinema yourself, sell it to a cruise ship, go on the festival circuit, get it given away with a magazine.

Recent years have proved to be an exciting time for documentaries, with the traditional models outlined above being broken to positive affect. Robert Greenwald's 'Outfoxed' is one such example of how to revolutionise the procedure. Self-released on DVD over the internet, the film maximised on grass-roots marketing, working with political organisation MoveOn.org.

Arthur Bradford followed a similar approach with 'How's Your News?' When the film didn't get a conventional theatrical release it was aired on HBO and the filmmaker and crew then took it on the road themselves: "If anyone wanted to screen it, as long as we could figure out a way of getting the cast there we would do it. We would do screenings in Portland, Boston, Montreaux and we would do that to continue to promote the film. It got to the point that every time I would think that it was time to forget about the film and move on to something else, some other opportunity would come up, like doing the SXSW music festival, where the cast performed a set on stage as backing vocalists to Polyphonic Spree." These screenings led to some acquisitions by local TV stations in places where they'd done public appearances, and they sold merchandise wherever they went. Keeping the attention up like this, Bradford was able to sell VHSs over the website, which eventually resulted in a company taking the DVD rights and giving an advance which allowed Arthur to re-author and update the film for DVD. Integrated websites can definitely be another channel for financing your films; in addition to the DVDs, the 'How's Your News?' website at www.howsyournews.com also sells audio CDs, t-shirts, stickers and hats, and keeps fans updated on the progress of a second film, which will be sold directly from the site.

Peter Broderick is a longstanding friend of Shooting People and a very clever LA-based executive producer, who was very active at the start of digital feature filmmaking and is now the 'Jonny Appleseed' of new distribution models for independent filmmakers. Peter is currently consulting with filmmakers about distribution strategies designed to maximise their film's audience, revenues and impact. He can be reached at upwards@earthlink.net. My thanks to him for sharing his ideas with me. Here's part of what he has to say in his own words; you can find more at http://dga.org/index2.php3 .

"Filmmakers who can make movies digitally at lower budgets are no longer wholly dependent on financiers for the resources and permission to make their films. Likewise, new distribution models are freeing them from dependence on a traditional distribution system that has been failing them. Powerful digital distribution tools — the DVD, digital projectors and the internet — are empowering independents to increasingly take their fate in their own hands and have a more direct relationship with their audiences. By effectively using these tools, filmmakers will be able to not only maximise the distribution opportunities

for their current films, but also find investors for subsequent projects designed to reach core audiences. These tools will also enable them to build and nurture a personal audience, which could ensure a long and fulfilling career".

I'm going to highlight Peter's very advice to independents in three points:

SPLIT THE RIGHTS. He advises producers not to sell world inclusive rights to the company offering the best advance. Instead, Peter is a huge advocate of the independent producer splitting up all their rights (TV, DVD, airline, etc.) and splitting up the territories of the world so that they can maximise the potential in each place.

SELL THE DVD DIRECT. He also very strongly advises everyone to keep a clause in their contracts giving them the right to sell their own DVD from their own website. You won't see much money out of traditional DVD sales after everyone has taken their cut and most importantly you won't know who bought them. Selling direct means you can make around £10 a unit and you start to build a relationship with the audience for your films.

WORK THE NICHE MARKETS. Many documentaries that do well in cinemas and on DVD rely on their appeal to a niche audience (motorcycles nuts, tango fans, teachers, activists). Niches are easier to market to than the 'broad audience' because they cluster around clubs, they read specialist publications that are cheaper to advertise in than national press, and because they are very handily networked by the internet into communities that can often be reached for no cost at all. Work out to whom your film appeals and how to reach them, cheaply.

So there we are. The rest of this section takes some of these areas in more detail, arming you with the how and who to try some of these different avenues. Good luck.

Jan Rofekamp is president and CEO of Films Transit International (www.filmstransit.com), the documentary distribution company that he founded in 1982. Headquartered in Montreal, with offices in New York and Amsterdam, Films Transit is one of the most successful and respected distributors, and it takes on roughly 20 documentaries a year, for cinematic and television distribution. In their catalogue are IDFA-winner 'Shape of the Moon', 'The Corporation', 'The Kidnapping of Ingrid Betancourt', 'The Education of Shelby Knox', as well as older, classic titles such as 'Stevie', 'Crumb', 'The Celluloid Closet', 'Power Trip', 'The Wonderful, Horrible Life of Leni Riefenstahl' and a host of other award-winning, big-name docs. Shooting People Documentary network patron Kevin Macdonald is also on the Films Transit books, with his account of his hero, 'A Brief History of Erol Morris'.

"I've just come from MIPTV at Cannes, which was very high-adrenaline, busy. There's a notion at the moment of documentary being more popular than ever. There are so many seminars telling us this, many festivals, the pitching forums, and even in some cases there are theatrical successes. But the question is, is there a market for all these films? Because however good the films are, any cinema distributor still might take one or two docs a year for theatrical release; they won't take more.

The DVD market is there but it's going towards very low consumer unit price, and by this I mean that you can buy a film on DVD extremely cheaply, and if that's so then the rights purchaser, who buys your film to put on the DVD, won't pay as much either.

Eighty per cent of our work is dealing with films for broadcast, and this, the first market, is the market that is not really growing. Swedish television, or BBC's Storyville, buy the same amount of documentaries as they did two or five years ago. Occasionally there is an opening: a new Channel, like Ch4's MORE FOUR but we have not seen the licence fees yet and we fear the worst.

There's more talent out there, so we're seeing also a lot of very good films, but this is problematic: as distributors, we have to work harder than before to make sure that it's your film that's sold, over another one. So we have to put in more effort at promotion, at the festivals. We have to have really attractive trailers, we have to have multiple versions ready right away. We can't come back later with a 60-minute version; it needs to be all there. So it's fair to say I'm a little worried.

At the key festivals at which you can launch films onto the world market, submissions are increasing wildly. For the Los Angeles Independent Film Festival this June, for example, Rachel Rosen the programming director was telling us that they've had two thousand submissions of docs. And they have eighteen slots. I'd say that yelling to the world that everyone should become a doc filmmaker is a bad idea. You get to the stage where everyone gets the enthusiasm, borrows cash, gets a camera, makes the film, and loses their money. There's a glut of films, and subjects are getting crowded. When your film does get made, and you take it to a festival, it's not going to be the only film there about, say, Peru. Even Albert Maysles, who's just been at Cannes with his film about Christo's Gates project, the one done in Central Park – they've known each other for twenty years, they collaborated on this account of what Christo was doing – and even with that, there's another French crew in Cannes with another film on exactly the same topic.

Eventually an audience will catch up, but it won't be through the usual channels. Broadcasters won't add to the documentaries they do purchase and screen. There's the increase in digital and satellite, specialised channels, but the problem is that they don't pay. They give a thousand dollars a pop, and in a market like that filmmakers and distributors can't make a living.

I think television will eventually be transforming into an on-demand system. There'll be a library of material, and individuals can demand whatever they're interested in, but each economic transaction is small, and to make money you need volume. Look at it now: a buyer for the BBC, for example, buys a film and up to sixty million people can see it. But how many people would actually ask for that film in an on-demand system? It'll be a matter of lots of tiny sums all adding up. The carrying system, the vehicle is now different. Of course the cost of the means of production has also gone down, with cheap professional-standard cameras, but it's still higher than the possible revenues. And licence fees have also gone right down, as buyers are ordered from above to decrease spending. Even Nick Fraser, with all he's done to champion documentary, is still dependent on word coming down from the office above; it's their decision. And when you do get docs they're often shown in late slots, after 11pm. Especially the lengthy ones. If you want prime time for your doc (generally) it will be with the one hour version.

As for the international market, we have two hundred sovereign nations in the world, and there are forty of them who buy docs. These forty are the ones who have some kind of public service broadcaster, and it's them who have had a documentary tradition. Every year when I buy my new paper agenda, I go through the two pages where they list the phone codes of every country, and I encircle the phone numbers for the countries with which we do business, where we sell our single docs; there's forty of them. It's not like for children's programming, or wildlife, or science. That kind of programming is seen in 150 countries!

Traditionally at Films Transit we've been in TV sales, which was the market, but now we do about 20% DVD and theatrical. There are only about five or six territories where the TV stations pay serious money. The rest pays very little. We launch films at major festivals: Berlin, Toronto, IDFA Amsterdam and Sundance.

For places that are in other contexts described as emerging markets – South America, China, etc – we don't work there because there's no public broadcast history, or if there is, there's no budget. As an example, we recently had a request from a Venezuelan broadcaster. They'd seen our catalogue, and sent us a nice, polite email explaining that they'd love to screen some of our films; there were about twenty that they were really keen on; but they could only offer $750. So we thought about this, and we replied that if we could find a good way, and do it efficiently, and they'd pay for transport, then we could come to an agreement, and we'd distribute the films to them for $750 each. But they said that all they had the money for was $750 for all twenty. And it just can't be done.

Another problem in some far away regions, we send a viewing VHS and broadcasters just air it. They copy it and transmit it from the VHS. With computer, broadband and internet technologies, everything's moving in the same direction, towards the shape of Video On Demand. At Cannes since a few years, there are people going round asking for Internet rights, but we had to say that unless you can guarantee some borders, some protection for any films you screen, we just can't do it. We have to ask, what's in it for the producers? And the people doing this are working for small companies, often experimental offshoots of the major, multi-million dollar entertainment companies, but because they're these tiny divisions, they say that they've got no cash. So we say: why should independent filmmakers subsidise your market expansion.

There are new companies, who offering to downstream films over the internet, but the problem is that nobody wants to be part of the experiment, not at this early stage. So they have the technology but you look at their site and they're not offering any good films. This way of doing things won't develop very fast because people just don't want to give away their great films, for no money; they want to wait until the technology settles down. That's my advice for filmmakers: sit on your butt and wait two or three years until things have stabilised. Then the distribution and the revenues will be better and the amateurs have been weeded out."

US documentary box office, 1982 to May 2005

Rank	Title	Studio	Lifetime Gross	Theatres	Date
1	Fahrenheit 9/11	Lions	$119,194,771	2011	6/23/04
2	Bowling for Columbine	UA	$21,576,018	248	36108
3	Winged Migration	SPC	$11,689,053	202	4/18/03
4	Super Size Me	IDP	$11,536,423	230	36711
5	Hoop Dreams	FL	$7,830,611	262	10/14/94
6	Tupac: Resurrection	Par.	$7,718,961	804	11/14/03
7	Roger and Me	WB	$6,706,368	265	12/22/89
8	Spellbound	Think	$5,728,581	117	4/30/03
9	Touching the Void	IFC	$4,593,598	137	1/23/04
10	The Fog of War	SPC	$4,198,566	261	12/19/03
11	Paris is Burning	Mira.	$3,779,620	91	32027
12	Imagine: John Lennon	WB	$3,753,977	561	30872
13	Step Into Liquid	Art.	$3,681,803	91	36379
14	The Corporation	Zeit.	$3,493,516	28	36621
15	Born Into Brothels	Think	$3,320,407	127	36749
16	Capturing the Friedmans	Magn.	$3,119,113	78	5/30/03
17	Crumb	Sony	$3,041,083	56	4/21/95
18	Unzipped	Mira.	$2,875,086	119	33335
19	When We Were Kings	Gram.	$2,789,985	92	10/25/96
20	Comedian	Mira.	$2,751,988	244	36108
21	My Architect	NYer	$2,750,707	39	36504
22	Control Room	Magn.	$2,589,616	74	5/21/04
23	The Endurance: Shackleton's Antarctic Adventure	Cow.	$2,453,083	40	35559
24	A Brief History of Time	Trit	$2,279,692	45	8/21/92
25	Riding Giants	SPC	$2,276,368	64	36775
26	Rivers and Tides	Roxie	$2,200,276	15	6/26/02
27	The Endless Summer II	NL	$2,155,385	302	32937
28	Beyond the Mat	Lions	$2,053,648	298	10/22/99
29	The Story of the Weeping Camel	Think	$1,763,052	55	36621
30	Life & Times of Hank Greenberg	Cow.	$1,712,385	31	35399
31	Vincent: The Life and Death of Vincent Van Gogh	Roxie	$1,577,480	16	8/19/88
32	The Wild Parrots of Telegraph Hill	Shad.	$1,555,614	50	37135
33	The Kid Stays in the Picture	Focus	$1,439,232	56	7/26/02
34	Microcosmos	Mira.	$1,433,210	43	33856
35	The Celluloid Closet	SPC	$1,400,591	38	3/15/96
36	Hearts of Darkness	Trit	$1,318,449	28	11/27/91
37	Anne Frank Remembered	SPC	$1,310,200	31	2/23/96
38	Brother's Keeper	CThnk	$1,305,915	15	32394
39	Dogtown and Z-Boys	SPC	$1,300,682	70	4/26/02
40	Startup.com	Art.	$1,283,356	35	35738
41	Metallica: Some Kind of Monster	IFC	$1,222,708	147	36775
42	The Thin Blue Line	Mira.	$1,209,846	23	8/26/88
43	Festival Express	Think	$1,174,079	43	7/23/04
44	American Movie	SPC	$1,165,795	29	34829
45	Enron: The Smartest Guys in the Room	Magn.	$1,079,756	98	4/22/05
46	The Eyes of Tammy Faye	Lions	$1,029,591	51	7/21/00
47	Paper Clips	Slow	$980,974	43	11/24/04
48	35 Up	Gold.	$922,872	21	1/15/92
49	The War Room	Oct.	$901,668	21	32577
50	Fast, Cheap and Out of Control	SPC	$878,960	40	34037

Rank	Title	Studio	Lifetime Gross	Theatres	Date
51	Marlene	Aliv	$852,676	6	30142
52	Visions of Light	Kino	$799,856	13	2/24/93
53	Trembling Before G-d	NYer	$788,896	8	10/24/01
54	To Be and to Have	NYer	$777,129	14	9/19/03
55	Listen Up: The Lives of Quincy Jones	WB	$776,699	111	31541
56	For All Mankind	Apol.	$770,132	9	31057
57	Lost in La Mancha	IFC	$732,393	24	1/31/03
58	The Big One	Mira.	$720,074	53	34610
59	Wigstock: The Movie	Gold.	$686,152	30	33486
60	Kurt and Courtney	Roxie	$668,228	12	2/27/98
61	Inside Deep Throat	Uni.	$656,114	27	37196
62	Pumping Iron 2: The Women	Cinc	$628,050	-	29649
63	Going Upriver: The Long War of John Kerry	Think	$614,138	163	36534
64	The Filth and the Fury	FL	$612,192	29	3/29/00
65	Dust to Glory	IFC	$600,470	80	36894
66	Road Scholar	Gold.	$597,564	16	7/16/93
67	Gunner Palace	Palm	$586,601	56	36983
68	Tibet: Cry of the Snow Lion	AL	$578,241	15	9/19/03
69	The Weather Underground	Shad.	$564,632	14	36255
70	Hands on a Hard Body	Prov.	$563,482	6	34613
71	Incident at Oglala	Mira.	$536,848	12	32359
72	Wild Man Blues	NL	$533,759	25	4/17/98
73	Sex Is...	Outs	$530,833	6	32693
74	A Great Day in Harlem	Castle	$527,034	8	2/17/95
75	Thelonious Monk: Straight, No Chaser	WB	$518,918	11	31056
76	The Trials of Henry Kissinger	FRun	$516,726	8	9/25/02
77	Mr. Death	Lions	$507,941	28	12/29/99
78	Outfoxed: Rupert Murdoch's War on Journalism	Libre	$461,572	18	36684
79	The Wonderful, Horrible Life of Leni Riefenstahl	Kino	$449,707	3	3/18/94
80	I Am Trying to Break Your Heart	Cow.	$445,522	13	7/26/02
81	Porn Star: The Legend of Ron Jeremy	Mael.	$421,516	7	11/30/01
82	The Last Days	Oct.	$421,432	32	34820
83	In the Realms of the Unreal	Wells	$401,834	13	12/22/04
84	Still, We Believe: The Boston Red Sox Movie	Think	$396,803	54	36711
85	End of the Century: The Story of the Ramones	Magn.	$391,950	10	8/20/04
86	Into the Arms of Strangers	WB	$382,807	18	9/15/00
87	Blind Spot: Hitler's Secretary	SPC	$378,382	12	1/24/03
88	The Hunting of the President	Reg.	$376,612	20	6/18/04
89	Genghis Blues	Roxie	$374,550	6	34705
90	The Decline of Western Civilization Part II: The Metal Years	NL	$373,743	21	30746
91	Keep the River on Your Right - A Modern Cannibal Tale	IFC	$373,366	15	3/30/01
92	Broadway: The Golden Age	Da.	$353,580	14	36835
93	Bukowski: Born Into This	Magn.	$318,816	8	5/28/04
94	Trekkies	ParC	$318,426	339	5/21/99
95	America's Heart and Soul	BV	$314,402	98	36562
96	Grass	Una.	$313,039	10	5/31/00
97	The Panama Deception	EPr	$309,596	11	7/31/92
98	Nico-Icon	Roxie	$306,691	4	33458
99	42 Up	FRun	$300,880	5	11/17/99
100	Bonhoeffer	FRun	$296,181	7	6/20/03Data

from www.boxofficemojo.com

A breakdown of feature documentaries released in the UK between 1990 and 2004

Information from the Uk Film Council

	Title	UK lifetime gross	Screens	Distributor	Opening date	
1	Fahrenheit 9/11	6,545,552	132	OPTIMUM	9-Jul	2004
2	Touching the Void	2,643,252	29	PATHE	12-Dec	2003
3	Ghosts of the Abyss	1,737,547	5	BVI	18-Apr	2003
4	Bowling for Columbine	1,667,625	28	MOMENTUM	15-Nov	2002
5	In Bed with Madonna	1,246,070	3	CARLTON	19-Jul	1991
6	Super Size Me	1,111,093	82	TARTAN	10-Sep	2004
7	Buena Vista Social Club	955,278	7	FILM FOUR	17-Sep	1999
8	Etre et Avoir	708,116	10	TARTAN	20-Jun	2003
9	When We Were Kings	545,637	19	UNIVERSAL	16-May	1997
10	Spellbound	484,540	13	METRODOME	10-Oct	2003
11	The Story of the Weeping Camel	441,489	19	UGC	9-Jul	2004
12	Capturing the Friedmans	388,238	25	TARTAN	9-Apr	2004
13	The Corporation	290,873	20	METRODOME	29-Oct	2004
14	Microcosmos	260,235	18	PATHE LTD.	16-May	1997
15	Lost in La Mancha	233,383	10	OPTIMUM	2-Aug	2002
16	My Architect	198,950	10	TARTAN	13-Aug	2004
17	The Fog of War	178,887	7	SONY	2-Apr	2004
18	Kurt and Courtney	161,796	6	DOWNTOWN	3-Jul	1998
19	Elvis: That's the Way it Is	124,179	21	BLUE DOLPHIN	16-Mar	2001
20	The Filth and the Fury	117,282	5	FILM FOUR	12-May	2000

UK DVD figures

Title	Label	Total units
In Bed with Madonna	MGM	13,377
When We Were Kings	Universal Pictures	54,593
Buena Vista Social Club	Cinema Club / Film 4	108,732
Bowling for Columbine	Momentum Pictures	184,187
Etre et Avoir	Tartan Video	15,430
Touching the Void	Film 4 / VCI	116,796
Spellbound	Metrodome	6,185
Ghosts of the Abyss	Walt Disney	10,615
Super Size Me	Tartan Video	44,453
Fahrenheit 9/11	Optimum Home Entertainment	161,243

© The official uk charts company 2005. These are the corresponding DVD unit sales of the top ten box office docs.

Chapter Eleven
Short documentaries

Introduction to shorts

Distribution of short documentaries is a distinct field. Be aware that there are not many mechanisms for your short documentary film to bring you any income. However, it's easier to persuade an audience to watch it.

Festivals are a good place for shorts, as they're easy to programme in compilation slots. At the end of this chapter, we list festivals that are exclusively for shorts. Chapter 12, Festivals and markets, which follows, includes festivals that take both long and short-form. Remember that while most festivals separate docs and fiction, at Sundance, shorts are categorised all together, and a documentary has won twice in the last three years: 'Terminal Bar', by Stefan Nadelman (2003) (see the interview with Stefan on page 208 below), and 'Family Portrait', by Patricia Riggen (2005).

Festivals expose your film to an ever-expanding network of audiences, consisting of other festival programmers, cinema programmers and distributors, as well as normal audiences. So although a short doc is unlikely to earn you large sums, it can have a very useful, slow-burning life touring the world and pulling interested parties into your orbit. It also works as a useful calling card, in that it takes a busy industry person less time to watch a five-minute short on DVD or via your site, than to sit through your 'Sorrow and the Pity'.

A notable aspect of the shorts world is that, in selecting and appreciating content, it can often be more innovative and less genre-bound than the features world. And short documentaries can be the place for formal and stylistic innovation. 'Snack and Drink', by Bob Sabiston and Tommy Palotta, used the technique of Rotoscoping in 1999, two years before Richard Linklater's feature drama 'Waking Life' (for which Sabiston was animation director) did the same, while Channel 4's strand The Slot (now Three Minute Wonders) gave the opportunity for producer Andy Glynne to experiment with animation accompanying real-life spoken testimony in his Animated Minds series in 2003.

The distribution outlets listed below are for the most part not doc-specific. They might include very few docs, but this is often because of lack of opportunity, not a policy decision. With non-theatrical, more and more opportunities are opening up for short docs on the Internet. Mostly there's no profit in this, but, again, it increases exposure. And DVD is a good format for collections. Cinema16 (www.cinema16.co.uk) hasn't yet included docs, but the principle is there.

Short docs are better placed than features to take advantage of the technological advances that are integrating film-watching into all niches of our lives. In June 2005, for example, the Rolling Stock film competition, run by Channel 4's Ideas Factory website for the creative industries, put short films into trains on the Midland Mainline network, while mobile phone companies are jostling to find the best delivery methods and content for short films.

The plain old internet has room for docs. There are sites to which you can upload or physically post in your film, and having a film online changes the distribution model: once it's there, any number of people, anywhere, can see it. There are competitions, such as the Ten Seconds Film Competition (www.tensecondfilms.com), for freely uploading a digital video of ten seconds. Voting by site visitors, then a panel, resulted in prizes of $1,000, $500 and $250. The competition is scheduled to run again.

The problem that comes hand in hand with exponentially expanding outlets is discernment: if everyone's short doc is on the web, how can a viewer with limited eyes and viewing time know that yours is the high quality doc that they really need to see? In the old-fashioned world, marketing and onside journalists were a key to this, and word of mouth, but online, there's more room for viral transmission (like word of mouth, but quicker and with a much larger ambit), and for peer-rating.

And in an very old-fashioned manner, a cinema might screen your short doc. One tip for this is to keep an eye on the Film Distributors' Association site www.launchingfilms.com to see whether in the months ahead there is a feature to be released that your short doc would go fantastically well with. Contact the cinema programmer and make the case that the audience's pleasure will be positively enhanced by the inclusion of your short before the feature. Nilesh Patel managed this with his short film 'A Love Supreme', which screened before the feature at several Picturehouse cinemas in 2002.

Short documentaries are hard to do well, but they can be worth it.

Stuart Bamforth works as a hired gun documentary director. But he's built up a successful oeuvre of independent short documentaries, including 'Kalbe's World' (2003), about a feisty young man in East London, 'Child of Bethlehem' (2004), about children in the Occupied Territories, and 'Tardis' (2004).

"With 'Kalbe's World', I funded it myself, and for distribution I just entered it into festivals. It won the audience vote at Raindance East, and a festival in Poland took it as well. I was quite new to the festival scene then, and was a bit disappointed that the film didn't travel well. The subject – this young British Asian guy in East London – works really well for people who recognise that environment and sense of humour, but it's hard to translate for foreign audiences. Sheffield turned it down, which was a major disappointment, especially as we got feedback that quite a few of the shorts that were accepted weren't as good. I thought of sending it to all the US festivals, but thought there wasn't much point at thirty-five pounds a time. If there were more festivals like Sheffield, though, I'd send it to all of them. What would I like from a festival ideally? That you don't have to pay, that the forms are clear and they let you know promptly; that if you did get in, they get you to participate with Q&As and so on, do your travel and accommodation and look after you; and I'd like there to be industry and the public watching, so you get exposure.

'Child of Bethlehem' came together because between TV and film commitments I do film workshops with kids, normally in the UK, but a colleague had a trip to Palestine planned, to run some video workshops with children there. So working with a Scottish charity called Tyger Tyger, there were four of us who spent a year or so fundraising. We got money from UNESCO, from the playwright David Hare, from collections at anti-war marches, all going towards running these workshops with the children. We went there in 2003. We had some troubles: the original rushes were confiscated by the Israeli authorities, and we spent a long time copying and retrieving them, and so on. But in the end it was fine, and Tower Hamlets Film Fund gave us the money to finish, which we did by editing the five vignettes made by the kids into one twenty minute film. That showed at Raindance East in 2005, and we did a private screening at The Other Cinema just before it closed in November 2004, which cost us £200 for the half hour slot. It won Best Documentary at Real to Reel in Glasgow, and was nominated for Best Editing too, which was great. It was in Blowing Up, the Clerkenwell Film and Video Festival, in Summer 2004, and the London Socialist Film Club screened it sort of by accident. They had a VHS viewing tape and when something in their programme fell through they put in our film at the very last minute. I sent it to the Human Rights Watch festival in New York as well, but haven't heard. It goes in dribs and drabs, with shorts. People get to hear about it, or they see it and pick up on it and it gradually goes on.

Then in 2004 the mobile phone company O2 approached me and my collaborator Rayna Nadeem. They were funding a project called Changing Voices, by commissioning four five-minute films, at £5,000 each, and although the other three were fiction, we made a short doc called 'The Tardis'. Each film was meant to feature a phone and picture messaging. They promised to put the four films into Bollywood cinemas as part of the trailers, and that worked, with the Cineworld chain, although another plan to get the short into all the indie cinemas fell through.

While I have enjoyed making shorts, I find it immensely tiresome trying to secure distribution. Perhaps I am being naive, but I feel that as a filmmaker I should have to make films, but I am completely useless at pushing the films once they have been made. So many people have seen my films and said, 'You know what, Channel 4 would love that!' It's a nice comment, but I could scream. Whenever I have sent anything to C4 or the Beeb, they always say, 'Great, but it doesn't fit what we are looking for at the moment.' They only seem willing to take stuff if it's a series or part of a pre-decided themed season. I thought that by going ahead and making the films myself I could side-step the whole commissioning process and be in a better position to sell a finished product to the broadcaster. Wrong again!

To be honest I do not feel that my films have had the exposure they deserve. 'Kalbe's World' took more than three years to make. I have had nothing but brilliant feedback on it, but still it has only really been screened less than five times. That's not a great return. In fact, I have never thought of it like that... I must stop making short films forthwith!!"

Distributors: live screenings

Future Shorts

✉ Future Shorts
C/O 10th Planet
68 - 70 Wardour Street
London W1F OTB

🖱 www.futureshorts.co.uk

Future Shorts is a fast-growing organisation on the shorts scene. There's no fee, and no pay for you, but it's a great opportunity to be seen in good company. You can submit a VHS / DVD and the application form that's available on the website.

Fabien Riggall founded exhibitor Future Shorts in June 2003 and it's been growing apace since then. www.futureshorts.com

"We started Future Shorts in June 2003 in a bar in Shepherd's Bush, because I was frustrated because I couldn't find an outlet for getting my film seen. We expanded from there, taking Future Shorts to Brussels, and the idea was formed of turning it into a network.

The idea suddenly turned into something far more ambitious. Now we programme sets of short films that screen in cinemas across the UK, with another 14 joining the network in April and May 2005, and we're already in Lisbon, Moscow and Toulouse, with plans for further international expansion. Eventually we'd like to have a monthly slot in

every independent cinema in the UK. We work in two sorts of venues: the traditional cinema environment, but also in more relaxed, live event venues, such as bars and clubs. We also have a presence at Glastonbury and other bigfestivals. We want use the digital projection networks that are emerging to get into villages, and use mobile cinemas, so film really gets everywhere. We also plan to expand with a project that we call Future Cinema, which involves going into degenerated areas, taking over disused carparks, etc, and getting films shown right down at that level.

We're going into distribution by setting up our own DVD label, so we'll acquire and commission shorts. The exhibition element of our work is non-profit; we negotiate with the rights holders for permission to show the shorts that they hold, as a courtesy screening. Because at the moment, distributors have the rights for all these short films, but they have no

time for organising events in which the films actually get seen; there's very little money in that. We've been running the events, but the more we grow, the more time and effort it takes to fix, with no corresponding rise in income. So we're expanding.

We're trying to get Film Council support, to help us increase our geographical spread for exhibition. This would help us source films more widely, as well. We see what we do as being of benefit both to the films, which get out there and find the audience they deserve, to the audiences, and to the medium of short film as well: the stronger and more extensive the distribution networks are, the more sense there is in making shorts, and making them really well.

At the moment I do all the programming. There's no restriction on what we include; it just has to be a good short film. I try to mix up the programming, so for example I'm currently putting together a short fiction piece, 'Magnetic North' by Miranda Pennell, which is set in Finland, lots of ice and expanses of white, and I'll put a music video from Chris Cunningham next to it. It's about increasing the audiences interest and engagement by putting together a range of things in an interesting way.

If we're successful in expanding properly, I don't want to control all the programming. I want the resources and the system to be in place, then it's there as an institutionalised channel for a whole range of programming to flow through. I'd like there to be this system in place; it goes some way towards making the environment in which, as a filmmaker myself, I'd like to work.

We welcome documentary submissions. See our website (www.futureshorts.com) for the submissions form, then you post in a copy. We will be changing the system so that all submissions come electronically, as MPEGs, which is quicker and much easier for us than unpacking and viewing the thirty or so films a week. But I love docs, and want to find ways of programming more. Ones that we've included in the past have been: Marc Isaacs' 'Lift', which has always gone down a storm with our audiences and been completely inspirational; Sophie Williams' film 'I Expect Joan Feels the Same', that she made when at Bournemouth Film School; and a film called 'Leon' made by Ian Sciacaluga as part of his 'Millennium Kids' series, a story about a slightly obese twelve-year-old. It's really charmingly told.

As for advice to independent shorts filmmakers, I'd say that the vital thing is not budget or format, but to focus on the story. Make it as simple as possible, and remember that you've got an audience at the end; you're not putting film in the camera just for practice. With good actors or characters, and a decent story well written, you're onto a winner."

Shortwave Films

 Shortwave Films
PO BOX 38443
London, SE16 4YT

 0778 869 2137

info@shortwavefilms.co.uk
www.shortwavefilms.co.uk

Shortwave does training, production and equipment hire, and they promote film and video artists through live events and festivals. For submissions, priority is given to digital or low budget productions, all genres welcome. The sound dub should be good and the piece should be under ten minutes in length (but 'exceptions can be made'); send a VHS or DVD viewing copy, SAE and brief synopsis. Screening is on betaSP or miniDV.

Distributors: across media

Shorts International

 Shorts International
25 Beak Street
Soho
London W1F 9RT

020 7734 2277

contactus@shortsinternational.com
www.shortsinternational.com
acquisitions: simon@shortsinternational.com

Shorts International (previously Brit Shorts) provides specialist programming of short films across all mediums, including broadcast, broadband, mobile phone operators and airlines, currently supply over ninety syndication partners worldwide. SI is open to documentaries, but the acquisitions manager points out that from the entire catalogue, documentary shorts form a tiny minority, with only a couple of acquisitions a year, and this number doesn't seem to be growing. But submissions are welcome: initially use the online submissions form and send a VHS. On selecting, the acquisitions department draws up a licensing agreement for exclusive distribution rights over a certain period. Sam Huntley's 'Polish Your Shoes' is one doc distributed by SI, and has had great success on the festival circuit.

Dazzle

 Dazzle
388 Old Street
London
EC1V 9LT

✆ 020 77397716

✍ studio@dazzlefilms.co.uk
sales@dazzlefilms.co.uk
www.dazzlefilms.co.uk

onedotzero

info@onedotzero.com

onedotzero holds a catalogue of short films and animation for worldwide distributino across all platforms. New films are considered for representation at any time, provided they fit the brief of 'new, original digital moving image of exceptional quality.'

Short Circuit Films

www.shortcircuitfilms.com

Short Circuit Films does not accept submissions but it tours the UKFC Digital Shorts winners (see Chapter 3, Nationwide Public Funding).

Distributors: non-theatrical, non-paying

Film Network

www.bbc.co.uk/dna/filmnetwork/

The Film Network is a BBC site, trialled between February and June 2005. It's meant to be a showcase for short films and profiles of the filmmakers, plus the site allows site users to comment on the films, exchange ideas and access advice sections. There's editorial control over what goes onto the site. The submissions process involves a form, film details, ensuring that rights and clearances are in order, and a hard copy of the film will be needed, preferably in digibeta. During the period for which an accepted film is licensed, the BBC has a non-exclusive right to make your film available through streaming technology and by way of download. After downloading, films self-destruct from the user's computer after a month. Once a film is selected, the site allows for rating by viewers, and encourages feedback. The Film Network is a project in development, but they plan to advance to enabling full-screen viewing quality, to having showcases of short film highlights from major UK film festivals, and to surgeries, how-tos and feedback on films from industry professionals.

Video Nation

www.bbc.co.uk/videonation

Video Nation was a very popular BBC initiative begun in 1993 in England and Wales. Contributors were given a Hi-8 camera for a year, during which time they filmed their everyday lives. Over ten thousand tapes were shot and submitted, from which about 1,300 were edited and screened on TV. The format really took off, and to the regular versions were added themed series such as African Shorts, Bitesize Britain (on food), and others. Viedo Nation came off-air in 2000, but the BFI began archiving all the material, and the series migrated to the Internet, where several hundred of the shorts remain for streamed viewing, and where the collection grows.

Video Nation isn't pitched at filmmakers but at normal people. The point is 'to reflect everyday life across the UK in all its rich diversity'. The production team gives training and advice on how to use the camcorder, and they do the editing, although the filmmaker can suggest changes, and has full control to decline that the film be shown at all. Video Nation is an early example of expanding the remit of documentary film by increasing access to the means of production and by assisting in distribution. And some of the short films aren't at all bad.

And there are various websites, including:

www.cinemabank.co.uk	Uploading costs £2 – 3 / month
www.ifilm.com	Films of under 45 minutes can be made available on the website for $75 for three months. Hard copy is needed, not self-uploading.
www.making-short-films.com	has a full listing of these and what they call 'online film festivals'.

Taking a different business model and cultural stance, there are organisations like www.ourmedia.org, which offer to hold any media for anybody, for free, forever, in return for the material being accessible for public viewing and use.

FourDocs

Later in summer 2005, Channel 4 will launch FourDocs, a broadband documentary channel that celebrates all aspects of the documentary genre.

Emily Renshaw-Smith, FourDocs producer, explains what it's all about:

"FourDocs is the result of a collaboration between More 4, Channel 4's free-to-air digital channel which launches in the autumn, Channel 4 New Media and Magic Lantern productions, a technology and production company.

Designed as an inspirational resource for groups and individuals interested in documentary, a key feature of the channel will be the ability for users to upload or download four-minute documentaries. Anyone with a story to tell will be able to submit their own film to FourDocs; all we ask is that it is four minutes long and complies with Channel 4's legal and technical standards. The upload process includes satisfying us that you've adhered to our legal guidelines with regard to copyright, libel, defamation, criminal behaviour, contributor consents, fairness and privacy and so on. The aim is for this upload process to be as simple as possible while ensuring your film has followed good filmmaking practice.

Once your film is uploaded, anyone using the site can watch it. The uploaded films are categorised in different ways: you can watch the most viewed, the most recently submitted, or the films with the highest ratings from viewers. In this way the best films will automatically rise to the top, further encouraging viewers to go away and film their own short-form documentary. If you wish, you can allow other people to download your film onto their own PCs. Under the new Creative Commons licences (www.creativecommons.org), you can also choose to allow people certain uses of your work without having to seek copyright clearances. For example, you could allow another viewer to use aspects of your work, but specify that this cannot be for commercial use. You can create your own FourDocs profile where you can keep track of uploaded films, reviews you have written and bookmark content from elsewhere on FourDocs. You can also create your own playlists of your favourite films a bit like you can with tracks on i-tunes. We will suggest monthly themes that you might like to make a film about for a special feature. There will be a blog with FourDocs news, and links through to the Channel 4 forum for discussion.

FourDocs will be curated with an emphasis on quality storytelling and technical proficiency. For this reason we are putting a lot of resources into advice and education. FourDocs Guides will provide advice on all aspects of filmmaking and there will be a moderated clinic to answer your questions. We are working with various partners on an archive of documentary films that will give you a sense of the history and progression of the documentary genre. Some of the films will have detailed commentaries like you might find on a DVD. We would hope to keep adding to the archive and to create seasons of films, depending on how many we can clear for viewing online.

And we will also have a rushes archive of free, already cleared material that can be downloaded and used by anyone making a film. Some we'll shoot ourselves, but we hope it will develop as more filmmakers donate material they've shot but don't need, in the spirit of collaboration and open access.

FourDocs will represent the democratisation of documentary filmmaking. We want everyone to feel they can take part, not just those already involved in the filmmaking world. Consequently we'll be targeting charities, community groups, schools and so on, especially outside of London, trying to get more people making films so FourDocs will give a diverse picture of life in the UK. It will also provide a space for new talent to experiment and showcase their work in a way that might not be open to them through terrestrial broadcast."

Festivals exclusively for short films

Clear the rights for any music or footage that you use in the film. In the rarest of occasions, a festival will agree to show your film without the rights fully cleared IF you have sought approval from the rights-holder and they have quoted you a price for eventual rights purchase and agreed that at this stage in the film's genesis you may show a cut using the music. This is all quite specific; in any other cases, you MUST have obtained the rights.

'Oscars-listed' means that films that have been in this festival become eligible for the Short Films category of the Academy Awards.

Bilbao International Festival of Documentary and Short Film

✉ Colón de Larreátegui no. 37, 4° dcha.
48009 BILBAO,
Spain

✆ +34.94 424 86 98

✉ info@zinebi.com
www.zinebi.com

Dates: 21st-26th Nov 2005

Deadline: September 1st 2005
Rules: under 45 minutes, completed since Jan 2004
Fees: none
Prizes: top prize of €6,000; many other categories

In 2004, there were 650 submissions of documentaries and 1,218 fiction. Ninety-four films were from the UK, with entries from throughout Asia, the Americas and Europe. The 2003 Gold Mikeldi prize of €3,000 for best documentary went to 'Kawah Ijen' ('The Solitary Crater', 2003, 20 mins) by Philip Mulroy, UK, a graduate of the NFTS. Oscars-listed.

Brief Encounters

✉ Watershed Media Centre
1 Canon's Road, Harbourside
Bristol BS1 5TX
UK

✆ 0117 915 0185

 info@brief-encounters.org.uk
www.brief-encounters.org.uk

Dates: 23rd –27th November 2005
Deadline: 10th June
Rules: 35mm, 16mm, Beta SP (PAL), DigiBeta, DVD; under 30 minutes, produced in preceding two years
Fees: none
Prizes: various

The UK's primary shorts festival. Welcomes docs in the general submissions but no separate strands. Also Animated Encounters takes place in April.

DepicT!

✉ (part of Brief Encounters)
Watershed Media Centre
1 Canon's Road
Bristol, BS1 5TX

 lucy.jefferies@brief-encounters.org.uk
www.depict.org

This competition invites new filmmakers to make a micro-movie of under 90 seconds. Films can be generated using any medium (eg. sequenced stills, digital, video, film) and must be submitted as uncompressed DV Pal encoded video (Quicktime). Short listed films will be promoted online, published on a DVD and screened at the Brief Encounters Bristol International Short Film Festival. A panel of distinguished industry professionals will select a winning film in each category. Their brief is to uncover distinctive voices – originality, style, clarity of idea and impact of idea. Emerging filmmakers from anywhere in the world may apply and £3,000 will be awarded to each winner. There is an annual September deadline for submissions.

Clermont-Ferrand International Short Film Festival

✉ (Sauve Qui Peut le Court Metrage)
6 Place Michel-de-l'Hospital
63058 Clermont-Ferrand cedex 1, FRANCE

☎ +33 473 91 65 73

🖰 info@clermont-filmfest.com
www.clermont-filmfest.com

2005 dates: 28th Jan – 5th Feb
Deadline: for 2005 fest, was October 2004
Rules: on 16mm, 35mm, digibeta; under 40 minutes, completed in prior two years
Fees: none
Prizes: largest €4,000

The largest shorts festival in the world. Various strands; the international competition includes roughly 80 films. In 2005 there were 49 docs submitted from the UK. 209 films of all genres were submitted, of which 12 were accepted. In 2004, British submissions included 'Across the Waters' (2004, 28', digibeta), by Sana Bilgrami, Scotland.

Market: In 2004, 4,015 competition entries resulted in 173 selected for competition, 1,615 entered into the Clermont-Ferrand Short Film Market, the main shorts market, with buyers mainly from France and Europe.

Oscars-listed.

Cracow International Festival of Short Films

✉ Cracow Film Foundation
ul. Pychowicka 7
30-364 Krakow
Poland

☎ +48 12 267 13 55

🖰 festiwal@apollofilm.pl
www.cracowfilmfestival.pl

✉ Festival Office
Kino KIJÓW
Al. Krasińskiego 34
30-101 Kraków

☎ +48 12/ 422 50 15, 12/ 433 74 00

🖰 festiwal@apollofilm.pl
www.cracowfilmfestival.pl

2005 dates: 31st May- 5th June 2005
Deadline: 31st January 2005
Rules: under 60 minutes, completed after Jan 2004
Fees: none
Prizes: Polish zloty 20,000 top prize
1,300 submissions in 2005.

In 2004 the Silver Dragon prize of 10,000 zloty was won by British Vivienne Jones for 'The House' (2003, 8'), an animation / live action film about a group of women with mental health problems.

Oscars-listed.

International Short Film Festival Hamburg

 Int. KurzFilmFestival Hamburg
Friedensallee 7
D-22765 Hamburg
Germany

📞 +49 40 39 10 63 23

✉ festival@shortfilm.com
http://www.shortfilm.com

Dates: 8th – 13th June 2005
Deadline: February / April
Rules: all formats, under 20 minutes
Fees: none
Prizes: International Competition major award €2,500; NoBudget award ("the independent realisation of an idea/concept with a small budget, but a big dose of enthusiasm and imagination") €1,500 and €1,250 prizes; Three-Minute Quickie award for up-to-three minute film on annual topic, this year is soccer, €500. NoBudget prize 2004 to 'Cultural Quarter' (2003, 10', Betacam), a doc by Mike Stubbs, England, on daily urban reality in an unspecified English suburb.

Oberhausen International Short Film Festival

✉ Internationale Kurzfilmtage Oberhausen gGmbH,
Grillostrasse 34
D-46045 Oberhausen
Germany

📞 +49 (0) 20 88 25 26 52

✉ info@kurzfilmtage.de
www.kurzfilmtage.de

2005 dates: 5th-10th May
Deadlines: entry window is September to mid-January
Rules: screening formats Super 8, 16mm and 35mm, Beta SP/PAL, S-VHS, DV and DVCAM; under 35

minutes, completed within previous 24 months
Fees: none
Prizes: €23,000 is the largest

Strong arts slant, a favourite of Werner Herzog. Every year the festival shows some 450 films and videos in about 60 programmes. About 150 of these are screened in the competitions, the others in the special programmes. The festival offers to purchase a selection of films each year to distribute non-commercially to museums, festivals, Goethe Institutes, etc. worldwide, as single films and curated into programmes.

In 2004, Special Mention of the International Jury went to 'Three Poems' by Spoon Jackson (Sweden, 2003 14', 35 mm) by Michel Wenzer, which came later in the year to Sheffield . In 2003, the Prize of the Ministry of Urban Development and Housing, Culture and Sport of NRW went to Marc Isaacs' 'Lift' (Great Britain 2001 25', Beta SP).

Market: All films submitted to the festival are included in the market (around 5000 in 2004), where they can be viewed on VHS and are included in the extensive catalogue, which appears in both hard copy (free to participating industry professionals; 12 euros to the public) and online. The online catalogue now stands at over 29,000 short films. The market has, with Clermont-Ferrand, a very high reputation with buyers, consisting of distributors, TV buyers, festival organisers and others from Australia, France, the USA, Austria, Sweden and many other countries purchasing on average about 200 films a year. Arte and 3sat are media partners to the festival and purchase films from the festival competition programs each year.

Oscars-listed.

Kinofilm: Manchester International Short Film Festival

Dates: 1st – 10th November 2005
Deadline: 16th June
Fees: £5
Prizes: awards in eight categories
Rules: under 20 minutes, produced within the last 18 months.

Resfest

 RESFEST Digital Film Festival
601 West 26th Street
11th Floor
New York, NY 10001
USA

 +1 212 320 3750

www.resfest.com

Dates: September to December
Deadlines and fees: 15th April 2005 fee $20; 13th May 2005 fee $25
Prizes: Audience Choice Awards
Rules: any format: film, analog/digital video or entirely on a computer; under 60 minutes, produced within the last two years.
A global touring festival (to over 30 cities including New York, San Francisco, Los Angeles, Tokyo, London, Sheffield, São Paulo, Melbourne and Cape Town) exploring the dynamic interplay of film, art,

music and design. A showcase of the best short experimental and innovative work, which combines screenings, live music events, parties, panel discussions and technology demonstrations. Other exhibition opportunities such as DVD and Internet release are possible. The cutting edge of short visual creative work touring the world, Resfest is good to be included in, with considerable attention from professionals in the creative fields.

credit: Darrin Noble

Over the course of a year Stefan Nadelman spent his free time making a film out of the thousands of photos his father had taken in the New York bar where he worked. Through flash animation, voice-over, music and newspaper articles, 'Terminal Bar' tells the soulful story of one of the roughest bars in New York and its patrons. 'Terminal Bar' won the jury prize for short film at the Sundance film festival, before going on to scoop a host of other awards on the festival circuit.

"The distribution just sort of fell in my lap; I wasn't really looking for it. RES Media Group aim to showcase the best of new film, music, art, design and technology through their magazine, the digital festival they run and DVDs. John at RES is a friend of mine and he said, 'We're going to put your film on the Best of RESfest DVD,' and I was like, 'OK so I'm going to be on a DVD,' and I thought that was it. On the back of that it got into a bunch of festivals. Sundance was the flood gates. After showing there all the other festivals started inviting me, because they read the competition results and if they haven't seen the film they'll start requesting it and it sort of snowballs from there.

At these festivals I began seeing this logo - Hypnotic - at the beginning of a lot of the short films. I learnt that they were a distributor and that sort of stuck in my head. Then at Aspen film festival I ran into Anna Lobell who works for Hypnotic, so I approached her and asked her if she'd seen 'Terminal Bar' and if she'd like to distribute it. She said, 'Well, I'll take a look at it, but we usually don't do documentaries,' and she was a little sceptical. Then I guess she saw it and found out the buzz, and after she went back to LA she contacted me and she was like, 'Yeah, let's work something out,' and I signed with them. So far they have secured distribution with the Sundance Channel, Corus Entertainment, HBO Latin America, Sky Italia (I think they show it on aeroplanes), Kunstkanaal Arts channel (a Dutch channel), RTV Spain; that's it so far, but it's an ongoing thing.

I managed to retain all the rights. Hypnotic take a cut and I don't have to pay anyone else except my Dad, but you know he's not expecting anything really. I've realised that you can't really make that much money. I haven't broken even from it because I spent around $13,000 for the film prints. I had four prints made and RES paid $6,000 towards that because John had agreed that if the film got into Sundance he'd help pay for a print, and of course they got their logo at the end of the film. Next time around I'll probably try to not do film prints and try to get it projected digitally or on high definition instead.

Maybe when Hypnotic gives me my first payment for the TV sales and RES pay me for the DVD sales I'll start seeing a little bit of money, but I have no idea how much money could come out of that. The way it works with the DVD is that there's a number of short films on it and so the percentage of the profits we'll get is based on time, so if mine's 22 minutes then I'm going to get more money than someone with a film of five minutes."

Rushes Soho Shorts Festival

✉ PO Box 2868
London W1A 5QL
UK

☎ 020 7851 6207

🖱 www.sohoshorts.com

Dates: 30th July - 5th August 2005
Rules: a VHS and Beta of each film required with submission. Up to twelve minutes, produced during the twelve months to 6th May 2005.
Prizes: various awards
Fees: none

Free daily screenings of all short-listed films in bars, cafes and cinemas throughout the West End. Three top short-listed winners in each of five categories are invited to a final judging session.

Tampere International Short Film Festival

✉ Tampere Film Festival
PO Box 305
33101 Tampere
Finland

☎ +358 33 146 6149

🖱 office@tamperefilmfestival.fi
www.tamperefilmfestival.fi

Dates: 8th –12th March 2006
Deadline: 1st December
Rules: 35mm, 16mm, Beta SP, DigiBeta, DVD, under 30 minutes.
Fees: none
Prizes: glory and cash

In 2005 The International Competition included 35 short films from 78 countries, selected from the 2,300 entries, and 800 guests, of whom 200 were non-Finnish. British entries included Andy Glynne's 'That Lightbulb Thing' and John Smith's 'Throwing Stones'; well-known United States documentary-maker Jay Rosenblatt was included with 'Phantom Limb'.

Market: mainly for Nordic, Baltic and European buyers, a free-entrance market for all submitted films and others, plus catalogue.

Oscars-listed

Other shorts festivals

Flickerfest, Australia
www.flickerfest.com.au

Vila do Conde International Short Film Festival
www.curtasmetragens.pt   2nd-10th July 2005

Vienna Independent Shorts Festival
www.shortfilmcompetition.at   July, for filmmakers aged under 35

Ohne Kohle (NO BUDGET) Independent VideoFilmfestival, Vienna
www.ohnekohle.net   July

Short Cuts Cologne
www.short-cuts-cologne.de   30th Nov-4th Dec 2005

Uppsala International Short Film Festival
www.shortfilmfestival.com   24th-30th October 2005

and

www.making-short-films.com

Chapter Twelve
Festivals and markets

Festivals overview

"You have a really nice time, they look after you, and you get to meet other filmmakers. The only sort of financial gain is either through distribution or prize money. 'Lift' was made for £40,000 and I've probably earned £10,000 in prize money – don't tell the tax man!" – Marc Isaacs

What are festivals for?

Festivals are a very important part of the picture for all filmmakers, documentary makers included. It's really good to get around the festivals, whether you have a film entered or to watch other people's work, get a broader sense of what's going on outside of your sphere of expertise and to meet possible future collaborators and funders. They are also enormous fun.

Director Arthur Howes: *"The whole film festival circuit is the only gratification for everything in the end because then you spend your year travelling and having a good time. Festivals are fundamental to getting your work seen, to getting distribution and also fundamental to being part of a community of all these filmmakers. Suddenly you meet all these people who are in the same boat as you and you're part of an international world club of people who all struggle to make films. In England you don't, well I don't meet other...I'm in contact with a few filmmakers but here everybody's very bound to TV. It seems that people in the UK have not managed to break away from the hold that television has."*

Festivals are effective places to get your film noticed and either sold or picked up by a sales agent. Most independent documentaries get accepted to festivals before they have any distribution deals made (this is particularly true of Sundance as producers know that if the film does well there and wins an award the value of the film will be enhanced) and if you get accepted by one of the majors you will probably be able to get a sales agent to help you sell it. The festival is often the place where your film will not only be judged by audiences and critics for the first time but also by the marketplace, which is a rather different thing. Festivals are often a strange mixture of both these elements or, as the designer of the Shooting People logo says; "Looks like art, smells like commerce".

Daniela Zanzotto: *"In 1997 I decided to take a break from my studies to try and make a film, just me and my camera. It was only going to be a 20-minute film that I was planning to finish in a summer. But I ended up spending a year and a half doing it and making a 52-minute film, 'If the Walls Could Speak'. It was self-funded (through my parents mostly).*
The festival circuit was crucial for its exposure. I managed to make two television sales (to France and Switzerland) and get a sales agent on board (Jane Balfour Films) because of them. It was screened at about fifteen festivals worldwide, a combination of documentary and general film festivals. And it won a couple of awards. I would never have been able to get funding for a first film with no filmmaking experience, but that film together with what it achieved allowed me to get funding for my second film, 'Kissed by Angels'.
I'd started filming this with no funding. I had no idea what kind of film I'd make with the material I was filming, and only after a funding opportunity came up for a 10-minute short did I decide to go for that. It was arts funding from Yorkshire Arts, and then I got regional funding from the Yorkshire Media Production Agency, and the rest from my parents, again. At the time I was living in Sheffield and that's where I shot the doc, which made me eligible for the regional funding. The exposure from the festival circuit was really good. The UK premier was at the Sheffield International Doc fest and it went to about 25 festivals worldwide, and got three awards. I made a sale to the Sundance doc channel in the US partly because of the two awards I got in the US. And the distribution company Britshorts in the UK contacted me after I won an award at the Kinofilm (Manchester) short film festival. It was, I think, their first short doc and they weren't quite sure how it would work. The sale to Channel 4 took about a year. I'd sent it in a first time and hadn't heard back. Sometime later I found out about the strand 'Outside' and thought it might fit in there. In the meantime Shooting People and Britshorts had organised a screening of shorts with a discussion on distributing short films. So I sent it to Channel 4 again, and this time they went for it."

At their best, festivals can offer financial rewards in terms of your film being purchased, in the form of prize money, or in winning you future commissions. They allow you to show your film to commissioning editors, distributors, journalists and other industry professionals, and to the public, in a way that lets you see how real audiences are reacting to your work. Festivals are a place to meet possible future collaborators, and your filmmaking peers. Sophie Fiennes, for example, met a co-funder for 'Hoover Street Revival' while she was at the IDFA pitching forum, and spotted her editor while watching films at the same festival. You can.

"Festivals are really important for the contacts, the opportunities. With 'McLibel', I was in Australia for a conference and just because I was there I went to the Sydney Women's Film Festival, and met this woman who was doing festival PR. She was brilliant and offered to do PR for me generally. She got me onto all these chat shows on ABC and they showed three minutes of the film. Distributors in the UK saw that and bought TV rights for the world and ended up selling it to about nine countries." – Franny Armstrong

"Festivals are fundamental to getting your work seen, to getting distribution and also fundamental to being part of a community of all these filmmakers. Suddenly you meet all these people who are in the same boat as you and you're part of an international world club of people who all struggle to make films." – Arthur Howes

Some festivals have a separate film market attached (like IDFA) and others just attract a lot of buyers who gather to see what's new (like Sundance). If you think your film has potential, then you should think carefully about which festival will be the best place to send it, and to what part of the festival. Entering your film into IDFA, for example, is not the same as entering it for the Docs for Sale catalogue. Each festival has its own tastes and preferences, your film may be accepted by one but not by another, and different festivals have different things to offer your film. Some will get you noticed by American distributors, for example, and others by European funders. Many experienced filmmakers plan their production schedule around the annual festival calendar to make sure their film will be finished in time to submit it to their first-choice festival.

The costs of festivals

Festivals cost money – some (Filmstock, Sundance, Raindance) charge an entry fee and not every festival pays for any or all of the costs if your film is selected. There is also the cost of making more than one master or film print and postage and shipping. What this means is that you must add festival costs to your original budget in order for you to exploit your film properly. This is likely to costs you a couple of thousand at an absolute minimum.

It can also literally be a full time job for you or an assistant to enter your film to festivals, handling the acceptances, organising the movement of master tapes and prints between them. The tip, by the way, is to get each festival to ship your master to the next festival as they usually only pay for one shipment, which is fine if you can arrange for your film to hop from festival to festival. You need to be damn organised or you will be continually missing festival entry deadlines and getting confused about where on their world tour your masters are.

Marc Isaacs: *"I would never pay to put my film in a festival unless I knew what the festival was. A lot of them ask for money and I'm really sceptical about that. With some festivals that have asked me for my films, and there's a fee, I have asked them to waive the fee and they've agreed. Some festivals I have paid for but they're the ones where I want the film to be shown, that are important for other reasons."*

Choosing which festivals to enter

Basically, you enter the best European and North American festivals first and work your way down and round through all the other smaller and further-flung festivals. A good film can spend two-to-three years on the festival circuit until it has exhausted all its possibilities and invitations. Too many filmmakers give up after a year or so because they are sick of the entry forms and get absorbed in a new project, but it is definitely worth taking the whole process to its final conclusion because you never know who will see the film at a smaller, more local festival that might prove invaluable to your career. It is also easy to make the mistake of thinking, 'Well, I never heard of that festival,' before checking it out and realising it has a huge cash prize or an amazingly high-profile jury. There are festivals that are just for films that have already been on television (Montreux, Banff), but apart from these, most require no previous transmission.

The big international festivals all prefer a world premier, so if you think your film is worth a pop, your first job is deciding which of these to go for. Most of the big festivals will accept not being a world premier if they like your film a lot, but they MUST be a regional (or in some cases national) premier. This means Sundance will not take anything that has played in North America, Cannes won't touch anything that has played outside its country of origin, Berlin is compatible with Sundance but not with Venice, the London and Edinburgh Festivals need to be the first national screening, so you have to choose which of those two you want (or go for Edinburgh in August and then try London in November if you don't get in).

Sirkka Moeller, programmer of the Sheffield International Documentary Festival, says, *"Once you've started to receive recognition for your film, as in any business, things grow from there. A valuable point about your film is the question of where it screened first. The larger festivals have strict stipulations about admissibility of films, depending on where else they've been seen, so think carefully about this. If you can, set the agenda by premiering your film prestigiously. If you're lucky enough to have a choice between Berlin and OxDox, for example, make sure you keep your sense of proportion and choose the right place to premier."*

If your film plays at one of the bigger festivals, reps from the smaller ones all over the world will watch your film there and start approaching you and asking for your film. The more festivals your film plays, the more requests you get and it becomes a job of sorting out which you want, or whether there is a bigger festival in that country for which you are still eligible. There are now so many festivals that many clash and then you need to decide whether to get multiple prints or masters and of course whether to attend yourself or send the film on its own.

The 'big three' film festivals - in Cannes, Venice and Berlin - include documentary but are not restricted to it. Sundance is an influential starting-point for independent films and filmmakers.

Rodrigo Vazquez' 'Condor: Axis of Evil' was included in Cannes 2003. *"First nobody wanted to make the film, then I got this small commission and we worked really hard to make the best of it. Then the commissioning editor said it was not up to scratch and then we got it into Cannes and suddenly it's the best film ever. The film went everywhere, it was sold to different countries and shown in cinemas in Paris. So it just goes to show that nobody knows anything."*

Lucy Walker's 'In the Devil's Playground' screened at Sundance in 2002. *" It's not just a launching pad for the film; it's also a real boost to your career and life in general. The way that they treat their filmmakers is wonderful in terms of introducing you to other filmmakers and giving you all kinds of support through the process and introducing you to resources like their labs and funds. Screening the film at Sundance has opened more doors for me than I could ever have imagined."*

The largest international festivals dedicated to documentary are IDFA in Amsterdam, and HotDocs in Toronto. Both of these have documentary markets attached, and pitching forums. In the UK, the Sheffield International Documentary Festival is the primary documentary festival, while the Edinburgh and London film festivals both incorporate documentary.

"Amsterdam was great; we got some sales and we met some very good people in case we ever did do documentary in a co-production way. But basically the first year you do the major festivals and the prize-givers, the second year you give the film to anyone that wants it." – Cairo Cannon

If your film doesn't get into a major festival, there is still plenty of advantage to working the smaller festival route, so don't be put off. There are hundreds of smaller festivals that accept documentary film or that are dedicated to it. Some are open simply to 'documentary', others have specific remits and interests: documentary and animation; children's documentary; anthropological documentary; human rights; wildlife.

Do some searching to find the ones that look right for your film – we have listed some of them at the end of this section. Remember that short films are often easier for a programmer to place, and many shorts festivals accept documentaries; see Chapter 11, Short docs, for more on this and for listings.

Festival guides

Festivals and their deadlines come and go; to make sure you're up to date, the internet is best. There's no one definitive guide, but with a mix of these resources, you can keep abreast of the fests.

www.britfilms.com/festivals	British Council online guide to festivals; hard copies also available.
www.screendaily.com	go via this site to Screen International's searchable festivals calendar
www.filmfestivals.com	a commercial enterprise with extensive listings and free mailing list for updates
www.making-short-films.com	good listings for shorts, online festivals, and festivals whose inclusion makes a film eligible to appear on IMDB
www.idfa.nl	festivals in the month ahead from the website of the big Amsterdam fest
www.creativexport.co.uk	government-funded portal for UK creative industries' export opportunities, searchable for festivals
http://web.docuinter.net	Czech-based Institute of Documentary Film has excellent listings of all sorts, including very thorough Eastern European festivals listings
www.eurofilmfest.org	the 200+ members of the European Coordination of Film Festivals share resources, arrange tours. Searchable database

Film publications such as Showreel (www.showreel.org) list news of festivals in their resources and news sections, and of course, keep an eye out for calls for entry on the Shooting People bulletins.

Submission notes

Make sure you're eligible for the festival. Read what they tell you to do and follow it carefully. The most common requirements are documentation and a VHS viewing copy of the film. Check whether the festival requires this viewing copy in NTSC or PAL format. If the film is accepted, you will usually need to provide a screening copy, on beta or, less frequently, 35mm. This starts to make your costs go up rapidly.

Some film festivals charge for submissions, some don't; do your own cost-benefit analysis. Look out for cheaper fees offered to early submissions and think about using Withoutabox, which arranges money off from some entry fees. If you're entering a little-known or a recently-begun festival that charges a submission fee, do check their reputation and look carefully at the terms on which you're handing over your money.

Check what formats the festival accepts for submission copies and for screening copies. Mostly the format is VHS or DVD, but you don't want your masterpiece screened on VHS.

Making copies of film, postage charges, and the large amount of time and attention that it can demand of you can make entering festivals seem an onerous task. Once you've taken the trouble to apply once, though, it makes it easier to do future submissions.

New electronic submissions systems such as Withoutabox can make the process much easier and cheaper. The basic service is free for filmmakers to join up and submit to festivals, with charges for additional services. www.withoutabox.com.

And when you're there?

Sophie Fiennes: *"At Locarno it screened in a cinema of 2000 people, all producers and distributors from all over, but it was French holiday so I went without having my sales people with me. I was the producer and director and it was very frustrating because you really have to be someone who knows people in these festivals otherwise you just don't know who's who. You're faced with hundreds of people going well done or hello and you don't know who anyone is and you don't get introduced to people. They should have geishas at festivals.*

You also have to be really careful about where you first show. It first showed at Urban World and Sundance and Tribeca both made contact wanting to see it because they'd heard about it. They didn't select it and I think if I'd been able to give either of them the US premiere then I would have had a lot better chance. With Urban World, because we finished the film so near to their time for the festival and I wasn't able to be there it didn't have that kind of birth. So you have to hold back your premier festival, really chose it carefully and when you go you have to go with a mission. Go with someone or know who you're trying to find.

But Edinburgh was great because several other festivals selected it from seeing it in Edinburgh. It's a great festival because they really put effort into helping people network and also you have things like the script factory doing things there. Because it's my own home country I kind of know how to network with the people there. Building those little relationships is really critical. I'm the producer of it but emotionally I'm the director, so you're not so good at selling yourself. It's important to go to festivals – you meet some brilliant people. You build up your network of contacts at festivals and then once you start to do that you know the homes you can go to. You get to know the landscape and the more people who know what you're doing, even if it's just a short, is good.

With a lot of documentary festivals there's always that responsibility of documentary to fulfil a certain social function. And I consider my documentary to be a more kind of experimental film, there's an obliquely provocative element in it, it's very visual and not polemically positioned and its not argued and positioned in a social sense, although it is a film about community. I think there's a certain kind of agenda with festivals like IDFA that they respond to certain kinds of films that are pushing for a certain kind of documentary interpretation. IDFA is a very important festival for anyone doing documentary but I think it's the difference between the generations, a difference between the people making films and the people who are in the position of power to commission them. Their mind set's different, there's a generation gap. I notice that younger people in particular really appreciate 'Hoover Street' because I think its language is reflective of something that young people are interested in seeing and want to make themselves. I feel that with IDFA there's a slightly kind of 70s mentality about documentary."

The big four international film festivals

55th Berlin International Film Festival

✉ Potsdamer Straße 5
D-10785 Berlin
Germany

✆ +49 30 259 20 0
fax: +49 30 259 20 299

✍ info@berlinale.de
www.berlinale.de

Dates: 9th – 19th February 2006, Berlin, Germany
Largest festival, covering everything from invited feature fiction to experimental and first-time shorts. Includes a co-production market and the Berlinale talent campus for filmmakers.

Submission deadline: November 2005 (IFSS Submission Deadline; 2 January 2006)
Fee: €50 to €125
Eligibility: depends on category, but must be produced in 12 months preceding festival and have been screened only in country of origin.
Awards: various categories and awards, all open to documentaries, with the largest cash prize of €25,000.

58th Cannes Film Festival

Festival de Cannes
Association Francaise du Festival International du Film
3, rue Amélie
75007 Paris - France

+33 (0) 1 53 59 61 00
fax: +33 (0)1 53 59 61 10

www.festival-cannes.fr

Dates: 11th – 22nd May 2005, Cannes, France
Ritziest festival, strictly for those within the industry.
Submission deadline: March
Fee: from free to €300
Eligibility: films produced during twelve months preceding the festival, screened only in country of origin, festival premiers, screening on 35mm.
Awards: various categories for submission and awards, both features and shorts. None specifically for documentary, but it's gaining momentum, with Michael Moore's documentary 'Fahrenheit 9/11' winning the Palme d'or (for best feature) in 2004. The Cinefondation category, for film schools, is not open to documentaries.

Cannes is so big and complex that there are various guides on how to make the most of it:
www.cannesguide.com/festival/
www.raindance.co.uk   (does training courses on Cannes)

Venice Film Festival

(62nd Mostra Internazionale d'Arte Cinematografica, part of La Biennale di Venezia, or Venice Biennale)
Ca' Giustinian
San Marco 1364
30124 Venice

+39 041 5218711
fax: +39 041 5227539

www.labiennale.org/en/cinema/

31st August- 10th September 2005, Venice, Italy
High-profile and classy, but open to the public.

Submission deadline: June 2005 (IFSS submission deadline 1st August 2005 - see below)
Fee: €50
Eligibility: 16mm or 35mm, must be of recent production, not screened outside country of origin or in Italy.
Awards: various categories and awards, none of which exclude documentaries.

Sundance 2005 Film Festival

 8857 West Olympic Blvd.
Suite 200, Beverly Hills
CA 90211-3605
USA

 +1 310 360 3605

www.sundance.org

19th – 29th January 2006, Park City, Utah, USA
High-profile festival of independent film. Good for new discoveries, but strong industry attention. Part of the Sundance Foundation.
Submission deadline: various dates in September 2005 (IFSS submission deadline 12 December 2005)
Fee: up to $50, depending on category and promptness
Eligibility: depends on category, but nothing that's been broadcast, including on the web. Not previously shown at more than two other festivals. Feature docs must be over fifty minutes.
Awards: jury and audience awards. US documentary, World Cinema: documentaries, directing, cinematography, freedom of expression, shorts awards.

John Cooper is Head of Programming at the Sundance Film Festival:

"We are a filter for the industry but our role is in exposure. If you have a small film there is hardly a better place to show it to get a bang for your buck. We show so few films, but we put a greater emphasis on documentaries compared to other festivals.

The number of documentaries submitted to the American documentary section has gone up over the years but not as much as you would think, even with the whole digital revolution; they hold at about four hundred a year. You would think everyone was shooting a documentary, and I think they are but also I think they learned that documentaries are a lot harder than people think.

With international docs it's different because Diane Weyermann, Head of the Sundance Documentary Institute, has seen so much of them that she is a huge asset. She doesn't programme but she is a part of the process and we start by seeing what she knows about. We don't get as many international docs submitted, just around two hundred, but in 2005 we start the World documentary award which might cause more people to start submitting.

I have been at Sundance sixteen years, but in the early years you couldn't talk people into going to the documentaries! They'd come and see the feature film but you'd open the door and there would be ten people there. They thought it was academic, they thought it was like church, they thought it was good for them.

If you are going to run a documentary festival then that is one thing but we are running a film festival that has a documentary section, and one of the first things we thought about was what was a good theatrical experience. So we were always looking for documentaries that worked in a cinematic setting and then audiences started to trust what we were doing.

I think the audiences have changed and that they have changed again since 9/11. American audiences were not willing to look at anything bad, were willing to stick their heads on the sand, but more people now are looking for truth, particularly young audiences who are the audiences of tomorrow. I don't see that they look at documentary film so different from a feature film. Their thing is still, 'Does it have subtitles or not?' – that's the next hurdle we have to get over!

It takes so much money to enter into the American consciousness. Even to get an American independent film noticed now when you release it takes five times more money than five years ago. It just costs so much and you have so much competition. You can't buy TV; it's too expensive, but newspaper even is tough. The best thing that has happened is with DVD sales where companies can make profit because they are spending $30 million on advertising now to get $30 million back from the box office. If it wasn't for DVD a lot of these companies would just be pulling back from releasing.

For selecting the docs for Sundance, we have three outside screeners, people we trust who watch all the films and write copy which we start processing, and each selects their favourites. Every film gets watched all the way at least by one person and in part by others. About half go through to the next stage and they get watched by the five of us programmers. My normal day at this time of year, the end of September, is that I get up at 5.30am and I start watching movies and I watch them all day long. We try to get to the point when we are sitting in a room with twenty more films than we need. Our discussions are so loud people come in our room and say, 'Wow, you guys are aggressive with each other,' but we know each other so well. We get really mean with each other and I always make everyone cry at least once. The great thing is that we have a set number, we can only take sixteen, so that's it. But we always have at the end that I hold up the cards with the film names on and let them fall to the floor. It's very dramatic but then at the end we pick up all the boards and go through them one more time to make sure and then we go away for the weekend. And you get to come back on Monday and say, 'I'm not really sure,' and films have come back off the floor to push out another film.

We look for a slate of films and sometimes a film that actually has obvious flaws in it still makes it into the festival if it has something different or special about it. You want a certain representation of things as well – not just subject matter but also stylistically, budget-wise. Like if you don't have one beautiful documentary shot on film you feel kinda weird. We don't get a lot of those anymore and I miss them. I do really like films where they have had a real good cinematographer with them. We get a lot of documentaries on a famous person, a portrait. It's popular and you can get money for that kind of thing but they really have to have something extra. We don't see enough really good political documentary. And I still like personal docs, I'm always a sucker for them and they have a lot of room for new aesthetic choice which can be really fun. Like 'Tarnation' which is some kind of hybrid, I mean, what is that? Is that a doc?

'Super Size Me' didn't win best documentary at Sundance, it won best director. I was surprised at first until I went back and watched it again and saw how clever he is at telling the story, a really good story teller."

Big festivals, good for docs

International Documentary Festival Amsterdam (IDFA)

International Documentary Filmfestival Amsterdam
Kleine-Gartmanplantsoen 10
1017 RR
Amsterdam
The Netherlands.

+31 (0) 20 6273329
Fax +31 (20) 6385388

info@idfa.nl
www.idfa.nl

17th – 27th November 2005, Amsterdam, Netherlands
Europe's largest documentary festival, broad ranging and accessible to filmmakers and audiences. Several categories of entry, plus retrospectives, experimental, themed strands and film-related events. Associated: the Pitching Forum for international television co-financing (see Chapter 6); Docs for Sale market.
Submissions deadline: 5th October 2005
Fee: none
Eligibility: 16mm, 35mm, betaSP, digibeta; films must be produced in the fifteen months preceding programme, and not previously shown in the Netherlands.
Awards: three competition programmes, other awards of cash, the largest of €12,500, and distribution.

Hot Docs Canadian International Documentary Festival

 110 Spadina Ave., Suite 333
Toronto, ON
M5V 2K4

 +1 416-203-2155
Fax: +1 416-203-0446

 www.hotdocs.ca

22nd April – 1st May 2005, Toronto, Canada
The major North American documentary festival, with over 1,400 delegates. With various strands and National Spotlight each year. Includes the Toronto Documentary Forum for pitching to international broadcasters and searching for co-financing (see Chapter 7, North America).
Submissions deadline: late deadline, 14th January 2005
Fee: C$35 – 100
Eligibility: 16mm, 35mm, betaSP; must be a Toronto premier, completed in the year preceding the festival.
Awards: C$20,000 total jury and audience prizes, in categories including features, shorts, international, first film, humanitarian.

Full Frame Documentary Film Festival

 www.fullframefest.org

7th – 10th April 2005, Durham, North Carolina, USA
Founded in 1998, this festival has grown to influential status as the USA's foremost documentary-dedicated festival. It includes new films, archive programmes and seminars. Some free accomodation for in-competition directors is offered.
Submissions deadline: November
Fee: $35 - 55
Eligibility: short docs of under 40 minutes, feature docs of 40 – 180 minutes.
Awards: cash prizes of up to $5,000 for jury, audience, shorts, emerging artist, and a prize for 'filmmakers that lay bare the seeds of war and the mechanisms that create war'. www.fullframefest.org
In 2004 there were 700 submissions, of which around 60 were selected for the main competition. The 2004 Grand Jury Award went to 'The Control Room', dir. Jehane Noujaim while Briton Phil Grabsky won an emerging artist award for 'The Boy Who Plays on the Buddhas of Bamiyan'. In 2005, British entries included Daniele Zanzotto's 'Battaglia' and 'Welcome to the Real World' by Barney Broomfield.

International Film Festival Rotterdam

 P.O. Box 21696
3001 AR Rotterdam
The Netherlands

+31 10 890.90.90
fax : +31 10 890.90.91

www.filmfestivalrotterdam.com

25th January -5th February 2006
Good for sales but also an interesting public programme of events and screenings. There is also the
CineMart annual co-production market, to which around 45 producers are invited to present their work to
potential funders.
Submissions window: June 2005 to 1st October 2005
Fee: none
Eligibility: 16mm, 25mm, betaSP, digibeta, Dvcam; priority to world and international premieres; must not
have been shown in The Netherlands
Awards: for new filmmakers' competition, three prizes of €10,000 and guaranteed TV release

Silverdocs

AFI Silver Theatre and Cultural Center
8633 Colesville Road
Silver Spring, MD 20910
USA

Phone: 301 495 6738
Fax: 301 495 6798

info@SILVERDOCS.com
www.silverdocs.com

14th – 19th June 2005
Set up by AFI (the American Film Institute) and the Discovery Channel.
Submissions window: 21st Oct 2004 - 4th March
Fee: $25 – $50
Eligibility: must not have been broadcast or screened theatrically before the festival; must have been
completed in the year before close of submissions.
Awards: Sterling Award of $5,000 in cash and prizes for a short doc (under 50 minutes), $2,000 for feature,
plus audience and jury awards. In 2004, 'Death in Gaza' directed by James Miller was joint winner of the
Sterling Award, with 'Original Child Bomb', dir. Carey Schonegevel.

Telluride

✉ Telluride Film Festival
379 State Street
Portsmouth, NH 03801

✆ 603 433 9202
Fax: 603 433 9206

🖰 mail@telluridefilmfestival.org
www.telluridefilmfestival.org

Dates: 2nd-5th September 2005
The auteur filmmaker's dream.
Submission window: May 1 - July 15, 2005
Fee: $35 - $95
Eligibility: screening formats 35mm or NTSC digibeta, shorts, long features, any genre
Awards: no prize, the glory is to be accepted into the exclusive screening programme of roughly fifteen shorts and thirty features and to rub shoulders with the crème of international cinema.

Thessaloniki

✉ Thessaloniki International Film Festival
9, _lexandras Avenue
11473 Athens
Greece

✆ +30 210 87 06 000
Fax: +30 210 64 48 143

🖰 newhorizons@filmfestival.gr
www.filmfestival.gr/docfestival

1st-10th April 2005
Films, retrospectives, market aimed at the TV networks of the region, pitching forum, workshops.
Submission deadlines:
Fee: none
Eligibility: docs under and over 45 minutes
Awards: largest cash prize is €12,000
In 2004 an audience award accompanied by a cash prize of €3,000 went to 'The Corporation', dir. Mark Achbar and Jennifer Abbott.

Yamagata International Documentary Film Festival

✉ YIDFF Organizing Committee Office (Yamagata Office)
2-3-25 Hatago-machi
Yamagata-shi
Yamagata-ken 990-8540
Japan

☎ 81-23-624-8368
fax: 81-23-624-9618

🖱 info@yidff.jp
www.city.yamagata.yamagata.jp/yidff/

2005 dates: 7th – 13th October 2005, Yamagata, Japan
Deadlines: 15th December 2004 for works completed by 31st October 2004; 15th April 2005 for works
completed after 1st November 2004.
Fee: none
Eligibility: 16mm, 35mm, video, produced in the two years before the festival and not released or television
in Japan, features only.
Awards: largest prize YEN 3 million, others.
Biennale, odd years. Roughly 15 films selected for the International Competition. YIDFF publishes
the twice-yearly Documentary Box, a journal covering recent trends in making and thinking about
documentaries.

Edinburgh International Film Festival

✉ 88 Lothian Road
Edinburgh
EH3 9BZ

☎ 0131 228 4051

🖱 info@edfilmfest.org.uk
www.edfilmfest.org.uk

17th – 28th August 2005, Edinburgh, Scotland, UK
Begun as a doc festival, roughly twenty percent of the programme is now documentary. Good programming,
open to public but strong focus on the UK film industry. Annual Guide to British Film omits docs but
they are included for screening in the Videotheque. Coincides with the Edinburgh International Television
Festival.
Submissions deadline: 19th April 2005
Fee: £25 to £95
Eligibility: no time limit preceding festival, but must not have had screening or broadcast in Britain.
Awards: range of awards for films of any genre (new directors, short films, best British) plus Grierson
Saltire award for short documentary from new director.

The Times bfi 49th London Film Festival

 London Film Festival
National Film Theatre
South Bank
London
SE1 8XT

✆ 020 7815 1322

🖰 www.lff.org.uk

19th October – 3rd November 2005
Mainly feature documentaries in this festival, which is friendly to general viewing audiences.
Submissions deadline: 15th July 2005
Fee: none
Eligibility: must be UK premier
Awards: various, none specifically for documentary.

OxDox

🖰 www.oxdox.com

21 - 28 October 2005.
Third year of a festival with a good range of films from round the world, archive, training sessions and plenty of directors present for discussion, in 2005 an emphasis on the accession states of the EU. Work in Progress workshop on 22nd – 23rd October.
Submissions deadline: mid-August 2005.

Sheffield International Documentary Festival

✉ International Documentary Festival Sheffield Ltd,
The Workstation
15 Paternoster Row
Sheffield
S1 2BX

✆ 0114 276 5141

🖰 info@sidf.co.uk
www.sidf.co.uk

Dates: 10th – 16th October 2005, Sheffield, UK
Deadline: 1st June
Fee: none
Prizes: only Jerwood First Cuts cash prize for student filmmakers
Rules: 16mm, 35mm, beta; films must be produced during the 20 months preceding. Not required to be premiers, but must not have been broadcast.
A mix of film programming from around the world from established names and newcomers, plus extensive

panel sessions, master classes and retrospectives. A delegate's pass giving access to all these is in the region of £200. No market, but most festival films and some non-accepted submissions can be viewed by delegates on VHS.

Steve Hewlett is the new Festival Chair. Of his aims for the festival, he says,
"Documentary making in the UK is changing. What used to be a largely television-financed (and focussed) business is emerging as something that will be much more recognisable to our colleagues and friends from Europe and the US. In addition to their craft, British documentary makers are having to learn the art of of business and deal-making. Co-production and co-financing are then the order of the day. The opportunities offered by new technology to connect film-makers with their audiences beyond traditional TV and to support and sustain the individual creative voice are both daunting and tremendously exciting. We intend that the Sheffield International Documentary Festival should evolve to help people meet the challenges of this new era so that in addition to the opportunities to watch outstanding documentaries, meet other film-makers and celebrate and debate the craft of documentary , Sheffield will also become a place to do business."

Sirkka Moeller is Festival Programmer of the Sheffield International Documentary Festival.
"Filmmakers often think of terms of finishing their film and then screening as soon as possible. But when it's made, after probably around a year of production, the clock starts ticking and gives you roughly two years to make commercial use of this film. If you can't put this time in after it's done, to concentrate on festivals, sales and distribution, then why bother finishing the film in the first place? But you should ask what you want the festival to do for you, and that in turn depends on the film. You need to be realistic about what the film can do, and can do for you. There's a line of continuity that runs through the production of your film and goes on through your use of festivals. If you've teamed up with a producer, make sure they're still with you for this difficult, time-consuming stage that is the festival stage. In some countries they've developed networks and groups to help filmmakers at this stage, but not really in the UK.

Before going to a festival, you should research it properly, finding out whether this is the right place for your film, seeing where it might fit into that festival. For example, a small-scale community project needs to be directed to a completely different festival than a big entertainment film. It's not quite right to think of any festival as being simply 'documentary', as even within these festivals there are subgenres. For example, there are festivals dedicated to architecture, or the Bristol wildlife documentary festival, and many others. At a general festival rather than a documentary-orientated one, there'll be more distributors, including television and theatrical, so that increases the potential audience for your documentary. Rotterdam, for example, is good for tapping into theatrical releases.

One of the early stages is submitting your film to a festival in the first place. It's important to think of your publicity material while you're making a film. You should stage your publicity shots with the still images in mind and get a proper shot. Some people, when they submit a film to a festival, provide too much supporting material with it, practically a four-page novel. Americans are good at submitting what's required. As a filmmaker, you should have in mind a logline of twenty-five words, a description of fifty, then longer or shorter as needed. You should be able to sum up your film in two or three sentences.

I've noticed that festival technicians can get annoyed at the low technical quality of films submitted to festivals, now that people are doing more of the filmmaking process themselves, guerilla-style. The quality of the film needs to be such that the audience actually enjoys the experience of watching it; this quality is vital, no matter how worthy the subject of the film might be.

You could classify the benefits of a documentary festival into four parts. The first advantage for filmmakers is that you get to show your film and receive feedback on it. This has the potential to be the most useful thing for the director: rather than your film going out on late-night television, where you don't know who's seen it or what their response is, at a festival you can actually learn from people what they think about your film. A second benefit of festivals is that inclusion of your film can lead to increased distribution. But there are some illusions about just what a film festival is, and what it should be. Film and cinema are a business, and as a filmmaker you can't expect everyone to be motivated just by art and culture. For a distributor to pick up your film, they have to think that there's commercial value to it. Filmmakers often complain, as well, that distributors take a lot of money out of the film, but they shouldn't forget that, for their part, the distributor will put a large amount of work into the film. Thirdly, festivals can be good for networking, but this does depend very much on what sort of personality you have, how much you like mingling and how much the festival encourages this, and the size of the festival. At Berlin, for example, if it was your first festival and you just turned up, you'd be lost. I'd recommend starting at Sheffield, which is the right size for you to be able to meet everybody, and then you can move on to other places once you know a few people. Finally, people sometimes forget that a festival is a great place simply for watching films. It's worthwhile going to one even if you haven't got a film included, just to see what the festival is like. Each one has its own profile, remit and audience.

The interesting thing is that you're working on an art form that's neglected by television, and this can lead to a greater sense of community among filmmakers and people at a festival. If programmers have an open-minded approach to selection, then you get a wide range of films, whatever the parameters of the festival. It's not the case the documentaries for festivals need to be over ninety minutes. Filmmakers often lack someone in the classic producer role, and they don't themselves have the ability to stop. I'd advise taking your film to people to show it to them, and then really listen to the advice they give. This will help you get to your audience. But it's rare for young filmmakers to accept criticism.

So do some research into festivals, and play to the strengths of your film. You need to take a careful look at the circumstances, think about what you're doing, and be ready to do some self-criticsm. I think some humility or realism is useful for filmmakers. You should aim high – I'm not just being discouraging – but don't lose touch with the real world that your film has to work in, or spend hundreds of pounds trying to place your film somewhere that isn't right for it. And vitally, make sure you've read the application forms for the festival right.

Different festivals have different agendas. In France, they're there to be part of the cultural agenda of the host city, in much the same way as a summer music festival might be, and the same in Italy. Some festivals are more like simply a season of films on show, but I think that to be a proper festival, it needs to attract some of the industry, and your peers within the industry such as other festival organisers, directors, producers and so on. It should go beyond just general public interest. A festival doesn't necessarily need to contribute to the economy of filmmaking. Cannes is exclusively for professionals, with suits busily talking into their mobile phones. Some have more room for journalists. Some filmmakers are only successful, or at least well-known, on the filmmaking circuit, and if that works for them, it's fine. John Smith, for example, is an experimental, humourous filmmaker whose work fits into the documentary category, but he tends to stay within the general festival circuit, and his work isn't that well know at documentary festivals. The same could apply to big cinematic documentaries, such as Nick Broomfield's work, because they're very well-received at general festivals not just documentary ones.

There are some success stories of films that have made good use of festivals. Marc Isaacs' 'Calais' has done very well at festivals. Brian Hill's 'Pornography' screened at Sheffield, where the audience really enjoyed it, the week before its television transmission, and this can be helpful for a film's general reception. Daniella Zanzotto's ten-minute short documentary 'Kissed by Angels' was shown at Sheffield in 2001, and after this she took part in the Bardonecchia pitching session, which resulted in her getting commissioning editors from Canada and Finland on board, and international distribution. From there, she had success at the Amsterdam pitching forums, gained contacts from two more countries, and is now in the process of editing a one-hour international piece. So doing well at festivals can help to build or cement your reputation, and I think that international commissioning editors and distributors do appreciate the filtering that a festival like Sheffield can do on their behalf.

For the future of the Sheffield International Documentary Festival, the ideal of the festival is to give a forum to UK documentary, and to give the outside world a window into what's happening in the UK. It's important that the process is two way, and we both bring in from the outside and show the best of new UK work. We're not just for distributors and commissioning editors, but also for filmmakers and audience; we'd like them to be inspired. But it is a challenge to find general public audiences for documentary, even though it's a rather glamourous time for docs in the cinema and in the media just now."

Also worth investigating

SXSW   www.sxsw.com
                                          new, upcoming film section of the music festival, with both competition
                                          and conferece. Plus SXSWClick, a multimedia fest that includes films
                                          under five minutes

Chicago Film Festival   www.chicagofilmfestival.org

Tribeca   www.tribecafilmfestival.org

Rio Documenta and Film Festival   Beth Ritto - Project Manager +55 (21) 2503-7778
                                          brasildocumenta@globosat.com.br . They don't promote hard overseas or
                                          make much information available, but if you want to access everything
                                          Brazil at once, this is where to do it.

Filmstock   www.filmstock.co.uk

                                          started small, in Luton, but growing in reputation, and is expanding to
                                          European tours

Cambridge   www.cambridgefilmfestival.org.uk
                                          organised at the epicentre of the Picturehouses empire

Raindance   www.raindance.co.uk
                                          at the heart of indy film in London

Special interest film festivals

What's your bag?

Anthropology: www.visualanthropology.net/fest.htm has listings of various anthropology and
                     ethnographic film festivals, including Parnu, July 2005; Royal Anthropological
                     Institute, Oxford, September 2005; Cinema du reel, Paris, March annually.

Architecture: www.atarax.sk
                     International Film Festival of Documentaries on Architecture, Slovakia

Aversion to editing: www.onetakefilmfestival.com, Zagreb, Croatia, November

                     www.straight8.net, London-based, international events

Bicyles: www.bicyclefilmfestival.com
                     international locations

Homosexuality: www.planetout.com/popcornq/fests
                     Planet Out's listing of over 150 gay and lesbian film festivals around the world

Human rights: www.oneworld.cz
                     International Human Rights Documentary Film Festival, Prague;

                     www.hrw.org/iff
                     Human Rights Watch International Film Festival, Seasons in New York, June,
                     London, March, and touring; for 2006, submissions window for the New York leg
                     only is September to December 2005.

Mountains: www.mountainfilm.co.uk
                     Kendall Mountain Film Festival is part of the Mountain Festival Alliance, which also
                     includes Trento in Italy and Banff in BC, Canada.

UK specialist: www.imagesofblackwomen.com
                  Black Women's Film Festival, London, March

                  www.africaatthepictures.co.uk
                  Africa at the Pictures, London, throughout 2005

                  www.llgff.org.uk
                  London Lesbian & Gay Film Festival, Spring

                  www.ukjewishfilmfestival.org.uk
                  Jewish Film Festival, Brighton then touring, Autumn

                  www.nmpft.org.uk/btm/2005
                  Bite the Mango, world cinema, Bradford, Sept

The list is endless…

Morgan Spurlock's first documentary 'Super Size Me' became the smash hit of Sundance 2004. In an interview with Jess Search at the 2004 Sheffield International Documentary Festival, he explains how the festival contributed to the inexorable progress of the film.

"I got the idea for the film at Thanksgiving 2002, that is, late November. I had just stuffed myself and I was sitting on the couch watching the tube when a news story came on about the two girls that were suing McDonald's. A spokesman for McDonald's came on and started talking about the lawsuit, saying, 'Our food is healthy, it's nutritious, it's good for you.' And I said, 'Come on, if it's that good for me, then realistically shouldn't I be able to eat it for thirty days straight with no side effects? Hmmm.' The light went on in my head – bing! – and I turned to my vegan girlfriend on the couch and said, 'I've got a great idea for a movie.'

The original germ idea was, I am going to make a film about fast food and obesity, that's it, cut and dry. I never saw it as television; my goal was always to make a feature film. So I had the idea. We were funding the whole movie ourselves. We had all the equipment; we had the friends and the people who already work for me. We had everything in place except for the research. So the minute I got the idea, the next day I started researching immediately and did nothing but research and work on this movie for seven weeks straight, and we were shooting by the end of January 2003. I was on the diet for the 30 days, but the filming went on for longer than that. A lot of the travel you see during the film, visiting fifteen states, we did during the thirty days. We finished the core shootings in mid May, but went back to do pick-ups all the way through to the end of the year. We finished the film not long before the Sundance deadline and submitted it around October of 2003.

My lawyer and sales agent is John Sloss who has a company called Cinetic. They fund and sell movies. When we made the film initially we showed it to them and their feelings were, and this was around mid-November, 'Yeah, it's funny. It's good, but we think it's just a TV sell and that's it.' And then suddenly we got into Sundance and that tune changed completely. We got into Sundance and the sales agents were, 'Oh my gosh, this is great. We gotta sell it. We'll get it into movie theatres.' And that was what I wanted. So after you get into Sundance, there is a check of credibility that suddenly goes by the film. You got into Sundance so that's one step done, that's one good thing.

We got the call the day after Thanksgiving, exactly one year later, after I'd got the idea; they make the announcement in December, and the festival's in January. As soon as I got accepted I called a friend of mine to get her to give me some money to make sure we could finish the film. So, I borrowed some money from her, and I cashed in an annuity from my grandparents, which was about $45,000. Because everybody who worked on the film had worked for free, and I had told people, 'If we get into Sundance I'm taking all of you to Sundance.' So I took twenty-five people to Sundance. Yeah. It was awesome.

We rented this huge, total fraternity house of a building, only one block off Main Street. It was a fantastic house and all twenty-five of us stayed there. A friend of mine who's a wardrobe supervisor made us ski jackets that said 'Super Size Me' on them, and everyone who went got a ski parka. A friend of mine in China, – Ron English, who did all the paintings in the film, also did our poster. He did a poster of an obese Ronald

McDonald for Sundance – so I sent that image to a friend of mine in China and he had a toy maker make 100 fat Ronald dolls that we took to Sundance. We made these obese Ronald dolls, and that was like the premium schwag for people. We had ski hats made. We made buttons that had the McDonald's logo and instead of saying McDonald's, it said 'obesity'. From the minute we got to Sundance we were branding the movie; you couldn't go anywhere without seeing somebody in a 'Super Size Me' jacket. We were giving hats out to all the parking attendants, every person who worked at the festival. We made bags, about 300 un-happy meals that on the side of the bag told all the wonderful facts about how many people have a heart attack in the United States a year, and what's inside the food, and how long it will take you to run off a Big Mac. And we were giving these out to journalists and people who helped us out, and volunteers at the festival. Just things that would continue to get the message out about the movie. By midway through even the first week it was everywhere, everybody knew about the film and it was incredible – even before we had our first screening.

And we finished the film. The print we screened at Sundance was on HD. We didn't have to have a 35 mm print. We screened on video, and cut the whole thing on Final Cut Pro 3 so we were outputting the video from our G4 to Dvcam, then we blow up in HD, which we screened on at the festival. We sent them the first print, which was about two weeks before our first screening. They called me up and said, 'There is something wrong with your video. There's video hits in it. There's all this degradation and artifacting in the video.' And I'm going, 'Oh my God.' So I go up to the dub house. They FedExed the tape back to me. We go up. We look at it. We see all of these video problems so they make me another tape. It's Monday now. Our film premiere's on Saturday. I say, 'Make this dub,' and they say, 'We're not going to be able to do it tonight, we'll have to do it tomorrow.' I said okay. So they made the print. They FedExed it to Sundance. So basically the first time the entire audience is watching the movie at our premiere is the first time I'm watching the movie because I have never seen this film. So I'm watching this tape going, 'Please let there be nothing wrong. Please, please.' And luckily there was nothing wrong with the video. It was perfect and, God, it was incredible. We got a standing ovation at the screening.

We had John Sloss from Cinetic on board because before I made the film my production company had created a show on the web called 'I Bet You Will' which was the first show in the United States ever to go from the web to the television. We sold that show to MTV and as soon as we'd sold it, I called him up and said, 'We just sold the show to MTV. We're a young production company. We're going to be doing a lot more over the years. I'd love to start to build a relationship with your company.' They said, 'We like the way you think.' Cinetic are a sales agent and financing company. At Sundance they sold 'Open Water', 'Napoleon Dynamite' and 'Super Size Me'. I think they took eight or nine films and they sold all eight or nine, which they do ever year. Every movie they take they sell, their track record is remarkable.

So at Sundance, there's a feeding frenzy with the distributors. They don't descend on me because they already knew John was selling the movie; they descended on the guys at Cinetic. It was interesting in the beginning after the first screening, it was a standing ovation, huge reception. Everybody loved the film so that was the vote of confidence. It tested well. Then the reviews started coming out the next day from press and all of the critics loved the movie. So then it was, 'Okay, great. Now let's see what happens with McDonald's.' Then during the festival rumors started coming out. People started saying, 'Well did you hear? Yeah, McDonald's is here. Their lawyers are in town. They're already suing you. They've shut down the film. They're here right now with cops. They're getting the print. They're taking the print from the theater. I saw them. I saw them taking the print away!'

A guy came to me and said, 'Did you hear about 'Super Size Me'? They took the prints away.' I said, 'Really? Wow, I better call somebody about that.' So I'm on the phone to Jeff Gilmore, the head of Sundance, saying, 'Is any of this true?' He's like, 'No, nobody's called us. None of this is true.' But it was interesting to see the concerns that people had, which was, will we be able to even release this movie or is it going to get squashed beforehand? We went in knowing there was a 99% chance a major studio would never put this movie out. And sure enough one by one, because the film exploded so fast, it was so overwhelming that everybody had to come do their due diligence on it because they needed to go back to their boss and say why they couldn't release this film everybody was talking about. And so one by one the major studios would come. And one by one they would leave the screenings and come up to me and say, 'Oh my God, Morgan, that movie was fantastic, but we could never put this out.' And they'd leave. Because these are companies that have to have their toys in the happy meals. They need the characters on the cups, the signs in the window. Losing that cross-marketing, that cross-promotion, for some of these major studios would be terrible. That's multi-millions of dollars of promotion that would just be gone.

In the United States the distributor that did take the film was a brand new company called Roadside Attractions that partnered with Samuel Goldwyn films. And Sam Goldwyn's been in the business for decades.

So it was nice to have the old blood and the new blood helping to push our movie out. By the end of 2004, the film will have played in more than sixty countries.

So January 2004 we're in Sundance, then the film was picked up, and in the cinemas in four months. It was out in May. Because we realised we couldn't wait. That is really fast, and had we been further along in having the film done, like had we had transfer print, an actually physical film, it would have come out even quicker, probably in March or April. Sometimes distributors hang about for a long time, and it can take up to eighteen months for a film to get from Sundance into the cinemas, but for us we realised there was such an explosion of the film from Sundance and so much dialogue about it that we wanted to try to capitalise on some of that. But we realised we couldn't because we had so much work to do in doing our blow-up to 35mm and the color correction for that and everything. Our final sound mix. Those things were just going to take time.

So since then, all my phone calls get returned now. It's fantastic. And the people I've gotten to meet! We were in New Zealand promoting the film and I got to the go on the set of 'King Kong' and meet Peter Jackson, which was the greatest day ever. We went on a tour of the Weta Workshop and Richard Taylor, four-time academy award winner, was taking Alex and me on a tour of the workshop, showing us, introducing me to every single person that works there and I am just like, oh God. It's crazy.

We're at Sundance and I met Robert Redford and I said, 'Hey, I'm Morgan Spurlock. I made 'Super Size Me.'' And he goes, 'Oh, Oh, OH! I've been carrying your movie around with me for months. I've been showing it to everybody.' And I'm just like, I can leave right now. Because his son-in-law is Eric Slosser who wrote 'Fast Food Nation'. A lot of people don't know that.

And we were at the Full Frame Film Festival and I met Michael Moore there. At Sundance everybody was asking me about Michael Moore and comparing this film to his. 'Do you like him? What do you think about him?' Everyone's waiting for me to say something bad. And I like Michael's movies very much and he definitely was an inspiration for me. So when we went to the Full Frame Film Festival he was speaking there and I thought, I really want to meet him when I get there. So I went walking up, I saw his wife Kathleen who produces all his movies. I introduced myself to her. She goes, 'Oh my gosh Morgan, thank you for all the nice things you said about Michael. Hold on, he's been dying to meet you. Michael, Michael.' And he turns around and says, 'Oh my god it's Morgan Spurlock.' And I went 'Hehehehehe!!'

Markets

Some festivals have markets running alongside, while some markets are independent of a festival. The aim of a market is different from a festival: it's to provide an environment in which buyers who work in television, film distribution and other industries that need films can find the product that they want. Each market produces a catalogue of all the films on offer, with thorough contact details of who's made what, how to contact them, and who's looking out for material of what type. Buyers can watch material chosen from the catalogue in videotheques, and can arrange meetings and do business. Filmmakers can have their films in the catalogue, at a price; they can attend the markets and buttonhole potential buyers, and some markets put on a programme of events and forums to bring buyers and sellers together. Markets have stands for exhibitors, usually taken by large companies, sales agents and organisations, but for the independent European filmmaker there is support from the MEDIA programme.

Support for your film at markets and festivals

MEDIA

One of the purposes of the whole MEDIA programme is to increase the good working of the European audiovisual industry, so it's in their interest to help UK filmmakers make the best of markets. To this end, MEDIA has a stand at several markets, under the protection of a (metaphorical) European Umbrella. MEDIA commissions another organisation to arrange the Umbrella, then has its own Stand within that. An

Umbrella gives the filmmakers access to meeting, office and screening facilities; consultancy and advice; sometimes inclusion in dedicated European market catalogues; and a very welcome discount on fees for attending the market.

Do contact your local MEDIA desk if you're thinking of attending a festival, to see what advice and practical help they can offer in your particular circumstances. Commissioning partners, including European Film Promotion (www.efp-online.com) and The Marketplace (www.marketplace-events.com), carry out other activities including funding and organisation, but the MEDIA website is the best place to look for prompt information about all schemes of relevance to British filmmakers. www.mediadesk.co.uk

The British Council

The British Council accepts roughly thirty documentaries a year, mainly shorts, made by British filmmakers, into the roster of British films that it supports abroad. If your film is accepted, the Council does the paperwork and pays for festival transportation for your film, and sometimes for you. At festivals including Cannes, Karlovy Vary, Venice, Toronto and Sundance, they arrange special screenings of British works. You may also be eligible for the grant-making Print Fund, for striking the first print of a short film. See www.britishcouncil.org.

Paul Howson is Head of Film.

UK Film Council International Film Sales Support Scheme

Following a pilot scheme to March 2005, the UK Film Council will again run a one-year IFSS Scheme for films accepted to film festivals: Cannes, Locarno, Venice, Toronto, Sundance, Rotterdam, Berlin. The aim is to support the international sale of UK films, to encourage their distribution and box office performance at home and abroad, and to promote UK skills and workers. Applications must come from sales agents or from a production company with one attached, and are awarded to assist films that qualify as: a British film for theatrical release of over 70 minutes and with a production budget of under £20 million, receiving its international festival premier at that festival, and with a budgetted marketing plan. The support consists of a grant of at least £1,500, to be used for production of subtitled prints; travel and accommodation for director and stars; a press campaign; and marketing items.

See the Film Council website at www.ukfilmcouncil.org.uk/funding/ifss/ for the deadlines for applying for support for the respective festivals.

Markets listings

MIPDOC, April, Cannes
MIPTV, April, Cannes
MIPCOM, October, Cannes

www.mipdoc.com
www.miptv.com
www.mipcom.com

2005 dates:
MIPDOC: 9th –10th April
MIPTV: 11th –15th April
MIPCOM: 17th – 21st October

Registration deadline: for inclusion in catalogue, 16th February. You can still attend by turning up on the day, but the fee is higher and you'll have lost the opportunity to appear in the official guide.
MIPTV participation fee: €960 + VAT when purchased before the event, and cheaper early bird offers available. MEDIA umbrella fee: €657.
MIPDOC distributor / seller's fee: €1,100 + VAT, MEDIA umbrella €610.

These are trade events for professionals from the audiovisual industry. They are both an opportunity to trade and a conference, including speakers who are heads of international companies, seminars, and learning. MIPDOC takes place directly before the main market MIPTV, and is aimed at distributors and broadcasters of documentary, although the other two markets do not exclude docs.

 John Edginton of Otmoor Productions, Oxford, is a veteran Cannes attender. His comments:

"Should you go to MIPDOC? A bit of advice from a small indie filmmaker who went: don't! MIPDOC is mainly attended by mainline distributors and documentary acquisitions execs from broadcasters, and is more geared up to people from Discovery or the History Channel searching for something to fit their formulas.

You pay almost double the cost of going to MIPTV itself for the doubtful privilege of having three titles in a catalogue that the execs peruse. They sit in screenings for two days. You (the small indie) hang about outside. At the end of day two you get a list of who watched your film. The theory is that you try and track down anyone who did watch it over the next few days at MIPTV, but by that stage their schedules are all locked in. It's an exercise in frustration. MIPDOC is definitely not good value for money, not conducive to pitching a product, and is not a place to attempt to talk pre-sales or co-productions.

Better to focus on MIPTV itself, and if you can identify your potential buyers beforehand, try and pre-arrange meetings with them to pitch your product. Definitely the best deal for small indies is to get in at half the price via the Media-funded 'Marketplace', which is open to all European indies (info@marketplace-events.com). Not only does it save you money, but there's a fantastic series of buyers' seminars all day long where you can meet and question virtually every TV exec that matters, from the US to Australia and Europe. Where else can you get to quiz the head of docs from ABC Australia, CBC Canada, Canal Plus France, ZDF Germany, the Sundance Channel in the US, all in a small room where you get the chance to pitch your projects to them informally after their session. If you're determined to go to MIPDOC you can get the Marketplace cut rate for entry there too.

The first time I went to MIPTV I was very green and unsure about why I was there. But I took with me a proposal for 'Our Father the Serial Killer', and tried to find people who were interested. It was a real learning experience and quite exhilarating. It was there that I first met Court TV and learnt they do docs (and now I'm developing a major proposal with them), but they also introduced me to Granada International, who were keen to put money in, and after a couple of days I had secured development money from both and they went on to fully fund the film. I eventually made two versions, one of which Granada sold to 'Everyman' on the BBC. Ironic because the BBC had rejected the original idea.

This was all especially good because it was in about 1999, when the prospect in England for docs looked quite depressing. So I'd really recommend that the first time you go to MIPTV or a market, make sure you have a target, a project to raise money for, something you're keen to sell. Work out a plan of action. Keep asking questions, getting moved on, networking like crazy. It's easy to get sidetracked by the stalls, events and parties, but if you can work it, it might well bring you the money that wasn't available in the UK."

Cannes Marché du Film

✉ 3, rue Amélie 75007
Paris

✆ +33 (0)1 53 59 61 30
fax : +33 (0)1 53 59 61 50

✉ marketinfo@festival-cannes.fr
www.cannesmarket.com

2005 dates: 11th –21st May
Deadlines: various in April: a month before the market is the cut-off date for appearing in the Market Guide; after that, online registration is possible until a fortnight before the market, then registering on the day is more expensive.
Fee: Marché registration €299; Producers' network €335; Short Film Corner films under 30 minutes €75, over 30 minutes €125, all inc. VAT. Early bird registration offers discounts. MEDIA umbrella discount €268.

The Cannes Marché du Film is the market attached to the Cannes Film Festival, which takes place at the same time. It's the major market for international film including docs. Registration also gives access to the online database. Applying to the Marché is completely separate from applying to the festival. Figures for 2004: 1,432 screenings, of which 545 were world premiers; 8,814 participants from 74 countries and from 2,612 companies present; 1450 buyers.

For independent producers who have in the last three years produced a feature film that's had theatrical release, there is the Producers' Network within the Marché, which aims to promote new partnerships between producers. The five hundred selected producers benefit from inclusion in the Market Guide and a specialised Producers' Catalogue and access to the market, plus additional networking benefits, breakfasts and seminars. In 2005 there is a new programme, the Atelier du Festival, in which 15 filmmakers from around the world will be invited to present their project and its financing at individual meetings. Registering with the Producers' Network gives automatic registration for the person (not the film) to the Marché and the Festival, but must be done by the deadline before the start of the Marché; you cannot turn up and register.

There is also the Short Film Corner, which in 2004 presented 450 films from 40 different countries, with over a hundred screening as world premiers. The Short Film Corner was run in conjunction with the Clermont-Ferrand festival, but they've terminated their association. Registration for the Short Film Corner gives access to all exhibition zones of the Festival and the Marché; your film is digitised and screened, and you get a year's access to the website www.shortfilmcorner.com, with continually updated news. The Short Film Corner catalogue lists all the short films and screening times, and this information is also published in the daily editions of the Film Français and Cannes Market News.

The European Film Market, Berlin

✉ Potsdamer Straße 5
D-10785 Berlin

✆ +49 30 259 20 623
fax +49 30 259 20 629

✉ contact: Frank Schirrmeister schirrmeister@berlinale.de
www.berlinale.de

2006 dates: 9th –19th February
2005 dates: 10th –20th February
In 2005, accreditation deadline was 15th December 2004; submissions deadline 10th January 2005.
Fee: accreditation for the Festival costs €50 and this is needed to obtain a Market Badge at €250, which
gives access to all screenings in the Market. During the Market, daily passes are also available at €20 for
access to the Market venue and stands, but with no access to the festival or screenings.
Films screening fee: 16mm or 35mm in a cinema, €190 per hour or part thereof; studio screening €160;
video screening €120, all inc. VAT.

There is a searchable public access database on the website of all films that have been included in the
Market. In 2005 these included Jeremy Gilley's 'Peace One Day' and Rupert Murray's 'Unknown White
Male'. Roughly five hundred new films are screened each year, with around 40% of the premieres shown in
the Berlinale programme presented at the same time in Market Screenings.

and

The Berlinale Co-Production Market

☏ +49 30 259 20 517
   fax +49 30 259 20 519

✉ coproductionmarket@berlinale.de

A two day event during the EFM to facilitate interaction between producers and financiers, distributors,
film fund operators and broadcasters. In September 2005, details will be available on the website of how
production companies can submit projects for which they're looking for co-production financing partners.
In December the Co-Production Market selects certain projects to be included in the Co-Production Market
Catalogue, which is sent to all Co-Pro Market participants in the month before the Market. This gives
time for the Market team to set up meetings between participants according to what's taken their fancy in
the catalogue. There are 25-minute private meetings, plus seminars, case studies and discussions for all
participants.

Sunny Side of the Doc

✉ Pôle Média
   Belle de Mai
   37-41 rue Guibal
   13003 Marseille
   France

☏ +33 (0)4 95 04 44 80
   Fax: +33 (0)4 91 84 38 34

✉ contact@sunnysideofthedoc.com
   www.sunnysideofthedoc.com

2005 dates: 29th June –2nd July
Registration deadline: 1st May
Fee: €1794 inc. VAT for a Blue Corner, which is two people and five programmes in the videotheque;
stands start at €3,707; to attend as a visitor with no projects costs €490 for the four days, €239 for one day.

Projects fall either into the 'works in development' category, or the 'commissioned projects', for which there's a supplemental fee of €299. In the first category, an exhibitor can include two (or more with extra charge) projects without commission, whether they're finished, or at the idea, synopsis or script stage. These projects are eligible for the 'Voyage / Discovery' prize of €10,000 and the Kodak prize of €2,500 worth of filmstock. They're included in the catalogue so all the attendants can see whether they want to fund them. You can also exhibit a work that has in place between 25% and 85% of the budget, with funding from an approved list of broadcasters. These go into a separate catalogue, and they're eligible for the Olivier Masson prize of €10,000, which in 2004 was won by 'Prostitution Behind the Veil', dir. Nahid Persson. You can also attend as a visitor, with access to a good range of seminars, discussion sessions, different yearly international focuses and screenings. There are on average 1,800 attendants of which 300 are commissioning editors.

Docs for Sale, International Documentary Festival Amsterdam

✉ Kleine-Gartmanplantsoen 10
1017 RR Amsterdam
The Netherlands

✆ +31 (0) 20 - 627 3329
fax. +31 (0)20 638 5388

🖳 docsforsale@idfa.nl
www.idfa.nl

Dates: 25th November –3rd December 2005
Deadline for entering a film: 1st October; for accreditation 11th October
Eligibility: documentaries of a creative nature completed after 1st September 2004
Fee: €185 inc. VAT, plus €100 if your film is also selected for the IDFA Festival (but submission to the Festival alone is free). Filmmakers with a film in Docs for Sale have access to the Docs for Sale desk and lobby.
For buyers, programmers and distributors, Docs for Sale visitors' passes cost €85, giving access to the desk, lobby and viewing facilities. To gain access to IDFA screenings and events, visitors need to buy a Guest Pass.

A major marketplace for the more independent side of documentary film, Docs for Sale consists of a video library and screening facilities consisting of 30 video booths, backed up by a database and catalogue listing around 350 films, consisting of works entered to Docs for Sale, selected films from the Festival, and completed docs that were pitched at previous pitching forums.

Xiaolu Guo made 'Concrete Revolution' on a shoestring budget over 2004.
"With 'Concrete Revolution', we took a rough cut to Amsterdam, and it's become the number one film being demanded for viewing there. Five distribution companies from France were all talking to me about wanting it, and I needed to choose the best one. I wanted to do that on a basis of passion and trust, just to have someone I trusted to get on with doing that business side. Making 'Concrete Revolution' I was in all the roles, and especially as a foreigner, it's hard to do all of those. But once the film was ready I felt I could hand it on, just give it away for other people to deal with. And now it's being distributed worldwide by Tele Images International, a distributor from France, who were one of the companies that I was speaking to at IDFA."

Doc Shop, Hot Docs Canadian International Documentary Festival

✉ 110 Spadina Ave., Suite 333
Toronto, ON
M5V 2K4

✆ +1 416-203-2155
Fax: +1 416-203-0446

🖱 www.hotdocs.ca

2005 dates: 23rd April – 1st May
Submissions window: September to March
Fee: ranging from US$25 to US$100

The Doc Shop generally includes all film submitted to the festival, with very little material of lesser production quality weeded out.

American Film Market

✉ 10850 Wilshire Boulevard, 9th Floor
Los Angeles, CA 90024-4311
USA

✆ Phone: 310 446 1000
Fax: 310 446 1600

🖱 AFM2005@ifta-online.org
www.americanfilmmarket.com

Dates: 2nd – 9th November 2005
Fee: to exhibit, vastly expensive for an indy filmmaker; to attend, starts at $250 / day.

Run by the IFTA (Independent Film & Television Alliance), the big American market for TV, cable and DVD distribution.

Chapter Thirteen
Competitions and awards

It's nice to get recognition, and in some cases a prize. Winning an award increases your visibility and makes it more likely that funders will invest in you in the future. Some festivals offer prizes, while some non-festival organisations exist just to draw attention and glory to your labours. In this chapter we describe a few of the more modest prizes, then work up to the big-time.

Smaller and specialised prizes

Jerwood First Cuts Documentary Award

 Sheffield International Documentary Festival
The Workstation
15 Paternoster Row
Sheffield
S1 2BX

 0114 276 5141

info@sidf.co.uk
www.sidf.co.uk

The Sheffield International Documentary Festival and the Jerwood Charity have created this new award that recognises the high quality of documentary work that students at UK film and media schools are producing. The Award celebrates new ways of storytelling as well as traditional forms of documentary and aims to give new talent a stepping-stone in their documentary career. An international jury of renowned documentary professionals will award a cash prize of £3,500 for the winning film during the Sheffield International Documentary Festival in November.

UK film students and course leaders are invited to submit documentary films and videos completed after 1st January of the previous year. Filmmakers eligible for the award must be either a UK citizen or a current UK resident and have been residing in the UK for the last three years. The film must have been produced while the filmmaker was studying at a UK Film or Media School or an equivalent course at a UK university. Films must not have been broadcast on terrestrial TV in the UK prior to the festival. They can be of any length and must have English dialogue or subtitles. In 2004 there was a July deadline for applications.

In 2004 the award went to 'The Mythologist' – an intriguing and stylish portrait of a latter-day Walter Mitty character, by NFTS student John Lundberg. *"On a practical level winning has made more people aware of 'The Mythologist' and interested in what I'm doing next. On a personal level having jury members such as Joan Churchill, Alan Hayling and Kevin Macdonald engaging with my work is very humbling, it's also done wonders for my self confidence."*

As well as awards for general filmmaking excellence, there is a range of special-interest prizes:

Mental Health Media Awards

356 Holloway Road
London
N7 6PA

020 7700 8171

 awards@mhmedia.com
www.mhmawards.org

Mental Health Media promotes the voice of mental health service users within the media and public discourse. Their annual awards recognise and celebrate the best portrayals of mental distress and reporting of mental health issues in the broadcast media. For a programme about mental health broadcast between 1st July 2004 and 30th June 2005, programme-makers should contact the awards office for an entry form, while anyone can also nominate a film via the website. Closing date for the 2005 awards is June 2005, with the award ceremony held in October in London.

In 2004 the TV Documentary award shortlist was:
'Adam Ant: The Madness of Prince Charming' (Planet Wild for Channel 4)
'An Artist's Guide to Schizophrenia' (Panglos Productions for The Community Channel)
'Animated Minds' (DFG and APT Films for Channel 4)
And the winner: 'O Flaen dy Lygaid: Camu Mlaen' (BBC for BBC Wales on S4C)

Rory Peck Trust

 The Rory Peck Trust
2 Grosvenor Gardens
London
SW1W 0DH

 020 7730 1411

 info@rorypecktrust.org

The Rory Peck Trust supports freelancers, 'an essential part of an open and free media', promoting their safety, and assisting them and dependents. Their annual award ceremony is in November. In 2004 the Rory Peck Award for Features was won by James Miller for 'Death in Gaza'.

One World Media Awards

 One World Broadcasting Trust
3-7 Euston Centre
Regent's Place
Off Euston Road
London NW1 3JG
United Kingdom

020 7874 7609

oneworld@owbt.org

The One World Broadcasting Trust exists to promote better-informed media communication between the developing world and the West. Its annual awards take place in June, with a March deadline for submissions, application via the website. The awards are open across media, with documentaries eligible.

In the 2004 ceremony, the Women in Society award went to Kim Longinotto for 'The Day I Will Never Forget', while the Television Documentary award was presented to 'Orphans of Nkandla' made by True Vision for BBC Four.

British Independent Film Awards

 81 Berwick Street
London, W1F 8TW

☏ 020 7287 3833

✉ info@bifa.org.uk
www.bifa.org.uk

Award ceremony dates: November 30th 2005, nominations announced 25th October
Deadlines: features 22nd Sept 2005; shorts 1st July.
Eligibility: intended for theatrical release, has had screening on general release or at British-based film festival between 1st Dec 04 and 30th Nov 05; not solely funded by a single studio; produced or majority co-produced by a British company OR with at least 51% of budget from a British source, OR qualifies as British under DCMS rules; 'sufficient creative elements' must be British.
Cost: no charge to enter but six screening copies needed for entry.
Shorts: must be submitted to the Raindance Film Festival (www.raindance.co.uk) to be considered for the Best British Short Film Award, application window 9th March to 1st July 05, cost £15 and up.
Prizes: a trophy, some financial rewards

Created in 1998, The British Independent Film Awards celebrate merit and achievement in independently funded British filmmaking and promote British films and filmmaking to a wider public. The BIFAs consider every eligible film for nomination. With the help of British-based film festivals and by tracking the release schedules, BIFA researchers set out to find everything that qualifies. Independent filmmakers can also submit their film directly for consideration.

Caletgories:

Best British Film
Best Achievement In Production
Best British Documentary
Best British Short Film
Best Director of a British Independent Film
Best Foreign Independent Film (above British requirements obviously don't apply for this category)
Best Technical Achievement
Most Promising Newcomer
The Douglas Hickox Award - is to be given to a British director for their debut feature film - £500
The Special Jury Prize

Films and prizes:
Nominations for Best British Documentary 2004:

'Touching the Void' Kevin Macdonald WINNER
'Aileen: Life & Death of a Serial Killer' Nick Broomfield
'Drowned Out' Franny Armstrong
'Peace One Day' Jeremy Gilley
'Trollywood' Madeleine Farley

And the 2003 winner was 'Bodysong', Simon Pummel
from a shortlist which also included:

'100 Doors', Kerri Davenport-Burton
'Bugs', Mike Slee
'Hoover Street Revival', Sophie Fiennes
'The Game of Their Lives', Daniel Gordon

Major British Prizes

Then the four big television documentary prizes are the Grierson, BAFTA, RTS and Broadcast:

Grierson Awards

Marc Isaacs (Grierson Best Newcomer 2002): *"If you make a film that is very personal and you take some risks by daring to do something different then you leave yourself open to failure. So winning awards (Grierson or whatever) knowing that others have connected with your work, of course it gives you the strength to carry on. Nobody wants to talk to themselves".*

awards administered by:

 Artichoke Productions Ltd
Netheravon
Wiltshire, SP4 9QP

01980 671102

awards@griersontrust.org
www.griersontrust.org

Timeframe from 2004:
Qualifying period 1 May 2003 – 30 April 2004. Closing date for entries 28th May 2004, shortlist announced July 2004, nominations announced October 2004, winners announced November 2004
Fee: yes

The Grierson Trust commemorates the pioneering Scottish documentary maker John Grierson (1898 – 1972), famous for 'Drifters' and 'Night Mail' and the man widely regarded as the father of the documentary. Each year, the Trust recognises the best documentary filmmaking from Britain and abroad through the Grierson Awards.

The Awards are for original UK productions only, with the exception of International Television and Cinema Awards. Entries must have been screened or broadcast to the public for the first time in the 12 months up to the submissions deadline. This includes scheduled screenings within recognised film, television and documentary festivals, and at public institutions such as museums and galleries. The awards seek to recognise documentaries which have made a significant contribution to the genre. The judges will be looking for evidence of quality, integrity, creativity, originality and overall excellence.

Awards are made in the following **categories**:
Best Documentary on a Contemporary Issue
Best Arts Documentary
Best Historical Documentary

Best Documentary on Science or the Natural World
Best Documentary Series or Strand
Best International Television Documentary
Best International Cinema Documentary
Best Newcomer (with £3000 cash prize), and
Most Entertaining Documentary
Trustees' Award (recognising the outstanding contribution to the art or craft of the documentary)

Some past winners...
Best Documentary on a Contemporary Issue
2004 'Terror in Moscow' Dan Reed
2003 'Crackhouse' Carl John
2002 'Kelly & her Sisters' Marilyn Gaunt
2001 'Correspondent: Killers don't cry' Clifford Bestall

Best Newcomer
2004 'The Boy Whose Skin Fell Off' Patrick Collerton
2003 'Chavez: Inside the Coup' Donnacha O'Brian & Kim Bartley
2002 'Lift' Marc Isaacs & 'This is Palestine' Azza El-Hassan
2001 'Fifteen' Daisy Asquith

BAFTA Awards

 The British Academy of Film & Television Arts
195 Piccadilly
London, W1 9LN

✆ 020 7734 0022

 www.bafta.org

The British Academy of Film & Television Arts is renowned for its high-profile Award ceremonies that promote and reward the best in film, television and interactive media. Entry forms are usually completed by UK distributors, but in the event that a distributor chooses not to register an eligible film for the awards, the film's producer may submit an entry form him or herself. Films are eligible if released within the awards year (1 January - 31 December). There is a November deadline for submissions and nominations will be announced in January of the following year, with the awards ceremony taking place in February. Entries are viewed by a jury which ultimately decides the winner. Each jury is made up of experts within the field relevant to the category under consideration. Nominations for British Academy Awards are made across a variety of different cagetories.

There are 19 **categories** in the Film Awards, of which the following are open to documentary films-makers:
The Fellowship
The Michael Balcon Award for outstanding British contribution to Cinema
The Alexander Korda Award for the outstanding British Film of the Year
The Carl Foreman Award for Special Achievement by a Director, Screenwriter or Producer in their first feature film
Short Film
Sound
Editing
Cinematography

Film Not in the English Language
David Lean Award for Best Achievement in Direction

In 2003, 'Touching the Void' was awarded the Alexander Korda Award for the Outstanding British Film of the Year. To date, it's the only documentary to have won a British Academy Film Award.

BAFTA Scotland

 BAFTA Scotland
249 West George Street
Glasgow
G2 4QE
Scotland

☏ 0141 302 1770

✉ info@baftascotland.co.uk
www.baftascotland.co.uk

Exists to promote and reward Scotland's screen industry. The annual prize ceremony is held in November, with winners in 2004 being:

Best Film Documentary 'Touch the Sound - A Sound Journey with Evelyn Glennie'

Best Television Documentary: David Peat for 'Gutted'

Bafta: The British Academy Television Awards - Production

Deadline for submissions: Dec, nominations announced 14th March 05, awards 17th April 2005, for films made in 2004
donnab@bafta.org

The entry form is sent to all BAFTA members, Independent Production Companies and Broadcasters. Entries cost £200. Forms are available each year between October and December. All programmes are then listed and sent to the members for voting purposes in January. The results produce a short list of four in each category. Broadcasters (BBC1, BBC2, ITV, Channel 4, Five and Sky) are notified of the top four and given the opportunity to add one programme per category at a cost of £500 per programme. This produces a short list, which is viewed by a jury to obtain the four nominations and a winner. If you wish to submit an entry but cannot pay the entry fee, you should explain your circumstances in writing to the British Academy Television Committee, which may reduce or waive the fee where appropriate.

The following award **categories** are open to Documentary:

Huw Wheldon award for factual series or strand:
for more than one factual programme linked through a unified approach, narrative or thematic development of subject matter.

Current Affairs:
programmes may be self-standing or part of a strand or series.

Flaherty Documentary Award:
for one-off documentaries, or single programmes within umbrella strands.

Films and prizes

Some past winners of the Flahery award:

2004 'Lager, Mum and Me (One Life)', Todd Austin, Min Clough
2003 'Feltham Sings', Brian Hill/Roger Graef
2002 'Kelly & her Sisters', Marilyn Guant
2001 '100% White', Leo Regan
2000 'Divorce Iranian Style', Kim Longinotto / Ziba Mir-Hosseini

and 2005 nominees:
'The Boy Whose Skin Fell Off', Patrick Collerton Yipp Films/C4
'The Brighton Bomb', BBC1
'The F***ing Fulfords', Optomen Television/C4
'The Orphans Of Nkandla', True Vision/BBC4

The British Academy Television Craft Awards

The British Academy Television Craft Awards were created in 2000, when the decision was taken to give behind-the-scenes talent their own dedicated ceremony. They take place in May, following the same submission procedures as the main television awards. The following categories are open to documentary:

Categories:
Editing Factual
Photography Factual
Sound Factual

Films and prizes:

New Director Factual. 2003 prize winners (presented in 2004):
ALT TV: 'Holiday Around My Bedroom', Jamie Jay Johnson Vashca Productions/C4
ALT TV: 'This Is A True Story', Paul Berczeller Diverse Productions/C4
'The Nine Lives of Alice Martineau', Oli Barry F Music TV/BBC3 WINNER
'Surviving Extremes: The Swamp', Will Anderson Keo Films/C4

2004 prize nominees announced 4th April 05, prize-giving 8th May
'The Boy Whose Skin Fell Off', Patrick Collerton Yipp Films/C4
'Holidays in the Danger Zone - Violent Coast (This World)', James Brabzon BBC/BBC2
'Who You Callin' A Nigger', Krishnendu Majumdar Diverse Productions/C4
'My Foetus', Julia Black Bivouac Productions/C4

RTS Awards

 Royal Television Society
Holborn Hall
100 Gray's Inn Road
London, WC1X 8AL

 020 7430 1000

info@rts.org.uk
www.rts.org.uk

The Royal Television Society is a forum for discussion and debate of all aspects of the television industry. The RTS rewards excellence, provides networking opportunities, and promotes professional development.

The society hosts awards ceremonies for Programme Making, Television Journalism, Sport, Education, Craft & Design, Technical Innovation and Student Television.

RTS Programme Awards

The RTS Awards seek to recognise programmes which have made a positive contribution to their genre: either because their originality in form or content has in some way moved the genre on, or perhaps created a new genre; or because their quality has set standards which other programme-makers can learn from and emulate. They span all genres of television programming and are held every March in London, for programmes first transmitted during the previous calendar year. Entries are accepted from broadcasting organisations, or staff and freelance technicians whose broadcasts are received in the UK. Entries must be endorsed by the television organisation or agency which transmitted or distributed the material and must have been networked. Broadcasters are limited as to the number of submissions they can make. Entry fee of £285, deadlines Dec / January.

Factual awards are made in the following **categories**:
Single Documentary - General
Documentary Series - General
History
Science & Natural History
Arts
Features and Factual Entertainment
Regional Programme
RTS International Award

Some past winners...
Single Documentary
2004 'Stealing a Nation: A Special Report by John Pilger', Granada for ITV
2003 'The Secret Policeman', BBC Documentaries
2002 'House of War', Diverse TV
2001 'Kelly & her Sisters', Marilyn Gaunt
2000 '100% White', Leo Regan

National and Regional Programme
This award is intended to cover Documentaries, Arts, Leisure and Drama. It is not intended for news or current affairs programmes. It is open to programmes made by an ITV Company or by a BBC Region and must have been shown first within a region. It does not have to reflect the particular region where it has been made. Up to one entry each from a BBC Region, an ITV Region and S4C.

Winners, 2004:
'My Name is Paul', BBC for BBC ONE NI

'Hidden Gifts: The Mystery of Angus MacPhee', Lansdowne Productions with Grampian TV (in association with YLE, SVT, VPRO, ZDF-3Sat and the Scottish Screen National Lottery Fund)

'Gutted', Tern Television Productions for BBC ONE Scotland

Documentary Series
2003 'The Last Peasants', Angus Macqueen
2002 'The Hunt for Britain's Paedophiles', BBC
2001 'Living with Cancer', BBC
2000 'Fifteen', Channel 4

RTS Student Television Awards
The RTS Student Television Awards recognise the best audiovisual work created by full- or part-time students as part of their course and are split into three strands: Animation, Factual and Non-Factual. The

factual award is for work that deals with news or social issues in documentary or reporting style and is separated into two categories: BTEC/ Undergraduate award and Postgraduate. The awards ceremony is held every May in central London. Documentary filmmaker Paul Watson is committee chair for the Student awards.

The awards are open to students attending educational institutions offering approved BTEC, degree and postgraduate courses in design, media and media-related studies and to film and television associations at these institutions. Timeframe: Entries produced in the 2003 / 2004 academic year can be entered for the 2004 awards, deadline July 04, application fee of £17, with the award ceremony the following May. Up to three entries in each category will be accepted from individual departments in each institution. The entering institution must undertake to clear the copyright in the event of the winning programme being broadcast.

For the 2003 awards, presented in 2004:
Undergraduate Factual Winner: 'High Flyers' by Jean Devlin & Shona Mullen, Dublin Institute of Technology

Postgraduate Factual Winner: 'Riles' by Ditsi Carolino, Sadhana Buxani, Valerio Bonelli, Peter Marquez, Martin Jensen & Bradley Miles, National Film and Television School

Broadcast Awards

 organised by Emap Media Events
33-39 Bowling Green Lane
London EC1R 0DA

☏ 020 7505 8000

🖱 www.broadcastnow.co.uk/awards/

Broadcast magazine is the standard publication for those working in television. Broadcast also organise regular conferences for production companies and producers to hear from broadcasters. The Broadcast Awards take place in January, with categories for Best Doc Programme and Doc Series.

2005 winner of Best Documentary Programme:
'The Secret Policeman', BBC for BBC One
Highly commended: 'The Boy Whose Skin Fell Off', Yipp Films for Channel 4

and the shortlist
'Orphans of Nkandla', True Vision Production for BBC Four
'The Protectors - Portrait of a Paedophile', Films of Record for BBC One
'The Secret Policeman', BBC for BBC one
'When Michael Portillo Became a Single Mum', BBC for BBC Two

and, aiming high:

Win yourself an Oscar! The Academy Awards

🖱 www.oscars.org

The Academy of Motion Picture Arts and Sciences is a US professional body, well known for dishing out statuettes to gown-wearing ladies and besuited men every February. The Academy says, 'Because the

Academy numbers among its members the ablest artists and craftsmen in the motion picture world, the Oscar represents the best achievements of the year in the opinion of those who themselves reside at the top of their craft.' And in case you're planning on going for the big one, here are just some of the hoops you'll have to jump through to qualify for nomination.

For both categories of Documentary Features and Documentary Shorts (40 mins or less):
The film must be publicly exhibited for paid admission in a commercial motion picture theatre in either Los Angeles County or the Borough of Manhattan in New York for a run of at least seven consecutive days.

In addition, one of the following two requirements must be met:
a) The film must have theatrical runs in at least four additional cities, lasting a minimum of two consecutive days. All screenings of the film must begin between 10:00 AM and midnight, and must commence by the day nominations are announced; or
b) If the exhibition requirements above are not met, then the film must be withheld from television and/or internet transmission for the nine months following the day nominations are announced

A Documentary Short Subject may have participated in a 'recognised' competitive film festival and MUST HAVE WON THE BEST DOCUMENTARY SHORT AWARD (or its equivalent). For the current list of eligible festivals, see our listing in Chapter 12, Festivals and Markets.

Public notification of the exhibition(s) is required in the form of paid advertising on the film page of a major newspaper. The ad copy must contain the dates, title and screening times of the film. The ad may either stand alone or appear in combination with the title of another film.

No television or internet transmission shall occur at any time prior to, or within the six months following, the first day of the qualifying run or the festival win.

Nominations will be determined by an averaged point system of voting using 10, 9.5, 9, 8.5, 8, 7.5, 7, 6.5 or 6. Those films receiving an average score of 8.0 or more shall be eligible for nomination. However, there may not be more than five nor fewer than three nominations.

The 2004 prize, for films made in 2004, awarded in 2005:
'Born into Brothels', dir. Ross Kauffman and Zana Briski (THINKFilm) A Red Light Films, Inc. Production

from a shortlist of:
'The Story of the Weeping Camel', Luigi Falorni and Byambasuren Davaa
'Super Size Me', Morgan Spurlock
'Tupac: Resurrection', Lauren Lazin and Karolyn Ali
'Twist of Faith', Kirby Dick and Eddie Schmidt

Past winners:
2003 'The Fog of War'
2002 'Bowling for Columbine'
2001 'Murder on a Sunday Morning'
2000 'Into the Arms of Strangers'

And the Best Documentary Short Subject category 2004:
Winner: 'Mighty Times: The Children's March', Robert Hudson and Bobby Houston
'Autism Is a World', Gerardine Wurzburg
'The Children of Leningradsky', Hanna Polak and Andrzej Celinski Hardwood, Hubert Davis and Erin Faith Young
'Sister Rose's Passion', Oren Jacoby and Steve Kalafer

John Battsek has produced a number of documentaries for both theatrical distribution and television. His first documentary, 'One Day in September', about the 1972 Munich Olympics massacre, won the 1999 Academy Award for Best Feature Length Documentary.

"The very early development of 'One Day in September' was funded by my company Passion Pictures. I went to director Kevin Macdonald with the idea and my business partner gave us a few grand so that we could go to Israel to research the story. Then Kevin got us a meeting with the News and Current Affairs department at the BBC. They said they'd fund the film and off the back of that my business partner agreed to give us a bit more money so that we could go back to Israel for further research. All along I had been looking elsewhere for the remainder of the money and I found a company in America called Non-fiction Films who said they would finance the rest of the film.

So eight months into the process we went to Israel with a bit of our own money, knowing that the BBC were definitely going to fund a chunk of it and that this American company were going to fund the rest. When we got back from Israel the Americans pulled out. I think that someone at the top of the company hadn't been in the loop and then once they heard about it they probably said, 'I don't want to make that,' which often happens, actually.

By this point I was talking to all sorts of other people. I'd never made a documentary before, so I had absolutely no idea what I was doing. All I could do was follow a certain instinct and go in the directions I thought one was supposed to go. So you go to the BBC and you go to whatever funding organisations there are. I don't even know how I got that relationship going with those Americans, but one thing rippled on to another, and when they were gone I started talking to some other people.

The producer, Sandy Lieberson, is a friend of Kevin's and he said that I should speak to this guy in Switzerland called Arthur Cohn. Arthur Cohn is a legend of filmmaking and documentary making in particular, and Sandy thought our film might be up his street. At the same moment the BBC told me they weren't going to make the film, so we'd lost pretty much everything at this point. They said I'd taken too much time and they weren't sure if they had the money anymore. That's when we went to see Nick Fraser and he very happily said, 'I'll take it off their hands and put it through my strand' (Storyville).

I rang Arthur Cohn up, clean out of the blue, and said, 'Sandy told me to call you, we're making a documentary, are you interested?' He said, 'I'm not interested, I don't make documentaries anymore'. And then he said, 'What's it about?' I told him, and asked if he'd like me to fax him a treatment. He read the treatment and 24 hours later he was in London. We met and suddenly this man was having a conversation with me like it was a foregone conclusion that we were going to be making this film. He also said, 'The film has got to be majority archive, because if you don't have archive you won't win the Oscar,' and he knows because he'd already won four. There was I, thinking, 'Christ, I'm desperately trying to figure out how I can make this film, and meeting anyone who will talk to me, and here's this guy not just talking to me about whether and if I'm going to make the film, but how I'm going to make it so that it wins an Oscar - it was pretty fucking ridiculous!

So there started a long and tempestuous relationship between myself and Arthur Cohn, who is my co-producer on the film and who in the end financed probably 50% of the film. Once Arthur was on board a great friend of mine, the producer Charles Steel, said you should go and talk to British Screen. British Screen jumped on board in seconds and came up with quite a lot of money. So it was British Screen, BBC, Arthur and that was pretty much it. Ultimately the film was financed by Arthur buying most of the rights that weren't already sold and splitting the rights between British Screen, BBC and Arthur Cohn. I don't even know what the total budget was, but it was probably about £600,000.

We definitely made 'One Day in September' hoping to make a piece of cinema, but the reality is that you never know. I'd worked for a distributor in this country for many years and my brother was head of Palace Pictures and is now head of Disney. So I knew enough about distribution to know that we wanted to make the film with a cinematic ambition, but ultimately the proof was in the pudding: if it doesn't feel like cinema, it doesn't feel like cinema. In those days it was post 'Hoop Dreams', 'When We Were Kings' and 'Crumb' and it was the beginning of a moment when documentary started to be taken much more seriously in terms of cinema, not like now where frankly people are gagging for documentaries for the cinema.

Once we realised we had a half-decent film I showed it to all the distributors over here. There were probably three who were genuinely interested in releasing it. As I said, it was in the early days of the renaissance of documentaries in the cinema and some distributors were definitely more than cautious. But one company in particular, Redbus, said they had to have it and I was delighted to have someone who would put some weight behind the film. Then we got Oscar-nominated and we got a book deal done so that Faber published a book to correspond with the film's release, all that sort of stuff. That whole journey took about two and a half years, from the day I had the idea, to the day it was released over here - it was a difficult and extremely painful process and great all at the same time."

Chapter Fourteen
High end distribution

Research by Maxyne Franklin

Overview

In October 2004, as part of Resfest at the NFT in London, Shooting People put on a panel discussion called 'The Year of the Documentary', in which representatives from three major British distributors gave their views on distribution and how it works for docs. The full transcript is at: http://shootingpeople.org/events/resdocs.php

"Documentary used to be a dirty word. But now it's become an asset; it's actually a selling point." – Jule Hartung, Metro Tartan

You've done the hard grind in getting your film funded but now you want to make sure that people see it in the cinema. This is where distributors and sales agents enter the picture, and you really need your producer to have their head on straight. To optimise your film's capability to reach the maximum audience, you need to be aware of who can help. Whilst self-distribution is definitely an option and becoming increasingly attractive, the big boys still rule the roost in this arena as they have the financial backing and the connections to give you mass exposure. "I think getting an agent to sell your film is actually pretty helpful. Although they take a big cut they're able to do the legwork that most filmmakers don't know how to do." – Arthur Bradford, director, 'How's Your News?'

A sales agent or producer's rep will take on your film (and usually a percentage cut around 30% on all advances and overages) and they'll work to show it off to international distributors (overages: the money coming to the sales agent and the producer after the distributor has got back the money they invested and the profit they require from the film). Both sales agents and producers' reps are key strategists. They will help you navigate the minefield of the distribution process, work as your connection to the theatrical and DVD distributor, the broadcaster and the press, and they'll explain the long-term ramifications of any deal. As Hugh Spearing of UK distributor Optimum notes, "Quite often the films we pick up come with a sales agent attached to them; already there's a relationship between the company and the agent." The distributor in turn is the company handling the theatrical release of the film in any given country, and may also be responsible for DVD and video sales. With producers' reps, sales agents and distributors alike, it's not advisable to make a deal with someone who asks you for a fee to represent your film; the rule of thumb is to only get involved with someone who takes a percentage of what they make for you. If your film doesn't get sold, they don't get paid.

This is what Sandi Dubowski's sales agents and distributor did for 'Trembling Before G-d':

"When we heard we were accepted to Sundance, I brought on board producer's rep Michael Roban who was attached to Lynda Hansen – they were responsible for selling the film. Even before Sundance, they were on the phone with distributors. They tried to get as many distributors as possible to see the film at our Sundance screenings with audiences and then they shipped prints and videos to Los Angeles and New York for others who could not attend. They continued the work selling the film in Berlin. We spent months talking to different companies and negotiating, and I finally selected New Yorker Films helmed by the legendary Dan Talbot. They had a stellar reputation, the strongest non-theatrical department of any US distributor, and their own DVD/video line which meant they didn't subcontract the job out so a director/producer would receive a mere percentage of a percentage. They also were very willing to have a director be actively involved in outreach, which some distributors definitely did not want. New Yorker Films became like family. They were fantastic to work with." www.newyorkerfilms.com

The problem with TV-funded documentaries

It still remains difficult to get UK documentaries in our own cinemas. In 2004 'Touching the Void' was the only UK documentary on traditional release in the UK. The reason is that almost all British documentaries are funded either entirely or to some degree by television. In the past, the broadcaster would usually have usurped all rights and even now that there are new PACT guidelines which allow producers to retain the theatrical rights, it is very hard for them to actually use them. Firstly, the producer needs to have had a clause inserted into their contract giving them a theatrical hold back window. This means that the TV company that funded them agrees not to screen the film until after it has been to the cinema and possibly been released on DVD too. This can mean the TV broadcaster is agreeing to pay now but wait an extra 18 months to two years to show the film. Broadcasters tend to have different views on whether it enhances a film for it to have been in the cinema first. Many such as HBO would rather have it sooner and show it first, so that any press the film is going to generate is attached to their screening and the project is more closely associated with the channel, rather than appearing just to be an after-the-fact acquisition. So if you think you have theatrical potential you must get the right to try for it in your TV contract. But even then there is a bigger problem awaiting you. With the TV rights now sold in your project it is unlikely a UK distributor will take your film. Because there is not much money to be made in the theatrical release and only a little from the DVD sales (documentary usually makes less than fiction films on DVD), the distributor usually makes their profit when they sell the TV rights. This makes foreign documentaries more attractive than domestic ones because the distributor is more likely to be able to acquire all rights, not just theatrical/DVD.

One notable exception to the rule was the excellent 'Etre et Avoir'. *"The problem with 'Etre et Avoir' was that the BBC had funded it so the terrestrial TV rights were gone by the time we could acquire it. But we saw so much potential in it that we picked it up anyway, for theatrical, DVD and other non-terrestrial channels"* – Jule Hartung, Metro Tartan.

How can you get a distributor?

Festivals. This is often the first place that you can raise awareness of your film and once the catalogues are released for the larger festivals this is when the phone starts ringing with calls from sales agents and distributors. As Josh Braun of producer's rep / sales agency Submarine says, "We're looking for films in the time leading up to Toronto or Sundance. The minute they make those announcements, that's when the producer's rep goes into high gear. We've seen what's been chosen and we make our pitch to represent those projects we feel have the potential to break out."

Whilst it's good to get your film into any number of festivals, the key festivals that double up as market places are Amsterdam, Berlin, Cannes, Toronto, Venice and Sundance. Unlike the others, Sundance has no official market infrastructure, and UK distributors are less likely to physically go there, but it does have an impressive documentary strand and as Tom Grievson of UK distributors Metrodome mentions, "We have friends over there and they'll give us a call and say, 'Oh this one's pretty cool.'" More often than not, the US sales agents and distributors will go to Sundance whilst the Brits wait to see what the buzz is and then go to Berlin.

The best advice when you're approached by distributors and agents is to try to speak to people who have used them (just look at their track record) and then go with your instincts. You're going to have a long relationship with this person, so be sure it's someone you feel you can trust. If there are multiple distributors and broadcasters showing an interest then it's definitely worth getting a sales agent who can carve out the best deals internationally and optimise on any bidding war; by doing this you should still come out with more, even after the agent's 30% fee.

Carefully consider your options when approaching the festivals, be sure to get your film in within the deadlines and be aware of the costs. Taking your film to Sundance could cost in the region of £5,000, even with the festival paying for the director's trip. You will need a high quality master (in the case of Cannes, a 35mm blow-up with subtitles is still required), posters, a strong press kit and visible give-aways; taking the British feature 'Unknown White Male' there in 2005, it was gratifying to see how many people wore the badge, building the film's hype and getting it into festival-goers' consciousness.

And without a festival?

The visibility of your film within these festivals cannot be underestimated, but even without that it is still possible to secure a sales agent and distributor. Using Jeff Blitz's 'Spellbound' as an example, the filmmakers sent it to Submarine's Josh Braun before Sundance and despite it not having been accepted by the festival, Josh took it on as a project – "I watched it and my jaw dropped to the floor, I couldn't believe how good it was" – and premiered it at Texas's SXSW (another rising festival) and the film went on to take over $5 million at the US box office. It was distributed in the UK by Metrodome. The re-make rights have recently been sold and original director Blitz is going on to make the fictional version. As David Koh of Palm Pictures says, "The most exciting thing is to find something that doesn't come from anywhere, it's just submitted and it's like a real discovery."

When asked what it is that draws them to a film and makes them want to distribute it, distributors return as one to the ideas of story and passion. Hugh Spearing: "At Optimum we did a documentary called 'Dark Days', which is amazing. That came about from a guy who was a social worker who made the film himself. He's got no interest in actually making films and he's never made anything else but he wanted to highlight that specific issue. He made it in a really amazing way. He probably could go on and make other very interesting films as well but he chose not to. That was one of those films where the person who acquired it just thought, 'I have to have that film,' and he met the guy and was really taken by his story. It can just be something like that, that gets you distribution."

Of all the distributors we've spoken to, none have said they won't take unsolicited materials but, as with anything, do your research and send an email synopsis first to avoid wasting your time and money.

Check the back catalogue of any company and be sure that your film matches their output. Arthur Howes explains, *"'Benjamin and His Brother' is distributed by DER (Documentary Educational Resources), an American distribution company set up by the filmmaker John Marshall. I was approached by several distributors at the Margaret Mead film festival and I quite liked DER and the people who run it. Even though they're not the most dynamic distributors they've got such an interesting collection of films that I didn't mind being in their company. They sell the film to universities and colleges. Every kind of prestigious college or university in the United States has a copy of 'Benjamin' now."*

Don't send the actual copy of the film completely on spec. Michael Thornton of Forward: "We have to be a bit protected on submissions, but anything that comes through a solicitor is inherently protected so that's fine. If we get sent a tape on its own it probably won't even be screened or opened. A filmmaker should mail us first to gauge our interest; we might tell them that we already have something similar, or we might not be the right home for it, in which case we might try and direct them to someplace else."

Follow the guidelines for submitting work, and don't send extra materials until requested or chase the company to confirm receipt of materials. If you're concerned about delivery, send it via registered post.

It's an unattractive truth but you should expect delays in the assessment of your film. But feel assured that it will most probably be watched. Distributors, producers' reps and broadcasters alike all have people to watch the films coming in and they want to find the next big thing as much as you and your film want to be it. Finally, it may sound like a cliché, but if you have connections, this is your time to use them. An introduction or a good word in someone's ear won't improve your film but it will certainly give it a good chance of being taken more seriously.

What does a distributor actually do?

A distributor takes your film to an audience. Usually a distributor will try and buy all rights for a minimum of ten years, including theatrical, video, DVD, TV terrestrial and non-terrestrial for their territory (the world is normally divided into 51 territories, for these purposes). Once you've struck a deal, the distributor will generally give you an advance (or minimum guarantee) and agree on a percentage of the profits from the different formats. Of the producer-distributor deal, Hugh Spearing from Optimum notes, "It varies with every film based on the potential that the sales company sees in the film and whether it's already screened at festivals or won any prizes." Once the licence – the rights for these formats in this territory for this time – is bought, the distributor will hold a screening for exhibitors, ie. programmers from the cinema chains. This is another crucial stage in the process as the exhibitor in turn needs to be convinced that the film is a viable product for them to show and get their return on. Hugh Spearing points out the dangers at this point:

"In 2004 we released 'The Agronomist', about Haiti, by Jonathan Demme, which we all loved. We brought it but ultimately it was released on just one print. In an Odeon cinema. They did watch it - the process is that when you've bought the film your get the print and screen it to all the exhibitors, the whole range of them. It can be quite hard to pin them down to come to a screening. But no-one really wanted to play the film and so we decided to completely downscale the ambition with it. It was a great story and we all liked it but it didn't seem to take anyone's attention in the

media or with the exhibitors. We didn't really have any access to cinemas with it. Things like that happen all the time, and all distributors end up downsizing things. It's worth pointing out that we're at the mercy of the exhibitors, and documentaries are hard to get into cinemas. They'll tell you what date you can screen the film, and it may not be what is best for the film. It is quite a struggle."

The better your distributor the better they can lobby, cajole and bargain with the cinemas to get the film in the number of screens you want around the country in a favourable release date. Distributors with clout and hot titles that cinemas are keen to have can broker deals so that they place other titles that the exhibitors are less convinced about.

Cinematic or theatrical release

But if they come on board, the exhibitor in collaboration with the distributor will devise a release strategy for the film in cinemas. This strategy is dependent on the number of screens, screen availability and other films that are due for release at that time. In addition, the distributor will co-ordinate the national press and marketing campaign. It helps if there's a catchy story behind the filmmaker or the film. 'Capturing the Friedmans' is often held up as an example of this: the director wanted to make a story about children's entertainers - clowns - in New York, and came across one who after a while came out with the information that he had a massive stash of home video, and an unusual home life... Of course the film itself is great, but hooks like this can help grab press attention.

As Jan Rofekamp and Diana Holtzberg point out in their article in the April 2005 issue of International Documentary Magazine (the magazine of the IDA; www.documentary.org), you the filmmaker should keep a close eye on, and universal access rights to, any material that's paid for by money advanced by the distributor. If, as is most commonly case, a US distributor takes your film first, make sure that for any subsequent distribution deals in other countries you can have access to negatives in a form that can be easily subtitled, to trailers, and to posters in a text-less form.

With documentaries in the UK, the norm is to open in London and key cities and then roll it out regionally over time, allowing word-of-mouth to build. The distributor advances the P&A fund (Prints and Advertising) and the clearances, but this money will eventually come out of the producer's pocket, as the advance needs to be recouped along with agreed costs (sometimes called COT or 'costs off the top') before any overages (percentage of income from sales) are due to the producer. The percentage the distributor will take varies for each stage of the process. The theatrical release will generally garner a 50/50 profit split between producer and distributor, but remember that this is after the recoupment of the advance and the 70% or thereabouts of box office income that the exhibitor will take for screening the film. The theatric release will rarely make either the distributor or the filmmaker any money but it's far from a vanity project and works to build reputation for the film, thereby enhancing TV and DVD sales. Tom Grievson says of the recent 'Bus 174', "In America it only went out in one cinema and it has done very well on DVD. We put it out on three cinemas to give it a good springboard so there would be lots written and people would learn a little bit more about it before it went on DVD." Ideally the film will pay for its own release but it's often little beyond that.

As pointed out, the theatrical release is often not financially beneficial within its own lifespan, but it does raise awareness of the film and can get the all-important national press attention and reviews, which you're unlikely to get by going striaght to DVD. In addition, TV sales are also becoming less lucrative, as the main UK terrestrial channels have very few slots for acquired documentaries, so the distributor will often sell films as a package. This happens where they have enough leverage, by virtue of a big seller such as 'Super Size Me', to require the channel to also buy smaller films. Again, this is another benefit of an established distributor, as it is far harder to sell your film individually in such a competitive market where so much is commissioned. The non-terrestrial channels such as BBC Four and the soon to be launched More4 have more air time to show acquired documentaries but often have smaller budgets and audience figures.

Where does all the money go?

Q: My film makes £100,000 at the cinema box office. How much do I get?

A: Very little

You, the producer / filmmaker, make a deal with a distributor. They come to an agreement with a cinema chain (the exhibitor) and plan to release the documentary in four screens, with a P&A spend of £24,000. Each print currently costs £5,000, leaving £4,000 for the whole marketing campaign.

The film opens, and the important figure is the box office take on the opening Friday, Saturday and Sunday nights, divided by the number of screens it's showing on (the capacity of the cinema doesn't count, for this). A take of £1K per screen is a bad figure, but say the film does respectably and the cinema lets it stay in that screen. Say your marketing spend was wisely used, you got good press, and the word-off-mouth recommendations had audiences flocking in. Say it runs phenomenally well for two weeks and brings in £25K per cinema, grossing £100,000.

A happy story?

Of this £100,000 taken in ticket money, 70% of the gross will go to the exhibitor, leaving £30,000. Less VAT at 17% is £24,750. The distributor then recoups their P&A spend of £24,000, leaving £750. If you have a 50/50 deal with the distributor on back end profits, you're both left at this point with £375. If a sales agent or producers rep struck the deal with the distributor for you, they get their 30% and you're left with returns from the cinematic release of £262 and 50 pence. If the distributor advanced you any money on taking the film, you've done well because they have still only made £375 on your film and will be hoping to make some money later down the line on DVD/ TV rights.

Edward Flectcher is founder and director of Soda Pictures, a UK distribution company he founded with Eve Gaberau in 2003 (www.sodapictures.com). Soda has released fiction features including 'The Saddest Music in the World', 'Afterlife', and in June 2005 it will release the documentary 'Czech Dream', dir. Filip Remunda and Vit Klusak. A DVD distribution arm of the company was launched earlier this year in conjunction with World Cinema Ltd handling sales.

Edward started his movie days managing cinemas in Croydon and Cambridge, before managing ICA Projects, the film distribution company of the Institute of Contemporary Arts. After five years, releasing films such as 'Atanarjuat: The Fast Runner', 'A One and a Two' and 'Ring', he left to launch Soda Pictures

Q: What brought you to distribution?

"It's not the case that I set up a distribution company because there was a particular problem that needed fixing; it was more a case that like any market there are always developments and opportunities. Some distributors are very successful by doing exactly same as they have always done, which is releasing similar films following similar strategies, according to a formula that works. But there are other companies that have changed much more over the past five years or so following shifts in the market, particularly for independent cinema.

In the not too distant past there were only five or so films released each week, of which maybe two were good, commercial US films, one poor one, and one or two were arthouse films. Arthouse films played in arthouse

cinemas, not in the Odeons etc. What has occured is a blurring of boundaries, a convergence between commercial and arthouse, working in both directions. Major studios have got involved with independent production, mainstream non-English cinema is now finding a theatrical release in the UK. Foreign Language no longer means auteur led arthouse cinema, which you could only see in regional art centres. It can mean commercial Korean thrillers in your local UGC mutiplex.

You can see the problem now for theatrical distributors just by looking at the newspaper. Look at the number of film reviews; there is simply too many films in too little space and the arts editors are not going to increase the space to cover all the releases. And for foreign language and documentaries reviews are critical in mobilising your core audience. We will spend money on advertising and promotions to make people choose to go and see our film, above the other films out that week and obviously we are very interested in how people make a decision about which film to see.

Our main problem though is securing enough cinemas to open a film with and then keeping a film there to give time for the word of mouth to grow. Independent films need this and without it your potential earnings for each film are reduced. It is obviously frustrating to have a film that can still be topping critics choice listings and have a week on week rising audience and then have no cinemas to play it in as each week another mass of films are released. Maybe we are now relying on DVD to make up for this hence DVD windows are getting shorter and release campaigns getting bigger."

Q: What's your advice to documentary filmmakers producing films now?

"Obviously there has been a new enthusiasm for documentary, i.e 'Spellbound', 'Super Size Me' or 'Fahrenheit 9/11'. But often successful types of film often bring inferior copies which contribute to a ending this new enthusiasm. When looking for a distributor I would advise one to do their research on what has been released and by whom. Consider the strengths of those documentaries released and the kind of campaigns and press they received. Look at building awareness in the industry by securing festival screenings.

Contemporary themes are good, with our documentary 'Czech Dream', about a campaign for a fictitious hypermarket, we'll be emphasizing the way that the films raises questions about advertising and manipulation, particularly in politics which has had some press here with the forthcoming general election. For a documentary to be release theatrically it does need the elements that other fiction features have, i.e. the heroism and landscapes of 'Touching the Void'. Having a niche audience to target helps, Football for example or music, two recent documentaries on the the Ramones and Metallica have performed very well.

Without either of these, I would think about some alternatives such as DVD or internet delivery. The technology is here and broadband take up is on the increase and there are number of film web sites concentrating on downloads from high definition digital masters via broadband and a set top box to your television. With very niche documentaries you may want to consider producing your own DVD's and selling them online yourself. And try link up with potential like-minded organisations or interest groups online to promote your sales."

After theatrical: DVD options

After the theatric release the distributor will release the film on DVD – ideally a more lucrative deal for the filmmaker, where a better percentage, up to 70% in the producer's favour, can be negotiated at the outset of the deal – and then sell through to television.

DVD sales and rental have increased enormously. As Tim de Lisle points out in a very good Guardian article accessible via http://film.guardian.co.uk/features/, in 2004, legal UK DVD sales of 197 million overtook the 174 million cinema tickets sold, and that's not counting the estimated 50 million pirate DVDs.

DocHouse director Elizabeth Wood points out that, *"Documentaries are different from fiction - they have a slower burn, they attract a smaller audience but for a longer time. People like to stop, watch again, re-visit. And for this type of film, the new distribution methods such as DVD that are becoming available are especially suitable."*

Sandi Dubowski has an extremely interesting story to tell about funding then screening and personally promoting his film about homosexuality and Judaism, 'Trembling Before G-d'. His labour-intensive and original approach didn't stop with its runaway success at festivals.
www.tremblingbeforeg-d.com

"Filmmakers need to grasp the rapidly shifting home video industry for two key reasons: the DVD medium can extend and expand the artistic life of a film; and the revenue it generates can wipe away the debt incurred by a theatrical release. For many independent filmmakers, particularly documentary makers, who finance their films through television sales, home video is often one of the rights they can retain and use to create real profit for themselves. As in all things independent, however, to maximise both revenue and the medium's creative potential, filmmakers must be prepared to play an active role in the development and production of their DVDs.

Extending the story:

At the Q&As following screenings of 'Trembling before G-d', people would ask, "What happened to the people in the film? Did the community see the film? What did they think?" DVDs offer an incredible opportunity to document not just the making of the film but also its subsequent movement in the world. Particularly for filmmakers whose films have catalyzed social change or stirred controversy, DVD can extend the meanings of their films in ways previously unimaginable. For me, there were such extraordinary changes in the lives of my subjects following my film's production that at one point I thought of filming a sequel — until I realised the DVD was just that. So I created a forty-minute featurette, 'Trembling on the Road', about the film's journey around the world, mixing footage from Brooklyn, Jerusalem, London, Mexico, Sundance, Ohio and beyond with updates on the lives of the film's subjects. I put out a special call on the Internet soliciting stories for the DVD. Among those who came forward was Shoshana, a Hasidic married woman who saw the film and for the first time learned of the existence of lesbians. She came out and a few weeks after left her husband and moved out of Williamsburg, Brooklyn. We filmed her story in Brooklyn's Hasidic neighborhood just before her life flipped 180 degrees. Orthodox people who in the film were closeted come out to their families in the DVD.

We were also awarded funding to launch a Trembling Before G-d Orthodox Education Project, for we trained eleven facilitators in Jerusalem who held screenings and led dialogues for two thousand teachers, school counselors and therapists across the nation, breaking the taboo on discussing the issue of homosexuality in the country's Orthodox (and secular) school systems. We created a fifteen-minute piece, 'Petach Lev: The Trembling Israeli Education Project', for the DVD about the experience.

Audience feedback:

In addition to documenting the communities that form around films, filmmakers can help create them, through linked websites with resources, glossaries, and chat rooms. As 'Trembling before G-d' generated enormous response through the Internet, I worked with a title designer to weave in art-directed excerpts from e-mail reactions to the film in 'Trembling on the Road'.

Enriching 'the making of…'

Filmmakers should free-associate and think of the DVD as a new art form with playful elasticity. I had fun while making my DVD by gathering footage I shot over six years and creating 'Mark: The Musical', a short that imagines an MTV–produced Hasidic music video. To ensure that they have dynamic elements for their immortal DVD, filmmakers should begin thinking of the disc on the first day of preproduction. Studio films do this routinely as home video executives weigh in at the first production meetings. Independents may not have all the resources of a studio, but there are things that can be done to ensure solid DVD extras.

- Save deleted scenes.
- License for the DVD archival pieces that may not make it into the film.
- Build into the budget a cinematographer who can shoot production B-roll.
- Develop story lines even if they are just for the DVD and Web site.
- Keep in mind multiple media while in production.

With regard to bonus materials in general, find out whether your distributor plans to release your film on a DVD-5 or a DVD-9. The former typically holds 133 minutes of playback video and the latter 240 minutes, so judge your time accordingly.

License one's own shorts:

A director's previous shorts can gain a new life on DVD, adding to the perceived value of the disc. I included on 'Trembling Before G-d' my short 'Tomboychik', a drag-themed tale made with my 88-year-old grandmother when I was 22.

Negotiating DVD production costs.

With my DVD, I was incredibly lucky to have a distributor, New Yorker Films, that was willing to alter the way it had traditionally done business. Our slow rollout across the US, hiring of outreach coordinators in more than a dozen cities, turning of cinemas into town halls and engaging various communities in more than 700 events was unparalleled. New Yorker invested in the production costs of the DVD (editors, shooting, tape stock, online, rights), which I was able to lower by securing in-kind online studio time and a fleet of interns. Such a strategy paid off when chains such as Blockbuster, aware of the reach and press generated, looked at the design and content of our deluxe two-disk DVD set and stocked their stores with the film. The massive press book that we were able to supply to major DVD/video chains made it clear that we had hundreds of stories on the film in every corner across the country and helped a big DVD buy. Video Store Magazine gave us unbelievable coverage, more than most Hollywood films get.

But in talking with various other distributors, none say they would have contractually guaranteed this kind of up-front support; all say they handle DVD creation on a case-by-case basis. While some home video companies and distributors are investing in bonus features and director's cuts, others are economising by dumping out bare-bones releases containing only a film, its theatrical trailer and maybe some outdated bios lifted from the press notes — and no consultation with the director/producers. How then do filmmakers guarantee that their video vision makes it to the DVD? The obvious answer is to build into a film's production or acquisition contract the responsibility for DVD creation, allocation of costs and authoring of additional materials and projects. However, this is easier said than done. Having deliverables ready when a video deal if signed is one strategy for building better DVDs. The larger video or distribution companies deal with a slew of releases and aren't staffed to track down and remaster deleted scenes or sometimes to even commission director's commentaries. By having these elements ready and mastered to DigiBetas, the filmmaker can induce a distributor into releasing a higher-quality DVD."

After theatrical: television acquisitions

Some broadcasters are open to the idea of buying completed films. The downside of this route is that you will rarely be paid enough to recoup your production costs, and if your film didn't appeal to a channel at the commissioning stage, you'd be lucky to find that, without any input from the channel, you had gone on to make the film in such a way as to completely tick their boxes. However, if your film is made and you're a director looking to raise your TV profile, it can be worth accepting a modest acquisition fee in exchange for getting your work out there.

For contacts of broadcasters and details of their acquisitions, see Chapter 2 for the UK, Chapter 8 for Europe, and Chapter 9 for the US.

Nikki Parrot had private funding for 'Footprints', a film about landmines.
"After it was finished we had a screening as part of the DocHouse. It was sold out and it got a great review in Time Out. We also had a Q & A with landmines charities and people got really involved in it and there were lots of petitions and stuff like that. Then I sent it to various people like Channel 4 and Channel Five to see if I could sell it and BBC Storyville. Nick Fraser just fell in love with it, so he bought it for the UK for a few transmissions.

Our investor Hans Geissendoerfer sold it to ARD which is part of the ARTE Deutschland network. Also German United Distributors, who Hans had previously worked with, took it on to sell it internationally. Although we're reviewing that arrangement because since making 'Footprints' I've become more involved in documentaries and I've made contacts through IDFA (the

International Documentary Film Festival in Amsterdam). I've realised that lots of people want to see it and I'd like to capitalise on that. It's not to say that United Distributors aren't good but they've got so many other projects, whereas I can just concentrate on selling that.

Geissendoerfer own the film outright and obviously they get more of a percentage of the sales than us because they put more money in, but eventually when they've made their money back, anything over that is a fifty-fifty split. The film hasn't recouped its initial outlay yet, so I want to keep pushing for sales and also it's important for the film to be seen by as many people as possible because the issue of cluster bombs is more relevant than ever."

'Sunny intervals and showers'

How do you get to the stage where a broadcaster will acquire your film? A distributor will have this as one of their aims, but Jonathan Goodman Levitt carved out his own route to this end. Jonathan came to the NFTS in 2000 as a Fulbright Scholar and began shooting what eventually became the film 'Sunny Intervals and Showers', a story of a doctor struggling to rebuild his marriage and career following diagnosis with manic depression. Funded primarily by credit cards and editing himself, Jonathan had a draft ready for screening by the Autumn of 2001.

"I showed a work-in-progress at the Royal Society of the Arts, but I was terribly unprepared for the screening. The cut screened was over three hours long, and I'm sure there were people who attended that would take a lot of convincing to look at anything of mine again. I should have just shown a few excerpts and led a discussion about the issues involved; now I would never agree to a screening before having a film in watchable shape, especially for a public audience. After that, in between increasingly frequent breaks to do other work necessitated by my finances, I developed a cut with the basic narrative before hiring a more experienced editor, Nick Thompson, to work with me during the final months.

It was a big break for us when the film was accepted to Sheffield in 2003 on the basis of a rough cut, as it was the only independently-financed UK feature to screen that year. The acceptance motivated me to pour more money into it as I thought we might sell it soon after the screening, and Sheffield Programmer Sirkka Moeller had been enormously supportive of the film since long before its completion.The screening itself was great, but it was also a wake-up call to the realities of the industry. I wasn't at all prepared to market the film, and it took me a while to understand that distribution was an entirely new process for which filmmaking itself doesn't prepare you.

Over the next year, we had a dozen or so festival screenings, including several at film festivals with a human rights theme, and almost invariably the film provoked a heated debate within audiences after each showing. I also began to send the film to commissioning editors, who either requested it or were eager to receive it when I asked. But I made the mistake of sending an 89-minute version because I didn't realise just how important it was to send a version, typically under an hour, that fits into an established slot. While feedback was positive, it took many months for the film to be viewed in some cases, and UK broadcasters are still deciding whether to air it. I've only shown the 60' minute version to one UK commissioning editor, who is now trying to pitch it directly to controllers on my behalf.

While I couldn't afford to spend as much time as I would have liked in trying to push the film, I had enough cash available and the will to re-edit the film into a television version, which I took to Docs for Sale at IDFA in 2004. I looked to that market as my last good chance to market my film effectively, so that I could sell it for television broadcast and finally focus more on new work. In part because I had done some research on broadcasters, in part because I had finally learned from experience to package my film as a product, a lot of broadcasters and distributors took an interest. The most important element of presenting it was to have it at an appropriate length for particular slots, and editors I asked were almost universally receptive to receiving a viewing copy. There was no slick presentation package; I've just used a small press pack that includes a synopsis, some stills, a filmmaker's statement. The most useful thing has been a page of reviews and quotes about the film. If I'd been more savvy I would have solicited comments from people, but as it was these were just comments and compliments that happened to come my way.

Although I was starting to get interest from broadcasters after IDFA, I decided recently to sign with a distributor because contracts are yet another area in which I'd be learning from scratch. It also seemed clear that most broadcasters would prefer dealing with companies with which they've worked before, rather than risk any problems with delivery. Beyond that, though, it has been very difficult to make new work while continuing to spend energy and headspace distributing 'Sunny Intervals and Showers'. So my distributor has the film now and is working to promote it. At first when I was looking at contracts I'd be blanching at the thought of them taking a 30 – 35% commission, but I learned that distribution is another area best left to specialists, at least for TV sales.

That said, I did retain some territories in which I was close to sales myself, and just made a first sale to the US satellite channel Link TV, after their Head of Acquisitions watched the film at the IDFA video library. It's only a few thousand dollars, but they say it's 'evergreen', continually relevant, and that there's a good chance the channel will re-acquisition it for several years. Whether other commissioners to whom I've recently sent copies eventually buy the film or not, I think it will be useful in funding future projects that they have been introduced to my work already. Somebody also suggested that whoever funds or acquires my next film might well want to leapfrog back and purchase 'Sunny Intervals' too. For educational and video / DVD sales, I'm going to launch a website soon to try self-distribution, but expect there's a good chance I'll eventually sign with a distributor for those sales too.

The thing about doing all this work by myself, moving towards what's getting to be successful distribution of the film, is that I now have a decent understanding of the market and my place in it. A couple of years ago I didn't think of myself as part of an industry at all. The film grew out of my passion to get people talking about discrimination against the mentally ill, and to create positive images of manic-depressives. It took a long time to view it as a product, and to realise that business concerns need to be part of my thinking. I won't be producing my next film, but I can now have conversations with producers on their level, and make specific suggestions of whom we should approach for funding, for example. With some luck, my working knowledge of the industry from distributing 'Sunny Intervals' will help us cobble together international co-productions much more quickly than we otherwise could."

Bear in mind that the progression through all these routes of selling the film isn't clear-cut.

As an indication of the complexity, Krysanne Katsoolis and Julie Goldman of Cactus 3 explain, "We've just finished a co-production on Hank Williams which was a co-production between PBS in the United States, the BBC in the UK, Universal for Home Video in the US and a UK-based sales agent. We've structured it so there's various versions: a theatrical version will play the festival circuit in the fall before it hits the TV window and Universal are cross-promoting with the television airing of the programme. Plus there will be a longer version for DVD and they'll be making a music video to go with it so we're fully promoting it and PBS will have a shorter version and the BBC and the sales agent will have a shorter version so they can sell it internationally. That's a good example of taking one film and the various ways to unpick it for the various markets and also using all the different distribution opportunitites. From festival, through broadcast, through video / dvd, promoting it with the music label. It's an example of all the pieces coming together really nicely.

David Koh of Palm Pictures points out: *"It's still early, but the trend now is towards split rights deal, where a cable company will team up with a theatrical company to buy the first window and work with a theatrical company to open it theatrically. We're doing that with Ondi Timoner's 'Dig!' and the Sundance channel, and 'Super Size Me' did it with another television partner. That seems like a new trend, in people experimenting with releasing windows, and it not being as black and white as it used to be. You would have your theatrical window, your TV window, your video window, but it's all getting mixed up now a bit. How it works is that the film would go simultaneously to a cable company and the theatrical company. The cable company will broadcast it once or twice. With 'Dig!' for example, we opened it October 21st 2004 in theatres, and Sundance Channel to broadcast it one or two times in October, to help it gain momentum. Then they'll fall back for a year, while we'll exploit the theatrical and video, and then they get it back for a year. Those type of deals are happening much more because then as a seller you can get a much bigger price from the combination of deals."*

And a tip for future possible income-generation, again from David Koh: *"The perception of documentary is changing and it's fertile ground for people looking for feature adaptations of documentaries. It's like with Korean films, for which nothing has come out that's been commercially successful in any way, but the studios have bought the remake rights to about ten of those in the past year and those rights are almost more viable than the actual film. It's the same with documentaries: studios are looking to docs to find ideas to make features out of. It's a valuable attribute of those films."*

Listings of distributors

Resources

www.filmfileeurope.com
Film Council and MEDIA-funded resource offering a searchable database of funders, distributors, films produced and production companies through Europe

The British Film Institute
Go via www.bfi.org.uk/facts/researchers for a listing of British theatrical distributors.
Go via www.bfi.org.uk/facts/distribution to access the pdf publication 'A Filmmakers Guide to Distribution and Exhibition'. Although written in 2001 so some of the smaller organisations mentioned in it are now defunct, it's by the extremely knowledgeable Jane Giles and still full of useful information.

The PACT Directory 2005 www.pact.co.uk
The PACT Directory now lists distributors. Shooting People members receive a 50% discount on the Directory, and can thereby buy the book for £25 instead of £50.
See www.shootingpeople.org/offers/pact.php for details.

Film Forum, New York
This independent cinema is a nirvana for documentary, and has the extremely useful practice of keeping a great record of films screened there plus details of each film's distributor:
www.filmforum.org/filmsource.html

INDEPENDENT CINEMA OFFICE

✉ 2nd Floor Kenilworth House
79-80 Margaret Street
London
W1W 8TA

✆ 020 7636 7120

✉ info@independentcinemaoffice.org.uk
www.independentcinemaoffice.org.uk

The ICO aims to develop and support independent film exhibition throughout the UK. It organises touring programmes of work that wouldn't otherwise receive a UK release, often derived from film festivals, but its main activities are advising cinemas about programming, booking films and working with the national and regional screen agencies. Head of Programming and Development Robin Baker explains, "We don't have the resources to view or tour all of the films that filmmakers submit to us, but it's very useful to be advised by email about brand new feature-length documentaries intended for cinema. If we believe that there is a theatric market for the film we will then contact the filmmakers for a tape and advise appropriate cinemas. Over the last year we have toured over 20 international feature documentaries (as well as many shorts) as part of our touring initiatives including 'Balseros', 'Madrid 11am', 'Repatriation', 'Arna's Children' and 'Behind Enemy Lines'. We have also been actively involved in ensuring that independently distributed documentaries such as 'Belonging', 'Peace One Day' and 'The Boy Who Plays on the Buddhas of Bamiyan' have received screenings in cinemas."

Independent Distributors UK

METRODOME

 5th Floor
33 Charlotte Street
London, W1T 1RR

020 7153 4421

 www.metrodomegroup.com

Docs include: 'The Corporation', 'Amandla!', 'Bus 174', 'Easy Riders, Raging Bulls', Nick Broomfield DVD box set, 'Spellbound'
Contact by email in the first instance: Sara Frain – sfrain@metrodomegroup.com

OPTIMUM RELEASING

22 Newman Street
London, W1T 1PH

020 7637 5403

 www.optimumreleasing.com

'The Agronomist', 'Aileen: Life and Death of a Serial Killer', 'Biggie & Tupac', 'Comandante', 'Dark Days', 'Fahrenheit 9/11', 'Muhammad Ali: The Greatest', 'Lost in La Mancha', 'Tarnation', 'Crumb', 'Festival Express'

Contact: Alison Neese, Acquisitions Assistant

Alison@optimumreleasing.com (can email with synopsis or send tape)

DOGWOOF PICTURES

Unit 2, Central Square
27 St. Mark Street
London E1 8EF

020 7488 0605

 www.dogwoofpictures.com

. Cinematic documentaries and docudramas

Contact via email to Anna Godas – anna@dogwoofpictures.com

TARTAN FILMS

 Atlantic House
5 Wardour Street
London W1D 6PV

 020 7494 1400

www.tartanvideo.com

Feature length Cinema documentaries: 'The Eyes of Tammy Faye', 'Etre Et Avoir', 'Basque Ball', 'Capturing the Friedmans', 'The Cockettes', 'Hoover Street Revival', 'Control Room', 'Super Size Me', 'My Architect'

Contact via email: Jane Giles, Head of Acquisitions – jgiles@tartanfilms.com

REDBUS

 Ariel House,
74A Charlotte Street,
London W1T 4QJ

020 7299 8800

www.films.redbus.co.uk
'One Day in September'

Contact: Chris Bailey

FORTISSIMO FILMS

 34, Tavistock Street
London, WC2E 7PB

020 7836 3637

www.fortissimo.nl

All contact should be made by email in the first instance to: Nicole@fortissimo-uk.com

3DD

190 Camden High Street,
London NW1 8QP

020 7428 1800

www.3dd-entertainment.co.uk

star based and musical docs and concerts

Contact via email: Rachel Job, Acquisitions Manager – Rachel@3DDtv.co.uk

SODA PICTURES

 3 Rupert Court
London
W1D 6DX

020 7287 7100

 www.sodapictures.com
info@sodapictures.com

'Czech Dream'

JOURNEYMAN PICTURES

Journalistic and current affairs documentaries
75a Walton Road
East Molesey, Surrey
KT8 0DP

020 8941 9994

www.journeyman.tv

'McLibel', 'Vietnam: Battle's Poison Cloud' 'How Arnold Won the West'

DOWNTOWN PICTURES

St. Georges House , 4th Floor
14-17 Wells Street
London W1P 3FP

020 7323 6604

'Kurt and Courtney'

FILM AND VIDEO UMBRELLA

 52 Bermondsey Street
London
SE1 3UD

020 7407 7755

 www.fvumbrella.com

Film, video and new media projects

Foreign distributors

FILMS TRANSIT

 Pieter Aertszstraat 112 hs,
1074 VT Amsterdam
The Netherlands

☎ +31 20.679 7954

🖱 www.filmstransit.com

Epic feature length documentaries and contemporary TV docs. Contact with synopsis via email: Barbara Truyen - barbaratruyen@filmstransit.com. (See Chapter 10 for our interview with Films Transit CEO Jan Rofekamp.)

FIRST HAND FILMS

 Zurich Office
Schaffhauserstrasse 359
8050 Zürich
Switzerland

☎ +41 1 312 20 60

🖱 www.firsthandfilms.com

Contacts via email: Joan Morselt or Gitte Hansen, Sales and Acquisitions: info@firsthandfilms.com

FORTISSIMO FILMS

 Head Office
Veemarkt 77-79
1019 DA Amsterdam
The Netherlands

☎ +31 20 627 32 15
Fax: +31 20 626 11 55

🖱 info@fortissimo.nl

✉ London Office
34 Tavistock Street , Covent Garden
London WC2E 7PB

☎ 020 7836 3637

🖱 nicole@fortissimo-uk.com

No unsolicited submissions.

TELE IMAGES INTERNATIONAL

✉ 64, rue Pierre Charron
75008 Paris
France

☏ +33 1 44 35 17 41
Fax: +33 1 44 35 17 62

🖱 www.teleimages.com

'Concrete Revolution'

7TH ART RELEASING

✉ 7551 Sunset Boulevard, Suite 104,
LA, CA 90046
USA

☏ +1 323 845 1455

🖱 www.7thart.com

'Balseros', 'Hidden in Plain Sight'

Stephen Kral, Acquisitions and Development

CINETIC MEDIA

✉ 555 W. 25th Street, 4th Floor
New York, NY 10001, USA

☏ +1 212 204 7979

🖱 www.cineticmedia.com

Sales agents for 'Control Room', 'The Yes Men', 'Super Size Me'

Contact via email: Dana O'Keefe - info@cineticmedia.com

DER: DOCUMENTARY EDUCATIONAL RESOURCES

✉ 101 Morse Street
Watertown, MA 02472
USA

☏ 800-569-6621 or 617-926-0491
fax. 617-926-9519

🖱 docued@der.org
www.der.org

Fostering cross-cultural understanding by quality ethnographic and documentary films from around the world.

'Jaguar', 'Benjamin and his Brother'

MAGNOLIA PICTURES

✉ 49 West 27th Street, 7th Floor
New York, NY 10001, USA

✆ +1 212 924 6701
fax +001 (212) 924-6742

🖱 www.magpictures.com

'Enron: the Smartest Guys in the Room', 'Capturing the Friedmans', 'Bukowski: Born into This'

Tom Quinn, Head of Acquisitions

PALM PICTURES

✉ 76 Ninth Avenue, Suite 1110
New York, NY 10011

✆ 212-320-3600
FAX: 212-320-3709

🖱 www.palmpictures.com

'Dig!', 'Stoked: the Rise and Fall of Gator'

ROADSIDE ATTRACTIONS

✉ 421 S. Beverly Drive, 8th Floor,
Beverly Hills, CA 90212, USA

✆ +1 310 789 4710

🖱 www.roadsideattractions.com

'Super Size Me'

They prefer to be contacted by sales reps and producers' agent, but you can mail in first instance to Eric d'Arbeloff: ericd@roadsideattractions.com

with title, logline, what stage the film is at and where it's been screened.

RO-CO FILM INTERNATIONAL

✉ 20 Hillcrest Road, Tiburon
CA 94920, USA

✆ +1 415 435 4631

www.rocofilms.com

'Born into Brothels', 'Promises', 'The Weather Underground'

Contact: send a VHS to Annie Roney, Managing Director

THINK FILM

155 Avenue of the Americas, 7th Floor
New York, NY 10013
USA

+1 646 293 9400
fax. +1 646 293 9407

www.thinkfilmcompany.com

'Mondovino', 'Born into Brothels'

Randy Manis, Sr. VP, Acquisitions & Business Affairs

WELLSPRING

419 Park Avenue South
New York, NY 10016, USA

+1 212 686 6777

www.wellspring.com

'Tarnation'

Head of Acquisitions: Marie Therese Guirgis

WOMEN MAKE MOVIES

Debra Zimmerman
462 Broadway, 5th floor
New York, NY 10013

212-925-0606
Fax: 212-925-2052

info@wmm.com
www.wmm.com

'Ferry Tales', 'The Man Who Stole my Mother's Face' 'The Kidnapping of Ingrid Betancourt', 'Beah: a Black Woman Speaks'

ZEITGEIST FILMS

 247 Centre Street
New York
NY 10013, USA

 +1 212 274 1989

www.zeitgeistfilms.com

Emily Russo, Co-founder

'Derrida', 'Manufacturing Consent'

Fax a one page synopsis marked for attention of Acquisitions to: 001 212 274 1644

Chapter Fifteen
DIY distribution

Introduction

If you want your film to have mainstream distribution through all the usual channels, bear in mind the warning from Michael Thornton of Forward: *"What filmmakers and distributors have to do is look at the issue through the eyes of the consumer, because at the end of the day that's the person who's going to have to be willing to put down ten dollars to buy the video or sit in the cinema."* And this mainstream consumer first of all has to be reached and told about your film, through some form of media, then they have to be intrigued enough to come and see it. It's not impossible, but there is a limited number of opportunities (parameters include: simply the number of cinemas and screens in the UK; the willingness of audiences to attend in their leisure time rather than follow another pursuit; the capacity of distributors, etc.), and however much the general public appetite for docs is growing, the are some films for which this head-on approach will be more suited than for others. We propose in this chapter a smorgasbord of alternative, more time-consuming, but perhaps more interesting routes to getting your documentary distributed. There are plenty of tips from distributors here, but the point is to adapt their knowledge to the circumstances of your film.

Franny Armstrong became a filmmaker to cover a story that had grabbed her attention: in 1995 a gardener and a postman had just lost the first stage of their legal battle against McDonald's. Ten years later, the story had changed somewhat, and Franny had been documenting it all. The distribution for 'McLibel' was as independent as the funding of it:

"I was at a film festival in Australia and the brilliant woman doing PR for the festival got me onto all these chat shows on ABC and they showed three minutes of the film. Distributors here, Journeyman, saw that and bought TV rights for the world and ended up selling it to about nine countries.

But DVDs are the only real way we'll make money from 'McLibel'. We made bits of money here and there when we sold it. First of all we sold it to BBC1, but they pulled out of broadcasting the film at the last minute and completely ripped us off, but that's another story. Then Channel 4 wanted to buy it, but that was a much more clear-cut legal problem. Alan Hayling wanted to buy it and the lawyers said no, end of story.

With regards to distribution there are some really important things that people don't know about, like Free Speech TV. Free Speech TV is an American satellite channel that transmits across the whole country, reaching over 17million homes .They programme their own material, but they don't have big budgets, so they can't afford to pay very much. But if you're prepared to give your film for very little, I think it's $500, you'll reach massive audiences. Then there's World Link and they have more money but less audience. They paid us $2000 for McLibel and they got 3 million people. We also have a distributor called TV Choice who sells to schools and colleges in the states and they're great too.

There are two things about having a commission, one is editorial control and two is copyright and on the subject of copyright. Channel 4 made a drama about 'McLibel' that was screened twice in the UK, end of story, they didn't even try and sell it internationally. We made a documentary about 'McLibel', it didn't screen in the UK but it screened all over the world. More than 20 million people have seen it and you can watch it on the internet, on VHS and on DVD. At its height we had 15 hundred people per month watching 'McLibel' or 'Drowned Out' on our website, which is huge for the internet. Then we started our pay-per-view and that was the end of our viewers, so we're going to go back to free view."

Since Shooting People's interview with Franny, 'McLibel' has had its theatrical premier in the Curzon Soho in London, and was finally acquired and screened by BBC Four. www.spannerfilms.net

Finding your audience

Tom Grieveson worked on 'The Corporation' in 2004 for distributors Metrodome. He works for an established distribution company, with a budget and with know-how, which is a different position to the independent lone filmmaker, but his comments on identifying and targeting your niche audience are relevant across the board.

"We identified three core audiences for the film outside of the traditional film-going audience. The first were the activists / students / NGOs. We saw this group as 'the converted' and we wanted to make them ACT and spread the word on the film among their networks. We also wanted to do lots of previews among this audience to help spread the buzz. Also a lot of these groups are working on projects very much linked to the messages in the film so we wanted to help them use the film to support their own campaigns. The second group we identified were the 'lifestyle hippies / chattering classes'. This is an audience that we thought would be interested in the film, but one that needed a nudge, to be spoon-fed the appeal of the film. We wanted to encourage this audience to BUY into the film and the messages and values attached to it. The third audience and probably the most difficult to reach we identified as the corporate footsoldiers. We believed that we needed to make this audience THINK about the actions of the companies they work for, and not criticise them as individuals. We want to tap into the issues raised and present them in a way that really makes this group think."

Tom also released 18-minute taster DVDs and educational resource packs, and he worked closely with the cinema to create an exhibition about video games and one of anti-corporate artwork, and to programme a month-long season of films linked to issues raised by 'The Corporation'. And all these methods of raising interest and broadening the discussion around the film were in addition to the normal posters and press marketing campaigns.

Your strategy will obviously depend on the subject, style and audience for the film, but these are indications of some of the ways to think laterally and stir up interest. The advantage of trying to distribute your own film is that you are already an expert on the topics covered in it, which should put you in good stead for knowing and already being in touch with the groups who might form an audience for it. Identify groups who already share information, and try to get them to spread the word to general audiences.

Marketing to your audience

Once you've identified an audience, you need to persuade them to watch your film. This calls for:
• Clear, attractive marketing material. You need a great photographic image or logo, and a set of texts that are effective whether the target audience catches a glimpse of your tagline, reads the press release, or whether they have the time to pore over the complete 'making of' and director's statement; and
• A way of disseminating it. Existing email listings bulletins are an obvious tool in this, but you could build up your own mailing list, remembering the legal obligation to include information on how to unsubscribe. Do not harvest addresses or spam people you don't know. It will not win you audiences.

Using cinemas and live screenings

Yes, there's a massive growth in DVD distribution, and if you're one of the happy few subscribed to BBC Four you can watch high-class independent docs in the Storyville strand. But there's something particular for both audiences and filmmakers about going to the cinema, and at the heart of that is the fact that real, breathing people are there watching, and you can talk to them at the end. As Arthur Howes puts it, *"With TV, you show your film – it's disposable, it's sandwiched between a couple of adverts – and then its over; it has no impact. So television has never been my focus. Films or videos have to be watched in cinemas. I want my films to appear in cinemas which are packed and audiences are responding, for me that's the romance of making films."*

Sandi Dubowski had phenomenal success both in promoting his film and in generating debate about its issues by his strategy of not rolling it out in cities across the US, but doing intensive live screenings with discussion around them. www.tremblingbeforeg-d.com

"Box office success came by extending our Sundance model into the theater – turning cinemas into town halls and approaching Trembling's release with the machinery of a precinct-by-precinct political campaign and armies of volunteers. We kept re-generating publicity and attendance through reaching out to different communities and mobilizing their email lists and contacts. All of our events and dialogues and discussions geometrically expanded the experience of attending Trembling for audiences. They turned cinemas into town halls, fostering engagement not just entertainment. When I chose theatrical release over a cable/TV Premiere, this was the reason - the sense of live presence as opposed to sitting safely in one's own world with your fridge and the remote. Too many filmmakers approach the festival and theatrical space as a pre-determined shape without the creativity that these spaces can embody. Most filmmakers come to a festival like Sundance with cell phone ready to make a deal, but forget the fact that it is even in Utah and what potential that could mean. Or they approach the theatrical space as just a place to unspool the film. What I learned is if we want voices of insight and debate heard and valued in a culture of corporate consolidation and merger, we must get smart. Filmmakers can see their distributors as partners so that their films do not fade. We can become the active element in making the difference between a distribution that creaks its way across a few cities, and distribution that creates a power surge as a film electrifies and galvanizes whatever ground it touches."

Sandi Dubowski in a Shooting People tee-shirt. Buy yours now via www.shootingpeople.org

To get into a bricks-and-mortar cinema, you can just ring up the programmer and ask. Most cinemas are keen to do private hires, with the price varying widely depending on screen capacity, time of day and location. But building relationships is more rewarding than just paying cash, and many cinemas are trying to develop a certain slot in their screening schedules for independent work. The cinema won't pay, but nor does the filmmaker pay to gain access to the screen, and if there's enough ticket income, there might even be financial recompense for the filmmakers, after the cinema has covered its costs. The benefit of this for the cinema is that it can bring in new, independent-oriented audiences into a quiet time-slot, and it's a lot more interesting for them than simply screening the latest blockbuster. A benefit of working with a cinema is that the physical infrastructure is there: seats, projection equipment, ticket booths, publicity. The downside is that they have high overheads to support all this infrastructure, and it is easier to cover these by programming mainstream films with the weight of a Hollywood juggernaut behind them, than by supporting independent documentary.

DocHouse

Elizabeth Wood is founder and director of DocHouse, the organisation that has already established a distinguished reputation through its documentary screenings at cinemas across the UK, and which is dedicated to promoting documentary through education, screenings, events and much more. www.dochouse.org

"The ultimate aim of DocHouse is to create a centre for documentary in the UK, a focus for the independent documentary community and a hub of activity for the public, media professionals, universities and cultural groups, one that's both physical and virtual. At the moment, documentary is fragmented across all media; we need to bring it together. In other words: a documentary centre that would hold the past, encourage the present, and promote the future.

So the physical side is to have a centre that would, first of all, have a much-needed videotheque, where anyone can come in, go to a viewing booth, and watch a documentary of their choice. A big problem at the moment is that there is an increasing audience for documentary, but there's no way to access docs by personal choice, and that ability really needs to become part of the culture. Television has atrophied into reality TV and factual entertainment, and it seems to have abandoned responsibility for independent, quality documentary making. Places such as the BFI and DocHouse's own existing archive do have the films there, but the question is how to create open access to them for the public, so that people become involved in and engaged with documentary as part of their cultural experience. In Paris, they have half a dozen such videotheques, all state-supported; we should be able to get one going, here in the UK.

So that would be the first stage, having a physical national centre, where anyone can view films, where there are also digital screening facilities, and a state-of-the-art venue for events and festivals. It could grow in time to include room for all the organisations involved in documentary: space for training, for a dedicated documentary production house, and eventually, for a stand-alone documentary film school, as almost all existing educational institutions have fiction as the priority.

The other, equally important, aspect of DocHouse is the virtual side, of building up a database of international and British documentary work, which would give fast-track access to world wide documentaries. The Internet offers the most important medium for fast-track access to the invaluable heritage of more than a century of brilliant documentary work. And this is access not only for the documentary community, but more importantly for the public, if the current surge in interest is to be sustained. Dochouse is working to fund these facilities, providing a spiritual home for documentary, and an umbrella for the many different independent activities that are emerging.

So to this ultimate plan, what DocHouse has done over the past three years, with virtually no funding, has already gained massive support and stimulated the docs environment within the film industry and with the public. We've continually run public screenings of documentaries since 2002, often followed by discussion and by sessions with the director, with increasing success. We began in The Other Cinema in London in October 2002, and we've now spread to four other London venues where we have regular, sold-out slots and we've screened at FACT Liverpool, and in York and Cambridge as well. We also have a presence on panels, at festivals, and so on. And what we've proved is that there is great demand for docs, and really keen audiences. In education, we've worked in conjunction with Tate Modern, running a course called 'Across Borders' in 2004; with the NFTS on our annual SummerDocs school, which takes people who have a burning idea for a film but perhaps not the confidence or the know how to realise it, and gives them an intensive seven-week training; and in 2004 we got funding from Film London to run a series of seminars and screenings called DocHistory, which, even to our surprise, was three times over-subscribed.

We find that about half the audiences to DocHouse screenings are dedicated documentarists, while half may have never been to the cinema to see a doc but come because they're interested in the subject matter. With the programming, we are aware of what our audiences want – a lot of the time it is information and insight that they feel they can no longer get from television – and we programme with current issues in mind. For example, at the time of the May 2005 British elections, the Iraq war has gone completely off the agenda for political debate on TV, so we've programmed a three week series on post-war Iraq, giving 'differing perspectives' in response, and we've had full audiences!

How to reach potential audiences? We use any means necessary: the cinemas include our events in their publicity, then we print posters which are distributed to all the cultural institutions and colleges around town; we have a growing email list and we use other outlets such as the Shooting People bulletins; we appear in an occasional radio slot. For mainstream press, Time Out has been fantastic, and we send press releases to all the papers, with occasional interest from the Guardian and the like.

For selection of our films, I curate the screenings and Gus Berger co-produces them with me. Mainly we search the festivals. We have two focuses: one is to bring the best of international documentary to screens here, and the second is to promote British documentary filmmakers. So, apart from a strong network in the UK documentary world - we get dozens of docs submitted to us for screenings - we attend festivals, get hold of copies of the best films, and decide from that what to screen. It has become more difficult to get 'hot docs' than when I first started looking for material for DocHouse screenings, in summer 2002, as more distributors are willing to take on documentaries. I used to have a free hand in grabbing the cream of the crop at, say, IDFA, for a British showcase screening, but that's not the case now. British distributors are picking up more and more docs. I don't mind; this is a good sign, as long as distributors are successful in picking up docs that prove viable at the box office! Also because of DocHouse's growing reputation, distributors are happy to give us a sneak preview screening, which to date has proved very successful. About seventy per cent of our screenings are international, and I'm very interested in making connections abroad. We have good links with institutions, distributors and festivals around the world.

We're looking forward to the Film Council's digital distribution network, as we would to anything that increases the quality of projection for docs. Most distributors have screening copies on DVD or Beta/Digi formats, so anything that helps high-quality screening can only be an advantage. If I could implement any other changes in the infrastructure of documentary, it would be to make the Film Council have a significant dedicated documentary budget, for development and distribution. In the past, documentary was seen as television and it wasn't seen as realistic to create proper distribution systems for docs by other means, as the distribution was controlled by big money, dominated by fiction. But now, technology is providing fantastic new opportunities for docs in particular. Documentaries are different from fiction: they have a slower burn, they attract a smaller audience but for a longer time. People like to stop, watch again, revisit. And for this type of film, the new distribution methods that are becoming available are especially suitable. With DVD, the web and site-specific screenings, you can have it that if you're interested in a particular subject – skateboarding, fashion, The World Bank, mountaineering, or anything – you can potentially gain access to docs on just this topic. Economically these new distribution methods have already proved very rewarding, if you witness the success of films like 'Outfoxed' and 'Unprecedented'.

I see the cinema, DVD and the web as the way towards a solid future for documentary: if, for example, kids at school are researching a topic, they need to have access to docs about that topic, so that it's normal to watch films that aren't just the latest blockbuster but feed their real interests, so that using and enjoying documentary is a normal part of our culture. If docs are used at that level, then the kids will also be willing to go to the cinema to see the smart docs, and it will be immaterial whether it is fact or fiction.

As advice for independent filmmakers working now, I'd say that the obvious thing is to use festivals, as that's where distributors look to pick it films. Metrodome, Optimum and Tartan are all good for docs. Still try for TV funding – BBC Storyville and the new More4 are still trying to keep indie docs on TV alive. If you can do it cheaply – make a taster and then try for co-production funding – Europe is a real source of cash. And think seriously about distribution on DVD. Looking at Robert Greenwald as an example, he was groundbreaking and made huge sums through his DVD distribution. Independent Distributors like Journeyman can help with this, they know about new DVD opportunities.

It's a great time for docs now: they're booming in cinemas, it's going mad on DVD. It's a great opportunity if we can just grasp the moment and create the future."

DocSpace

Amy Hardie is director of DocSpace, based in Edinburgh. DocSpace is the British partner of CinemaNet Europe, a MEDIA-funded project to increase distribution of independent films through a digital distribution network. It launched in November 2004 with simultaneous screenings in eight countries and a satellite-linked Q&A with director Jeremy Gilley, whose 'Peace One Day' was the opening film. DocSpace currently shows an unreleased doc once monthly across its UK cinema network.

www.cinemaneteurope.com
www.docspace.org

"I was - I am - a filmmaker, and in 2000 I appeared on a panel at the Edinburgh Film Festival discussing documentary audiences. What we ended up talking about was the fact that at festivals, people can't seem to get enough of documentaries. In this context, they're extremely in demand, but, elsewhere, beyond the festival circuit, you can't get enough films or audiences. I said that I'd find out why. At that time, I really felt as though if I wanted to see good docs, I had to get on a plane, fly somewhere else where they were screening.

So I started interviewing, asking why 35mm cinema on film, in the UK, was so difficult, and, as a second question, looking at what the barriers to digital distribution were, at the time. I did these interviews and asked questions, basing some of the queries on work done by Docuzone in the Netherlands. I had input from various figures in the docs world as well. Karen Cooper, for example, from Film Forum in New York, and Kees Ryninks in the Netherlands. He'd overseen some research in audiences in the Netherlands, and I used that as a basis for original research I carried out with cinema audience in Scotland. I was also very struck by work done by Cam Haynes in Canada. He'd done a lot on marketing films to groups in outlying towns, raising the profile of films with specific audiences. He offered films to audiences who then aranged their own screenings for their own groups. It is a form of ambassadorial marketing that I've adapted for Docspace. His tactics increased revenue streams by up to 25% for distributors in Canada. What I found from my research, and what was in the report that I subsequently sent round the industry, was, firstly, that digital screening was the thing that could make niche audiences financially viable, and secondly, details of the audiences. We found that documentary audiences tend not to watch TV, and when they chose to see a film at the cinema they go on the basis of subject matter.

Armed with this information, I launched an action plan at the next year's Edinburgh Film Festival, in 2002. I had Diane Weyermann of the Sundance Foundation, Storyville's Nick Fraser, Murray Weston from the British Universities Film and Video Council, for an educational perspective, and we set out how we wanted to capitalise on what the research had shown: by using digital; by building on word of mouth, so that there's time for a film to be in the cinema and for audiences to gradually come to it, rather than the situation in which by the time word has spread about a good film, it's been moved on from the screens; by marketing films to a documentary audience and thinking of them as a community. We gained the endorsement of distributors, exhibitors, broadcasters.

The next stage was the pilot project. I worked with Kees Ryninks, who'd been in discussion with the MEDIA programme. Kees already had a digital documentary distribution network up and running in the Netherlands, through which they'd increased distribution for cinema documentaries by 150%. Why is Holland so forward-thinking? They've always had a real commitment to public sector funding for documentary. Their film fund, for example, has a dedicated head of documentary, who is Kees. I'd really lobby for that in the UK, for the Film Council, Scottish Screen and others. Documentary filmmakers and audiences have different needs from fiction filmmakers, there's a different relation between them and the broadcasters, and there should be an official position that reflects and assists that.

So from MEDIA we received £2.2 million for a two-year pilot which was the European DocuZone, or EDZ, which became CinemaNet Europe, launched in November 2004. There's no particular significance in the name change; we wanted to stress we were an independent digital network. CNE is not exclusively for documentaries; the independent digital cinema network will benefit all independent filmmaking. As for the Film Council's designation of docs in with other arthouse and 'specialized' cinema, well, it's better than nothing, having docs recognised in this way.

What we find, though, is that docs work in society in a different way than do animation, fiction, other genres. For example, we've been sending out docs to tiny island communities in Scotland, and they're not just for watching, they're a focus for debate. Jeremy Gilley's film 'Peace One Day' was the British launch film for CNE, and we find that with every screening of it, the audience is stirred up and wants to take the debate further, and each screening leads on to about five more, there's so much demand.

We find the films we screen by putting out calls for submissions. We did the first call in 2004 to find the film to represent the UK in the opening weekend of CNE, as well as putting out the word across broadcasaters and festivals and groups like Dochouse and DFG – it was through Nick Fraser that we came across 'Peace One Day'. We were very restricted in what we could select because it had to be a film that had had no TV broadcast throughout Europe, but this was a fantastic find. From other countries we had Werner Herzog's 'The White Diamond', Jos de Putter's 'The Damned and the Sacred', and the Emmy-winning Slovakian film 'The Power of Good'. From British feature docs, we received about seventy feature docs in that call, with a huge variety in the quality. As well as the launch, there was one call for submissions in conjunction with the human rights and media group Media 19, who are organising the film programme to launch the new Nobel Peace Centre. And we've put in spring 2005 put out a call for ecological and environmental docs, for our first themed season. We've had 137 entries, the highlights of which will be shown by DocSpace in the UK, starting in June in Glasgow and Edinburgh. I'm amazed at how many documentaries are being made without *funding. Or, if they're for TV, the director's making a secret cinema cut as well. And I'm delighted by this: docs need to be in the public sphere, seen on the big screen, so that the audience can engage aesthetically and emotionally, and the film is out in the community. It's very different from radio documentary, as well, in that with radio you're listening alone, wherever you happen to be, in the kitchen or in the car, whereas with cinema you're there together; it's a shared journey.*

There's a good sense of those involved in the world of British documentary working together. We're working with the broadcasters, with film festivals. We're coperating more closely with festivals if we can schedule our releases up to eighteen months in advance – provided tv agree to that holdback. Currently there can be a problem: if a filmmaker submits a film to us and we screen it, that can hurt their festival chances. But if it's programmed that far in advance, they have the assurance that their film will be screened by us, but it can still go into festivals. With broadcasters, we're discussing getting cinema versions of BBC-produced documentaries. And with filmmakers, we're working on improving the distribution contract model, so that we could get funding back to filmmakers straight away, rather than the current slow process they have to endure. We're also developing preview contracts, to make this sort of distribution more filmmaker-friendly. The current seven-year contracts with distributors don't help to get the films to wider audiences. And with venues, although we have ten cinemas round the UK who we work with who are second to none, we're also trying to offer programming to arts centres, small community halls and other places. In a year's time, ideally, we'd be in more venues. We'd like to be able to digitally equip tiny venues throughout the country, so that they could fully participate in the European agenda. We're also looking closely at satellite. At the launch of CNE, we held a hi-definition materclass with director Jeremy Gilley, with live questioning coming to him from audiences in Amsterdam, Vienna, Berlin, Glasgow – right across Europe, and everyone concerned thought this was an extremely promising new form of communication. It's live, direct, flexible. So we're looking to equip more cinemas with satellite.

If I could make changes in the structure of how documentary distribution currently works? I think I'd like to see broadcasters work very closely with us, as soon as they commission, to develop cinematic versions of films right from the start. We're talking about this with them now. I would also set up a head of Documentary in each of the public funding bodies, to ensure that these documentaries not only get funded, but get shown to the widest possible audience, both in the UK and internationally.

My other intervention would be to do with the Film Council's digital screen network. The key to this is going to be the interoperability throughout Europe and internationally, and also the cost of encoding the films so that they're available for distribution through the network. I'd like a guarantee that the system is open and interoperable, and subsidised encoding centres round the nation, to increase access to this facility and to prevent the network being too London-centric.

It's early days for DocSpace; we're still putting together our staff and premises and so on. At the moment we have a researcher, a technical specialist, a manager, a intern in Edinburgh and one in London, and me as the head. But it's a good start, and we've set out towards our aim, which is to answer the question, 'What can we do to improve things for documentary filmmakers, and for audiences?'"

The UK Film Council Digital Screen Network

The Film Council set up its distribution department in 2002, with the aim of increasing the range and breadth of film-going in the UK. So far the Department has implemented schemes to increase access to cinemas for disabled audiences, to provide digital equipment for small and non-theatrical local film organisations, and there is a forthcoming audience education and development scheme.

The largest project to date, though, is the Digital Screen Network, funded in August 2004 to the tune of £13 million by money from Arts Council England.

The aim is 'to create a network of screens dedicated to the exhibition of specialised films in locations across the UK where there is no such provision currently' (UKFC website). Between 150 and 200 cinemas will participate in the scheme, in which the selected contractor Arts Alliance Digital Cinema will install, maintain and upgrade digital projection equipment, train cinema staff, and manage the conversion and distribution of films in the new format. To gain acceptance to the scheme, the cinemas undertake: to make conversions to accommodate the equipment; to pay an annual usage charge starting at approximately £3000 / year; to do marketing; and, vitally, to increase to an agreed minimum per week the number of specialised films they show, a category which includes documentary. In the application process, cinemas with no specialised programming had to undertake to start some, while cinemas that already include specialised programming had to propose how they would increase and broaden their provision. Successful cinemas will report back quarterly to the Film Council to ensure that they are hitting their shows-per week-quota.

The successful cinemas are due to be announced in June 2005 (after this book has gone to print; check the Film Council website at www.ukfilmcouncil.org.uk for details), with a rough timescale being that the first installation of equipment will take place by Autumn, with 50 cinemas equipped by the end of 2005 and all 200 completed by the end of 2006. The scheme will run for four years after the end of this installation period.

Alex Stolz is the Distribution and Exhibition Executive at the UKFC. This is how he explains what the impact of the Network might be on documentary filmmakers.

"The aim of the Digital Screen Network scheme is to grow the market for non-mainstream and specialised film, which includes documentary. We think of docs as being similar to a foreign-language fiction film, or perhaps an American arthouse movie, in that they provide an alternative to the mainstream Hollywood-style cinema experience: audiences here might go to a doc in one cinema visit, and to one of these others the next, but they wouldn't necessarily go exclusively to documentaries. The role of the Film Council is to put the infrastructure into place, but then we take a step back. We won't be programming the screens in the network – that will be down to the cinemas as it is now – but the participating sites will be contractually obliged to screen a minimum amount of specialised product which we will of course monitor.

The one exception to the no programming is that there's the possibility of a nationally co-ordinated showing of a film that's centrally booked by the Film Council. The idea is that we can truly maximize the marketing and publicity potential for specialised film by 'uniting' the network for one-off shows. E.g. 'tonight at a hundred and fifty cinemas nationwide the restored version of 'Gone With the Wind' will be showing in high definition', etc.

For documentaries (and other specialised films) that currently do make it to release, there will be a facility in place to help convert the film to digital distribution versions, which is much cheaper that striking a 35mm print. To access this there needs to be an existing digital master of the film. Ideally this would be in high definition, but other formats, such as digibeta, would also be ok if the producer/distributor/exhibitor is happy with the quality. The projection equipment is the highest spec currently on the market and in order to truly maximise potential of it you will want to go hi-def. However, if your movie was shot in grainy low-def digital, 16mm or similar then there would be little upside in going hi-def as its not going to improve what's already there. Basically the facility will ensure the filmmaker's vision is represented accurately on screen – and the great thing is that it will look that good every single time it is shown! On supplying the master to the service provider, the cost would involve a one-off fee in the region of £2,000 – 4,000 plus approx £80 per copy delivered to the cinema as opposed to about £1,500 for each 35mm print. Of course the vastly increased cost-effectiveness of digital over 35mm is the main reason behind the scheme.

So it will be more cost-effective for distributors, and they'll find it cheaper to reach a larger audience. Although it's unconnected to the Network, the Film Council also runs the £2 million Prints and Advertising fund, which supports distributors in their marketing of larger-budget specialised films, and in theory a film could benefit from both these schemes. 'Capturing the Friedmans' and 'Super Size Me' were both docs whose distribution was supported by the P&A fund.

And for non-released docs, although this isn't the main thrust of the Network, it could make it easier to get through to audiences. The equipment is very simple; you can plug-and-play other devices such as DVD or mini-DV, so it would be possible for independent doc-makers to go individually to cinemas trying to get them to show their films, on a local basis. Of course you can do this now, but the equipment will be in place to make it easier, and each individual cinema will have their quota of specialised films to show each week, so they'll have an incentive to be a bit more receptive to approaches. Another of the criteria for selecting the cinemas for the Network was how they proposed to make additional use of the equipment, in terms of making it available to local colleges, students, and community filmmaking groups. So that's another way the Network could be useful for more grass-roots documentary-makers to screen their films."

There's some curiosity as to whether the Film Council's strategy of investing in the distribution channels will have an effect on the product that's being distributed – that is, your actual film – but it's a new initiative and we await the results with interest.

Beyond cinemas

There are also many ways of taking your film to a live audience without going to an actual cinema. Film clubs and screening societies are a good grassroots resource, as are universities and colleges. Particularly if your local higher education institute has a film studies or film production department, it's worthwhile getting in touch and seeing what sort of screenings and events they organise. If the answer is 'not much', then you could suggest starting something: they should have screening equipment and empty rooms in the evening.

By their nature, grassroots societies tend to come and go, depending on individuals being willing to put in the time, so look locally for events currently running near you. Your Regional Screen Agency website will have news, while the Shooting People events calendar also lists screening nights, and calls for entries appear in the bulletins so you can see who's actively seeking material to show. The good thing about screening events is that the audiences tend to be made up of filmmakers, so they're good for meeting potential collaborators, swapping tips, and seeing what your peers are up to.

Director Kersti Uibo:
"'Narrow is the Gate' has been showing at festivals, and I have also been organising film screenings in small art cinemas in Belgium, Germany, Estonia, and Russia. The screenings started on a small scale. I showed it to a local Amnesty International group in London where I live and I showed it in Brixton prison - it's really up to me how much I could show it. I do the screenings for free because I got funding for the film - for some reason I never thought of doing the screenings for money. You can set up screenings in your locality and as it is about the situation in Kosovo lots of people are interested in it. We have discussions afterwards on the Balkans and on Kosovo, especially now because it very much relates to the Iraqi war. It's the sort of film that doesn't date. In many ways my film about Kosovo is also about Iraq and Afghanistan - it's about the same issues. I can see that there is still life in it - unexpected invitations keep coming."

DVD

Domestic computer equipment allows you to burn your own DVD for the few pence it costs to buy the blank discs, or you can get higher quality and a large number authored for you by a facility for as cheap as a pound or so a throw. But once you hold the material in your hand, the question of marketing and distribution is still there. Luke Morris paved the way in the UK with his Cinema16 collection of short films (www.cinema16.co.uk), which had good press attention and sells through the website and through some independent bookshops. Warp Films released Chris Morris' BAFTA-winning short 'My Wrongs...'

on DVD, and because they're an off-shoot of established record label Warp Records, they have the infrastructure in place to get the film into big record shops. There, consumers are completely au fait with the idea that you might buy music from Warp, but a disc with a film on is equally convenient. Filmmaker Simon Tzu raises the point, however, that the film industry doesn't yet really know how to sell DVDs: *"For most of us the viability of a cinema release is a moot point as the budgets we are currently able to raise probably dictate a straight-to-DVD release anyway. If that is successful we might just be able to raise the capital for something which will go first to the cinema. In order for it to be successful the film needs to be good (of course!) but the DVD release also needs to be handled properly. This is where the industry is pretty immature. Realistically speaking there should be far more direct-to-DVD distributors than there are. The costs and infrastructure required for a company distributing DVDs directly are probably similar to those of a small book or music publisher, yet there are far fewer small DVD distributors than small music or book publishers. In fact small book and music publishers might be just the people to push the next wave of films going out via direct DVD distribution."*

And indeed there is a crop of new DVD distributors with new ideas. Luke Morris of Cinema16 fame has recently joined Warp to create a European-focused, direct-to-DVD business which will undoubtedly do interesting things in interesting ways. An alternative is a new British business launched by Cauri Jaye. www.myriadmovies.com is a service to make your documentary into a DVD and get it advertised and sold on-line (saving you a lot of the hassle of getting your film ready for sale) but the marketing will be left up to you to do yourself. The service launches in August 2005.

In the United States things are also changing. Docurama (www.docurama.com) calls itself 'the first and only video label dedicated exclusively to critically acclaimed and cutting edge documentaries', and it last year made deals with POV and Sundance Channel to carry their titles. Docurama now has well over 100 titles, including great documentaries like 'Same River Twice', which played at Sundance but didn't originally sign theatrical/network TV deals (partly because of the extensive 1970's nude scenes in the film. It was then shown in theatres in 80 cities via a distributor, and televised nationally on the Sundance Channel.) Docurama's top three sellers are Pennebaker's Dylan film 'Don't Look Back', 'Porn Star: The Legend of Ron Jeremy' and 'The Weather Underground'. Other interesting developments include Morgan Spurlock's plans with his new company Warrior Poets to help documentaries by other directors that are struggling to get distribution. Morgan will be releasing them straight to DVD under his label – as a sort of Super Size stamp of approval. The idea is to reach the American audiences who don't generally watch docs and persuade them to give other documentaries a go. Plans are still being drawn up but watch for the new web site at www.warriorpoets.com.

Online distribution

By Simon Tzu

Sometimes, although there is an audience for one's film it is just not a large enough market to excite a broadcaster or a distributor. While it is possible to press DVDs and sell them via a website, often you are

Jason Massot self-funded 'Seafarers' in 2003, and organised three live screenings of it. The Picturehouse chain were talking of touring it, but by 2005 Jason's strategy had changed to, *"I'm going to resubmit it to some festivals and see if anyone bites. I'm starting to realise that self-funded films take a very long time to get out there. One of the things that I've been doing which has been really fun is selling DVDs of the film off my website and it's had quite a good response. I have email correspondence with everyone who buys it and we get into chats about it. I've no idea how they find my website, but I've had a pilot from Air Alaska write in saying I want to buy your film so I got chatting to him about what it's like to be a pilot for Air Alaska and that kind of interaction feels really good. It all feels very cottage industry, but I know in music I've always admired that way of doing things – not worrying about official structures or channels or streams of funding and all the rest of it."*

Robert Greenwald's 'Outfoxed' was first seen on July 13th 2004 at The New School University in New York City and then went immediately on sale on DVD over the internet at the modest price of $10. Five days later Moveon.org held a network of 3,000 interactive house parties which involved an incredible 25,000 people in a simultaneous screening and panel discussion. That kick-started the word-of-mouth phenomenon and over 50,000 DVD copies have now been sold, keeping it consistently in the amazon.com top three DVD titles. This was not the first Greenwald documentary with alternative distribution build into the initial plan. 'Uncovered: The Truth About the Iraq War' has accumulated sales of 120,000, but the latest twist is that distributors, seeing the popularity of the films on DVD, are now offering them cinematic runs, reversing the accepted wisdom that the role of a theatrical release is to build the prospects of the DVD release later down the line. Although Robert has said that theatrical release is the least important aspect of this film, he explained to Shooting People, *"We never planned for theatrical release, so it is a nice addition to our efforts to reach as many people as possible. With films that have a social message and in which my goal is to reach as wide an audience as quickly as possible, I think this new model we have created, of DVD via website and house parties and simultaneous commercial theatrical screening works very well. Each one serves to spread the word and encourage the other form of distribution; the cumulative results have been spectacular: hundreds of thousands of people seeing the films in theatres, at schools, at screenings of clubs, union halls, churches, etc.I think the notion of a certain order and time frame for windows will be changing quickly. I love having my films seen with groups of people, in theatres, in screenings, in homes.*

I think new technology has unleashed a creative outburst from filmmakers who are exploding with energy, ideas, passion. They now have the tools to do them inexpensively, intimately and quickly, and we are not going away. These films can be creative, they can help bring ideas to people all over the country and they re-affirm the integral role that film can and should play in a society.

Television will always be one of the ways that people see documentaries but having them seen in theatres, in groups, in public space with people coming together in the group experience is the way films benefit. If it is ten people in a living room, or a hundred people in a theatre, or two hundred in a union hall, film uniquely brings people together, and film and audience benefit from the group experience."

competing for attention with many other forms of entertainment, and people who have done this have been disappointed with sales. Once the dreams of riches have faded, making the film available for download online becomes a far more attractive option. Why do you want to do this? In a word: exposure. With online distribution you can reach the world. What are the chances otherwise that some family in Botswana might see your film? With exposure you can begin to build a following for your work and should this following grow large enough it can be converted into sales and commissions.

2005 is the year that internet downloads became a viable distribution mechanism, mainly through BitTorrent, a cunning peer-to-peer mechanism for making large films available without incurring large bandwidth costs. People have already started downloading movies in earnest and the phenomenon is growing so rapidly that BitTorrent now accounts for one third of all traffic on the internet. Bigger hard drives and faster net connections are driving this trend.

One example of how the world has already changed: Gary Lerhaupt, a graduate student in computer science at Stanford, became fascinated with 'Outfoxed', Robert Greenwald's documentary critical of Fox News, and thought more people should see it. So he convinced the film's producer to let him put a chunk of it on his website for free, as a 500-Mbyte torrent. Within two months, nearly 1,500 people downloaded it. That's almost 750 gigs of traffic, which could have cost tens of thousands of dollars in bandwidth fees. But to get the ball rolling, Lerhaupt's site needed to serve up only five gigs. After that, the peers took over and hosted it themselves. His bill for that bandwidth? $4. There are drinks at Starbucks that cost more. "It's amazing - I'm a movie distributor," he says. "If I had my own content, I'd be a TV station."

BitTorrent is a file-downloading protocol. In BitTorrent, files are split up into chunks (on the order of a thousand per file), and the downloaders of a file barter for chunks of it by uploading and downloading them in a tit-for-tat-like manner to prevent parasitic behavior. Each peer is responsible for maximising its own download rate by contacting suitable peers, and peers with high upload rates will with high probability also be able to download with high speeds. When a peer has finished downloading a file, it may become a seed by staying online for a while and sharing the file for free, i.e., without bartering. To find a file in BitTorrent format, users access websites which act as global directories of available files.

BitTorrent makes it possible to distribute films at their highest quality without incurring huge bandwidth bills. It makes Internet film distribution possible. Find out more at www.bittorrent.com

Video streaming has many downsides: it requires specialised software and hardware to manage on both the client and server side and it costs a fortune if your film is at all popular; it has to be done in low quality due to bandwidth restrictions and it does not allow one to fast forward or rewind. Downloadable films have none of these restrictions but streaming is still alive because programme makers fear piracy.

It is impossibly to technologically prevent piracy. If the film can be made available to legitimate users for watching then its encryption system can be cracked. Most major feature films are available for download on the internet BEFORE their official cinema release. Extensive measures to prevent piracy are not only doomed to failure (and present an attractive challenge for the crackers) but will also make it much more difficult for legitimate users to watch your film.

If you intend to charge for a film, the easiest way to do so is to ask for an online payment on your website before directing users to where they can download the BitTorrent file.

Mainstream internet film distribution is coming. Soon Apple will extend iTunes to offer films and Amazon, Google and Yahoo are all currently testing film download technology. The success of iTunes' online music sales has paved the way for the MPAA and studios' acceptance of the principal of film downloads.

However it will take some time for these organisations to work out the deals and launch their services – in the meantime using BitTorrent and a bit of marketing nous, any filmmaker can have their work seen around the world.

Listings

City Screen is a UK-wide exhibition chain, working through the chain of 18 Picturehouse cinemas, and with almost as many cinemas again under contract for programming services.

City Screen
Hardy House
16 – 18 Beak Street
London W1F 9RD

Tel. 020 7734 4342
enquiries@picturehouses.co.uk
www.picturehouses.co.uk

Encouragingly, there are far too many independent cinemas in the UK to list them here. To find ones in your area, go via your Regional Screen Agency. Screen South West, for example, lists all the cinemas in the region, while Scottish Screen supports nine 'cultural cinemas' across Scotland: The Belmont, Aberdeen; Dundee Contemporary Arts; Robbey Burns Centre, Dumfries; Edinburgh Filmhouse; Glasgow Film Theatre; Screen Machine mobile cinema in the Highlands and Islands; Eden Court Theatre, Inverness; Adam Smith Theatre, Kirkcaldy; MacRobert Cinema, Stirling.

The British Federation of Film Societies represents many but not all of the film societies in the UK.

British Federation of Film Societies
The Ritz Building
Mount Pleasant Campus
SWANSEA
SA1 6ED

Telephone 01792 481170
bffs-admin@sihe.ac.uk
www.bffs.org.uk

And regional contacts (as at April 2005)

North-West England	Chris Coffey - 01744 817130
South West England	Brian Clay - 0117 9420378
Yorkshire	Richard Fort - 01535 653471
Scotland	Ian Kerr - 01324 558089
Wales	Carol Phillips - 01600 780263

Ring them up to see what goes on in your area, or contact the head office for other regions.

Appendix

Appendix: checklist

A checklist of common mistakes to avoid whilst making your doc (so you can finish it and get it seen)

1) Get release forms – get them. They don't need to be super-complex but they need to prove the person knew what sort of film you were interviewing them for and what you had hoped to do with the film once you'd made it.

2) Only use archive and music you can afford to clear. Cost it before you lock your picture and bear in mind that tracing the owners and negotiating usage may take weeks, so start as soon as possible.

3) Picture and sound quality: is this film for cinema, TV or just for DVD? At festivals your film may have to stand up on a big screen and sound tracks that are fine on your TV at home can fall apart in a large venue. Distributors will always prefer films that look and sound professional, even if we filmmakers appreciate innovative, hand-held use of the DV camera.

4) Good journalism: get your facts right. You are responsible for the facts that your contributors spit out, not just what appears in commentary. Have you fact-checked? And fairness: has your film paid respect to both sides of the story? Have allegations about people or companies been put to them to reply to? (See the longer guidelines in the Shooting People documentary resources at www.shootingpeople.org, the BBC producers' guidelines or the OFCOM rules).

5) Be ethical in your approach – a good rule of thumb before you do something is to ask if it would ruin your reputation or the film's if discovered by the press after the film was released. You must be happy to admit it and defend it.

6) Make sure you have the rights. Get contracts with the other people who work on your film, even if it is unpaid, to clarify who owns the film once it is made. Particularly essential to clarify is the ownership position between producer and director, and between them and the camera operator. If you have finance for your documentary, what does the contract say about who has the different distribution rights?

7) Get great stills whilst you are making the film. They are essential later and screen grabs are an expense and look rubbish. They don't need to be observational shots – set one up if you need to, but get something iconic. Also get a couple of shots of the documentary being made, people holding cameras looking serious, etc.

8) Do a proper safety assessment of the project and get insurance to cover the people on your project and the equipment. Accidents aren't always preventable but if you have put time and thought into precautions and accidents are covered by the insurance then you are more likely to be able to weather them financially and emotionally. If you are going abroad, think even more carefully about what could possibly go wrong and what the plan would be if it did. Check the Foreign Office website for info on where you are going and what the risk status is. If it is considered risky, consult with people who have filmed there recently and with your insurers.

9) If your film makes allegations (whether they are against the world's biggest corporation or some bloke at your local chip shop) then get a media lawyer to look at it when you have a first cut. (Failing that, ask an experienced TV documentary executive producer – TV docs are quite closely policed so they will be aware of most issues). Make sure you make your point without laying yourself open to being sued.

10) Budget for distribution. Make sure you can afford to make good-looking packaged copies, enter festivals and attend them – and remember that most won't pay for short filmmakers to go.

Appendix: training

Dedicated documentary training

Documentary Filmmakers Group   www.dfglondon.com
Short courses in London and intensive training at FilmFarm in Poland for documentary filmmakers.

The National Film and Television School   www.nftsfilm-tv.ac.uk
An MA in documentary and a seven-week summer school, Beaconsfield.

Metropolitan Film School, London   www.metfilmschool.co.uk
An 8-week documentary filmmaking course.

Undercurrents   www.undercurrents.org
Training for community filmmakers and activist video.

MA degrees in documentary practice

Brunel   www.brunel.ac.uk

Goldsmiths   www.goldsmiths.ac.uk

Luton   www.luton.ac.uk

Lincoln   www.lincoln.ac.uk

Royal Holloway   www.rhul.ac.uk

Surrey Institute of Art and Design   www.surrart.ac.uk

Salford   www.salford.ac.uk

University of Wales, Newport (a BA)   www.newport.ac.uk

Bodies promoting skills development

Skillset   www.skillset.org
The national body for promoting skills within the audiovisual industry, through which UK Film Council support for training is routed.

BECTU   www.bectu.org.uk
The independent union for those working in broadcast and film.

New Producers Alliance   www.newproducer.co.uk
Trade body for producers.

PACT   www.pact.co.uk
UK film industry's main trade association.

Film and Television Freelance Training   www.ft2.org.uk
Training for freelancers in the industry.

General filmmaking courses

Raindance, London   www.raindance.co.uk/courses

Panico, London   www.panicofilms.com/courses

London Film School   www.lfs.com

London Film Academy www.londonfilmacademy.com

Edinburgh Mediabase www.edinburghmediabase.com

Glasgow Media Access Center (G-MAC) www.g-mac.co.uk

Wildeye, for wildlife filmmaking training www.wildeye.co.uk

Education listings

British Council sites:

Education UK www.educationuk.org
Allows a search of film-related UK courses and qualifications; and

Brit Films www.britfilms.com
Has a somewhat patchy listing of courses, workshops and providers.

Ideas Factory www.ideasfactory.com
A Channel 4 website providing information on the creative industries.

Learndirect www.learndirect-advice.co.uk
A government service promoting post-16 learning and employability

 And keep an eye on the Shooting People documentary bulletins for news of upcoming training.

Appendix: the Shooting People documentary network

Patrons: Kevin Macdonald, Albert Maysles, Morgan Spurlock, Mike Figgis, Penny Woolcock

The network

The Shooting People documentary network brings you a daily bulletin of work, questions, answers, festivals, screenings, discussion, collaboration, debate... Anything to do with being an independent documentary filmmaker, we cover it.

Being a Shooter gives you access to our website and resources, and allows you to fill out a Shooter's card so that other people can learn about you and access you online.

But most importantly, being a Shooter gives you a direct link to the most vibrant community of documentary filmmakers working today, both in the UK and abroad. Join today at www.shootingpeople.org

Shooters benefit from special offers:

Lovefilm
A six week free trial, then a monthly subscription charge of £13.99 for full SP members – save £12 a year

Screen International
A year's subscription for just £27 quarterly – save £36 a year

Kay's Production Manual
The directory of film and TV production for £40 – this 50% discount saves you £40

Broadcast
Fifty issues for £85 a year – a saving of £55

Pact Directory
Buy the Directory of Independent Producers 2005 for £25 – a 50% discount saving you £25

European Documentary Network
Get a year's membership of EDN, which includes subscription to DOX magazine and a copy of the EDN TV Guide, for €77 – a 30% discount

Get Your Documentary Funded and Distributed
Shooters can buy a copy of this book for £15 – a £10 discount on the full price www.shootingpeople.org/docsbook

And more
And all of this for £30 a year.

Index

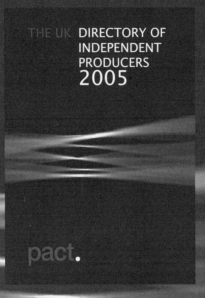

UNKNOWN WHITE MALE

THE TRUE STORY OF A MAN WHO FORGOT HIMSELF

SUNDANCE WORLD DOCUMENTARY
COMPETITION 2005

A FILMFOUR AND SPECTRE PRODUCTION
WWW.UNKNOWNWHITEMALE.CO.UK

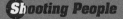

The year in fests

fold out chart ⤵

Festivals with markets:

Australian Int. Docu.Conference	www.aidc.com.au
Berlin International Film Festival	www.berlinale.de
Cannes Film Festival	www.festival-cannes.fr
Hot Docs	www.hotdocs.ca
IDFA (International Documentary Festival Amsterdam)	www.idfa.nl
Thessaloniki Documentary Festival	www.filmfestival.gr/docfestival/

Festivals without markets:

Chicago International Film Festival	www.chicagofilmfestival.com
Cinema du Reel: Int Fest of Documentary Films	www.bpi.fr
DocAviv (the Tel Aviv International Documentary Film Festival)	www.docaviv.co.il
DocPoint	www.docpoint.info/eng
DocuDays: Beirut International Documentary Festival	www.docudays.com
Edinburgh International Film Festival	www.edfilmfest.org.uk
Encounters South African Documentary Festival	www.encounters.co.za
FESPACO	www.fespaco.bf
Filmstock International Film Festival	www.filmstock.co.uk
Full Frame Documentary Film Festival	www.fullframefest.org
Human Rights Watch International Film Festival	www.hrw.org/iff
International Documentary Festival of Marseille	www.fidmarseille.org
International Documentary Film Festival Jihlava	www.dokument-festival.cz/
International Leipzig Festival for Documentary and Animated Film	www.dokfestival-leipzig.de
International Munich Documentary Film Festival	www.dokfest-muenchen.de
It's All True Documentary Festival (Sao Paolo)	www.itsalltrue.com.br
Karlovy Vary International Film Festival	www.kviff.com
Kassel Documentary Film and Video Festival	www.filmladen.de/dokfest
Leeds International Film Festival	www.leedsfilm.com
Locarno International Film Festival	www.pardo.ch
OxDox (Oxford Documentary Film Festival)	www.oxdox.com
Parnu International Documentary and Anthropology Film Festival	www.chaplin.ee/english/filmfestival
Raindance East	www.raindance.co.uk/east
Raindance Film Festival / British Independent Film Awards	www.raindance.co.uk
Sheffield International Documentary Festival	www.sidf.co.uk
Silverdocs	www.silverdocs.com
Sundance Film Festival	www.sundance.org
SXSW	www.sxsw.com
Telluride Film Festival	www.telluridefilmfestival.org
the Times bfi London Film Festival	www.lff.org.uk
Tribeca Film Festival	www.tribecafilmfestival.com
Venice Film Festival	www.labiennale.org/en/cinema
Yamagata International Documentary Film Festival	www.city.yamagata.yamagata.jp/yidff